The Stones of Venice by John Ruskin

Volume I (of III)

John Ruskin was born on February 8th, 1819 at 54, Hunter Street, Brunswick Square, London.

Ruskin is now recognised as the pre-eminent English art critic of the Victorian era. His talents and interests were diverse and complex. He was also an art patron, draughtsman, water-colourist, a prominent social thinker and philanthropist.

His writing was across subjects from geology, architecture, myth, ornithology and literature to education, botany and political economy. As well Ruskin also wrote essays and treatises, poetry and lectures, travel guides and manuals, letters and even a fairy tale.

Ruskin's earliest writings were initially elaborate but over the course of his long career he gradually moved to a far plainer form which communicated his ideas in a simpler and more effective way. All his writings have a common core of emphasising the connections between nature, art and society.

He first came to widespread attention with the first volume of Modern Painters, published in 1843, an extended essay in defence of the work of the painter J. M. W. Turner in which he argued that the principal role of the artist is "truth to nature". (He would later on the death of Turner be an executor of his will).

From the 1850s he championed the Pre-Raphaelites who were much influenced by his ideas. As his style developed so did his social concerns and increasingly he voiced and wrote about his social and political issues. Unto This Last (1860, 1862) marked the shift in emphasis. In 1869, Ruskin became the first Slade Professor of Fine Art at the University of Oxford, where he established the Ruskin School of Drawing.

In 1871, he began his monthly "letters to the workmen and labourers of Great Britain", published under the title Fors Clavigera (1871–1884). During the publication of this complex and deeply personal work, he developed the principles underlying his ideal society. As a result, he founded the Guild of St George, an organisation that still endures to this day.

John Ruskin died on January 20th, 1900 at age 80 at Brantwood in Coniston, Lancashire.

Part of his numerous writings concerned his work on Venice in three volumes: The Stones of Venice. He visited Venice in November 1849 with his wife, Effie, and stayed at the water-fronted Hotel Danieli. Their six-year marriage was never consummated and for Effie, Venice provided an opportunity to socialise, while for Ruskin it was a venue to engage in more solitary studies. In particular, he made a point of drawing the Ca' d'Oro and the Doge's Palace, or Palazzo Ducale, fearing they would be destroyed by the occupying Austrian troops.

Ruskin made extensive sketches and notes for the three-volume work, which soon developed from a technical history of Venetian architecture, from the Romanesque to the Renaissance, into a broad cultural history. Cleverly Ruskin managed to reflect his own view of contemporary England and to weave in a warning about the moral and spiritual health of society. Ruskin argued that Venice had slowly deteriorated. Its cultural achievements had been compromised, and its society corrupted, by the decline of true Christian faith. Instead of revering the divine, Renaissance artists honoured themselves, arrogantly celebrating human sensuousness.

It is a work of immense worth both culturally and artistically.

VENICE. FROM A PAINTING BY J. M. W. TURNER.

Index of Contents

THE STONES OF VENICE

VOLUME I

THE FOUNDATIONS

PREFACE

In the course of arranging the following essay, I put many things aside in my thoughts to be said in the Preface, things which I shall now put aside altogether, and pass by; for when a book has been advertised a year and a half, it seems best to present it with as little preface as possible.

Thus much, however, it is necessary for the reader to know, that, when I planned the work, I had materials by me, collected at different times of sojourn in Venice during the last seventeen years, which it seemed to me might be arranged with little difficulty, and which I believe to be of value as illustrating the history of Southern Gothic. Requiring, however, some clearer assurance respecting certain points of chronology, I went to Venice finally in the autumn of 1849, not doubting but that the dates of the principal edifices of the ancient city were either ascertained, or ascertainable without extraordinary research. To my consternation, I found that the Venetian antiquaries were not agreed within a century as to the date of the building of the façades of the Ducal Palace, and that nothing was known of any other civil edifice of the early city, except that at some time or other it had been fitted up for somebody's reception, and been thereupon fresh painted. Every date in question was determinable only by internal evidence, and it became necessary for me to examine not only every one of the older palaces, stone by stone, but every fragment throughout the city which afforded any clue to the formation of its styles. This I did as well as I could, and I believe there will be found, in the following pages, the only existing account of the details of early Venetian architecture on which dependence can be placed, as far as it goes. I do not care to point out the deficiencies of other works on this subject; the reader will find, if he examines them, either that the buildings to which I shall specially direct his attention have been hitherto undescribed, or else that there are great discrepancies between previous descriptions and mine: for which discrepancies I may be permitted to give this single and sufficient reason, that my account of every building is based on personal examination and measurement of it, and that my taking the pains so to examine what I had to describe, was a subject of grave surprise to my Italian friends. The work of the Marchese Selvatico is, however, to be distinguished with respect; it is clear in arrangement, and full of useful, though vague, information; and I have found cause to adopt, in great measure, its views of the chronological succession of the edifices of Venice. I shall have cause hereafter to quarrel with it on other grounds, but not without expression of gratitude for the assistance it has given me. Fontana's "Fabbriche di Venezia" is also historically valuable, but does not attempt to give architectural detail. Cicognara, as is now generally known, is so inaccurate as hardly to deserve mention.

Indeed, it is not easy to be accurate in an account of anything, however simple. Zoologists often disagree in their descriptions of the curve of a shell, or the plumage of a bird, though they may lay their specimen on the table, and examine it at their leisure; how much greater becomes the likelihood of error in the description of things which must be in many parts observed from a distance, or under unfavorable circumstances of light and shade; and of which many of the distinctive features have been worn away by time. I believe few people have any idea of the cost of truth in these things; of the expenditure of time necessary to make sure of the simplest facts, and of the strange way in which separate observations will sometimes falsify each other, incapable of reconcilement, owing to some imperceptible inadvertency. I am ashamed of the number of times in which I have had to say, in the following pages, "I am not sure," and I claim for them no authority, as if they were thoroughly sifted from error, even in what they more confidently state. Only, as far as my time, and strength, and mind served me, I have endeavored down to the smallest matters, to ascertain and speak the truth.

Nor was the subject without many and most discouraging difficulties, peculiar to itself. As far as my inquiries have extended, there is not a building in Venice, raised prior to the sixteenth century, which has not sustained essential change in one or more of its most important features. By far the greater number present examples of three or four different styles, it may be successive, it may be accidentally associated; and, in many instances, the restorations or additions have gradually replaced the entire structure of the ancient fabric, of which nothing but the name remains, together with a kind of identity, exhibited in the anomalous association of the modernized portions: the Will of the old building asserted through them all, stubbornly, though vainly, expressive; superseded by codicils, and falsified by misinterpretation; yet animating what would otherwise be a mere group of fantastic masque, as embarrassing to the antiquary, as to the mineralogist, the epigene crystal, formed by materials of one substance modelled on the perished crystals of another. The church of St. Mark's itself, harmonious as its structure may at first sight appear, is an epitome of the changes of Venetian architecture from the tenth to the nineteenth century. Its crypt, and the line of low arches which support the screen, are apparently the earliest portions; the lower stories of the main fabric are of the eleventh and twelfth centuries, with later Gothic interpolations; the pinnacles are of the earliest fully developed Venetian Gothic (fourteenth century); but one of them, that on the projection at the eastern extremity of the Piazzetta de Leoni, is of far finer, and probably earlier workmanship than all the rest. The southern range of pinnacles is again inferior to the northern and western, and visibly of later date. Then the screen, which most writers have described as part of the original fabric, bears its date inscribed on its architrave, 1394, and with it are associated a multitude of small screens, balustrades, decorations of the interior building, and probably the rose window of the south transept. Then come the interpolated traceries of the front and sides; then the crocketings of the upper arches, extravagances of the incipient Renaissance: and, finally, the figures which carry the waterspouts on the north side—utterly barbarous seventeenth or eighteenth century work—connect the whole with the plastered restorations of the year 1844 and 1845. Most of the palaces in Venice have sustained interpolations hardly less numerous; and those of the Ducal Palace are so intricate, that a year's labor would probably be insufficient altogether to disentangle and define them. I therefore gave up all thoughts of obtaining a perfectly clear chronological view of the early architecture; but the dates necessary to the main purposes of the book the reader will find well established; and of the evidence brought forward for those of less importance, he is himself to judge. Doubtful estimates are never made grounds of argument; and the accuracy of the account of the buildings themselves, for which alone I pledge myself, is of course entirely independent of them.

In like manner, as the statements briefly made in the chapters on construction involve questions so difficult and so general, that I cannot hope that every expression referring to them will be found free from error: and as the conclusions to which I have endeavored to lead the reader are thrown into a form the validity of which depends on that of each successive step, it might be argued, if fallacy or weakness could be detected in one of them, that all the subsequent reasonings were valueless. The reader may be assured, however, that it is not so; the method of proof used in the following essay being only one out of many which were in my choice, adopted because it seemed to me the shortest and simplest, not as being the strongest. In many cases, the conclusions are those which men of quick feeling would arrive at instinctively; and I then sought to discover the reasons of what so strongly recommended itself as truth. Though these reasons could every one of them, from the beginning to the end of the book, be proved insufficient, the truth of its conclusions would remain the same. I should only regret that I had dishonored them by an ill-grounded defence; and endeavor to repair my error by a better one.

I have not, however, written carelessly; nor should I in any wise have expressed doubt of the security of the following argument, but that it is physically impossible for me, being engaged quite as much with mountains, and clouds, and trees, and criticism of painting, as with architecture, to verify, as I should desire, the expression of every sentence bearing upon empirical and technical matters. Life is not long enough; nor does a day pass by without causing me to feel more bitterly the impossibility of carrying out to the extent which I should desire, the separate studies which general criticism continually forces me to undertake. I can only assure the reader, that he will find the certainty of every statement I permit myself to make, increase with its importance; and that, for the security of the final conclusions of the following essay, as well as for the resolute veracity of its account of whatever facts have come under my own immediate cognizance, I will pledge myself to the uttermost.

It was necessary, to the accomplishment of the purpose of the work (of which account is given in the First Chapter), that I should establish some canons of judgment, which the general reader should thoroughly understand, and, if it pleased him, accept, before we took cognizance, together, of any architecture whatsoever. It has taken me more time and trouble to do this than I expected; but, if I have succeeded, the thing done will be of use for many other purposes than that to which it is now put. The establishment of these canons, which I have called "the Foundations," and some account of the connection of Venetian architecture with that of the rest of Europe, have filled the present volume. The second will, I hope, contain all I have to say about Venice itself.

It was of course inexpedient to reduce drawings of crowded details to the size of an octavo volume,—I do not say impossible, but inexpedient; requiring infinite pains on the part of the engraver, with no result except farther pains to the beholder. And as, on the other hand, folio books are not easy reading, I determined to separate the text and the unreducible plates. I have given, with the principal text, all the illustrations absolutely necessary to the understanding of it, and, in the detached work, such additional text as has special reference to the larger illustrations.

A considerable number of these larger plates were at first intended to be executed in tinted lithography; but, finding the result unsatisfactory, I have determined to prepare the principal subjects for mezzotinting,—a change of method requiring two new drawings to be made of every subject; one a carefully penned outline for the etcher, and then a finished drawing upon the etching. This work does not proceed fast, while I am also occupied with the completion of the text; but the numbers of it will appear as fast as I can prepare them.

For the illustrations of the body of the work itself, I have used any kind of engraving which seemed suited to the subjects—line and mezzotint, on steel, with mixed lithographs and woodcuts, at considerable loss of uniformity in the appearance of the volume, but, I hope, with advantage, in rendering the character of the architecture it describes. And both in the plates and the text I have aimed chiefly at clear intelligibility; that any one, however little versed in the subject, might be able to take up the book, and understand what it meant forthwith. I have utterly failed of my purpose, if I have not made all the essential parts of the essay intelligible to the least learned, and easy to the most desultory readers, who are likely to take interest in the matter at all. There are few passages which even require so much as an acquaintance with the elements of Euclid, and these may be missed, without harm to the sense of the rest, by every reader to whom they may appear mysterious; and the architectural terms necessarily employed (which are very few) are explained as they occur, or in a note; so that, though I may often be found trite or tedious, I trust that I shall not be obscure. I am especially anxious to rid this essay of ambiguity, because I want to gain the ear of all kinds of persons. Every man has, at some time of his life, personal interest in architecture. He has influence on the design of some public building; or he has to buy, or build, or alter his own house. It signifies less whether the knowledge of other arts be general or not; men may live without buying pictures or statues: but, in architecture, all must in some way commit themselves; they must do mischief, and waste their money, if they do not know how to turn it to account. Churches, and shops, and warehouses, and cottages, and small row, and place, and terrace houses, must be built, and lived in, however joyless or inconvenient. And it is assuredly intended that all of us should have knowledge, and act upon our knowledge, in matters with which we are daily concerned, and not to be left to the caprice of architects or mercy of contractors. There is not, indeed, anything in the following essay bearing on the special forms and needs of modern buildings; but the principles it inculcates are universal; and they are illustrated from the remains of a city which should surely be interesting to the men of London, as affording the richest existing examples of architecture raised by a mercantile community, for civil uses, and domestic magnificence.

DENMARK HILL,
February, 1851.

THE STONES OF VENICE

CHAPTER I

THE QUARRY

§ I. Since the first dominion of men was asserted over the ocean, three thrones, of mark beyond all others, have been set upon its sands: the thrones of Tyre, Venice, and England. Of the First of these great powers only the memory remains; of the Second, the ruin; the Third, which inherits their greatness, if it forget their example, may be led through prouder eminence to less pitied destruction.

The exaltation, the sin, and the punishment of Tyre have been recorded for us, in perhaps the most touching words ever uttered by the Prophets of Israel against the cities of the stranger. But we read them as a lovely song; and close our ears to the sternness of their warning: for the very depth of the Fall of Tyre has blinded us to its reality, and we forget, as we watch the bleaching of the rocks between the sunshine and the sea, that they were once "as in Eden, the garden of God."

Her successor, like her in perfection of beauty, though less in endurance of dominion, is still left for our beholding in the final period of her decline: a ghost upon the sands of the sea, so weak—so quiet,—so bereft of all but her loveliness, that we might well doubt, as we watched her faint reflection in the mirage of the lagoon, which was the City, and which the Shadow.

I would endeavor to trace the lines of this image before it be for ever lost, and to record, as far as I may, the warning which seems to me to be uttered by every one of the fast-gaining waves, that beat, like passing bells, against the STONES OF VENICE.

§ II. It would be difficult to overrate the value of the lessons which might be derived from a faithful study of the history of this strange and mighty city: a history which, in spite of the labor of countless chroniclers, remains in vague and disputable outline,—barred with brightness and shade, like the far away edge of her own ocean, where the surf and the sand-bank are mingled with the sky. The inquiries in which we have to engage will hardly render this outline clearer, but their results will, in some degree, alter its aspect; and, so far as they bear upon it at all, they possess an interest of a far higher kind than that usually belonging to architectural investigations. I may, perhaps, in the outset, and in few words, enable the general reader to form a clearer idea of the importance of every existing expression of Venetian character through Venetian art, and of the breadth of interest which the true history of Venice embraces, than he is likely to have gleaned from the current fables of her mystery or magnificence.

§ III. Venice is usually conceived as an oligarchy: She was so during a period less than the half of her existence, and that including the days of her decline; and it is one of the first questions needing severe examination, whether that decline was owing in any wise to the change in the form of her government, or altogether, as assuredly in great part, to changes, in the character of the persons of whom it was composed.

The state of Venice existed Thirteen Hundred and Seventy-six years, from the first establishment of a consular government on the island of the Rialto,[1] to the moment when the General-in-chief of the French army of Italy pronounced the Venetian republic a thing of the past. Of this period, Two Hundred and Seventy-six[2] years were passed in a nominal subjection to the cities of old Venetia, especially to Padua, and in an agitated form of democracy, of which the executive appears to have been entrusted to tribunes,[3] chosen, one by the inhabitants of each of the principal islands. For six hundred years,[4] during which the power of Venice was continually on the increase, her government was an elective monarchy, her King or doge possessing, in early times at least, as much independent authority as any other European sovereign, but an authority gradually subjected to limitation, and shortened almost daily of its prerogatives, while it increased in a spectral and incapable magnificence. The final government of the nobles, under the image of a king, lasted for five hundred years, during which Venice reaped the fruits of her former energies, consumed them,—and expired.

§ IV. Let the reader therefore conceive the existence of the Venetian state as broadly divided into two periods: the first of nine hundred, the second of five hundred years, the separation being marked by what was called the "Serrar del Consiglio;" that is to say, the final and absolute distinction of the nobles from the commonalty, and the establishment of the government in their hands to the exclusion alike of the influence of the people on the one side, and the authority of the doge on the other.

Then the first period, of nine hundred years, presents us with the most interesting spectacle of a people struggling out of anarchy into order and power; and then governed, for the most part, by the worthiest and noblest man whom they could find among them,[5] called their Doge or Leader, with an aristocracy gradually and resolutely forming itself around him, out of which, and at last by which, he was chosen; an aristocracy owing its origin to the accidental numbers, influence, and wealth of some among the families of the fugitives from the older Venetia, and gradually organizing itself, by its unity and heroism, into a separate body.

This first period includes the rise of Venice, her noblest achievements, and the circumstances which determined her character and position among European powers; and within its range, as might have been anticipated, we find the names of all her hero princes,—of Pietro Urseolo, Ordalafo Falier, Domenico Michieli, Sebastiano Ziani, and Enrico Dandolo.

§ V. The second period opens with a hundred and twenty years, the most eventful in the career of Venice—the central struggle of her life—stained with her darkest crime, the murder of Carrara—disturbed by her most dangerous internal sedition, the conspiracy of Falier—oppressed by her most fatal war, the war of Chiozza—and distinguished by the glory of her two noblest citizens (for in this period the heroism of her citizens replaces that of her monarchs), Vittor Pisani and Carlo Zeno.

I date the commencement of the Fall of Venice from the death of Carlo Zeno, 8th May, 1418;[6] the visible commencement from that of another of her noblest and wisest children, the Doge Tomaso Mocenigo, who expired five years later. The reign of Foscari followed, gloomy with pestilence and war; a war in which large acquisitions of territory were made by subtle or fortunate policy in Lombardy, and disgrace, significant as irreparable, sustained in the battles on the Po at Cremona, and in the marshes of Caravaggio. In 1454, Venice, the first of the states of Christendom, humiliated herself to the Turk: in the same year was established the Inquisition of State,[7] and from this period her government takes the perfidious and mysterious form under which it is usually conceived. In 1477, the great Turkish invasion spread terror to the shores of the lagoons; and in 1508 the league of Cambrai marks the period usually assigned as the commencement of the decline of the Venetian power;[8] the commercial prosperity of Venice in the close of the fifteenth century blinding her historians to the previous evidence of the diminution of her internal strength.

§ VI. Now there is apparently a significative coincidence between the establishment of the aristocratic and oligarchical powers, and the diminution of the prosperity of the state. But this is the very question at issue; and it appears to me quite undetermined by any historian, or determined by each in accordance with his own prejudices. It is a triple question: first, whether the oligarchy established by the efforts of individual ambition was the cause, in its subsequent operation, of the Fall of Venice; or (secondly) whether the establishment of the oligarchy itself be not the sign and evidence, rather than the cause, of national enervation; or (lastly) whether, as I rather think, the history of Venice might not be written almost without reference to the construction of her senate or the prerogatives of her Doge. It is the history of a people eminently at unity in itself, descendants of Roman race, long disciplined by adversity, and compelled by its position either to live nobly or to perish:—for a thousand years they fought for life; for three hundred they invited death: their battle was rewarded, and their call was heard.

§ VII. Throughout her career, the victories of Venice, and, at many periods of it, her safety, were purchased by individual heroism; and the man who exalted or saved her was sometimes (oftenest) her king, sometimes a noble, sometimes a citizen. To him no matter, nor to her: the real question is, not so much what names they bore, or with what powers they were entrusted, as how they were trained; how they were made masters of themselves, servants of their country, patient of distress, impatient of dishonor; and what was the true reason of the change from the time when she could find saviours among those whom she had cast into prison, to that when the voices of her own children commanded her to sign covenant with Death.[9]

§ VIII. On this collateral question I wish the reader's mind to be fixed throughout all our subsequent inquiries. It will give double interest to every detail: nor will the interest be profitless; for the evidence which I shall be able to deduce from the arts of Venice will be both frequent and irrefragable, that the decline of her political prosperity was exactly coincident with that of domestic and individual religion.

I say domestic and individual; for—and this is the second point which I wish the reader to keep in mind—the most curious phenomenon in all Venetian history is the vitality of religion in private life, and its deadness in public policy. Amidst the enthusiasm, chivalry, or fanaticism of the other states of Europe, Venice stands, from first to last, like a masked statue; her coldness impenetrable, her exertion only aroused by the touch of a secret spring. That spring was her commercial interest,—this the one motive of all her important political acts, or enduring national animosities. She could forgive insults to her honor, but never rivalship in her commerce; she calculated the glory of her conquests by their value, and estimated their justice by their facility. The fame of success remains, when the motives of attempt are forgotten; and the casual reader of her history may perhaps be surprised to be reminded, that the expedition which was commanded by the noblest of her princes, and whose results added most to her military glory, was one in which while all Europe around her was wasted by the fire of its devotion, she first calculated the highest price she could exact from its piety for the armament she furnished, and then, for the advancement of her own private interests, at once broke her faith[10] and betrayed her religion.

§ IX. And yet, in the midst of this national criminality, we shall be struck again and again by the evidences of the most noble individual feeling. The tears of Dandolo were not shed in hypocrisy, though they could not blind him to the importance of the conquest of Zara. The habit of assigning to religion a direct influence over all his own actions, and all the affairs of his own daily life, is remarkable in every great Venetian during the times of the prosperity of the state; nor are instances wanting in which the private feeling of the citizens reaches the sphere of their policy, and even becomes the guide of its course where the scales of expediency are doubtfully balanced. I sincerely trust that the inquirer would be disappointed who should endeavor to trace any more immediate reasons for their adoption of the cause of Alexander III. against Barbarossa, than the piety which was excited by the character of their suppliant, and the noble pride which was provoked by the insolence of the emperor. But the heart of Venice is shown only in her hastiest councils; her worldly spirit recovers the ascendency whenever she has time to calculate the probabilities of advantage, or when they are sufficiently distinct to need no calculation; and the entire subjection of private piety to national policy is not only remarkable throughout the almost endless series of treacheries and tyrannies by which her empire was enlarged and maintained, but symbolised by a very singular circumstance in the building of the city itself. I am aware of no other city of Europe in which its cathedral was not the principal feature. But the principal church in Venice was the chapel attached to the palace of her prince, and called the "Chiesa Ducale." The patriarchal church,[11] inconsiderable in size and mean in decoration, stands on the outermost islet of the Venetian group, and its name, as well as its site, is probably unknown to the greater number of travellers passing hastily through the city. Nor is it less worthy of remark, that the two most important temples of Venice, next to the ducal chapel, owe their size and magnificence, not to national effort, but to the energy of the Franciscan and Dominican monks, supported by the vast organization of those great societies on the mainland of Italy, and countenanced by the most pious, and perhaps also, in his generation, the most wise, of all the princes of Venice,[12] who now rests beneath the roof of one of those very temples, and whose life is not satirized by the images of the Virtues which a Tuscan sculptor has placed around his tomb.

§ X. There are, therefore, two strange and solemn lights in which we have to regard almost every scene in the fitful history of the Rivo Alto. We find, on the one hand, a deep and constant tone of individual religion characterising the lives of the citizens of Venice in her greatness; we find this spirit influencing them in all the familiar and immediate concerns of life, giving a peculiar dignity to the conduct even of their commercial transactions, and confessed by them with a simplicity of faith that may well put to shame the hesitation with which a man of the world at present admits (even if it be so in reality) that religious feeling has any influence over the minor branches of his conduct. And we find as the natural consequence of all this, a healthy serenity of mind and energy of will expressed in all their actions, and a habit of heroism which never fails them, even when the immediate motive of action ceases to be praiseworthy. With the fulness of this spirit the prosperity of the state is exactly correspondent, and with its failure her decline, and that with a closeness and precision which it will be one of the collateral objects of the following essay to demonstrate from such accidental evidence as the field of its inquiry presents. And, thus far, all is natural and simple. But the stopping short of this religious faith when it appears likely to influence national action, correspondent as it is, and that most strikingly, with several characteristics of the temper of our present English legislature, is a subject, morally and politically, of the most curious interest and complicated difficulty; one, however, which the range of my present inquiry will not permit me to approach, and for the treatment of which I must be content to furnish materials in the light I may be able to throw upon the private tendencies of the Venetian character.

§ XI. There is, however, another most interesting feature in the policy of Venice which will be often brought before us; and which a Romanist would gladly assign as the reason of its irreligion; namely, the magnificent and successful struggle which she maintained against the temporal authority of the Church of Rome. It is true that, in a rapid survey of her career, the eye is at first arrested by the strange drama to which I have already alluded, closed by that ever memorable scene in the portico of St. Mark's,[13] the central expression in most men's thoughts of the unendurable elevation of the pontifical power; it is true that the proudest thoughts of Venice, as well as the insignia of her prince, and the form of her chief festival, recorded the service thus rendered to the Roman Church. But the enduring sentiment of years more than balanced the enthusiasm of a moment; and the bull of Clement V., which excommunicated the Venetians and their doge, likening them to Dathan, Abiram, Absalom, and Lucifer, is a stronger evidence of the great tendencies of the Venetian government than the umbrella of the doge or the ring of the Adriatic. The humiliation of Francesco Dandolo blotted out the shame of Barbarossa, and the total exclusion of ecclesiastics from all share in the councils of Venice became an enduring mark of her knowledge of the spirit of the Church of Rome, and of her defiance of it.

To this exclusion of Papal influence from her councils, the Romanist will attribute their irreligion, and the Protestant their success.[14] The first may be silenced by a reference to the character of the policy of the Vatican itself; and the second by his own shame, when he reflects that the English legislature sacrificed their principles to expose themselves to the very danger which the Venetian senate sacrificed theirs to avoid.

§ XII. One more circumstance remains to be noted respecting the Venetian government, the singular unity of the families composing it,—unity far from sincere or perfect, but still admirable when contrasted with the fiery feuds, the almost daily revolutions, the restless successions of families and parties in power, which fill the annals of the other states of Italy. That rivalship should sometimes be ended by the dagger, or enmity conducted to its ends under the mask of law, could not but be anticipated where the fierce Italian spirit was subjected to so severe a restraint: it is much that jealousy appears usually unmingled with illegitimate ambition, and that, for every instance in which private passion sought its gratification through public danger, there are a thousand in which it was sacrificed to the public advantage. Venice may well call upon us to note with reverence, that of all the towers which are still seen rising like a branchless forest from her islands, there is but one whose office was other than that of summoning to prayer, and that one was a watch-tower only: from first to last, while the palaces of the other cities of Italy were lifted into sullen fortitudes of rampart, and fringed with forked battlements for the javelin and the bow, the sands of Venice never sank under the weight of a war tower, and her roof terraces were wreathed with Arabian imagery, of golden globes suspended on the leaves of lilies.[15]

§ XIII. These, then, appear to me to be the points of chief general interest in the character and fate of the Venetian people. I would next endeavor to give the reader some idea of the manner in which the testimony of Art bears upon these questions, and of the aspect which the arts themselves assume when they are regarded in their true connexion with the history of the state.

1st. Receive the witness of Painting.

It will be remembered that I put the commencement of the Fall of Venice as far back as 1418.

Now, John Bellini was born in 1423, and Titian in 1480. John Bellini, and his brother Gentile, two years older than he, close the line of the sacred painters of Venice. But the most solemn spirit of religious faith animates their works to the last. There is no religion in any work of Titian's: there is not even the smallest evidence of religious temper or sympathies either in himself, or in those for whom he painted. His larger sacred subjects are merely themes for the exhibition of pictorial rhetoric,—composition and color. His minor works are generally made subordinate to purposes of portraiture. The Madonna in the church of the Frari is a mere lay figure, introduced to form a link of connexion between the portraits of various members of the Pesaro family who surround her.

Now this is not merely because John Bellini was a religious man and Titian was not. Titian and Bellini are each true representatives of the school of painters contemporary with them; and the difference in their artistic feeling is a consequence not so much of difference in their own natural characters as in their early education: Bellini was brought up in faith; Titian in formalism. Between the years of their births the vital religion of Venice had expired.

§ XIV. The vital religion, observe, not the formal. Outward observance was as strict as ever; and doge and senator still were painted, in almost every important instance, kneeling before the Madonna or St. Mark; a confession of faith made universal by the pure gold of the Venetian sequin. But observe the great picture of Titian's in the ducal palace, of the Doge Antonio Grimani kneeling before Faith: there is a curious lesson in it. The figure of Faith is a coarse portrait of one of Titian's least graceful female models: Faith had become carnal. The eye is first caught by the flash of the Doge's armor. The heart of Venice was in her wars, not in her worship.

The mind of Tintoret, incomparably more deep and serious than that of Titian, casts the solemnity of its own tone over the sacred subjects which it approaches, and sometimes forgets itself into devotion; but the principle of treatment is altogether the same as Titian's: absolute subordination of the religious subject to purposes of decoration or portraiture.

The evidence might be accumulated a thousandfold from the works of Veronese, and of every succeeding painter,—that the fifteenth century had taken away the religious heart of Venice.

§ XV. Such is the evidence of Painting. To collect that of Architecture will be our task through many a page to come; but I must here give a general idea of its heads.

Philippe de Commynes, writing of his entry into Venice in 1495, says,—

"Chascun me feit seoir au meillieu de ces deux ambassadeurs qui est l'honneur d'Italie que d'estre au meillieu; et me menerent au long de la grant rue, qu'ilz appellent le Canal Grant, et est bien large. Les gallees y passent à travers et y ay ven navire de quatre cens tonneaux ou plus pres des maisons: et est la plus belle rue que je croy qui soit en tout le monde, et la mieulx maisonnee, et va le long de la ville. Les maisons sont fort grandes et haultes, et de bonne pierre, et les anciennes toutes painctes; les aultres faictes depuis cent ans: toutes ont le devant de marbre blanc, qui leur vient d'Istrie, à cent mils de là, et encores maincte grant piece de porphire et de sarpentine sur le devant.... C'est la plus triumphante cité que j'aye jamais vene et qui plus faict d'honneur à ambassadeurs et estrangiers, et qui plus saigement se gouverne, et où le service de Dieu est le plus sollempnellement faict: et encores qu'il y peust bien avoir d'aultres faultes, si je croy que Dieu les a en ayde pour la reverence qu'ilz portent au service de l'Eglise."[16]

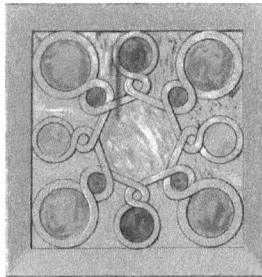

Plate I. Wall-Veil-Decoration. CA'TREVISAN CA'DARIO

§ XVI. This passage is of peculiar interest, for two reasons. Observe, first, the impression of Commynes respecting the religion of Venice: of which, as I have above said, the forms still remained with some glimmering of life in them, and were the evidence of what the real life had been in former times. But observe, secondly, the impression instantly made on Commynes' mind by the distinction between the elder palaces and those built "within this last hundred years; which all have their fronts of white marble brought from Istria, a hundred miles away, and besides, many a large piece of porphyry and serpentine upon their fronts."

On the opposite page I have given two of the ornaments of the palaces which so struck the French ambassador.[17] He was right in his notice of the distinction. There had indeed come a change over Venetian architecture in the fifteenth century; and a change of some importance to us moderns: we English owe to it our St. Paul's Cathedral, and Europe in general owes to it the utter degradation or destruction of her schools of architecture, never since revived. But that the reader may understand this, it is necessary that he should have some general idea of the connexion of the architecture of Venice with that of the rest of Europe, from its origin forwards.

§ XVII. All European architecture, bad and good, old and new, is derived from Greece through Rome, and colored and perfected from the East. The history of architecture is nothing but the tracing of the various modes and directions of this derivation. Understand this, once for all: if you hold fast this great connecting clue, you may string all the types of successive architectural invention upon it like so many beads. The Doric and the Corinthian orders are the roots, the one of all Romanesque, massy-capitaled buildings—Norman, Lombard, Byzantine, and what else you can name of the kind; and the Corinthian of all Gothic, Early English, French, German, and Tuscan. Now observe: those old Greeks gave the shaft; Rome gave the arch; the Arabs pointed and foliated the arch. The shaft and arch, the frame-work and strength of architecture, are from the race of Japheth: the spirituality and sanctity of it from Ismael, Abraham, and Shem.

§ XVIII. There is high probability that the Greek received his shaft system from Egypt; but I do not care to keep this earlier derivation in the mind of the reader. It is only necessary that he should be able to refer to a fixed point of origin, when the form of the shaft was first perfected. But it may be incidentally observed, that if the Greeks did indeed receive their Doric from Egypt, then the three families of the earth have each contributed their part to its noblest architecture: and Ham, the servant of the others, furnishes the sustaining or bearing member, the shaft; Japheth the arch; Shem the spiritualisation of both.

§ XIX. I have said that the two orders, Doric and Corinthian, are the roots of all European architecture. You have, perhaps, heard of five orders; but there are only two real orders, and there never can be any more until doomsday. On one of these orders the ornament is convex: those are Doric, Norman, and what else you recollect of the kind. On the other the ornament is concave: those are Corinthian, Early English, Decorated, and what else you recollect of that kind. The transitional form, in which the ornamental line is straight, is the centre or root of both. All other orders are varieties of those, or phantasms and grotesques altogether indefinite in number and species.[18]

§ XX. This Greek architecture, then, with its two orders, was clumsily copied and varied by the Romans with no particular result, until they begun to bring the arch into extensive practical service; except only that the Doric capital was spoiled in endeavors to mend it, and the Corinthian much varied and enriched with fanciful, and often very beautiful imagery. And in this state of things came Christianity: seized upon the arch as her own; decorated it, and delighted in it; invented a new Doric capital to replace the spoiled

Roman one: and all over the Roman empire set to work, with such materials as were nearest at hand, to express and adorn herself as best she could. This Roman Christian architecture is the exact expression of the Christianity of the time, very fervid and beautiful—but very imperfect; in many respects ignorant, and yet radiant with a strong, childlike light of imagination, which flames up under Constantine, illumines all the shores of the Bosphorus and the Ægean and the Adriatic Sea, and then gradually, as the people give themselves up to idolatry, becomes Corpse-light. The architecture sinks into a settled form—a strange, gilded, and embalmed repose: it, with the religion it expressed; and so would have remained for ever,—so does remain, where its languor has been undisturbed.[19] But rough wakening was ordained for it.

§ XXI. This Christian art of the declining empire is divided into two great branches, western and eastern; one centred at Rome, the other at Byzantium, of which the one is the early Christian Romanesque, properly so called, and the other, carried to higher imaginative perfection by Greek workmen, is distinguished from it as Byzantine. But I wish the reader, for the present, to class these two branches of art together in his mind, they being, in points of main importance, the same; that is to say, both of them a true continuance and sequence of the art of old Rome itself, flowing uninterruptedly down from the fountain-head, and entrusted always to the best workmen who could be found—Latins in Italy and Greeks in Greece; and thus both branches may be ranged under the general term of Christian Romanesque, an architecture which had lost the refinement of Pagan art in the degradation of the empire, but which was elevated by Christianity to higher aims, and by the fancy of the Greek workmen endowed with brighter forms. And this art the reader may conceive as extending in its various branches over all the central provinces of the empire, taking aspects more or less refined, according to its proximity to the seats of government; dependent for all its power on the vigor and freshness of the religion which animated it; and as that vigor and purity departed, losing its own vitality, and sinking into nerveless rest, not deprived of its beauty, but benumbed and incapable of advance or change.

§ XXII. Meantime there had been preparation for its renewal. While in Rome and Constantinople, and in the districts under their immediate influence, this Roman art of pure descent was practised in all its refinement, an impure form of it—a patois of Romanesque—was carried by inferior workmen into distant provinces; and still ruder imitations of this patois were executed by the barbarous nations on the skirts of the empire. But these barbarous nations were in the strength of their youth; and while, in the centre of Europe, a refined and purely descended art was sinking into graceful formalism, on its confines a barbarous and borrowed art was organising itself into strength and consistency. The reader must therefore consider the history of the work of the period as broadly divided into two great heads: the one embracing the elaborately languid succession of the Christian art of Rome; and the other, the imitations of it executed by nations in every conceivable phase of early organisation, on the edges of the empire, or included in its now merely nominal extent.

§ XXIII. Some of the barbaric nations were, of course, not susceptible of this influence; and when they burst over the Alps, appear, like the Huns, as scourges only, or mix, as the Ostrogoths, with the enervated Italians, and give physical strength to the mass with which they mingle, without materially affecting its intellectual character. But others, both south and north of the empire, had felt its influence, back to the beach of the Indian Ocean on the one hand, and to the ice creeks of the North Sea on the other. On the north and west the influence was of the Latins; on the south and east, of the Greeks. Two nations, pre-eminent above all the rest, represent to us the force of derived mind on either side. As the central power is eclipsed, the orbs of reflected light gather into their fulness; and when sensuality and idolatry had done their work, and the religion of the empire was laid asleep in a glittering sepulchre, the living light rose upon both horizons, and the fierce swords of the Lombard and Arab were shaken over its golden paralysis.

§ XXIV. The work of the Lombard was to give hardihood and system to the enervated body and enfeebled mind of Christendom; that of the Arab was to punish idolatry, and to proclaim the spirituality of worship. The Lombard covered every church which he built with the sculptured representations of bodily exercises—hunting and war.[20] The Arab banished all imagination of creature form from his temples, and proclaimed from their minarets, "There is no god but God." Opposite in their character and mission, alike in their magnificence of energy, they came from the North and from the South, the glacier torrent and the lava stream: they met and contended over the wreck of the Roman empire; and the very centre of the struggle, the point of pause of both, the dead water of the opposite eddies, charged with embayed fragments of the Roman wreck, is VENICE.

The Ducal palace of Venice contains the three elements in exactly equal proportions—the Roman, Lombard, and Arab. It is the central building of the world.

§ XXV. The reader will now begin to understand something of the importance of the study of the edifices of a city which includes, within the circuit of some seven or eight miles, the field of contest between the three pre-eminent architectures of the world:—each architecture expressing a condition of religion; each an erroneous condition, yet necessary to the correction of the others, and corrected by them.

§ XXVI. It will be part of my endeavor, in the following work, to mark the various modes in which the northern and southern architectures were developed from the Roman: here I must pause only to name the distinguishing characteristics of the great families. The Christian Roman and Byzantine work is round-arched, with single and well-proportioned shafts; capitals imitated from classical Roman; mouldings more or less so; and large surfaces of walls entirely covered with imagery, mosaic, and paintings, whether of scripture history or of sacred symbols.

The Arab school is at first the same in its principal features, the Byzantine workmen being employed by the caliphs; but the Arab rapidly introduces characters half Persepolitan, half Egyptian, into the shafts and capitals: in his intense love of excitement he points the arch and writhes it into extravagant foliations; he banishes the animal imagery, and invents an ornamentation of his own (called Arabesque) to replace it: this not being adapted for covering large surfaces, he concentrates it on features of interest, and bars his surfaces with horizontal lines of color, the expression of the level of the Desert. He retains the dome, and adds the minaret. All is done with exquisite refinement.

§ XXVII. The changes effected by the Lombard are more curious still, for they are in the anatomy of the building, more than its decoration. The Lombard architecture represents, as I said, the whole of that of the northern barbaric nations. And this I believe was, at first, an imitation in wood of the Christian Roman churches or basilicas. Without staying to examine the whole structure of a basilica, the reader will easily understand thus much of it: that it had a nave and two aisles, the nave much higher than the aisles; that the nave was separated from the aisles by rows of shafts, which supported, above, large spaces of flat or dead wall, rising above the aisles, and forming the upper part of the nave, now called the clerestory, which had a gabled wooden roof.

These high dead walls were, in Roman work, built of stone; but in the wooden work of the North, they must necessarily have been made of horizontal boards or timbers attached to uprights on the top of the nave pillars, which were themselves also of wood.[21] Now, these uprights were necessarily thicker than the rest of the timbers, and formed vertical square pilasters above the nave piers. As Christianity extended and civilisation increased, these wooden structures were changed into stone; but they were literally petrified, retaining the form which had been made necessary by their being of wood. The upright pilaster above the nave pier remains in the stone edifice, and is the first form of the great distinctive feature of Northern architecture—the vaulting shaft. In that form the Lombards brought it into Italy, in the seventh century, and it remains to this day in St. Ambrogio of Milan, and St. Michele of Pavia.

§ XXVIII. When the vaulting shaft was introduced in the clerestory walls, additional members were added for its support to the nave piers. Perhaps two or three pine trunks, used for a single pillar, gave the first idea of the grouped shaft. Be that as it may, the arrangement of the nave pier in the form of a cross accompanies the superimposition of the vaulting shaft; together with corresponding grouping of minor shafts in doorways and apertures of windows. Thus, the whole body of the Northern architecture, represented by that of the Lombards, may be described as rough but majestic work, round-arched, with grouped shafts, added vaulting shafts, and endless imagery of active life and fantastic superstitions.

§ XXIX. The glacier stream of the Lombards, and the following one of the Normans, left their erratic blocks, wherever they had flowed; but without influencing, I think, the Southern nations beyond the sphere of their own presence. But the lava stream of the Arab, even after it ceased to flow, warmed the whole of the Northern air; and the history of Gothic architecture is the history of the refinement and spiritualisation of Northern work under its influence. The noblest buildings of the world, the Pisan-Romanesque, Tuscan (Giottesque) Gothic, and Veronese Gothic, are those of the Lombard schools themselves, under its close and direct influence; the various Gothics of the North are the original forms of the architecture which the Lombards brought into Italy, changing under the less direct influence of the Arab.

§ XXX. Understanding thus much of the formation of the great European styles, we shall have no difficulty in tracing the succession of architectures in Venice herself. From what I said of the central character of Venetian art, the reader is not, of course, to conclude that the Roman, Northern, and Arabian elements met together and contended for the mastery at the same period. The earliest element was the pure Christian Roman; but few, if any, remains of this art exist at Venice; for the present city was in the earliest times only one of many settlements formed on the chain of marshy islands which extend from the mouths of the Isonzo to those of the Adige, and it was not until the beginning of the ninth century that it became the seat of government; while the cathedral of Torcello, though Christian Roman in general form, was rebuilt in the eleventh century, and shows evidence of Byzantine workmanship in many of its details. This cathedral, however, with the church of Santa Fosca at Torcello, San Giacomo di Rialto at Venice, and the crypt of St. Mark's, forms a distinct group of buildings, in which the Byzantine influence is exceedingly slight; and which is probably very sufficiently representative of the earliest architecture on the islands.

§ XXXI. The Ducal residence was removed to Venice in 809, and the body of St. Mark was brought from Alexandria twenty years later. The first church of St. Mark's was, doubtless, built in imitation of that destroyed at Alexandria, and from which the relics of the saint had been obtained. During the ninth, tenth, and eleventh centuries, the architecture of Venice seems to have been formed on the same model, and is almost identical with that of Cairo under the caliphs,[22] it being quite immaterial whether the reader chooses to call both Byzantine or both Arabic; the workmen being certainly Byzantine, but forced to the invention of new forms by their Arabian masters, and bringing these forms into use in whatever other parts of the world they were employed.

To this first manner of Venetian architecture, together with vestiges as remain of the Christian Roman, I shall devote the first division of the following inquiry. The examples remaining of it consist of three noble churches (those of Torcello, Murano, and the greater part of St. Mark's), and about ten or twelve fragments of palaces.

§ XXXII. To this style succeeds a transitional one, of a character much more distinctly Arabian: the shafts become more slender, and the arches consistently pointed, instead of round; certain other changes, not to be enumerated in a sentence, taking place in the capitals and mouldings. This style is almost exclusively secular. It was natural for the Venetians to imitate the beautiful details of the Arabian dwelling-house, while they would with reluctance adopt those of the mosque for Christian churches.

I have not succeeded in fixing limiting dates for this style. It appears in part contemporary with the Byzantine manner, but outlives it. Its position is, however, fixed by the central date, 1180, that of the elevation of the granite shafts of the Piazetta, whose capitals are the two most important pieces of detail in this transitional style in Venice. Examples of its application to domestic buildings exist in almost every street of the city, and will form the subject of the second division of the following essay.

§ XXXIII. The Venetians were always ready to receive lessons in art from their enemies (else had there been no Arab work in Venice). But their especial dread and hatred of the Lombards appears to have long prevented them from receiving the influence of the art which that people had introduced on the mainland of Italy. Nevertheless, during the practice of the two styles above distinguished, a peculiar and very primitive condition of pointed Gothic had arisen in ecclesiastical architecture. It appears to be a feeble reflection of the Lombard-Arab forms, which were attaining perfection upon the continent, and would probably, if left to itself, have been soon merged in the Venetian-Arab school, with which it had from the first so close a fellowship, that it will be found difficult to distinguish the Arabian ogives from those which seem to have been built under this early Gothic influence. The churches of San Giacopo dell'Orio, San Giovanni in Bragora, the Carmine, and one or two more, furnish the only important examples of it. But, in the thirteenth century, the Franciscans and Dominicans introduced from the continent their morality and their architecture, already a distinct Gothic, curiously developed from Lombardic and Northern (German?) forms; and the influence of the principles exhibited in the vast churches of St. Paul and the Frari began rapidly to affect the Venetian-Arab school. Still the two systems never became united; the Venetian policy repressed the power of the church, and the Venetian artists resisted its example; and thenceforward the architecture of the city becomes divided into ecclesiastical and civil: the one an ungraceful yet powerful form of the Western Gothic, common to the whole peninsula, and only showing Venetian sympathies in the adoption of certain characteristic mouldings; the other a rich, luxuriant, and entirely original Gothic, formed from the Venetian-Arab by the influence of the Dominican and Franciscan architecture, and especially by the engrafting upon the Arab forms of the most novel feature of the Franciscan work, its traceries. These various forms of Gothic, the distinctive architecture of Venice, chiefly represented by the churches of St. John and Paul, the Frari, and San Stefano, on the ecclesiastical side, and by the Ducal palace, and the other principal Gothic palaces, on the secular side, will be the subject of the third division of the essay.

§ XXXIV. Now observe. The transitional (or especially Arabic) style of the Venetian work is centralised by the date 1180, and is transformed gradually into the Gothic, which extends in its purity from the middle of the thirteenth to the beginning of the fifteenth century; that is to say, over the precise period which I have described as the central epoch of the life of Venice. I dated her decline from the year 1418; Foscari became doge five years later, and in his reign the first marked signs appear in architecture of that mighty change which Philippe de Commynes notices as above, the change to which London owes St. Paul's, Rome St. Peter's, Venice and Vicenza the edifices commonly supposed to be their noblest, and Europe in general the degradation of every art she has since practised.

§ XXXV. This change appears first in a loss of truth and vitality in existing architecture all over the world. (Compare "Seven Lamps," chap. ii.) All the Gothics in existence, southern or northern, were corrupted at once: the German and French lost themselves in every species of extravagance; the English Gothic was confined, in its insanity, by a strait-waistcoat of perpendicular lines; the Italian efforesced on the mainland into the meaningless ornamentation of the Certosa of Pavia and the Cathedral of Como (a style sometimes ignorantly called Italian Gothic), and at Venice into the insipid confusion of the Porta della Carta and wild crockets of St. Mark's. This corruption of all architecture, especially ecclesiastical, corresponded with, and marked the state of religion over all Europe,—the peculiar degradation of the Romanist superstition, and of public morality in consequence, which brought about the Reformation.

§ XXXVI. Against the corrupted papacy arose two great divisions of adversaries, Protestants in Germany and England, Rationalists in France and Italy; the one requiring the purification of religion, the other its destruction. The Protestant kept the religion, but cast aside the heresies of Rome, and with them her arts, by which last rejection he injured his own character, cramped his intellect in refusing to it one of its noblest exercises, and materially diminished his influence. It may be a serious question how far the Pausing of the Reformation has been a consequence of this error.

The Rationalist kept the arts and cast aside the religion. This rationalistic art is the art commonly called Renaissance, marked by a return to pagan systems, not to adopt them and hallow them for Christianity, but to rank itself under them as an imitator and pupil. In Painting it is headed by Giulio Romano and Nicolo Poussin; in Architecture by Sansovino and Palladio.

§ XXXVII. Instant degradation followed in every direction,—a flood of folly and hypocrisy. Mythologies ill understood at first, then perverted into feeble sensualities, take the place of the representations of Christian subjects, which had become blasphemous under the treatment of men like the Caracci. Gods without power, satyrs without rusticity, nymphs without innocence, men without humanity, gather into idiot groups upon the polluted canvas, and scenic affectations encumber the streets with preposterous marble. Lower and lower declines the level of abused intellect; the base school of landscape[23] gradually usurps the place of the historical painting, which had sunk into prurient pedantry,—the Alsatian sublimities of Salvator, the confectionery idealities of Claude, the dull manufacture of Gaspar and Canaletto, south of the Alps, and on the north the patient devotion of besotted lives to delineation of bricks and fogs, fat cattle and ditchwater. And thus Christianity and morality, courage, and intellect, and art all crumbling together into one wreck, we are hurried on to the fall of Italy, the revolution in France, and the condition of art in England (saved by her Protestantism from severer penalty) in the time of George II.

§ XXXVIII. I have not written in vain if I have heretofore done anything towards diminishing the reputation of the Renaissance landscape painting. But the harm which has been done by Claude and the Poussins is as nothing when compared to the mischief effected by Palladio, Scamozzi, and Sansovino. Claude and the Poussins were weak men, and have had no serious influence on the general mind. There is little harm in their works being purchased at high prices: their real influence is very slight, and they may be left without grave indignation to their poor mission of furnishing drawing-rooms and assisting stranded conversation. Not so the Renaissance architecture. Raised at once into all the magnificence of which it was capable by Michael Angelo, then taken up by men of real intellect and imagination, such as Scamozzi, Sansovino, Inigo Jones, and Wren, it is impossible to estimate the extent of its influence on the European mind; and that the more, because few persons are concerned with painting, and, of those few, the larger number regard it with slight attention; but all men are concerned with architecture, and have at some time of their lives serious business with it. It does not much matter that an individual loses two or three hundred pounds in buying a bad picture, but it is to be regretted that a nation should lose two or three hundred thousand in raising a ridiculous building. Nor is it merely wasted wealth or distempered conception which we have to regret in this Renaissance architecture: but we shall find in it partly the root, partly the expression, of certain dominant evils of modern times—over-sophistication and ignorant classicalism; the one destroying the healthfulness of general society, the other rendering our schools and universities useless to a large number of the men who pass through them.

Now Venice, as she was once the most religious, was in her fall the most corrupt, of European states; and as she was in her strength the centre of the pure currents of Christian architecture, so she is in her decline the source of the Renaissance. It was the originality and splendor of the palaces of Vicenza and Venice which gave this school its eminence in the eyes of Europe; and the dying city, magnificent in her dissipation, and graceful in her follies, obtained wider worship in her decrepitude than in her youth, and sank from the midst of her admirers into the grave.

§ XXXIX. It is in Venice, therefore, and in Venice only that effectual blows can be struck at this pestilent art of the Renaissance. Destroy its claims to admiration there, and it can assert them nowhere else. This, therefore, will be the final purpose of the following essay. I shall not devote a fourth section to Palladio, nor weary the reader with successive chapters of vituperation; but I shall, in my account of the earlier architecture, compare the forms of all its leading features with those into which they were corrupted by the Classicalists; and pause, in the close, on the edge of the precipice of decline, so soon as I have made its depths discernible. In doing this I shall depend upon two distinct kinds of evidence:—the first, the testimony borne by particular incidents and facts to a want of thought or of feeling in the builders; from which we may conclude that their architecture must be bad:—the second, the sense, which I doubt not I shall be able to excite in the reader, of a systematic ugliness in the architecture itself. Of the first kind of testimony I shall here give two instances, which may be immediately useful in fixing in the readers mind the epoch above indicated for the commencement of decline.

§ XL. I must again refer to the importance which I have above attached to the death of Carlo Zeno and the doge Tomaso Mocenigo. The tomb of that doge is, as I said, wrought by a Florentine; but it is of the same general type and feeling as all the Venetian tombs of the period, and it is one of the last which retains it. The classical element enters largely into its details, but the feeling of the whole is as yet unaffected. Like all the lovely tombs of Venice and Verona, it is a sarcophagus with a recumbent figure above, and this figure is a faithful but tender portrait, wrought as far as it can be without painfulness, of the doge as he lay in death. He wears his ducal robe and bonnet—his head is laid slightly aside upon his pillow—his hands are simply crossed as they fall. The face is emaciated, the features large, but so pure and lordly in their natural chiselling, that they must have looked like marble even in their animation. They are deeply worn away by thought and death; the veins on the temples branched and starting; the skin gathered in sharp folds; the brow high-arched and shaggy; the eye-ball magnificently large; the curve of the lips just veiled by the light mustache at the side; the beard short, double, and sharp-pointed: all noble and quiet; the white sepulchral dust marking like light the stern angles of the cheek and brow.

This tomb was sculptured in 1424, and is thus described by one of the most intelligent of the recent writers who represent the popular feeling respecting Venetian art.

"Of the Italian school is also the rich but ugly (ricco ma non bel) sarcophagus in which repose the ashes of Tomaso Mocenigo. It may be called one of the last links which connect the declining art of the Middle Ages with that of the Renaissance, which was in its rise. We will not stay to particularise the defects of each of the seven figures of the front and sides, which represent the cardinal and theological virtues; nor will we make any remarks upon those which stand in the niches above the pavilion, because we consider them unworthy both of the age and reputation of the Florentine school, which was then with reason considered the most notable in Italy."[24]

It is well, indeed, not to pause over these defects; but it might have been better to have paused a moment beside that noble image of a king's mortality.

§ XLI. In the choir of the same church, St. Giov. and Paolo, is another tomb, that of the Doge Andrea Vendramin. This doge died in 1478, after a short reign of two years, the most disastrous in the annals of Venice. He died of a pestilence which followed the ravage of the Turks, carried to the shores of the lagoons. He died, leaving Venice disgraced by sea and land, with the smoke of hostile devastation rising in the blue distances of Friuli; and there was raised to him the most costly tomb ever bestowed on her monarchs.

§ XLII. If the writer above quoted was cold beside the statue of one of the fathers of his country, he atones for it by his eloquence beside the tomb of the Vendramin. I must not spoil the force of Italian superlative by translation.

"Quando si guarda a quella corretta eleganza di profili e di proporzioni, a quella squisitezza d'ornamenti, a quel certo sapore antico che senza ombra d'imitazione traspare da tutta l'opera"—&c. "Sopra ornatissimo zoccolo fornito di squisiti intagli s'alza uno stylobate"—&c. "Sotto le colonne, il predetto stilobate si muta leggiadramente in piedistallo, poi con bella novità di pensiero e di effetto va coronato da un fregio il più gentile che veder si possa"—&c. "Non puossi lasciar senza un cenno l'arca dove sta chiuso il doge; capo lavoro di pensiero e di esecuzione," &c.

There are two pages and a half of closely printed praise, of which the above specimens may suffice; but there is not a word of the statue of the dead from beginning to end. I am myself in the habit of considering this rather an important part of a tomb, and I was especially interested in it here, because Selvatico only echoes the praise of thousands. It is unanimously declared the chef d'oeuvre of Renaissance sepulchral work, and pronounced by Cicognara (also quoted by Selvatico)

"Il vertice a cui l'arti Veneziane si spinsero col ministero del scalpello,"—"The very culminating point to which the Venetian arts attained by ministry of the chisel."

To this culminating point, therefore, covered with dust and cobwebs, I attained, as I did to every tomb of importance in Venice, by the ministry of such ancient ladders as were to be found in the sacristan's keeping. I was struck at first by the excessive awkwardness and want of feeling in the fall of the hand towards the spectator, for it is thrown off the middle of the body in order to show its fine cutting. Now the Mocenigo hand, severe and even stiff in its articulations, has its veins finely drawn, its sculptor having justly felt that the delicacy of the veining expresses alike dignity and age and birth. The Vendramin hand is far more laboriously cut, but its blunt and clumsy contour at once makes us feel that all the care has been thrown away, and well it may be, for it has been entirely bestowed in cutting gouty wrinkles about the joints. Such as the hand is, I looked for its fellow. At first I thought it had been broken off, but, on clearing away the dust, I saw the wretched effigy had only one hand, and was a mere block on the inner side. The face, heavy and disagreeable in its features, is made monstrous by its semi-sculpture. One side of the forehead is wrinkled elaborately, the other left smooth; one side only of the doge's cap is chased; one cheek only is finished, and the other blocked out and distorted besides; finally, the ermine robe, which is elaborately imitated to its utmost lock of hair and of ground hair on the one side, is blocked out only on the other: it having been supposed throughout the work that the effigy was only to be seen from below, and from one side.

§ XLIII. It was indeed to be so seen by nearly every one; and I do not blame—I should, on the contrary, have praised—the sculptor for regulating his treatment of it by its position; if that treatment had not involved, first, dishonesty, in giving only half a face, a monstrous mask, when we demanded true portraiture of the dead; and, secondly, such utter coldness of feeling, as could only consist with an extreme of intellectual and moral degradation: Who, with a heart in his breast, could have stayed his hand as he drew the dim lines of the old man's countenance—unmajestic once, indeed, but at least sanctified by the solemnities of death—could have stayed his hand, as he reached the bend of the grey forehead, and measured out the last veins of it at so much the zecchin?

I do not think the reader, if he has feeling, will expect that much talent should be shown in the rest of his work, by the sculptor of this base and senseless lie. The whole monument is one wearisome aggregation of that species of ornamental flourish, which, when it is done with a pen, is called penmanship, and when done with a chisel, should be called chiselmanship; the subject of it being chiefly fat-limbed boys sprawling on dolphins, dolphins incapable of swimming, and dragged along the sea by expanded pocket-handkerchiefs.

But now, reader, comes the very gist and point of the whole matter. This lying monument to a dishonored doge, this culminating pride of the Renaissance art of Venice, is at least veracious, if in nothing else, in its testimony to the character of its sculptor. He was banished from Venice for forgery in 1487.[25]

§ XLIV. I have more to say about this convict's work hereafter; but I pass at present, to the second, slighter, but yet more interesting piece of evidence, which I promised.

The ducal palace has two principal façades; one towards the sea, the other towards the Piazzetta. The seaward side, and, as far as the seventh main arch inclusive, the Piazzetta side, is work of the early part of the fourteenth century, some of it perhaps even earlier; while the rest of the Piazzetta side is of the fifteenth. The difference in age has been gravely disputed by the Venetian antiquaries, who have examined many documents on the subject, and quoted some which they never examined. I have myself collated most of the written documents, and one document more, to which the Venetian antiquaries never thought of referring,—the masonry of the palace itself.

§ XLV. That masonry changes at the centre of the eighth arch from the sea angle on the Piazzetta side. It has been of comparatively small stones up to that point; the fifteenth century work instantly begins with larger stones, "brought from Istria, a hundred miles away."[26] The ninth shaft from the sea in the lower arcade, and the seventeenth, which is above it, in the upper arcade, commence the series of fifteenth century shafts. These two are somewhat thicker than the others, and carry the party-wall of the Sala del Scrutinio. Now observe, reader. The face of the palace, from this point to the Porta della Carta, was built at the instance of that noble Doge Mocenigo beside whose tomb you have been standing; at his instance, and in the beginning of the reign of his successor, Foscari; that is to say, circa 1424. This is not disputed; it is only disputed that the sea façade is earlier; of which, however, the proofs are as simple as they are incontrovertible: for not only the masonry, but the sculpture, changes at the ninth lower shaft, and that in the capitals of the shafts both of the upper and lower arcade: the costumes of the figures introduced in the sea façade being purely Giottesque, correspondent with Giotto's work in the Arena Chapel at Padua, while the costume on the other capitals is Renaissance-Classic: and the lions' heads between the arches change at the same point. And there are a multitude of other evidences in the statues of the angels, with which I shall not at present trouble the reader.

§ XLVI. Now, the architect who built under Foscari, in 1424 (remember my date for the decline of Venice, 1418), was obliged to follow the principal forms of the older palace. But he had not the wit to invent new capitals in the same style; he therefore clumsily copied the old ones. The palace has seventeen main arches on the sea façade, eighteen on the Piazzetta side, which in all are of course carried by thirty-six pillars; and these pillars I shall always number from right to left, from the angle of the palace at the Ponte della Paglia to that next the Porta della Carta. I number them in this succession, because I thus have the earliest shafts first numbered. So counted, the 1st, the 18th, and the 36th, are the great supports of the angles of the palace; and the first of the fifteenth century series, being, as above stated, the 9th from the sea on the Piazzetta side, is the 26th of the entire series, and will always in future be so numbered, so that all numbers above twenty-six indicate fifteenth century work, and all below it, fourteenth century, with some exceptional cases of restoration.

Then the copied capitals are: the 28th, copied from the 7th; the 29th, from the 9th; the 30th, from the 10th; the 31st, from the 8th; the 33rd, from the 12th; and the 34th, from the 11th; the others being dull inventions of the 15th century, except the 36th, which is very nobly designed.

§ XLVII. The capitals thus selected from the earlier portion of the palace for imitation, together with the rest, will be accurately described hereafter; the point I have here to notice is in the copy of the ninth capital, which was decorated (being, like the rest, octagonal) with figures of the eight Virtues:—Faith, Hope, Charity, Justice, Temperance, Prudence, Humility (the Venetian antiquaries call it Humanity!), and Fortitude. The Virtues of the fourteenth century are somewhat hard-featured; with vivid and living expression, and plain every-day clothes of the time. Charity has her lap full of apples (perhaps loaves), and is giving one to a little child, who stretches his arm for it across a gap in the leafage of the capital. Fortitude tears open a lion's jaws; Faith lays her hand on her breast, as she beholds the Cross; and Hope is praying, while above her a hand is seen emerging from sunbeams—the hand of God (according to that of Revelations, "The Lord God giveth them light"); and the inscription above is, "Spes optima in Deo."

§ XLVIII. This design, then, is, rudely and with imperfect chiselling, imitated by the fifteenth century workmen: the Virtues have lost their hard features and living expression; they have now all got Roman noses, and have had their hair curled. Their actions and emblems are, however, preserved until we come to Hope: she is still praying, but she is praying to the sun only: The hand of God is gone.

Is not this a curious and striking type of the spirit which had then become dominant in the world, forgetting to see God's hand in the light He gave; so that in the issue, when that light opened into the Reformation, on the one side, and into full knowledge of ancient literature on the other, the one was arrested and the other perverted?

§ XLIX. Such is the nature of the accidental evidence on which I shall depend for the proof of the inferiority of character in the Renaissance workmen. But the proof of the inferiority of the work itself is not so easy, for in this I have to appeal to judgments which the Renaissance work has itself distorted. I felt this difficulty very forcibly as I read a slight review of my former work, "The Seven Lamps," in "The Architect:" the writer noticed my constant praise of St. Mark's: "Mr. Ruskin thinks it a very beautiful building! We," said the Architect, "think it a very ugly building." I was not surprised at the difference of opinion, but at the thing being considered so completely a subject of opinion. My opponents in matters of painting always assume that there is such a thing as a law of right, and that I do not understand it: but my architectural adversaries appeal to no law, they simply set their opinion against mine; and indeed there is no law at present to which either they or I can appeal. No man can speak with rational decision of the merits or demerits of buildings: he may with obstinacy; he may with resolved adherence to previous prejudices; but never as if the matter could be otherwise decided than by a majority of votes, or pertinacity of partizanship. I had always, however, a clear conviction that there was a law in this matter: that good architecture might be indisputably discerned and divided from the bad; that the opposition in their very nature and essence was clearly visible; and that we were all of us just as unwise in disputing about the matter without reference to principle, as we should be for debating about the genuineness of a coin, without ringing it. I felt also assured that this law must be universal if it were conclusive; that it must enable us to reject all foolish and base work, and to accept all noble and wise work, without reference to style or national feeling; that it must sanction the design of all truly great nations and times, Gothic or Greek or Arab; that it must cast off and reprobate the design of all foolish nations and times, Chinese or Mexican, or modern European: and that it must be easily applicable to all possible architectural inventions of human mind. I set myself, therefore, to establish such a law, in full belief that men are intended, without excessive difficulty, and by use of their general common sense, to know good things from bad; and that it is only because they will not be at the pains required for the discernment, that the world is so widely encumbered with forgeries and basenesses. I found the work simpler than I had hoped; the reasonable things ranged themselves in the order I required, and the foolish things fell aside, and took themselves away so soon as they were looked in the face. I had then, with respect to Venetian architecture, the choice, either to establish each division of law in a separate form, as I came to the features with which it was concerned, or else to ask the reader's patience, while I followed out the general inquiry first, and determined with him a code of right and wrong, to which we might together make retrospective appeal. I thought this the best, though perhaps the dullest way; and in these first following pages I have therefore endeavored to arrange those foundations of criticism, on which I shall rest in my account of Venetian architecture, in a form clear and simple enough to be intelligible even to those who never thought of architecture before. To those who have, much of what is stated in them will be well known or self-evident; but they must not be indignant at a simplicity on which the whole argument depends for its usefulness. From that which appears a mere truism when first stated, they will find very singular consequences sometimes following,—consequences altogether unexpected, and of considerable importance; I will not pause here to dwell on their importance, nor on that of the thing itself to be done; for I believe most readers will at once admit the value of a criterion of right and wrong in so practical and costly an art as architecture, and will be apt rather to doubt the possibility of its attainment than dispute its usefulness if attained. I invite them, therefore, to a fair trial, being certain that even if I should fail in my main purpose, and be unable to induce in my reader the confidence of judgment I desire, I shall at least receive his thanks for the suggestion of consistent reasons, which may determine hesitating choice, or justify involuntary preference. And if I should succeed, as I hope, in making the Stones of Venice touchstones, and detecting, by the mouldering of her marble, poison more subtle than ever was betrayed by the rending of her crystal; and if thus I am enabled to show the baseness of the schools of architecture and nearly every other art, which have for three centuries been predominant in Europe, I believe the result of the inquiry may be serviceable for proof of a more vital truth than any at which I have hitherto hinted. For observe: I said the Protestant had despised the arts, and the Rationalist corrupted them. But what has the Romanist done meanwhile? He boasts that it was the papacy which raised the arts; why could it not support them when it was left to its own strength? How came it to yield to Classicalism which was based on infidelity, and to oppose no barrier to innovations, which have reduced the once faithfully conceived imagery of its worship to stage decoration? Shall we not rather find that Romanism, instead of being a promoter of the arts, has never shown itself capable of a single great conception since the separation of Protestantism from its side?[27] So long as, corrupt though it might be, no clear witness had been borne against it, so that it still included in its ranks a vast number of faithful Christians, so long its arts were noble. But the witness was borne—the error made apparent; and Rome, refusing to hear the testimony or forsake the falsehood, has been struck from that instant with an intellectual palsy, which has not only incapacitated her from any further use of the arts which once were her ministers, but has made her worship the shame of its own shrines, and her worshippers their destroyers. Come, then, if truths such as these are worth our thoughts; come, and let us know, before we enter the streets of the Sea city, whether we are indeed to submit ourselves to their undistinguished enchantment, and to look upon the last changes which were wrought on the lifted forms of her palaces, as we should on the capricious towering of summer clouds in the sunset, ere they sank into the deep of night; or whether, rather, we shall not behold in the brightness of their accumulated marble, pages on which the sentence of her luxury was to be written until the waves should efface it, as they fulfilled—"God has numbered thy kingdom, and finished it."

FOOTNOTES:

[1] Appendix 1, "Foundation of Venice."

[2] Appendix 2, "Power of the Doges."

[3] Sismondi, Hist. des Rép. Ital., vol. i. ch. v.

[4] Appendix 3, "Serrar del Consiglio."

[5] "Ha saputo trovar modo che non uno, non pochi, non molti, signoreggiano, ma molti buoni, pochi migliori, e insiememente, un ottimo solo." (Sansovino.) Ah, well done, Venice! Wisdom this, indeed.

[6] Daru, liv. xii. ch. xii.

[7] Daru, liv. xvi. cap. xx. We owe to this historian the discovery of the statutes of the tribunal and date of its establishment.

[8] Ominously signified by their humiliation to the Papal power (as before to the Turkish) in 1509, and their abandonment of their right of appointing the clergy of their territories.

[9] The senate voted the abdication of their authority by a majority of 512 to 14. (Alison, ch. xxiii.)

[10] By directing the arms of the Crusaders against a Christian prince. (Daru, liv. iv. ch. iv. viii.)

[11] Appendix 4, "San Pietro di Castello."

[12] Tomaso Mocenigo, above named, § V.

[13] "In that temple porch,
(The brass is gone, the porphyry remains,)
Did BARBAROSSA fling his mantle off,
And kneeling, on his neck receive the foot
Of the proud Pontiff—thus at last consoled
For flight, disguise, and many an aguish shake
On his stone pillow."

I need hardly say whence the lines are taken: Rogers' "Italy" has, I believe, now a place in the best beloved compartment of all libraries, and will never be removed from it. There is more true expression of the spirit of Venice in the passages devoted to her in that poem, than in all else that has been written of her.

[14] At least, such success as they had. Vide Appendix 5, "The Papal Power in Venice."

[15] The inconsiderable fortifications of the arsenal are no exception to this statement, as far as it regards the city itself. They are little more than a semblance of precaution against the attack of a foreign enemy.

[16] Mémoires de Commynes, liv. vii. ch. xviii.

[17] Appendix 6, "Renaissance Ornaments."

[18] Appendix 7, "Varieties of the Orders."

[19] The reader will find the weak points of Byzantine architecture shrewdly seized, and exquisitely sketched, in the opening chapter of the most delightful book of travels I ever opened,—Curzon's "Monasteries of the Levant."

[20] Appendix 8, "The Northern Energy."

[21] Appendix 9, "Wooden Churches of the North."

[22] Appendix 10, "Church of Alexandria."

[23] Appendix 11, "Renaissance Landscape."

[24] Selvatico, "Architettura di Venezia," p. 147.

[25] Selvatico, p. 221.

[26] The older work is of Istrian stone also, but of different quality.

[27] Appendix 12, "Romanist Modern Art."

CHAPTER II

THE VIRTUES OF ARCHITECTURE

§ I. We address ourselves, then, first to the task of determining some law of right which we may apply to the architecture of all the world and of all time; and by help of which, and judgment according to which, we may easily pronounce whether a building is good or noble, as, by applying a plumb-line, whether it be perpendicular.

The first question will of course be: What are the possible Virtues of architecture?

In the main, we require from buildings, as from men, two kinds of goodness: first, the doing their practical duty well: then that they be graceful and pleasing in doing it; which last is itself another form of duty.

Then the practical duty divides itself into two branches,—acting and talking:—acting, as to defend us from weather or violence; talking, as the duty of monuments or tombs, to record facts and express feelings; or of churches, temples, public edifices, treated as books of history, to tell such history clearly and forcibly.

We have thus, altogether, three great branches of architectural virtue, and we require of any building,—

1. That it act well, and do the things it was intended to do in the best way.

2. That it speak well, and say the things it was intended to say in the best words.

3. That it look well, and please us by its presence, whatever it has to do or say.[28]

§ II. Now, as regards the second of these virtues, it is evident that we can establish no general laws. First, because it is not a virtue required in all buildings; there are some which are only for covert or defence, and from which we ask no conversation. Secondly, because there are countless methods of expression, some conventional, some natural: each conventional mode has its own alphabet, which evidently can be no subject of general laws. Every natural mode is instinctively employed and instinctively understood, wherever there is true feeling; and this instinct is above law. The choice of conventional methods depends on circumstances out of calculation, and that of natural methods on sensations out of control; so that we can only say that the choice is right, when we feel that the means are effective; and we cannot always say that it is wrong when they are not so.

A building which recorded the Bible history by means of a series of sculptural pictures, would be perfectly useless to a person unacquainted with the Bible beforehand; on the other hand, the text of the Old and New Testaments might be written on its walls, and yet the building be a very inconvenient kind of book, not so useful as if it had been adorned with intelligible and vivid sculpture. So, again, the power of exciting emotion must vary or vanish, as the spectator becomes thoughtless or cold; and the building may be often blamed for what is the fault of its critic, or endowed with a charm which is of its spectator's creation. It is not, therefore, possible to make expressional character any fair criterion of excellence in buildings, until we can fully place ourselves in the position of those to whom their expression was originally addressed, and until we are certain that we understand every symbol, and are capable of being touched by every association which its builders employed as letters of their language. I shall continually endeavor to put the reader into such sympathetic temper, when I ask for his judgment of a building; and in every work I may bring before him I shall point out, as far as I am able, whatever is peculiar in its expression; nay, I must even depend on such peculiarities for much of my best evidence respecting the character of the builders. But I cannot legalize the judgment for which I plead, nor insist upon it if it be refused. I can neither force the reader to feel this architectural rhetoric, nor compel him to confess that the rhetoric is powerful, if it have produced no impression on his own mind.

§ III. I leave, therefore, the expression of buildings for incidental notice only. But their other two virtues are proper subjects of law,—their performance of their common and necessary work, and their conformity with universal and divine canons of loveliness: respecting these there can be no doubt, no ambiguity. I would have the reader discern them so quickly that, as he passes along a street, he may, by a glance of the eye, distinguish the noble from the ignoble work. He can do this, if he permit free play to his natural instincts; and all that I have to do for him is to remove from those instincts the artificial restraints which prevent their action, and to encourage them to an unaffected and unbiassed choice between right and wrong.

§ IV. We have, then, two qualities of buildings for subjects of separate inquiry: their action, and aspect, and the sources of virtue in both; that is to say, Strength and Beauty, both of these being less admired in themselves, than as testifying the intelligence or imagination of the builder.

For we have a worthier way of looking at human than at divine architecture: much of the value both of construction and decoration, in the edifices of men, depends upon our being led by the thing produced or adorned, to some contemplation of the powers of mind concerned in its creation or adornment. We are not so led by divine work, but are content to rest in the contemplation of the thing created. I wish the reader to note this especially: we take pleasure, or should take pleasure, in architectural construction altogether as the manifestation of an admirable human intelligence; it is not the strength, not the size, not the finish of the work which we are to venerate: rocks are always stronger, mountains always larger, all natural objects more finished; but it is the intelligence and resolution of man in overcoming physical difficulty which are to be the source of our pleasure and subject of our praise. And again, in decoration or beauty, it is less the actual loveliness of the thing produced, than the choice and invention concerned in the production, which are to delight us; the love and the thoughts of the workman more than his work: his work must always be imperfect, but his thoughts and affections may be true and deep.

§ V. This origin of our pleasure in architecture I must insist upon at somewhat greater length, for I would fain do away with some of the ungrateful coldness which we show towards the good builders of old time. In no art is there closer connection between our delight in the work, and our admiration of the workman's mind, than in architecture, and yet we rarely ask for a builder's name. The patron at whose cost, the monk through whose dreaming, the foundation was laid, we remember occasionally; never the man who verily did the work. Did the reader ever hear of William of Sens as having had anything to do with Canterbury Cathedral? or of Pietro Basegio as in anywise connected with the Ducal Palace of Venice? There is much ingratitude and injustice in this; and therefore I desire my reader to observe carefully how much of his pleasure in building is derived, or should be derived, from admiration of the intellect of men whose names he knows not.

§ VI. The two virtues of architecture which we can justly weigh, are, we said, its strength or good construction, and its beauty or good decoration. Consider first, therefore, what you mean when you say a building is well constructed or well built; you do not merely mean that it answers its purpose,—this is much, and many modern buildings fail of this much; but if it be verily well built, it must answer this purpose in the simplest way, and with no over-expenditure of means. We require of a light-house, for instance, that it shall stand firm and carry a light; if it do not this, assuredly it has been ill built; but it may do it to the end of time, and yet not be well built. It may have hundreds of tons of stone in it more than were needed, and have cost thousands of pounds more than it ought. To pronounce it well or ill built, we must know the utmost forces it can have to resist, and the best arrangements of stone for encountering them, and the quickest ways of effecting such arrangements: then only, so far as such arrangements have been chosen, and such methods used, is it well built. Then the knowledge of all difficulties to be met, and of all means of meeting them, and the quick and true fancy or invention of the modes of applying the means to the end, are what we have to admire in the builder, even as he is seen through this first or inferior part of his work. Mental power, observe: not muscular nor mechanical, nor technical, nor empirical,—pure, precious, majestic, massy intellect; not to be had at vulgar price, nor received without thanks, and without asking from whom.

§ VII. Suppose, for instance, we are present at the building of a bridge: the bricklayers or masons have had their centring erected for them, and that centring was put together by a carpenter, who had the line of its curve traced for him by the architect: the masons are dexterously handling and fitting their bricks, or, by the help of machinery, carefully adjusting stones which are numbered for their places. There is probably in their quickness of eye and readiness of hand something admirable; but this is not what I ask the reader to admire: not the carpentering, nor the bricklaying, nor anything that he can presently see and understand, but the choice of the curve, and the shaping of the numbered stones, and the appointment of that number; there were many things to be known and thought upon before these were decided. The man who chose the curve and numbered the stones, had to know the times and tides of the river, and the strength of its floods, and the height and flow of them, and the soil of the banks, and the endurance of it, and the weight of the stones he had to build with, and the kind of traffic that day by day would be carried on over his bridge,—all this specially, and all the great general laws of force and weight, and their working; and in the choice of the curve and numbering of stones are expressed not only his knowledge of these, but such ingenuity and firmness as he had, in applying special means to overcome the special difficulties about his bridge. There is no saying how much wit, how much depth of thought, how much fancy, presence of mind, courage, and fixed resolution there may have gone to the placing of a single stone of it. This is what we have to admire,—this grand power and heart of man in the thing; not his technical or empirical way of holding the trowel and laying mortar.

§ VIII. Now there is in everything properly called art this concernment of the intellect, even in the province of the art which seems merely practical. For observe: in this bridge-building I suppose no reference to architectural principles; all that I suppose we want is to get safely over the river; the man who has taken us over is still a mere bridge-builder,—a builder, not an architect: he may be a rough, artless, feelingless man, incapable of doing any one truly fine thing all his days. I shall call upon you to despise him presently in a sort, but not as if he were a mere smoother of mortar; perhaps a great man, infinite in memory, indefatigable in labor, exhaustless in expedient, unsurpassable in quickness of thought. Take good heed you understand him before you despise him.

§ IX. But why is he to be in anywise despised? By no means despise him, unless he happen to be without a soul,[29] or at least to show no signs of it; which possibly he may not in merely carrying you across the river. He may be merely what Mr. Carlyle rightly calls a human beaver after all; and there may be nothing in all that ingenuity of his greater than a complication of animal faculties, an intricate bestiality,—nest or hive building in its highest development. You need something more than this, or the man is despicable; you need that virtue of building through which he may show his affections and delights; you need its beauty or decoration.

§ X. Not that, in reality, one division of the man is more human than another. Theologists fall into this error very fatally and continually; and a man from whom I have learned much, Lord Lindsay, has hurt his noble book by it, speaking as if the spirit of the man only were immortal, and were opposed to his intellect, and the latter to the senses; whereas all the divisions of humanity are noble or brutal, immortal or mortal, according to the degree of their sanctification; and there is no part of the man which is not immortal and divine when it is once given to God, and no part of him which is not mortal by the second death, and brutal before the first, when it is withdrawn from God. For to what shall we trust for our distinction from the beasts that perish? To our higher intellect?—yet are we not bidden to be wise as the serpent, and to consider the ways of the ant?—or to our affections? nay; these are more shared by the lower animals than our intelligence. Hamlet leaps into the grave of his beloved, and leaves it,—a dog had stayed. Humanity and immortality consist neither in reason, nor in love; not in the body, nor in the animation of the heart of it, nor in the thoughts and stirrings of the brain of it,—but in the dedication of them all to Him who will raise them up at the last day.

§ XI. It is not, therefore, that the signs of his affections, which man leaves upon his work, are indeed more ennobling than the signs of his intelligence; but it is the balance of both whose expression we need, and the signs of the government of them all by Conscience; and Discretion, the daughter of Conscience. So, then, the intelligent part of man being eminently, if not chiefly, displayed in the structure of his work, his affectionate part is to be shown in its decoration; and, that decoration may be indeed lovely, two things are needed: first, that the affections be vivid, and honestly shown; secondly, that they be fixed on the right things.

§ XII. You think, perhaps, I have put the requirements in wrong order. Logically I have; practically I have not: for it is necessary first to teach men to speak out, and say what they like, truly; and, in the second place, to teach them which of their likings are ill set, and which justly. If a man is cold in his likings and dislikings, or if he will not tell you what he likes, you can make nothing of him. Only get him to feel quickly and to speak plainly, and you may set him right. And the fact is, that the great evil of all recent architectural effort has not been that men liked wrong things: but that they either cared nothing about any, or pretended to like what they did not. Do you suppose that any modern architect likes what he builds, or enjoys it? Not in the least. He builds it because he has been told that such and such things are fine, and that he should like them. He pretends to like them, and gives them a false relish of vanity. Do you seriously imagine, reader, that any living soul in London likes triglyphs?[30]—or gets any hearty enjoyment out of pediments?[31] You are much mistaken. Greeks did: English people never did,—never will. Do you fancy that the architect of old Burlington Mews, in Regent Street, had any particular satisfaction in putting the blank triangle over the archway, instead of a useful garret window? By no manner of means. He had been told it was right to do so, and thought he should be admired for doing it. Very few faults of architecture are mistakes of honest choice: they are almost always hypocrisies.

§ XIII. So, then, the first thing we have to ask of the decoration is that it should indicate strong liking, and that honestly. It matters not so much what the thing is, as that the builder should really love it and enjoy it, and say so plainly. The architect of Bourges Cathedral liked hawthorns; so he has covered his porch with hawthorn,—it is a perfect Niobe of May. Never was such hawthorn; you would try to gather it forthwith, but for fear of being pricked. The old Lombard architects liked hunting; so they covered their work with horses and hounds, and men blowing trumpets two yards long. The base Renaissance architects of Venice liked masquing and fiddling; so they covered their work with comic masks and musical instruments. Even that was better than our English way of liking nothing, and professing to like triglyphs.

§ XIV. But the second requirement in decoration, is a sign of our liking the right thing. And the right thing to be liked is God's work, which He made for our delight and contentment in this world. And all noble ornamentation is the expression of man's delight in God's work.

§ XV. So, then, these are the two virtues of building: first, the signs of man's own good work; secondly, the expression of man's delight in better work than his own. And these are the two virtues of which I desire my reader to be able quickly to judge, at least in some measure; to have a definite opinion up to a certain point. Beyond a certain point he cannot form one. When the science of the building is great, great science is of course required to comprehend it; and, therefore, of difficult bridges, and light-houses, and harbor walls, and river dykes, and railway tunnels, no judgment may be rapidly formed. But of common buildings, built in common circumstances, it is very possible for every man, or woman, or child, to form judgment both rational and rapid. Their necessary, or even possible, features are but few; the laws of their construction are as simple as they are interesting. The labor of a few hours is enough to render the reader master of their main points; and from that moment he will find in himself a power of judgment which can neither be escaped nor deceived, and discover subjects of interest where everything before had appeared barren. For though the laws are few and simple, the modes of obedience to them are not so. Every building presents its own requirements and difficulties; and every good building has peculiar appliances or contrivances to meet them. Understand the laws of structure, and you will feel the special difficulty in every new building which you approach; and you will know also, or feel instinctively,[32] whether it has been wisely met or otherwise. And an enormous number of buildings, and of styles of buildings, you will be able to cast aside at once, as at variance with these constant laws of structure, and therefore unnatural and monstrous.

§ XVI. Then, as regards decoration, I want you only to consult your own natural choice and liking. There is a right and wrong in it; but you will assuredly like the right if you suffer your natural instinct to lead you. Half the evil in this world comes from people not knowing what they do like, not deliberately setting themselves to find out what they really enjoy. All people enjoy giving away money, for instance: they don't know that,—they rather think they like keeping it; and they do keep it under this false impression, often to their great discomfort. Every body likes to do good; but not one in a hundred finds this out. Multitudes think they like to do evil; yet no man ever really enjoyed doing evil since God made the world.

So in this lesser matter of ornament. It needs some little care to try experiments upon yourself: it needs deliberate question and upright answer. But there is no difficulty to be overcome, no abstruse reasoning to be gone into; only a little watchfulness needed, and thoughtfulness, and so much honesty as will enable you to confess to yourself and to all men, that you enjoy things, though great authorities say you should not.

§ XVII. This looks somewhat like pride; but it is true humility, a trust that you have been so created as to enjoy what is fitting for you, and a willingness to be pleased, as it was intended you should be. It is the child's spirit, which we are then most happy when we most recover; only wiser than children in that we are ready to think it subject of thankfulness that we can still be pleased with a fair color or a dancing light. And, above all, do not try to make all these pleasures reasonable, nor to connect the delight which you take in ornament with that which you take in construction or usefulness. They have no connection; and every effort that you make to reason from one to the other will blunt your sense of beauty, or confuse it with sensations altogether inferior to it. You were made for enjoyment, and the world was filled with things which you will enjoy, unless you are too proud to be pleased by them, or too grasping to care for what you cannot turn to other account than mere delight. Remember that the most beautiful things in the world are the most useless; peacocks and lilies for instance; at least I suppose this quill I hold in my hand writes better than a peacock's would, and the peasants of Vevay, whose fields in spring time are as white with lilies as the Dent du Midi is with its snow, told me the hay was none the better for them.

§ XVIII. Our task therefore divides itself into two branches, and these I shall follow in succession. I shall first consider the construction of buildings, dividing them into their really necessary members or features; and I shall endeavor so to lead the reader forward from the foundation upwards, as that he may find out for himself the best way of doing everything, and having so discovered it, never forget it. I shall give him stones, and bricks, and straw, chisels, and trowels, and the ground, and then ask him to build; only helping him, as I can, if I find him puzzled. And when he has built his house or church, I shall ask him to ornament it, and leave it to him to choose the ornaments as I did to find out the construction: I shall use no influence with him whatever, except to counteract previous prejudices, and leave him, as far as may be, free. And when he has thus found out how to build, and chosen his forms of decoration, I shall do what I can to confirm his confidence in what he has done. I shall assure him that no one in the world could, so far, have done better, and require him to condemn, as futile or fallacious, whatever has no resemblance to his own performances.

FOOTNOTES:

[28] Appendix 13, "Mr. Fergusson's System."

[29] Appendix 14, "Divisions of Humanity."

[30] Triglyph. Literally, "Three Cut." The awkward upright ornament with two notches in it, and a cut at each side, to be seen everywhere at the tops of Doric colonnades, ancient and modern.

[31] Pediment. The triangular space above Greek porticoes, as on the Mansion House or Royal Exchange.

[32] Appendix 15: "Instinctive Judgments."

CHAPTER III

THE SIX DIVISIONS OF ARCHITECTURE

§ I. The practical duties of buildings are twofold.

They have either (1), to hold and protect something; or (2), to place or carry something.

1. Architecture of Protection. This is architecture intended to protect men or their possessions from violence of any kind, whether of men or of the elements. It will include all churches, houses, and treasuries; fortresses, fences, and ramparts; the architecture of the hut and sheepfold; of the palace and the citadel: of the dyke, breakwater, and sea-wall. And the protection, when of living creatures, is to be

understood as including commodiousness and comfort of habitation, wherever these are possible under the given circumstances.

2. Architecture of Position. This is architecture intended to carry men or things to some certain places, or to hold them there. This will include all bridges, aqueducts, and road architecture; light-houses, which have to hold light in appointed places; chimneys to carry smoke or direct currents of air; staircases; towers, which are to be watched from or cried from, as in mosques, or to hold bells, or to place men in positions of offence, as ancient moveable attacking towers, and most fortress towers.

§ II. Protective architecture has to do one or all of three things: to wall a space, to roof it, and to give access to it, of persons, light, and air; and it is therefore to be considered under the three divisions of walls, roofs, and apertures.

We will take, first, a short, general view of the connection of these members, and then examine them in detail: endeavoring always to keep the simplicity of our first arrangement in view; for protective architecture has indeed no other members than these, unless flooring and paving be considered architecture, which it is only when the flooring is also a roof; the laying of the stones or timbers for footing being pavior's or carpenter's work, rather than architect's; and, at all events, work respecting the well or ill doing of which we shall hardly find much difference of opinion, except in points of æsthetics. We shall therefore concern ourselves only with the construction of walls, roofs, and apertures.

§ III. 1. Walls.—A wall is an even and united fence, whether of wood, earth, stone, or metal. When meant for purposes of mere partition or enclosure, it remains a wall proper: but it has generally also to sustain a certain vertical or lateral pressure, for which its strength is at first increased by some general addition to its thickness; but if the pressure becomes very great, it is gathered up into piers to resist vertical pressure, and supported by buttresses to resist lateral pressure.

If its functions of partition or enclosure are continued, together with that of resisting vertical pressure, it remains as a wall veil between the piers into which it has been partly gathered; but if it is required only to resist the vertical or roof pressure, it is gathered up into piers altogether, loses its wall character, and becomes a group or line of piers.

On the other hand, if the lateral pressure be slight, it may retain its character of a wall, being supported against the pressure by buttresses at intervals; but if the lateral pressure be very great, it is supported against such pressure by a continuous buttress, loses its wall character, and becomes a dyke or rampart.

§ IV. We shall have therefore (A) first to get a general idea of a wall, and of right construction of walls; then (B) to see how this wall is gathered into piers; and to get a general idea of piers and the right construction of piers; then (C) to see how a wall is supported by buttresses, and to get a general idea of buttresses and the right construction of buttresses. This is surely very simple, and it is all we shall have to do with walls and their divisions.

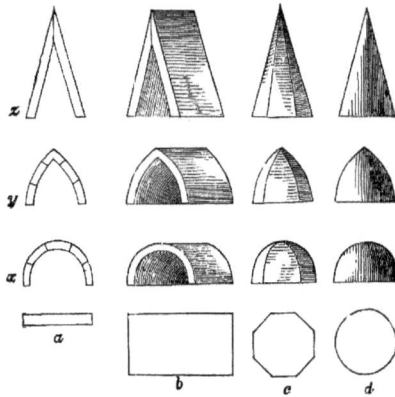

Fig. I.

§ V. 2. Roofs.—A roof is the covering of a space, narrow or wide. It will be most conveniently studied by first considering the forms in which it may be carried over a narrow space, and then expanding these on a wide plan; only there is some difficulty here in the nomenclature, for an arched roof over a narrow space has (I believe) no name, except that which belongs properly to the piece of stone or wood composing such a roof, namely, lintel. But the reader will have no difficulty in understanding that he is first to consider roofs on the section only, thinking how best to construct a narrow bar or slice of them, of whatever form; as, for instance, x, y, or z, over the plan or area a, Fig. I. Having done this, let him imagine these several divisions, first moved along (or set side by side) over a rectangle, b, Fig. I., and then revolved round a point (or crossed at it) over a polygon, c, or circle, d, and he will have every form of simple roof: the arched section giving successively the vaulted roof and dome, and the gabled section giving the gabled roof and spire.

As we go farther into the subject, we shall only have to add one or two forms to the sections here given, in order to embrace all the uncombined roofs in existence; and we shall not trouble the reader with many questions respecting cross-vaulting, and other modes of their combination.

§ VI. Now, it also happens, from its place in buildings, that the sectional roof over a narrow space will need to be considered before we come to the expanded roof over a broad one. For when a wall has been gathered, as above explained, into piers, that it may better bear vertical pressure, it is generally necessary that it should be expanded again at the top into a continuous wall before it carries the true roof. Arches or lintels are, therefore, thrown from pier to pier, and a level preparation for carrying the real roof is made above them. After we have examined the structure of piers, therefore, we shall have to see how lintels or arches are thrown from pier to pier, and the whole prepared for the superincumbent roof; this arrangement being universal in all good architecture prepared for vertical pressures: and we shall then examine the condition of the great roof itself. And because the structure of the roof very often introduces certain lateral pressures which have much to do with the placing of buttresses, it will be well to do all this before we examine the nature of buttresses, and, therefore, between parts (B) and (C) of the above plan, § IV. So now we shall have to study: (A) the construction of walls; (B) that of piers; (C) that of lintels or arches prepared for roofing; (D) that of roofs proper; and (E) that of buttresses.

§ VII. 3. Apertures.—There must either be intervals between the piers, of which intervals the character will be determined by that of the piers themselves, or else doors or windows in the walls proper. And, respecting doors or windows, we have to determine three things: first, the proper shape of the entire aperture; secondly, the way in which it is to be filled with valves or glass; and thirdly, the modes of protecting it on the outside, and fitting appliances of convenience to it, as porches or balconies. And this will be our division F; and if the reader will have the patience to go through these six heads, which include every possible feature of protective architecture, and to consider the simple necessities and fitnesses of each, I will answer for it, he shall never confound good architecture with bad any more. For, as to architecture of position, a great part of it involves necessities of construction with which the spectator cannot become generally acquainted, and of the compliance with which he is therefore never expected to judge,—as in chimneys, light-houses, &c.: and the other forms of it are so closely connected with those of protective architecture, that a few words in Chap. XIX. respecting staircases and towers, will contain all with which the reader need be troubled on the subject.

CHAPTER IV

THE WALL BASE

§ I. Our first business, then, is with Wall, and to find out wherein lies the true excellence of the "Wittiest Partition." For it is rather strange that, often as we speak of a "dead" wall, and that with considerable disgust, we have not often, since Snout's time, heard of a living one. But the common epithet of opprobrium is justly bestowed, and marks a right feeling. A wall has no business to be dead. It ought to have members in its make, and purposes in its existence, like an organized creature, and to answer its ends in a living and energetic way; and it is only when we do not choose to put any strength nor organization into it, that it offends us by its deadness. Every wall ought to be a "sweet and lovely wall." I do not care about its having ears; but, for instruction and exhortation, I would often have it to "hold up its fingers." What its necessary members and excellences are, it is our present business to discover.

§ II. A wall has been defined to be an even and united fence of wood, earth, stone, or metal. Metal fences, however, seldom, if ever, take the form of walls, but of railings; and, like all other metal constructions, must be left out of our present investigation; as may be also walls composed merely of light planks or laths for purposes of partition or inclosure. Substantial walls, whether of wood or earth (I use the word earth as including clay, baked or unbaked, and stone), have, in their perfect form, three distinct members;—the Foundation, Body or Veil, and Cornice.

§ III. The foundation is to the wall what the paw is to an animal. It is a long foot, wider than the wall, on which the wall is to stand, and which keeps it from settling into the ground. It is most necessary that this great element of security should be visible to the eye, and therefore made a part of the structure above ground. Sometimes, indeed, it becomes incorporated with the entire foundation of the building, a vast table on which walls or piers are alike set: but even then, the eye, taught by the reason, requires some additional preparation or foot for the wall, and the building is felt to be imperfect without it. This foundation we shall call the Base of the wall.

§ IV. The body of the wall is of course the principal mass of it, formed of mud or clay, of bricks or stones, of logs or hewn timber; the condition of structure being, that it is of equal thickness everywhere, below and above. It may be half a foot thick, or six feet thick, or fifty feet thick; but if of equal thickness everywhere, it is still a wall proper: if to its fifty feet of proper thickness there be added so much as an inch of thickness in particular parts, that added thickness is to be considered as some form of buttress or pier, or other appliance.[33]

In perfect architecture, however, the walls are generally kept of moderate thickness, and strengthened by piers or buttresses; and the part of the wall between these, being generally intended only to secure privacy, or keep out the slighter forces of weather, may be properly called a Wall Veil. I shall always use this word "Veil" to signify the even portion of a wall, it being more expressive than the term Body.

§ V. When the materials with which this veil is built are very loose, or of shapes which do not fit well together, it sometimes becomes necessary, or at least adds to security, to introduce courses of more solid material. Thus, bricks alternate with rolled pebbles in the old walls of Verona, and hewn stones with brick in its Lombard churches. A banded structure, almost a stratification of the wall, is thus produced; and the courses of more solid material are sometimes decorated with carving. Even when the wall is not thus banded through its whole height, it frequently becomes expedient to lay a course of stone, or at least of more carefully chosen materials, at regular heights; and such belts or bands we may call String courses. These are a kind of epochs in the wall's existence; something like periods of rest and reflection in human life, before entering on a new career. Or else, in the building, they correspond to the divisions of its stories within, express its internal structure, and mark off some portion of the ends of its existence already attained.

§ VI. Finally, on the top of the wall some protection from the weather is necessary, or some preparation for the reception of superincumbent weight, called a coping, or Cornice. I shall use the word Cornice for both; for, in fact, a coping is a roof to the wall itself, and is carried by a small cornice as the roof of the building by a large one. In either case, the cornice, small or large, is the termination of the wall's existence, the accomplishment of its work. When it is meant to carry some superincumbent weight, the cornice may be considered as its hand, opened to carry something above its head; as the base was considered its foot: and the three parts should grow out of each other and form one whole, like the root, stalk, and bell of a flower.

These three parts we shall examine in succession; and, first, the Base.

§ VII. It may be sometimes in our power, and it is always expedient, to prepare for the whole building some settled foundation, level and firm, out of sight. But this has not been done in some of the noblest buildings in existence. It cannot always be done perfectly, except at enormous expense; and, in reasoning upon the superstructure, we shall never suppose it to be done. The mind of the spectator does not conceive it; and he estimates the merits of the edifice on the supposition of its being built upon the ground. Even if there be a vast table land of foundation elevated for the whole of it, accessible by steps all round, as at Pisa, the surface of this table is always conceived as capable of yielding somewhat to superincumbent weight, and generally is so; and we shall base all our arguments on the widest possible supposition, that is to say, that the building stands on a surface either of earth, or, at all events, capable of yielding in some degree to its weight.

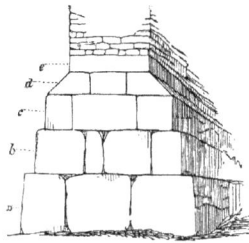

Fig. II.

§ VIII. Now, let the reader simply ask himself how, on such a surface, he would set about building a substantial wall, that should be able to bear weight and to stand for ages. He would assuredly look about for the largest stones he had at his disposal, and, rudely levelling the ground, he would lay these well together over a considerably larger width than he required the wall to be (suppose as at a, Fig. II.), in order to equalise the pressure of the wall over a large surface, and form its foot. On the top of these he would perhaps lay a second tier of large stones, b, or even the third, c, making the breadth somewhat less each time, so as to prepare for the pressure of the wall on the centre, and, naturally or necessarily, using somewhat smaller stones above than below (since we supposed him to look about for the largest first), and cutting them more neatly. His third tier, if not his second, will probably appear a sufficiently secure foundation for finer work; for if the earth yield at all, it will probably yield pretty equally under the great mass of masonry now knit together over it. So he will prepare for the wall itself at once by sloping off the next tier of stones to the right diameter, as at d. If there be any joints in this tier within the wall, he may perhaps, for further security, lay a binding stone across them, e, and then begin the work of the wall veil itself, whether in bricks or stones.

§ IX. I have supposed the preparation here to be for a large wall, because such a preparation will give us the best general type. But it is evident that the essential features of the arrangement are only two, that is to say, one tier of massy work for foundation, suppose c, missing the first two; and the receding tier or real foot of the wall, d. The reader will find these members, though only of brick, in most of the considerable and independent walls in the suburbs of London.

§ X. It is evident, however, that the general type, Fig. II., will be subject to many different modifications in different circumstances. Sometimes the ledges of the tiers a and b may be of greater width; and when the building is in a secure place, and of finished masonry, these may be sloped off also like the main foot d. In Venetian buildings these lower ledges are exposed to the sea, and therefore left rough hewn; but in fine work and in important positions the lower ledges may be bevelled and decorated like the upper, or another added above d; and all these parts may be in different proportions, according to the disposition of the building above them. But we have nothing to do with any of these variations at present, they being all more or less dependent upon decorative considerations, except only one of very great importance, that is to say, the widening of the lower ledge into a stone seat, which may be often done in buildings of great size with most beautiful effect: it looks kind and hospitable, and preserves the work above from violence. In St. Mark's at Venice, which is a small and low church, and needing no great foundation for the wall veils of it, we find only the three members, b, c, and d. Of these the first rises about a foot above the pavement of St. Mark's Place, and forms an elevated dais in some of the recesses of the porches, chequered red and white; c forms a seat which follows the line of the walls, while its basic character is marked by its also carrying certain shafts with which we have here no concern; d is of white marble; and all are enriched and decorated in the simplest and most perfect manner possible, as we shall see in Chap. XXV. And thus much may serve to fix the type of wall bases, a type oftener followed in real practice than any other we shall hereafter be enabled to determine: for wall bases of necessity must be solidly built, and the architect is therefore driven into the adoption of the right form; or if he deviate from it, it is generally in meeting some necessity of peculiar circumstances, as in obtaining cellars and underground room, or in preparing for some grand features or particular parts of the wall, or in some mistaken idea of decoration,—into which errors we had better not pursue him until we understand something more of the rest of the building: let us therefore proceed to consider the wall veil.

FOOTNOTES:

[33] *Many walls are slightly sloped or curved towards their tops, and have buttresses added to them (that of the Queen's Bench Prison is a curious instance of the vertical buttress and inclined wall); but in all such instances the slope of the wall is properly to be considered a condition of incorporated buttress.*

CHAPTER V

THE WALL VEIL

§ I. The summer of the year 1849 was spent by the writer in researches little bearing upon his present subject, and connected chiefly with proposed illustrations of the mountain forms in the works of J. M. W. Turner. But there are sometimes more valuable lessons to be learned in the school of nature than in that of Vitruvius, and a fragment of building among the Alps is singularly illustrative of the chief feature which I have at present to develope as necessary to the perfection of the wall veil.

It is a fragment of some size; a group of broken walls, one of them overhanging; crowned with a cornice, nodding some hundred and fifty feet over its massy flank, three thousand above its glacier base, and fourteen thousand above the sea,—a wall truly of some majesty, at once the most precipitous and the strongest mass in the whole chain of the Alps, the Mont Cervin.

§ II. It has been falsely represented as a peak or tower. It is a vast ridged promontory, connected at its western root with the Dent d'Erin, and lifting itself like a rearing horse with its face to the east. All the way along the flank of it, for half a day's journey on the Zmutt glacier, the grim black terraces of its foundations range almost without a break; and the clouds, when their day's work is done, and they are weary, lay themselves down on those foundation steps, and rest till dawn, each with his leagues of grey mantle stretched along the grisly ledge, and the cornice of the mighty wall gleaming in the moonlight, three thousand feet above.

§ III. The eastern face of the promontory is hewn down, as if by the single sweep of a sword, from the crest of it to the base; hewn concave and smooth, like the hollow of a wave: on each flank of it there is set a buttress, both of about equal height, their heads sloped out from the main wall about seven hundred feet below its summit. That on the north is the most important; it is as sharp as the frontal angle of a bastion, and sloped sheer away to the north-east, throwing out spur beyond spur, until it terminates in a long low curve of russet precipice, at whose foot a great bay of the glacier of the Col de Cervin lies as level as a lake. This spur is one of the few points from which the mass of the Mont Cervin is in anywise approachable. It is a continuation of the masonry of the mountain itself, and affords us the means of examining the character of its materials.

§ IV. Few architects would like to build with them. The slope of the rocks to the north-west is covered two feet deep with their ruins, a mass of loose and slaty shale, of a dull brick-red color, which yields beneath the foot like ashes, so that, in running down, you step one yard, and slide three. The rock is indeed hard beneath, but still disposed in thin courses of these cloven shales, so finely laid that they look in places more like a heap of crushed autumn leaves than a rock; and the first sensation is one of unmitigated surprise, as if the mountain were upheld by miracle; but surprise becomes more intelligent reverence for the great builder, when we find, in the middle of the mass of these dead leaves, a course of living rock, of quartz as white as the snow that encircles it, and harder than a bed of steel.

§ V. It is one only of a thousand iron bands that knit the strength of the mighty mountain. Through the buttress and the wall alike, the courses of its varied masonry are seen in their successive order, smooth and true as if laid by line and plummet,[34] but of thickness and strength continually varying, and with silver cornices glittering along the edge of each, laid by the snowy winds and carved by the sunshine,—stainless ornaments of the eternal temple, by which "neither the hammer nor the axe, nor any tool, was heard while it was in building."

§ VI. I do not, however, bring this forward as an instance of any universal law of natural building; there are solid as well as coursed masses of precipice, but it is somewhat curious that the most noble cliff in Europe, which this eastern front of the Cervin is, I believe, without dispute, should be to us an example of the utmost possible stability of precipitousness attained with materials of imperfect and variable character; and, what is more, there are very few cliffs which do not display alternations between compact and friable conditions of their material, marked in their contours by bevelled slopes when the bricks are soft, and vertical steps when they are harder. And, although we are not hence to conclude that it is well to introduce courses of bad materials when we can get perfect material, I believe we may conclude with great certainty that it is better and easier to strengthen a wall necessarily of imperfect substance, as of brick, by introducing carefully laid courses of stone, than by adding to its thickness; and the first impression we receive from the unbroken aspect of a wall veil, unless it be of hewn stone throughout, is that it must be both thicker and weaker than it would have been, had it been properly coursed. The decorative reasons for adopting the coursed arrangement, which we shall notice hereafter, are so weighty, that they would alone be almost sufficient to enforce it; and the constructive ones will apply universally, except in the rare cases in which the choice of perfect or imperfect material is entirely open to us, or where the general system of the decoration of the building requires absolute unity in its surface.

Fig. III.

§ VII. As regards the arrangement of the intermediate parts themselves, it is regulated by certain conditions of bonding and fitting the stones or bricks, which the reader need hardly be troubled to consider, and which I wish that bricklayers themselves were always honest enough to observe. But I hardly know whether to note under the head of æsthetic or constructive law, this important principle, that masonry is always bad which appears to have arrested the attention of the architect more than absolute conditions of strength require. Nothing is more contemptible in any work than an appearance of the slightest desire on the part of the builder to direct attention to the way its stones are put together, or of any trouble taken either to show or to conceal it more than was rigidly necessary: it may sometimes, on the one hand, be necessary to conceal it as far as may be, by delicate and close fitting, when the joints would interfere with lines of sculpture or of mouldings; and it may often, on the other hand, be delightful to show it, as it is delightful in places to show the anatomy even of the most delicate human frame: but studiously to conceal it is the error of vulgar painters, who are afraid to show that their figures have bones; and studiously to display it is the error of the base pupils of Michael Angelo, who turned heroes' limbs into surgeons' diagrams,—but with less excuse than theirs, for there is less interest in the anatomy displayed. Exhibited masonry is in most cases the expedient of architects who do not know how to fill up blank spaces, and many a building, which would have been decent enough if let alone, has been scrawled over with straight lines, as in Fig. III., on exactly the same principles, and with just the same amount of intelligence as a boy's in scrawling his copy-book when he cannot write. The device was thought ingenious at one period of architectural history; St. Paul's and Whitehall are covered with it, and it is in this I imagine that some of our modern architects suppose the great merit of those buildings to consist. There is, however, no excuse for errors in disposition of masonry, for there is but one law upon the subject, and that easily complied with, to avoid all affectation and all unnecessary expense, either in showing or concealing. Every one knows a building is built of separate stones; nobody will ever object to seeing that it is so, but nobody wants to count them. The divisions of a church are much like the divisions of a sermon; they are always right so long as they are necessary to edification, and always wrong when they are thrust upon the attention as divisions only. There may be neatness in carving when there is richness in feasting; but I have heard many a discourse, and seen many a church wall, in which it was all carving and no meat.

FOOTNOTES:

[34] On the eastern side: violently contorted on the northern and western.

CHAPTER VI

THE WALL CORNICE

§ I. We have lastly to consider the close of the wall's existence, or its cornice. It was above stated, that a cornice has one of two offices: if the wall have nothing to carry, the cornice is its roof, and defends it from the weather; if there is weight to be carried above the wall, the cornice is its hand, and is expanded to carry the said weight.

There are several ways of roofing or protecting independent walls, according to the means nearest at hand: sometimes the wall has a true roof all to itself; sometimes it terminates in a small gabled ridge, made of bricks set slanting, as constantly in the suburbs of London; or of hewn stone, in stronger work; or in a single sloping face, inclined to the outside. We need not trouble ourselves at present about these small roofings, which are merely the diminutions of large ones; but we must examine the important and constant member of the wall structure, which prepares it either for these small roofs or for weights above, and is its true cornice.

§ II. The reader will, perhaps, as heretofore, be kind enough to think for himself, how, having carried up his wall veil as high as it may be needed, he will set about protecting it from weather, or preparing it for weight. Let him imagine the top of the unfinished wall, as it would be seen from above with all the joints, perhaps uncemented, or imperfectly filled up with cement, open to the sky; and small broken materials filling gaps between large ones, and leaving cavities ready for the rain to soak into, and loosen and dissolve the cement, and split, as it froze, the whole to pieces. I am much mistaken if his first impulse would not be to take a great flat stone and lay it on the top; or rather a series of such, side by side, projecting well over the edge of the wall veil. If, also, he proposed to lay a weight (as, for instance, the end of a beam) on the wall, he would feel at once that the pressure of this beam on, or rather among, the small stones of the wall veil, might possibly dislodge or disarrange some of them; and the first impulse would be, in this case, also to lay a large flat stone on the top of all to receive the beam, or any other weight, and distribute it equally among the small stones below, as at a, Fig. IV.

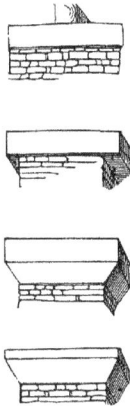

Fig. IV.

§ III. We must therefore have our flat stone in either case; and let b, Fig. IV., be the section or side of it, as it is set across the wall. Now, evidently, if by any chance this weight happen to be thrown more on the edges of this stone than the centre, there will be a chance of these edges breaking off. Had we not better, therefore, put another stone, sloped off to the wall, beneath the projecting one, as at c. But now our cornice looks somewhat too heavy for the wall; and as the upper stone is evidently of needless thickness, we will thin it somewhat, and we have the form d. Now observe: the lower or bevelled stone here at d corresponds to d in the base (Fig. II., page 59). That was the foot of the wall; this is its hand. And the top stone here, which is a constant member of cornices, corresponds to the under stone c, in Fig. II., which is a constant member of bases. The reader has no idea at present of the enormous importance of these members; but as we shall have to refer to them perpetually, I must ask him to compare them, and fix their relations well in his mind: and, for convenience, I shall call the bevelled or sloping stone, X, and the upright edged stone, Y. The reader may remember easily which is which; for X is an intersection of two slopes, and may therefore properly mean either of the two sloping stones; and

Y is a figure with a perpendicular line and two slopes, and may therefore fitly stand for the upright stone in relation to each of the sloping ones; and as we shall have to say much more about cornices than about bases, let X and Y stand for the stones of the cornice, and Xb and Yb for those of the base, when distinction is needed.

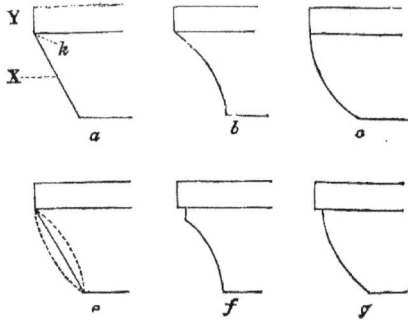

Fig. V.

§ IV. Now the form at d, Fig. IV., is the great root and primal type of all cornices whatsoever. In order to see what forms may be developed from it, let us take its profile a little larger—a, Fig. V., with X and Y duly marked. Now this form, being the root of all cornices, may either have to finish the wall and so keep off rain; or, as so often stated, to carry weight. If the former, it is evident that, in its present profile, the rain will run back down the slope of X; and if the latter, that the sharp angle or edge of X, at k, may be a little too weak for its work, and run a chance of giving way. To avoid the evil in the first case, suppose we hollow the slope of X inwards, as at b; and to avoid it in the second case, suppose we strengthen X by letting it bulge outwards, as at c.

§ V. These (b and c) are the profiles of two vast families of cornices, springing from the same root, which, with a third arising from their combination (owing its origin to æsthetic considerations, and inclining sometimes to the one, sometimes to the other), have been employed, each on its third part of the architecture of the whole world throughout all ages, and must continue to be so employed through such time as is yet to come. We do not at present speak of the third or combined group; but the relation of the two main branches to each other, and to the line of origin, is given at e, Fig. V.; where the dotted lines are the representatives of the two families, and the straight line of the root. The slope of this right line, as well as the nature of the curves, here drawn as segments of circles, we leave undetermined: the slope, as well as the proportion of the depths of X and Y to each other, vary according to the weight to be carried, the strength of the stone, the size of the cornice, and a thousand other accidents; and the nature of the curves according to æsthetic laws. It is in these infinite fields that the invention of the architect is permitted to expatiate, but not in the alteration of primitive forms.

§ VI. But to proceed. It will doubtless appear to the reader, that, even allowing for some of these permissible variations in the curve or slope of X, neither the form at b, nor any approximation to that form, would be sufficiently undercut to keep the rain from running back upon it. This is true; but we have to consider that the cornice, as the close of the wall's life, is of all its features that which is best fitted for honor and ornament. It has been esteemed so by almost all builders, and has been lavishly decorated in modes hereafter to be considered. But it is evident that, as it is high above the eye, the fittest place to receive the decoration is the slope of X, which is inclined towards the spectator; and if we cut away or hollow out this slope more than we have done at b, all decoration will be hid in the shadow. If, therefore, the climate be fine, and rain of long continuance not to be dreaded, we shall not hollow the stone X further, adopting the curve at b merely as the most protective in our power. But if the climate be one in which rain is frequent and dangerous, as in alternations with frost, we may be compelled to consider the cornice in a character distinctly protective, and to hollow out X farther, so as to enable it thoroughly to accomplish its purpose. A cornice thus treated loses its character as the crown or honor of the wall, takes the office of its protector, and is called a DRIPSTONE. The dripstone is naturally the attribute of Northern buildings, and therefore especially of Gothic architecture; the true cornice is the attribute of Southern buildings, and therefore of Greek and Italian architecture; and it is one of their peculiar beauties, and eminent features of superiority.

§ VII. Before passing to the dripstone, however, let us examine a little farther into the nature of the true cornice. We cannot, indeed, render either of the forms b or c, Fig. V., perfectly protective from rain, but we can help them a little in their duty by a slight advance of their upper ledge. This, with the form b, we can best manage by cutting off the sharp upper point of its curve, which is evidently weak and useless; and we shall have the form f. By a slight advance of the upper stone c, we shall have the parallel form g.

These two cornices, f and g, are characteristic of early Byzantine work, and are found on all the most lovely examples of it in Venice. The type a is rarer, but occurs pure in the most exquisite piece of composition in Venice—the northern portico of St. Mark's; and will be given in due time.

§ VIII. Now the reader has doubtless noticed that these forms of cornice result, from considerations of fitness and necessity, far more neatly and decisively than the forms of the base, which we left only very generally determined. The reason is, that there are many ways of building foundations, and many good ways, dependent upon the peculiar accidents of the ground and nature of accessible materials. There is also room to spare in width, and a chance of a part of the arrangement being concealed by the ground, so as to modify height. But we have no room to spare in width on the top of a wall, and all that we do must be thoroughly visible; and we can but have to deal with bricks, or stones of a certain degree of fineness, and not with mere gravel, or sand, or clay,—so that as the conditions are limited, the forms become determined; and our steps will be more clear and certain the farther we advance. The sources of a river are usually half lost among moss and pebbles, and its first movements doubtful in direction; but, as the current gathers force, its banks are determined, and its branches are numbered.

§ IX. So far of the true cornice: we have still to determine the form of the dripstone.

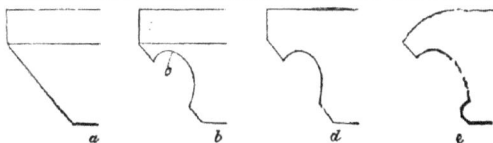

Fig. VI.

We go back to our primal type or root of cornice, a of Fig. V. We take this at a in Fig. VI., and we are to consider it entirely as a protection against rain. Now the only way in which the rain can be kept from running back on the slope of X is by a bold hollowing out of it upwards, b. But clearly, by thus doing, we shall so weaken the projecting part of it that the least shock would break it at the neck, c; we must therefore cut the whole out of one stone, which will give us the form d. That the water may not lodge on the upper ledge of this, we had better round it off; and it will better protect the joint at the bottom of the slope if we let the stone project over it in a roll, cutting the recess deeper above. These two changes are made in e: e is the type of dripstones; the projecting part being, however, more or less rounded into an approximation to the shape of a falcon's beak, and often reaching it completely. But the essential part of the arrangement is the up and under cutting of the curve. Wherever we find this, we are sure that the climate is wet, or that the builders have been bred in a wet country, and that the rest of the building will be prepared for rough weather. The up cutting of the curve is sometimes all the distinction between the mouldings of far-distant countries and utterly strange nations.

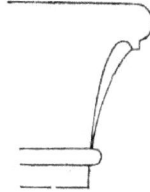

Fig. VII.

Fig. VII. representing a moulding with an outer and inner curve, the latter undercut. Take the outer line, and this moulding is one constant in Venice, in architecture traceable to Arabian types, and chiefly to the early mosques of Cairo. But take the inner line; it is a dripstone at Salisbury. In that narrow interval between the curves there is, when we read it rightly, an expression of another and mightier curve,—the orbed sweep of the earth and sea, between the desert of the Pyramids, and the green and level fields through which the clear streams of Sarum wind so slowly.

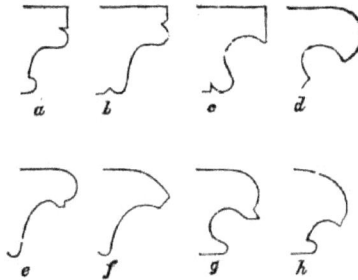

Fig. VIII.

And so delicate is the test, that though pure cornices are often found in the north,—borrowed from classical models,—so surely as we find a true dripstone moulding in the South, the influence of Northern builders has been at work; and this will be one of the principal evidences which I shall use in detecting Lombard influence on Arab work; for the true Byzantine and Arab mouldings are all open to the sky and light, but the Lombards brought with them from the North the fear of rain, and in all the Lombardic Gothic we instantly recognize the shadowy dripstone: a, Fig. VIII., is from a noble fragment at Milan, in the Piazza dei Mercanti; b, from the Broletto of Como. Compare them with c and d; both from Salisbury; e and f from Lisieux, Normandy; g and h from Wenlock Abbey, Shropshire.

§ X. The reader is now master of all that he need know about the construction of the general wall cornice, fitted either to become a crown of the wall, or to carry weight above. If, however, the weight above become considerable, it may be necessary to support the cornice at intervals with brackets; especially if it be required to project far, as well as to carry weight; as, for instance, if there be a gallery on top of the wall. This kind of bracket-cornice, deep or shallow, forms a separate family, essentially connected with roofs and galleries; for if there be no superincumbent weight, it is evidently absurd to put brackets to a plain cornice or dripstone (though this is sometimes done in carrying out a style); so that, as soon as we see a bracket put to a cornice, it implies, or should imply, that there is a roof or gallery above it. Hence this family of cornices I shall consider in connection with roofing, calling them "roof cornices," while what we have hitherto examined are proper "wall cornices." The roof cornice and wall cornice are therefore treated in division D.

We are not, however, as yet nearly ready for our roof. We have only obtained that which was to be the object of our first division (A); we have got, that is to say, a general idea of a wall and of the three essential parts of a wall; and we have next, it will be remembered, to get an idea of a pier and the essential parts of a pier, which were to be the subjects of our second division (B).

CHAPTER VII

THE PIER BASE

§ I. In § III. of Chap. III., it was stated that when a wall had to sustain an addition of vertical pressure, it was first fitted to sustain it by some addition to its own thickness; but if the pressure became very great, by being gathered up into PIERS.

I must first make the reader understand what I mean by a wall's being gathered up. Take a piece of tolerably thick drawing-paper, or thin Bristol board, five or six inches square. Set it on its edge on the table, and put a small octavo book on the edge or top of it, and it will bend instantly. Tear it into four strips all across, and roll up each strip tightly. Set these rolls on end on the table, and they will carry the small octavo perfectly well. Now the thickness or substance of the paper employed to carry the weight is exactly the same as it was before, only it is differently arranged, that is to say, "gathered up."[35] If therefore a wall be gathered up like the Bristol board, it will bear greater weight than it would if it remained a wall veil. The sticks into which you gather it are called Piers. A pier is a coagulated wall.

§ II. Now you cannot quite treat the wall as you did the Bristol board, and twist it up at once; but let us see how you can treat it. Let A, Fig. IX., be the plan of a wall which you have made inconveniently and expensively thick, and which still appears to be slightly too weak for what it must carry: divide it, as at B, into equal spaces, a, b, a, b, &c. Cut out a thin slice of it at every a on each side, and put the slices you cut out on at every b on each side, and you will have the plan at B, with exactly the same quantity of bricks. But your wall is now so much concentrated, that, if it was only slightly too weak before, it will be stronger now than it need be; so you may spare some of your space as well as your bricks by cutting off the corners of the thicker parts, as suppose c, c, c, c, at C: and you have now a series of square piers connected by a wall veil, which, on less space and with less materials, will do the work of the wall at A perfectly well.

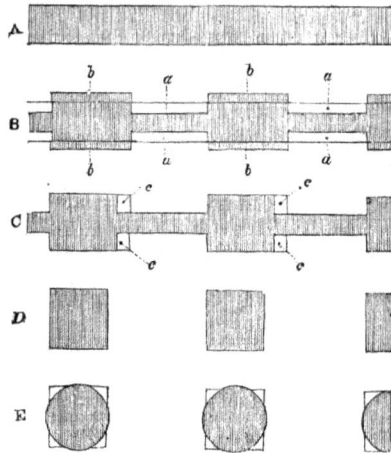

Fig. IX.

§ III. I do not say how much may be cut away in the corners c, c,—that is a mathematical question with which we need not trouble ourselves: all that we need know is, that out of every slice we take from the "b's" and put on at the "a's," we may keep a certain percentage of room and bricks, until, supposing that we do not want the wall veil for its own sake, this latter is thinned entirely away, like the girdle of the Lady of Avenel, and finally breaks, and we have nothing but a row of square piers, D.

§ IV. But have we yet arrived at the form which will spare most room, and use fewest materials. No; and to get farther we must apply the general principle to our wall, which is equally true in morals and mathematics, that the strength of materials, or of men, or of minds, is always most available when it is applied as closely as possible to a single point.

Let the point to which we wish the strength of our square piers to be applied, be chosen. Then we shall of course put them directly under it, and the point will be in their centre. But now some of their materials are not so near or close to this point as others. Those at the corners are farther off than the rest.

Now, if every particle of the pier be brought as near as possible to the centre of it, the form it assumes is the circle.

The circle must be, therefore, the best possible form of plan for a pier, from the beginning of time to the end of it. A circular pier is called a pillar or column, and all good architecture adapted to vertical support is made up of pillars, has always been so, and must ever be so, as long as the laws of the universe hold.

The final condition is represented at E, in its relation to that at D. It will be observed that though each circle projects a little beyond the side of the square out of which it is formed, the space cut off at the angles is greater than that added at the sides; for, having our materials in a more concentrated arrangement, we can afford to part with some of them in this last transformation, as in all the rest.

§ V. And now, what have the base and the cornice of the wall been doing while we have been cutting the veil to pieces and gathering it together?

The base is also cut to pieces, gathered together, and becomes the base of the column.

The cornice is cut to pieces, gathered together, and becomes the capital of the column. Do not be alarmed at the new word, it does not mean a new thing; a capital is only the cornice of a column, and you may, if you like, call a cornice the capital of a wall.

We have now, therefore, to examine these three concentrated forms of the base, veil, and cornice: first, the concentrated base, still called the BASE of the column; then the concentrated veil, called the SHAFT of the column; then the concentrated cornice, called the CAPITAL of the column.

And first the Base:—

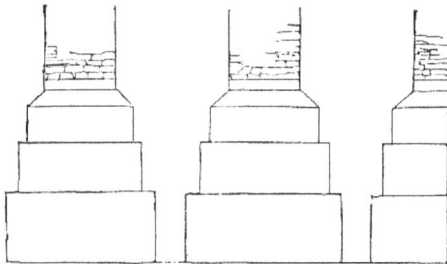

Fig. X.

§ VI. Look back to the main type, Fig. II., page 55, and apply its profiles in due proportion to the feet of the pillars at E in Fig. IX. p. 72: If each step in Fig. II. were gathered accurately, the projection of the entire circular base would be less in proportion to its height than it is in Fig. II.; but the approximation to the result in Fig. X. is quite accurate enough for our purposes. (I pray the reader to observe that I have not made the smallest change, except this necessary expression of a reduction in diameter, in Fig. II. as it is applied in Fig. X., only I have not drawn the joints of the stones because these would confuse the outlines of the bases; and I have not represented the rounding of the shafts, because it does not bear at present on the argument.) Now it would hardly be convenient, if we had to pass between the pillars, to have to squeeze ourselves through one of those angular gaps or brêches de Roland in Fig. X. Our first impulse would be to cut them open; but we cannot do this, or our piers are unsafe. We have but one other resource, to fill them up until we have a floor wide enough to let us pass easily: this we may perhaps obtain at the first ledge, we are nearly sure to get it at the second, and we may then obtain access to the raised interval, either by raising the earth over the lower courses of foundation, or by steps round the entire building.

Fig. XI. is the arrangement of Fig. X. so treated.

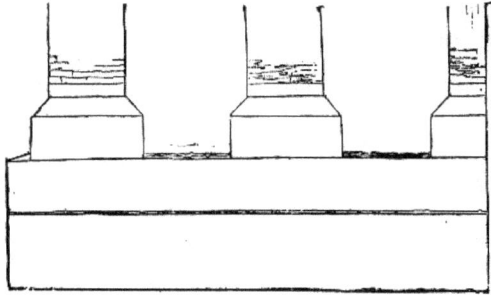

Fig. XI.

§ VII. But suppose the pillars are so vast that the lowest chink in Fig. X. would be quite wide enough to let us pass through it. Is there then any reason for filling it up? Yes. It will be remembered that in Chap. IV. § VIII. the chief reason for the wide foundation of the wall was stated to be "that it might equalise its pressure over a large surface;" but when the foundation is cut to pieces as in Fig. X., the pressure is thrown on a succession of narrowed and detached spaces of that surface. If the ground is in some places more disposed to yield than in others, the piers in those places will sink more than the rest, and this distortion of the system will be probably of more importance in pillars than in a wall, because the adjustment of the weight above is more delicate; we thus actually want the weight of the stones between the pillars, in order that the whole foundation may be bonded into one, and sink together if it sink at all: and the more massy the pillars, the more we shall need to fill the intervals of their foundations. In the best form of Greek architecture, the intervals are filled up to the root of the shaft, and the columns have no independent base; they stand on the even floor of their foundation.

§ VIII. Such a structure is not only admissible, but, when the column is of great thickness in proportion to its height, and the sufficient firmness, either of the ground or prepared floor, is evident, it is the best of all, having a strange dignity in its excessive simplicity. It is, or ought to be, connected in our minds with the deep meaning of primeval memorial. "And Jacob took the stone that he had put for his pillow, and set it up for a pillar." I do not fancy that he put a base for it first. If you try to put a base to the rock-piers of Stonehenge, you will hardly find them improved; and two of the most perfect buildings in the world, the Parthenon and Ducal palace of Venice, have no bases to their pillars: the latter has them, indeed, to its upper arcade shafts; and had once, it is said, a continuous raised base for its lower ones: but successive elevations of St. Mark's Place have covered this base, and parts of the shafts themselves, with an inundation of paving stones; and yet the building is, I doubt not, as grand as ever. Finally, the two most noble pillars in Venice, those brought from Acre, stand on the smooth marble surface of the Piazzetta, with no independent bases whatever. They are rather broken away beneath, so that you may look under parts of them, and stand (not quite erect, but leaning somewhat) safe by their own massy weight. Nor could any bases possibly be devised that would not spoil them.

§ IX. But it is otherwise if the pillar be so slender as to look doubtfully balanced. It would indeed stand quite as safely without an independent base as it would with one (at least, unless the base be in the form of a socket). But it will not appear so safe to the eye. And here for the first time, I have to express and apply a principle, which I believe the reader will at once grant,—that features necessary to express security to the imagination, are often as essential parts of good architecture as those required for security itself. It was said that the wall base was the foot or paw of the wall. Exactly in the same way, and with clearer analogy, the pier base is the foot or paw of the pier. Let us, then, take a hint from nature. A foot has two offices, to bear up, and to hold firm. As far as it has to bear up, it is uncloven, with slight projection,—look at an elephant's (the Doric base of animality);[36] but as far as it has to hold firm, it is divided and clawed, with wide projections,—look at an eagle's.

§ X. Now observe. In proportion to the massiness of the column, we require its foot to express merely the power of bearing up; in fact, it can do without a foot, like the Squire in Chevy Chase, if the ground only be hard enough. But if the column be slender, and look as if it might lose its balance, we require it to look as if it had hold of the ground, or the ground hold of it, it does not matter which,—some expression of claw, prop, or socket. Now let us go back to Fig. XI., and take up one of the bases there, in the state in which we left it. We may leave out the two lower steps (with which we have nothing more to do, as they have become the united floor or foundation of the whole), and, for the sake of greater clearness, I shall not draw the bricks in the shaft, nor the flat stone which carries them, though the reader is to suppose them remaining as drawn in Fig. XI.; but I shall only draw the shaft and its two essential members of base, Xb and Yb, as explained at p. 65, above: and now, expressing the rounding of these numbers on a somewhat larger scale, we have the profile a, Fig. XII.; b, the perspective appearance of such a base seen from above; and c, the plan of it.

§ XI. Now I am quite sure the reader is not satisfied of the stability of this form as it is seen at b; nor would he ever be so with the main contour of a circular base. Observe, we have taken some trouble to reduce the member Yb into this round form, and all that we have gained by so doing, is this unsatisfactory and unstable look of the base; of which the chief reason is, that a circle, unless enclosed by right lines, has never an appearance of fixture, or definite place,[37]—we suspect it of motion, like an orb of heaven; and the second is, that the whole base, considered as the foot of the shaft, has no grasp nor hold: it is a club-foot, and looks too blunt for the limb,—it wants at least expansion, if not division.

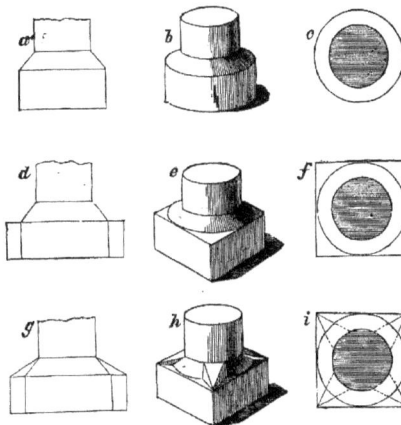

Fig. XII.

§ XII. Suppose, then, instead of taking so much trouble with the member Yb, we save time and labor, and leave it a square block. Xb must, however, evidently follow the pillar, as its condition is that it slope to the very base of the wall veil, and of whatever the wall veil becomes. So the corners of Yb will project beyond the circle of Xb, and we shall have (Fig. XII.) the profile d, the perspective appearance e, and the plan f. I am quite sure the reader likes e much better than he did b. The circle is now placed, and we are not afraid of its rolling away. The foot has greater expansion, and we have saved labor besides, with little loss of space, for the interval between the bases is just as great as it was before,—we have only filled up the corners of the squares.

But is it not possible to mend the form still further? There is surely still an appearance of separation between Xb and Yb, as if the one might slip off the other. The foot is expanded enough; but it needs some expression of grasp as well. It has no toes. Suppose we were to put a spur or prop to Xb at each corner, so as to hold it fast in the centre of Yb. We will do this in the simplest possible form. We will have the spur, or small buttress, sloping straight from the corner of Yb up to the top of Xb, and as seen from above, of the shape of a triangle. Applying such spurs in Fig. XII., we have the diagonal profile at g, the perspective h, and the plan i.

§ XIII. I am quite sure the reader likes this last base the best, and feels as if it were the firmest. But he must carefully distinguish between this feeling or imagination of the eye, and the real stability of the structure. That this real stability has been slightly increased by the changes between b and h, in Fig. XII., is true. There is in the base h somewhat less chance of accidental dislocation, and somewhat greater solidity and weight. But this very slight gain of security is of no importance whatever when compared with the general requirements of the structure. The pillar must be perfectly secure, and more than secure, with the base b, or the building will be unsafe, whatever other base you put to the pillar. The changes are made, not for the sake of the almost inappreciable increase of security they involve, but in order to convince the eye of the real security which the base b appears to compromise. This is especially the case with regard to the props or spurs, which are absolutely useless in reality, but are of the highest importance as an expression of safety. And this will farther appear when we observe that they have been above quite arbitrarily supposed to be of a triangular form. Why triangular? Why should not the spur be made wider and stronger, so as to occupy the whole width of the angle of the square, and to become a complete expansion of Xb to the edge of the square? Simply because, whatever its width, it has, in reality, no supporting power whatever; and the expression of support is greatest where it assumes a form approximating to that of the spur or claw of an animal. We shall, however, find hereafter, that it ought indeed to be much wider than it is in Fig. XII., where it is narrowed in order to make its structure clearly intelligible.

§ XIV. If the reader chooses to consider this spur as an æsthetic feature altogether, he is at liberty to do so, and to transfer what we have here said of it to the beginning of Chap. XXV. I think that its true place is here, as an expression of safety, and not a means of beauty; but I will assume only, as established, the form e of Fig. XII., which is absolutely, as a construction, easier, stronger, and more perfect than b. A word or two now of its materials. The wall base, it will be remembered, was built of stones more neatly cut as they were higher in place; and the members, Y and X, of the pier base, were the highest members of the wall base gathered. But, exactly in proportion to this gathering or concentration in form, should, if possible, be the gathering or concentration of substance. For as the whole weight of the building is now to rest upon few and limited spaces, it is of the greater importance that it should be there received by solid masonry. Xb and Yb are therefore, if possible, to be each of a single stone; or, when the shaft is small, both cut out of one block, and especially if spurs are to be added to Xb. The reader must not be angry with me for stating things so self-evident, for these are all necessary steps in the chain of argument which I must not break. Even this change from detached stones to a single block is not without significance; for it is part of the real service and value of the member Yb to provide for the reception of the shaft a surface free from joints; and the eye always conceives it as a firm covering over all inequalities or fissures in the smaller masonry of the floor.

§ XV. I have said nothing yet of the proportion of the height of Yb to its width, nor of that of Yb and Xb to each other. Both depend much on the height of shaft, and are besides variable within certain limits, at the architect's discretion. But the limits of the height of Yb may be thus generally stated. If it looks so thin as that the weight of the column above might break it, it is too low; and if it is higher than its own width, it is too high. The utmost admissible height is that of a cubic block; for if it ever become higher than it is wide, it becomes itself a part of a pier, and not the base of one.

§ XVI. I have also supposed Yb, when expanded from beneath Xb, as always expanded into a square, and four spurs only to be added at the angles. But Yb may be expanded into a pentagon, hexagon, or polygon; and Xb then may have five, six, or many spurs. In proportion, however, as the sides increase in number, the spurs become shorter and less energetic in their effect, and the square is in most cases the best form.

§ XVII. We have hitherto conducted the argument entirely on the supposition of the pillars being numerous, and in a range. Suppose, however, that we require only a single pillar: as we have free space round it, there is no need to fill up the first ranges of its foundations; nor need we do so in order to equalise pressure, since the pressure to be met is its own alone. Under such circumstances, it is well to exhibit the lower tiers of the foundation as well as Yb and Xb. The noble bases of the two granite pillars of the Piazzetta at Venice are formed by the entire series of members given in Fig. X., the lower courses expanding into steps, with a superb breadth of proportion to the shaft. The member Xb is of course circular, having its proper decorative mouldings, not here considered; Yb is octagonal, but filled up into a square by certain curious groups of figures representing the trades of Venice. The three courses below are octagonal, with their sides set across the angles of the innermost octagon, Yb. The shafts are 15 feet in circumference, and the lowest octagons of the base 56 (7 feet each side).

§ XVIII. Detached buildings, like our own Monument, are not pillars, but towers built in imitation of Pillars. As towers they are barbarous, being dark, inconvenient, and unsafe, besides lying, and pretending to be what they are not. As shafts they are barbarous, because they were designed at a time when the Renaissance architects had introduced and forced into acceptance, as de rigueur, a kind of columnar high-heeled shoe,—a thing which they called a pedestal, and which is to a true base exactly what a Greek actor's cothurnus was to a Greek gentleman's sandal. But the Greek actor knew better, I believe, than to exhibit or to decorate his cork sole; and, with shafts as with heroes, it is rather better to put the sandal off than the cothurnus on. There are, indeed, occasions on which a pedestal may be necessary; it may be better to raise a shaft from a sudden depression of plinth to a level with others, its companions, by means of a pedestal, than to introduce a higher shaft; or it may be better to place a shaft of alabaster, if otherwise too short for our purpose, on a pedestal, than to use a larger shaft of coarser material; but the pedestal is in each case a make-shift, not an additional perfection. It may, in the like manner, be sometimes convenient for men to walk on stilts, but not to keep their stilts on as ornamental parts of dress. The bases of the Nelson Column, the Monument, and the column of the Place Vendôme, are to the shafts, exactly what highly ornamented wooden legs would be to human beings.

§ XIX. So far of bases of detached shafts. As we do not yet know in what manner shafts are likely to be grouped, we can say nothing of those of grouped shafts until we know more of what they are to support.

Lastly; we have throughout our reasoning upon the base supposed the pier to be circular. But circumstances may occur to prevent its being reduced to this form, and it may remain square or rectangular; its base will then be simply the wall base following its contour, and we have no spurs at the angles. Thus much may serve respecting pier bases; we have next to examine the concentration of the Wall Veil, or the Shaft.

FOOTNOTES:

[35] *The experiment is not quite fair in this rude fashion; for the small rolls owe their increase of strength much more to their tubular form than their aggregation of material; but if the paper be cut up into small strips, and tied together firmly in three or four compact bundles, it will exhibit increase of strength enough to show the principle. Vide, however, Appendix 16, "Strength of Shafts."*

[36] *Appendix 17, "Answer to Mr. Garbett."*

[37] *Yet more so than any other figure enclosed by a curved line: for the circle, in its relations to its own centre, is the curve of greatest stability. Compare § XX. of Chap. XX.*

CHAPTER VIII

THE SHAFT

§ I. We have seen in the last Chapter how, in converting the wall into the square or cylindrical shaft, we parted at every change of form with some quantity of material. In proportion to the quantity thus surrendered, is the necessity that what we retain should be good of its kind, and well set together, since everything now depends on it.

It is clear also that the best material, and the closest concentration, is that of the natural crystalline rocks; and that, by having reduced our wall into the shape of shafts, we may be enabled to avail ourselves of this better material, and to exchange cemented bricks for crystallised blocks of stone. Therefore, the general idea of a perfect shaft is that of a single stone hewn into a form more or less elongated and cylindrical. Under this form, or at least under the ruder one of a long stone set upright, the conception of true shafts appears first to have occurred to the human mind; for the reader must note this carefully, once for all, it does not in the least follow that the order of architectural features which is most reasonable in their arrangement, is most probable in their invention. I have theoretically deduced shafts from walls, but shafts were never so reasoned out in architectural practice. The man who first propped a thatched roof with poles was the discoverer of their principle; and he who first hewed a long stone into a cylinder, the perfecter of their practice.

§ II. It is clearly necessary that shafts of this kind (we will call them, for convenience, block shafts) should be composed of stone not liable to flaws or fissures; and therefore that we must no longer continue our argument as if it were always possible to do what is to be done in the best way; for the style of a national architecture may evidently depend, in great measure, upon the nature of the rocks of the country.

Our own English rocks, which supply excellent building stone from their thin and easily divisible beds, are for the most part entirely incapable of being worked into shafts of any size, except only the granites and whinstones, whose hardness renders them intractable for ordinary purposes;—and English architecture therefore supplies no instances of the block shaft applied on an extensive scale; while the facility of obtaining large masses of marble has in Greece and Italy been partly the cause of the adoption of certain noble types of architectural form peculiar to those countries, or, when occurring elsewhere, derived from them.

We have not, however, in reducing our walls to shafts, calculated on the probabilities of our obtaining better materials than those of which the walls were built; and we shall therefore first consider the form of shaft which will be best when we have the best materials; and then consider how far we can imitate, or how far it will be wise to imitate, this form with any materials we can obtain.

§ III. Now as I gave the reader the ground, and the stones, that he might for himself find out how to build his wall, I shall give him the block of marble, and the chisel, that he may himself find out how to shape his column. Let him suppose the elongated mass, so given him, rudely hewn to the thickness which he has calculated will be proportioned to the weight it has to carry. The conditions of stability will require that some allowance be made in finishing it for any chance of slight disturbance or subsidence of the ground below, and that, as everything must depend on the uprightness of the shaft, as little chance should be left as possible of its being thrown off its balance. It will therefore be prudent to leave it slightly thicker at the base than at the top. This excess of diameter at the base being determined, the reader is to ask himself how most easily and simply to smooth the column from one extremity to the other. To cut it into a true straight-sided cone would be a matter of much trouble and nicety, and would incur the continual risk of chipping into it too deep. Why not leave some room for a chance stroke, work it slightly, very slightly convex, and smooth the curve by the eye between the two extremities? you will save much trouble and time, and the shaft will be all the stronger.

Fig. XIII.

This is accordingly the natural form of a detached block shaft. It is the best. No other will ever be so agreeable to the mind or eye. I do not mean that it is not capable of more refined execution, or of the application of some of the laws of æsthetic beauty, but that it is the best recipient of execution and subject of law; better in either case than if you had taken more pains, and cut it straight.

§ IV. You will observe, however, that the convexity is to be very slight, and that the shaft is not to bulge in the centre, but to taper from the root in a curved line; the peculiar character of the curve you will discern better by exaggerating, in a diagram, the conditions of its sculpture.

Let a, a, b, b, at A, Fig. XIII., be the rough block of the shaft, laid on the ground; and as thick as you can by any chance require it to be; you will leave it of this full thickness at its base at A, but at the other end you will mark off upon it the diameter c, d, which you intend it to have at the summit; you will then take your mallet and chisel, and working from c and d you will roughly knock off the corners, shaded in the figure, so as to reduce the shaft to the figure described by the inside lines in A and the outside lines in B; you then proceed to smooth it, you chisel away the shaded parts in B, and leave your finished shaft of the form of the inside lines e, g, f, h.

The result of this operation will be of course that the shaft tapers faster towards the top than it does near the ground. Observe this carefully; it is a point of great future importance.

§ V. So far of the shape of detached or block shafts. We can carry the type no farther on merely structural considerations: let us pass to the shaft of inferior materials.

Unfortunately, in practice, this step must be soon made. It is alike difficult to obtain, transport, and raise, block shafts more than ten or twelve feet long, except in remarkable positions, and as pieces of singular magnificence. Large pillars are therefore always composed of more than one block of stone. Such pillars are either jointed like basalt columns, and composed of solid pieces of stone set one above another; or they are filled up towers, built of small stones cemented into a mass, with more or less of regularity: Keep this distinction carefully in mind, it is of great importance; for the jointed column, every stone composing which, however thin, is (so to speak) a complete slice of the shaft, is just as strong as the block pillar of one stone, so long as no forces are brought into action upon it which would have a tendency to cause horizontal dislocation. But the pillar which is built as a filled-up tower is of course liable to fissure in any direction, if its cement give way.

But, in either case, it is evident that all constructive reason of the curved contour is at once destroyed. Far from being an easy or natural procedure, the fitting of each portion of the curve to its fellow, in the separate stones, would require painful care and considerable masonic skill; while, in the case of the filled-up tower, the curve outwards would be even unsafe; for its greatest strength (and that the more in proportion to its careless building) lies in its bark, or shell of outside stone; and this, if curved outwards, would at once burst outwards, if heavily loaded above.

If, therefore, the curved outline be ever retained in such shafts, it must be in obedience to æsthetic laws only.

§ VI. But farther. Not only the curvature, but even the tapering by straight lines, would be somewhat difficult of execution in the pieced column. Where, indeed, the entire shaft is composed of four or five blocks set one upon another, the diameters may be easily determined at the successive joints, and the stones chiselled to the same slope. But this becomes sufficiently troublesome when the joints are numerous, so that the pillar is like a pile of cheeses; or when it is to be built of small and irregular stones. We should be naturally led, in the one case, to cut all the cheeses to the same diameter; in the other to build by the plumb-line; and in both to give up the tapering altogether.

§ VII. Farther. Since the chance, in the one case, of horizontal dislocation, in the other, of irregular fissure, is much increased by the composition of the shaft out of joints or small stones, a larger bulk of shaft is required to carry the given weight; and, cæteris paribus, jointed and cemented shafts must be thicker in proportion to the weight they carry than those which are of one block.

We have here evidently natural causes of a very marked division in schools of architecture: one group composed of buildings whose shafts are either of a single stone or of few joints; the shafts, therefore, being gracefully tapered, and reduced by successive experiments to the narrowest possible diameter proportioned to the weight they carry: and the other group embracing those buildings whose shafts are of many joints or of small stones; shafts which are therefore not tapered, and rather thick and ponderous in proportion to the weight they carry; the latter school being evidently somewhat imperfect and inelegant as compared with the former.

It may perhaps appear, also, that this arrangement of the materials in cylindrical shafts at all would hardly have suggested itself to a people who possessed no large blocks out of which to hew them; and that the shaft built of many pieces is probably derived from, and imitative of the shaft hewn from few or from one.

§ VIII. If, therefore, you take a good geological map of Europe, and lay your finger upon the spots where volcanic influences supply either travertin or marble in accessible and available masses, you will probably mark the points where the types of the first school have been originated and developed. If, in the next place, you will mark the districts where broken and rugged basalt or whinstone, or slaty sandstone, supply materials on easier terms indeed, but fragmentary and unmanageable, you will probably distinguish some of the birthplaces of the derivative and less graceful school. You will, in the first case, lay your finger on Pæstum, Agrigentum, and Athens; in the second, on Durham and Lindisfarne.

The shafts of the great primal school are, indeed, in their first form, as massy as those of the other, and the tendency of both is to continual diminution of their diameters: but in the first school it is a true diminution in the thickness of the independent pier; in the last, it is an apparent diminution, obtained by giving it the appearance of a group of minor piers. The distinction, however, with which we are concerned is not that of slenderness, but of vertical or curved contour; and we may note generally that while throughout the whole range of Northern work, the perpendicular shaft appears in continually clearer development, throughout every group which has inherited the spirit of the Greek, the shaft retains its curved or tapered form; and the occurrence of the vertical detached shaft may at all times, in European architecture, be regarded as one of the most important collateral evidences of Northern influence.

§ IX. It is necessary to limit this observation to European architecture, because the Egyptian shaft is often untapered, like the Northern. It appears that the Central Southern, or Greek shaft, was tapered or curved on æsthetic rather than constructive principles; and the Egyptian which precedes, and the Northern which follows it, are both vertical, the one because the best form had not been discovered, the other because it could not be attained. Both are in a certain degree barbaric; and both possess in combination and in their ornaments a power altogether different from that of the Greek shaft, and at least as impressive if not as admirable.

§ X. We have hitherto spoken of shafts as if their number were fixed, and only their diameter variable according to the weight to be borne. But this supposition is evidently gratuitous; for the same weight may be carried either by many and slender, or by few and massy shafts. If the reader will look back to Fig. IX., he will find the number of shafts into which the wall was reduced to be dependent altogether upon the length of the spaces a, b, a, b, &c., a length which was arbitrarily fixed. We are at liberty to make these spaces of what length we choose, and, in so doing, to increase the number and diminish the diameter of the shafts, or vice versâ.

§ XI. Supposing the materials are in each case to be of the same kind, the choice is in great part at the architect's discretion, only there is a limit on the one hand to the multiplication of the slender shaft, in the inconvenience of the narrowed interval, and on the other, to the enlargement of the massy shaft, in the loss of breadth to the building.[38] That will be commonly the best proportion which is a natural mean between the two limits; leaning to the side of grace or of grandeur according to the expressional intention of the work. I say, commonly the best, because, in some cases, this expressional invention may prevail over all other considerations, and a column of unnecessary bulk or fantastic slightness be adopted in order to strike the spectator with awe or with surprise.[39] The architect is, however, rarely in practice compelled to use one kind of material only; and his choice lies frequently between the employment of a larger number of solid and perfect small shafts, or a less number of pieced and cemented large ones. It is often possible to obtain from quarries near at hand, blocks which might be cut into shafts eight or twelve feet long and four or five feet round, when larger shafts can only be obtained in distant localities; and the question then is between the perfection of smaller features and the imperfection of larger. We shall find numberless instances in Italy in which the first choice has been boldly, and I think most wisely made; and magnificent buildings have been composed of systems of small but perfect shafts, multiplied and superimposed. So long as the idea of the symmetry of a perfect shaft remained in the builder's mind, his choice could hardly be directed otherwise, and the adoption of the built and tower-like shaft appears to have been the result of a loss of this sense of symmetry consequent on the employment of intractable materials.

§ XII. But farther: we have up to this point spoken of shafts as always set in ranges, and at equal intervals from each other. But there is no necessity for this; and material differences may be made in their diameters if two or more be grouped so as to do together the work of one large one, and that within, or nearly within, the space which the larger one would have occupied.

§ XIII. Let A, B, C, Fig. XIV., be three surfaces, of which B and C contain equal areas, and each of them double that of A: then supposing them all loaded to the same height, B or C would receive twice as much weight as A; therefore, to carry B or C loaded, we should need a shaft of twice the strength needed to carry A. Let S be the shaft required to carry A, and S2 the shaft required to carry B or C; then S3 may be divided into two shafts, or S2 into four shafts, as at S3, all equal in area or solid contents;[40] and the mass A might be carried safely by two of them, and the masses B and C, each by four of them.

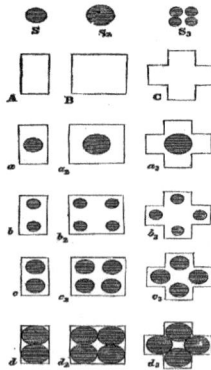

Fig. XIV.

Now if we put the single shafts each under the centre of the mass they have to bear, as represented by the shaded circles at a, a2, a3, the masses A and C are both of them very ill supported, and even B insufficiently; but apply the four and the two shafts as at b, b2, b3, and they are supported satisfactorily. Let the weight on each of the masses be doubled, and the shafts doubled in area, then we shall have such arrangements as those at c, c2, c3; and if again the shafts and weight be doubled, we shall have d, d2, d3.

§ XIV. Now it will at once be observed that the arrangement of the shafts in the series of B and C is always exactly the same in their relations to each other; only the group of B is set evenly, and the group of C is set obliquely,—the one carrying a square, the other a cross.

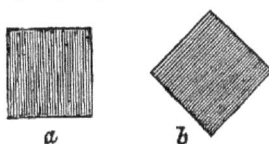

a   *b*

Fig. XV.

You have in these two series the primal representations of shaft arrangement in the Southern and Northern schools; while the group b, of which b2 is the double, set evenly, and c2 the double, set obliquely, is common to both. The reader will be surprised to find how all the complex and varied forms of shaft arrangement will range themselves into one or other of these groups; and still more surprised to find the oblique or cross set system on the one hand, and the square set system on the other, severally distinctive of Southern and Northern work. The dome of St. Mark's, and the crossing of the nave and transepts of Beauvais, are both carried by square piers; but the piers of St. Mark's are set square to the walls of the church, and those of Beauvais obliquely to them: and this difference is even a more essential one than that between the smooth surface of the one and the reedy complication of the other. The two squares here in the margin (Fig. XV.) are exactly of the same size, but their expression is altogether different, and in that difference lies one of the most subtle distinctions between the Gothic and Greek spirit,—from the shaft, which bears the building, to the smallest decoration. The Greek square is by preference set evenly, the Gothic square obliquely; and that so constantly, that wherever we find the level or even square occurring as a prevailing form, either in plan or decoration, in early northern work, there we may at least suspect the presence of a southern or Greek influence; and, on the other hand, wherever the oblique square is prominent in the south, we may confidently look for farther evidence of the influence of the Gothic architects. The rule must not of course be pressed far when, in either school, there has been determined search for every possible variety of decorative figures; and accidental circumstances may reverse the usual system in special cases; but the evidence drawn from this character is collaterally of the highest value, and the tracing it out is a pursuit of singular interest. Thus, the Pisan Romanesque might in an instant be pronounced to have been formed under some measure of Lombardic influence, from the oblique squares set under its arches; and in it we have the spirit of northern Gothic affecting details of the southern;—obliquity of square, in magnificently shafted Romanesque. At Monza, on the other hand, the levelled square is the characteristic figure of the entire decoration of the façade of the Duomo, eminently giving it southern character; but the details are derived almost entirely from the northern Gothic. Here then we have southern spirit and northern detail. Of the cruciform outline of the load of the shaft, a still more positive test of northern work, we shall have more to say in the 28th Chapter; we must at present note certain farther changes in the form of the grouped shaft, which open the way to every branch of its endless combinations, southern or northern.

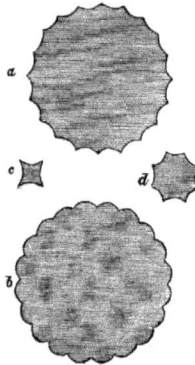

Fig. XVI.

§ XV. 1. If the group at d3, Fig. XIV., be taken from under its loading, and have its centre filled up, it will become a quatrefoil; and it will represent, in their form of most frequent occurrence, a family of shafts, whose plans are foiled figures, trefoils, quatrefoils, cinquefoils, &c.; of which a trefoiled example, from the Frari at Venice, is the third in Plate II., and a quatrefoil from Salisbury the eighth. It is rare, however, to find in Gothic architecture shafts of this family composed of a large number of foils, because multifoiled shafts are seldom true grouped shafts, but are rather canaliculated conditions of massy piers. The representatives of this family may be considered as the quatrefoil on the Gothic side of the Alps; and the Egyptian multifoiled shaft on the south, approximating to the general type, b, Fig. XVI.

§ XVI. Exactly opposed to this great family is that of shafts which have concave curves instead of convex on each of their sides; but these are not, properly speaking, grouped shafts at all, and their proper place is among decorated piers; only they must be named here in order to mark their exact opposition to the foiled system. In their simplest form, represented by c, Fig. XVI., they have no representatives in good architecture, being evidently weak and meagre; but approximations to them exist in late Gothic, as in the vile cathedral of Orleans, and in modern cast-iron shafts. In their fully developed form they are the Greek Doric, a, Fig. XVI., and occur in caprices of the Romanesque and Italian Gothic: d, Fig. XVI., is from the Duomo of Monza.

§ XVII. 2. Between c3 and d3 of Fig. XIV. there may be evidently another condition, represented at 6, Plate II., and formed by the insertion of a central shaft within the four external ones. This central shaft we may suppose to expand in proportion to the weight it has to carry. If the external shafts expand in the same proportion, the entire form remains unchanged; but if they do not expand, they may (1) be pushed out by the expanding shaft, or (2) be gradually swallowed up in its expansion, as at 4, Plate II. If they are pushed out, they are removed farther from each other by every increase of the central shaft; and others may then be introduced in the vacant spaces; giving, on the plan, a central orb with an ever increasing host of satellites, 10, Plate II.; the satellites themselves often varying in size, and perhaps quitting contact with the central shaft. Suppose them in any of their conditions fixed, while the inner shaft expands, and they will be gradually buried in it, forming more complicated conditions of 4, Plate II. The combinations are thus altogether infinite, even supposing the central shaft to be circular only; but their infinity is multiplied by many other infinities when the central shaft itself becomes square or crosslet on the section, or itself multifoiled (8, Plate II.) with satellite shafts eddying about its recesses and angles, in every possible relation of attraction. Among these endless conditions of change, the choice of the architect is free, this only being generally noted: that, as the whole value of such piers depends, first, upon their being wisely fitted to the weight above them, and, secondly, upon their all working together: and one not failing the rest, perhaps to the ruin of all, he must never multiply shafts without visible cause in the disposition of members superimposed:[41] and in his multiplied group he should, if possible, avoid a marked separation between the large central shaft and its satellites; for if this exist, the satellites will either appear useless altogether, or else, which is worse, they will look as if they were meant to keep the central shaft together by wiring or caging it in; like iron rods set round a supple cylinder,—a fatal fault in the piers of Westminster Abbey, and, in a less degree, in the noble nave of the cathedral of Bourges.

§ XVIII. While, however, we have been thus subdividing or assembling our shafts, how far has it been possible to retain their curved or tapered outline? So long as they remain distinct and equal, however close to each other, the independent curvature may evidently be retained. But when once they come in contact, it is equally evident that a column, formed of shafts touching at the base and separate at the top, would appear as if in the very act of splitting asunder. Hence, in all the closely arranged groups, and especially those with a central shaft, the tapering is sacrificed; and with less cause for regret, because it was a provision against subsidence or distortion, which cannot now take place with the separate members of the group. Evidently, the work, if safe at all, must be executed with far greater accuracy and stability when its supports are so delicately arranged, than would be implied by such precaution. In grouping shafts, therefore, a true perpendicular line is, in nearly all cases, given to the pier; and the reader will anticipate that the two schools, which we have already found to be distinguished, the one by its perpendicular and pieced shafts, and the other by its curved and block shafts, will be found divided also in their employment of grouped shafts;—it is likely that the idea of grouping, however suggested, will be fully entertained and acted upon by the one, but hesitatingly by the other; and that we shall find, on the one hand, buildings displaying sometimes massy piers of small stones, sometimes clustered piers of rich complexity, and on the other, more or less regular succession of block shafts, each treated as entirely independent of those around it.

§ XIX. Farther, the grouping of shafts once admitted, it is probable that the complexity and richness of such arrangements would recommend them to the eye, and induce their frequent, even their unnecessary introduction; so that weight which might have been borne by a single pillar, would be in preference supported by four or five. And if the stone of the country, whose fragmentary character first occasioned the building and piecing of the large pier, were yet in beds consistent enough to supply shafts of very small diameter, the strength and simplicity of such a construction might justify it, as well as its grace. The fact, however, is that the charm which the multiplication of line possesses for the eye has always been one of the chief ends of the work in the grouped schools; and that, so far from employing the grouped piers in order to the introduction of very slender block shafts, the most common form in which such piers occur is that of a solid jointed shaft, each joint being separately cut into the contour of the group required.

§ XX. We have hitherto supposed that all grouped or clustered shafts have been the result or the expression of an actual gathering and binding together of detached shafts. This is not, however, always so: for some clustered shafts are little more than solid piers channelled on the surface, and their form appears to be merely the development of some longitudinal furrowing or striation on the original single shaft. That clustering or striation, whichever we choose to call it, is in this case a decorative feature, and to be considered under the head of decoration.

§ XXI. It must be evident to the reader at a glance, that the real serviceableness of any of these grouped arrangements must depend upon the relative shortness of the shafts, and that, when the whole pier is so lofty that its minor members become mere reeds or rods of stone, those minor members can no longer be charged with any considerable weight. And the fact is, that in the most complicated Gothic arrangements, when the pier is tall and its satellites stand clear of it, no real work is given them to do, and they might all be removed without endangering the building. They are merely the expression of a great consistent system, and are in architecture what is often found in animal anatomy,—a bone, or process of a bone, useless, under the ordained circumstances of its life, to the particular animal in which it is found, and slightly developed, but yet distinctly existent, and representing, for the sake of absolute consistency, the same bone in its appointed, and generally useful, place, either in skeletons of all animals, or in the genus to which the animal itself belongs.

§ XXII. Farther: as it is not easy to obtain pieces of stone long enough for these supplementary shafts (especially as it is always unsafe to lay a stratified stone with its beds upright) they have been frequently composed of two or more short shafts set upon each other, and to conceal the unsightly junction, a flat stone has been interposed, carved into certain mouldings, which have the appearance of a ring on the shaft. Now observe: the whole pier was the gathering of the whole wall, the base gathers into base, the veil into the shaft, and the string courses of the veil gather into these rings; and when this is clearly expressed, and the rings do indeed correspond with the string courses of the wall veil, they are perfectly admissible and even beautiful; but otherwise, and occurring, as they do in the shafts of Westminster, in the middle of continuous lines, they are but sorry make-shifts, and of late since gas has been invented, have become especially offensive from their unlucky resemblance to the joints of gas-pipes, or common water-pipes. There are two leaden ones, for instance, on the left hand as one enters the abbey at Poet's Corner, with their solderings and funnels looking exactly like rings and capitals, and most disrespectfully mimicking the shafts of the abbey, inside.

Thus far we have traced the probable conditions of shaft structure in pure theory; I shall now lay before the reader a brief statement of the facts of the thing in time past and present.

§ XXIII. In the earliest and grandest shaft architecture which we know, that of Egypt, we have no grouped arrangements, properly so called, but either single and smooth shafts, or richly reeded and furrowed shafts, which represent the extreme conditions of a complicated group bound together to sustain a single mass; and are indeed, without doubt, nothing else than imitations of bundles of reeds, or of clusters of lotus:[42] but in these shafts there is merely the idea of a group, not the actual function or structure of a group; they are just as much solid and simple shafts as those which are smooth, and merely by the method of their decoration present to the eye the image of a richly complex arrangement.

§ XXIV. After these we have the Greek shaft, less in scale, and losing all suggestion or purpose of suggestion of complexity, its so-called flutings being, visibly as actually, an external decoration.

§ XXV. The idea of the shaft remains absolutely single in the Roman and Byzantine mind; but true grouping begins in Christian architecture by the placing of two or more separate shafts side by side, each having its own work to do; then three or four, still with separate work; then, by such steps as those above theoretically pursued, the number of the members increases, while they coagulate into a single mass; and we have finally a shaft apparently composed of thirty, forty, fifty, or more distinct members; a shaft which, in the reality of its service, is as much a single shaft as the old Egyptian one; but which differs from the Egyptian in that all its members, how many soever, have each individual work to do, and a separate rib of arch or roof to carry: and thus the great Christian truth of distinct services of the individual soul is typified in the Christian shaft; and the old Egyptian servitude of the multitudes, the servitude inseparable from the children of Ham, is typified also in that ancient shaft of the Egyptians, which in its gathered strength of the river reeds, seems, as the sands of the desert drift over its ruin, to be intended to remind us for ever of the end of the association of the wicked. "Can the rush grow up without mire, or the flag grow without water?—So are the paths of all that forget God; and the hypocrite's hope shall perish."

§ XXVI. Let the reader then keep this distinction of the three systems clearly in his mind: Egyptian system, an apparent cluster supporting a simple capital and single weight; Greek and Roman system, single shaft, single weight; Gothic system, divided shafts, divided weight: at first actually and simply divided, at last apparently and infinitely divided; so that the fully formed Gothic shaft is a return to the Egyptian, but the weight is divided in the one and undivided in the other.

§ XXVII. The transition from the actual to the apparent cluster, in the Gothic, is a question of the most curious interest; I have thrown together the shaft sections in Plate II. to illustrate it, and exemplify what has been generally stated above.[43]

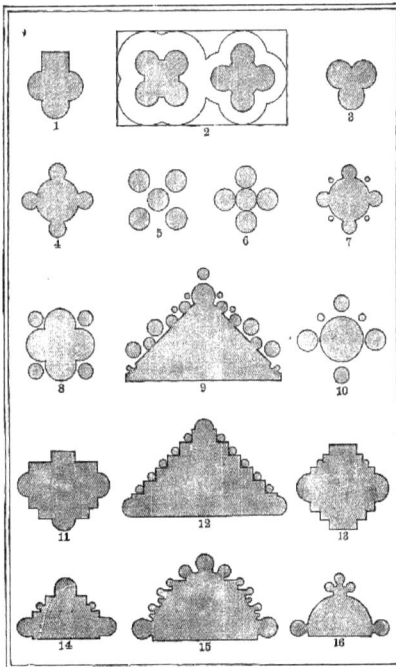

Plate II. PLANS OF PIERS.

1. The earliest, the most frequent, perhaps the most beautiful of all the groups, is also the simplest; the two shafts arranged as at b or c, (Fig. XIV.) above, bearing an oblong mass, and substituted for the still earlier structure a, Fig. XIV. In Plate XVII. (Chap. XXVII.) are three examples of the transition: the one on the left, at the top, is the earliest single-shafted arrangement, constant in the rough Romanesque windows; a huge hammer-shaped capital being employed to sustain the thickness of the wall. It was rapidly superseded by the double shaft, as on the right of it; a very early example from the cloisters of the Duomo, Verona. Beneath, is a most elaborate and perfect one from St. Zeno of Verona, where the group is twice complicated, two shafts being used, both with quatrefoil sections. The plain double shaft, however, is by far the most frequent, both in the Northern and Southern Gothic, but for the most part early; it is very frequent in cloisters, and in the singular one of St. Michael's Mount, Normandy, a small pseudo-arcade runs along between the pairs of shafts, a miniature aisle. The group is employed on a magnificent scale, but ill proportioned, for the main piers of the apse of the cathedral of Coutances, its purpose being to conceal one shaft behind the other, and make it appear to the spectator from the nave as if the apse were sustained by single shafts, of inordinate slenderness. The attempt is ill-judged, and the result unsatisfactory.

Fig. XVII.

§ XXVIII. 2. When these pairs of shafts come near each other, as frequently at the turnings of angles (Fig. XVII.), the quadruple group results, b 2, Fig. XIV., of which the Lombardic sculptors were excessively fond, usually tying the shafts together in their centre, in a lover's knot. They thus occur in Plate V., from the Broletto of Como; at the angle of St. Michele of Lucca, Plate XXI.; and in the balustrade of St. Mark's. This is a group, however, which I have never seen used on a large scale.[44]

§ XXIX. 3. Such groups, consolidated by a small square in their centre, form the shafts of St. Zeno, just spoken of, and figured in Plate XVII., which are among the most interesting pieces of work I know in Italy. I give their entire arrangement in Fig. XVIII.: both shafts have the same section, but one receives a half turn as it ascends, giving it an exquisite spiral contour: the plan of their bases, with their plinth, is given at 2, Plate II.; and note it carefully, for it is an epitome of all that we observed above, respecting the oblique and even square. It was asserted that the oblique belonged to the north, the even to the south: we have here the northern Lombardic nation naturalised in Italy, and, behold, the oblique and even quatrefoil linked together; not confused, but actually linked by a bar of stone, as seen in Plate XVII., under the capitals.

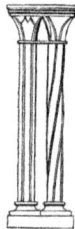

Fig. XVIII.

4. Next to these, observe the two groups of five shafts each, 5 and 6, Plate II., one oblique, the other even. Both are from upper stories; the oblique one from the triforium of Salisbury; the even one from the upper range of shafts in the façade of St. Mark's at Venice.[45]

§ XXX. Around these central types are grouped, in Plate II., four simple examples of the satellitic cluster, all of the Northern Gothic: 4, from the Cathedral of Amiens; 7, from that of Lyons (nave pier); 8, the same from Salisbury; 10, from the porch of Notre Dame, Dijon, having satellites of three magnitudes: 9 is one of the piers between the doors of the same church, with shafts of four magnitudes, and is an instance of the confusion of mind of the Northern architects between piers proper and jamb mouldings (noticed farther in the next chapter, § XXXI.): for this fig. 9, which is an angle at the meeting of two jambs, is treated like a rich independent shaft, and the figure below, 12, which is half of a true shaft, is treated like a meeting of jambs.

All these four examples belonging to the oblique or Northern system, the curious trefoil plan, 3, lies between the two, as the double quatrefoil next it unites the two. The trefoil is from the Frari, Venice, and has a richly worked capital in the Byzantine manner,—an imitation, I think, of the Byzantine work by the Gothic builders: 1 is to be compared with it, being one of the earliest conditions of the cross shaft, from the atrium of St. Ambrogio at Milan. 13 is the nave pier of St. Michele at Pavia, showing the same condition more fully developed: and 11 another nave pier from Vienne, on the Rhone, of far more distinct Roman derivation, for the flat pilaster is set to the nave, and is fluted like an antique one. 12 is the grandest development I have ever seen of the cross shaft, with satellite shafts in the nooks of it: it is half of one of the great western piers of the cathedral of Bourges, measuring eight feet each side, thirty-two round.[46] Then the one below (15) is half of a nave pier of Rouen Cathedral, showing the mode in which such conditions as that of Dijon (9) and that of Bourges (12) were fused together into forms of inextricable complexity (inextricable I mean in the irregularity of proportion and projection, for all of them are easily resolvable into simple systems in connexion with the roof ribs). This pier of Rouen is a type of the last condition of the good Gothic; from this point the small shafts begin to lose shape, and run into narrow fillets and ridges, projecting at the same time farther and farther in weak tongue-like sections, as described in the "Seven Lamps." I have only here given one example of this family, an unimportant but sufficiently characteristic one (16) from St. Gervais of Falaise. One side of the nave of that church is Norman, the other Flamboyant, and the two piers 14 and 16 stand opposite each other. It would be useless to endeavor to trace farther the fantasticism of the later Gothic shafts; they become mere aggregations of mouldings very sharply and finely cut, their bases at the same time running together in strange complexity and their capitals diminishing and disappearing. Some of their conditions, which, in their rich striation, resemble crystals of beryl, are very massy and grand; others, meagre, harsh, or effeminate in themselves, are redeemed by richness and boldness of decoration; and I have long had it in my mind to reason out the entire harmony of this French Flamboyant system, and fix its types and possible power. But this inquiry is foreign altogether to our present purpose, and we shall therefore turn back from the Flamboyant to the Norman side of the Falaise aisle, resolute for the future that all shafts of which we may have the ordering, shall be permitted, as with wisdom we may also permit men or cities, to gather themselves into companies, or constellate themselves into clusters, but not to fuse themselves into mere masses of nebulous aggregation.

FOOTNOTES:

[38] In saying this, it is assumed that the interval is one which is to be traversed by men; and that a certain relation of the shafts and intervals to the size of the human figure is therefore necessary. When shafts are used in the upper stories of buildings, or on a scale which ignores all relation to the human figure, no such relative limits exist either to slenderness or solidity.

[39] Vide the interesting discussion of this point in Mr. Fergusson's account of the Temple of Karnak, "Principles of Beauty in Art," p. 219.

[40] I have assumed that the strength of similar shafts of equal height is as the squares of their diameters; which, though not actually a correct expression, is sufficiently so for all our present purposes.

[41] How far this condition limits the system of shaft grouping we shall see presently. The reader must remember, that we at present reason respecting shafts in the abstract only.

[42] The capitals being formed by the flowers, or by a representation of the bulging out of the reeds at the top, under the weight of the architrave.

[43] I have not been at the pains to draw the complicated piers in this plate with absolute exactitude to the scale of each: they are accurate enough for their purpose: those of them respecting which we shall have farther question will be given on a much larger scale.

[44] The largest I remember support a monument in St. Zeno of Verona; they are of red marble, some ten or twelve feet high.

[45] The effect of this last is given in Plate VI. of the folio series.

[46] The entire development of this cross system in connexion with the vaulting ribs, has been most clearly explained by Professor Willis (Architecture of Mid. Ages, Chap. IV.); and I strongly recommend every reader who is inclined to take pains in the matter, to read that chapter. I have been contented, in my own text, to pursue the abstract idea of shaft form.

CHAPTER IX

THE CAPITAL

§ I. The reader will remember that in Chap. VII. § V. it was said that the cornice of the wall, being cut to pieces and gathered together, formed the capital of the column. We have now to follow it in its transformation.

We must, of course, take our simplest form or root of cornices (a, in Fig. V., above). We will take X and Y there, and we must necessarily gather them together as we did Xb and Yb in Chap. VII. Look back to the tenth paragraph of Chap. VII., read or glance it over again, substitute X and Y for Xb and Yb, read capital for base, and, as we said that the capital was the hand of the pillar, while the base was its foot, read also fingers for toes; and as you look to the plate, Fig. XII., turn it upside down. Then h, in Fig. XII., becomes now your best general form of block capital, as before of block base.

§ II. You will thus have a perfect idea of the analogies between base and capital; our farther inquiry is into their differences. You cannot but have noticed that when Fig. XII. is turned upside down, the square stone (Y) looks too heavy for the supporting stone (X); and that in the profile of cornice (a of Fig. V.) the proportions are altogether different. You will feel the fitness of this in an instant when you consider that the principal function of the sloping part in Fig. XII. is as a prop to the pillar to keep it from slipping aside; but the function of the sloping stone in the cornice and capital is to carry weight above. The thrust of the slope in the one case should therefore be lateral, in the other upwards.

§ III. We will, therefore, take the two figures, e and h of Fig. XII., and make this change in them as we reverse them, using now the exact profile of the cornice a,—the father of cornices; and we shall thus have a and b, Fig. XIX.

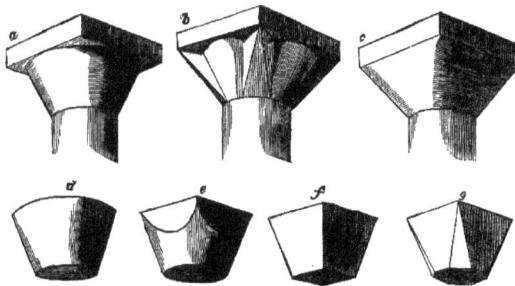

Fig. XIX.

Both of these are sufficiently ugly, the reader thinks; so do I; but we will mend them before we have done with them: that at a is assuredly the ugliest,—like a tile on a flower-pot. It is, nevertheless, the father of capitals; being the simplest condition of the gathered father of cornices. But it is to be observed that the diameter of the shaft here is arbitrarily assumed to be small, in order more clearly to show the general relations of the sloping stone to the shaft and upper stone; and this smallness of the shaft diameter is inconsistent with the serviceableness and beauty of the arrangement at a, if it were to be realised (as we shall see presently); but it is not inconsistent with its central character, as the representative of every species of possible capital; nor is its tile and flower-pot look to be regretted, as it may remind the reader of the reported origin of the Corinthian capital. The stones of the cornice, hitherto called X and Y, receive, now that they form the capital, each a separate name; the sloping stone is called the Bell of the capital, and that laid above it, the Abacus. Abacus means a board or tile: I wish there were an English word for it, but I fear there is no substitution possible, the term having been long fixed, and the reader will find it convenient to familiarise himself with the Latin one.

§ IV. The form of base, e of Fig. XII., which corresponds to this first form of capital, a, was said to be objectionable only because it looked insecure; and the spurs were added as a kind of pledge of stability to the eye. But evidently the projecting corners of the abacus at a, Fig. XIX., are actually insecure; they may break off, if great weight be laid upon them. This is the chief reason of the ugliness of the form; and the spurs in b are now no mere pledges of apparent stability, but have very serious practical use in supporting the angle of the abacus. If, even with the added spur, the support seems insufficient, we may fill up the crannies between the spurs and the bell, and we have the form c.

Thus a, though the germ and type of capitals, is itself (except under some peculiar conditions) both ugly and insecure; b is the first type of capitals which carry light weight; c, of capitals which carry excessive weight.

§ V. I fear, however, the reader may think he is going slightly too fast, and may not like having the capital forced upon him out of the cornice; but would prefer inventing a capital for the shaft itself, without reference to the cornice at all. We will do so then; though we shall come to the same result.

The shaft, it will be remembered, has to sustain the same weight as the long piece of wall which was concentrated into the shaft; it is enabled to do this both by its better form and better knit materials; and it can carry a greater weight than the space at the top of it is adapted to receive. The first point, therefore, is to expand this space as far as possible, and that in a form more convenient than the circle for the adjustment of the stones above. In general the square is a more convenient form than any other; but the hexagon or octagon is sometimes better fitted for masses of work which divide in six or eight directions. Then our first impulse would be to put a square or hexagonal stone on the top of the shaft, projecting as far beyond it as might be safely ventured; as at a, Fig. XX. This is the abacus. Our next idea would be to put a conical shaped stone beneath this abacus, to support its outer edge, as at b. This is the bell.

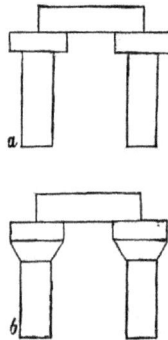

Fig. XX.

§ VI. Now the entire treatment of the capital depends simply on the manner in which this bell-stone is prepared for fitting the shaft below and the abacus above. Placed as at a, in Fig. XIX., it gives us the simplest of possible forms; with the spurs added, as at b, it gives the germ of the richest and most elaborate forms: but there are two modes of treatment more dexterous than the one, and less elaborate than the other, which are of the highest possible importance,—modes in which the bell is brought to its proper form by truncation.

§ VII. Let d and f, Fig. XIX., be two bell-stones; d is part of a cone (a sugar-loaf upside down, with its point cut off); f part of a four-sided pyramid. Then, assuming the abacus to be square, d will already fit the shaft, but has to be chiselled to fit the abacus; f will already fit the abacus, but has to be chiselled to fit the shaft.

From the broad end of d chop or chisel off, in four vertical planes, as much as will leave its head an exact square. The vertical cuttings will form curves on the sides of the cone (curves of a curious kind, which the reader need not be troubled to examine), and we shall have the form at e, which is the root of the greater number of Norman capitals.

From f cut off the angles, beginning at the corners of the square and widening the truncation downwards, so as to give the form at g, where the base of the bell is an octagon, and its top remains a square. A very slight rounding away of the angles of the octagon at the base of g will enable it to fit the circular shaft closely enough for all practical purposes, and this form, at g, is the root of nearly all Lombardic capitals.

If, instead of a square, the head of the bell were hexagonal or octagonal, the operation of cutting would be the same on each angle; but there would be produced, of course, six or eight curves on the sides of e, and twelve or sixteen sides to the base of g.

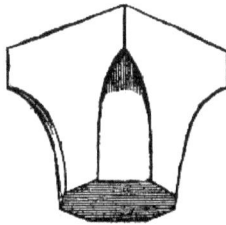

Fig. XXI.

§ VIII. The truncations in e and g may of course be executed on concave or convex forms of d and f; but e is usually worked on a straight-sided bell, and the truncation of g often becomes concave while the bell remains straight; for this simple reason,—that the sharp points at the angles of g, being somewhat difficult to cut, and easily broken off, are usually avoided by beginning the truncation a little way down the side of the bell, and then recovering the lost ground by a deeper cut inwards, as here, Fig. XXI. This is the actual form of the capitals of the balustrades of St. Mark's: it is the root of all the Byzantine Arab capitals, and of all the most beautiful capitals in the world, whose function is to express lightness.

§ IX. We have hitherto proceeded entirely on the assumption that the form of cornice which was gathered together to produce the capital was the root of cornices, a of Fig. V. But this, it will be remembered, was said in § VI. of Chap. VI. to be especially characteristic of southern work, and that in northern and wet climates it took the form of a dripstone.

Accordingly, in the northern climates, the dripstone gathered together forms a peculiar northern capital, commonly called the Early English,[47] owing to its especial use in that style.

There would have been no absurdity in this if shafts were always to be exposed to the weather; but in Gothic constructions the most important shafts are in the inside of the building. The dripstone sections of their capitals are therefore unnecessary and ridiculous.

§ X. They are, however, much worse than unnecessary.

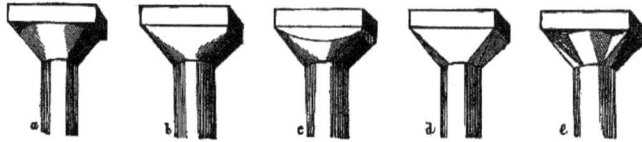

Fig. XXII.

The edge of the dripstone, being undercut, has no bearing power, and the capital fails, therefore, in its own principal function; and besides this, the undercut contour admits of no distinctly visible decoration; it is, therefore, left utterly barren, and the capital looks as if it had been turned in a lathe. The Early English capital has, therefore, the three greatest faults that any design can have: (1) it fails in its own proper purpose, that of support; (2) it is adapted to a purpose to which it can never be put, that of keeping off rain; (3) it cannot be decorated.

The Early English capital is, therefore, a barbarism of triple grossness, and degrades the style in which it is found, otherwise very noble, to one of second-rate order.

§ XI. Dismissing, therefore, the Early English capital, as deserving no place in our system, let us reassemble in one view the forms which have been legitimately developed, and which are to become hereafter subjects of decoration. To the forms a, b, and c, Fig. XIX., we must add the two simplest truncated forms e and g, Fig. XIX., putting their abaci on them (as we considered their contours in the bells only), and we shall have the five forms now given in parallel perspective in Fig. XXII., which are the roots of all good capitals existing, or capable of existence, and whose variations, infinite and a thousand times infinite, are all produced by introduction of various curvatures into their contours, and the endless methods of decoration superinduced on such curvatures.

§ XII. There is, however, a kind of variation, also infinite, which takes place in these radical forms, before they receive either curvature or decoration. This is the variety of proportion borne by the different lines of the capital to each other, and to the shafts. This is a structural question, at present to be considered as far as is possible.

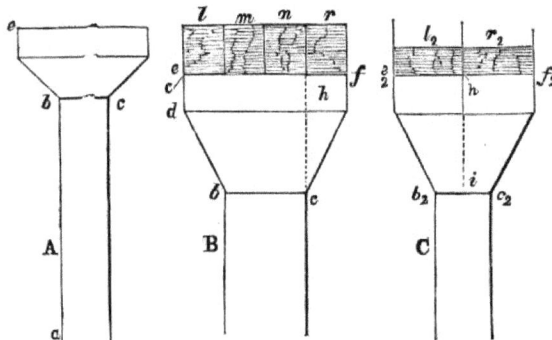

Fig. XXIII.

§ XIII. All the five capitals (which are indeed five orders with legitimate distinction; very different, however, from the five orders as commonly understood) may be represented by the same profile, a section through the sides of a, b, d, and e, or through the angles of c, Fig. XXII. This profile we will put on the top of a shaft, as at A, Fig. XXIII., which shaft we will suppose of equal diameter above and below for the sake of greater simplicity: in this simplest condition, however, relations of proportion exist between five quantities, any one or any two, or any three, or any four of which may change, irrespective of the others. These five quantities are:

1. The height of the shaft, a b;
2. Its diameter, b c;
3. The length of slope of bell, b d;
4. The inclination of this slope, or angle c b d;
5. The depth of abacus, d e.

For every change in any one of these quantities we have a new proportion of capital: five infinities, supposing change only in one quantity at a time: infinity of infinities in the sum of possible changes.

It is, therefore, only possible to note the general laws of change; every scale of pillar, and every weight laid upon it admitting, within certain limits, a variety out of which the architect has his choice; but yet fixing limits which the proportion becomes ugly when it approaches, and dangerous when it exceeds. But the inquiry into this subject is too difficult for the general reader, and I shall content myself with proving four laws, easily understood and generally applicable; for proof of which if the said reader care not, he may miss the next four paragraphs without harm.

§ XIV. 1. The more slender the shaft, the greater, proportionally, may be the projection of the abacus. For, looking back to Fig. XXIII., let the height a b be fixed, the length d b, the angle d b c, and the depth d e. Let the single quantity b c be variable, let B be a capital and shaft which are found to be perfectly safe in proportion to the weight they bear, and let the weight be equally distributed over the whole of the abacus. Then this weight may be represented by any number of equal divisions, suppose four, as l, m, n, r, of brickwork above, of which each division is one fourth of the whole weight; and let this weight be placed in the most trying way on the abacus, that is to say, let the masses l and r be detached from m and n, and bear with their full weight on the outside of the capital. We assume, in B, that the width of abacus e f is twice as great as that of the shaft, b c, and on these conditions we assume the capital to be safe.

But b c is allowed to be variable. Let it become b2 c2 at C, which is a length representing about the diameter of a shaft containing half the substance of the shaft B, and, therefore, able to sustain not more than half the weight sustained by B. But the slope b d and depth d e remaining unchanged, we have the capital of C, which we are to load with only half the weight of l, m, n, r, i.e., with l and r alone. Therefore the weight of l and r, now represented by the masses l2, r2, is distributed over the whole of the capital. But the weight r was adequately supported by the projecting piece of the first capital h f c: much more is it now adequately supported by i h, f2 c2. Therefore, if the capital of B was safe, that of C is more than safe. Now in B the length e f was only twice b c; but in C, e2 f2 will be found more than twice that of b2 c2. Therefore, the more slender the shaft, the greater may be the proportional excess of the abacus over its diameter.

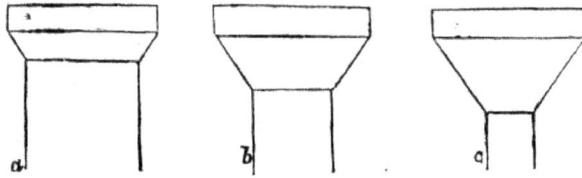

Fig. XXIV.

§ XV. 2. The smaller the scale of the building, the greater may be the excess of the abacus over the diameter of the shaft. This principle requires, I think, no very lengthy proof: the reader can understand at once that the cohesion and strength of stone which can sustain a small projecting mass, will not sustain a vast one overhanging in the same proportion. A bank even of loose earth, six feet high, will sometimes overhang its base a foot or two, as you may see any day in the gravelly banks of the lanes of Hampstead: but make the bank of gravel, equally loose, six hundred feet high, and see if you can get it to overhang a hundred or two! much more if there be weight above it increased in the same proportion. Hence, let any capital be given, whose projection is just safe, and no more, on its existing scale; increase its proportions every way equally, though ever so little, and it is unsafe; diminish them equally, and it becomes safe in the exact degree of the diminution.

Let, then, the quantity e d, and angle d b c, at A of Fig. XXIII., be invariable, and let the length d b vary: then we shall have such a series of forms as may be represented by a, b, c, Fig. XXIV., of which a is a proportion for a colossal building, b for a moderately sized building, while c could only be admitted on a very small scale indeed.

§ XVI. 3. The greater the excess of abacus, the steeper must be the slope of the bell, the shaft diameter being constant.

This will evidently follow from the considerations in the last paragraph; supposing only that, instead of the scale of shaft and capital varying together, the scale of the capital varies alone. For it will then still be true, that, if the projection of the capital be just safe on a given scale, as its excess over the shaft diameter increases, the projection will be unsafe, if the slope of the bell remain constant. But it may be rendered safe by making this slope steeper, and so increasing its supporting power.

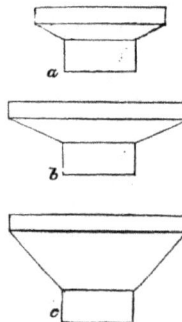

Fig. XXV.

Thus let the capital a, Fig. XXV., be just safe. Then the capital b, in which the slope is the same but the excess greater, is unsafe. But the capital c, in which, though the excess equals that of b, the steepness of the supporting slope is increased, will be as safe as b, and probably as strong as a.[48]

§ XVII. 4. The steeper the slope of the bell, the thinner may be the abacus.

The use of the abacus is eminently to equalise the pressure over the surface of the bell, so that the weight may not by any accident be directed exclusively upon its edges. In proportion to the strength of these edges, this function of the abacus is superseded, and these edges are strong in proportion to the steepness of the slope. Thus in Fig. XXVI., the bell at a would carry weight safely enough without any abacus, but that at c would not: it would probably have its edges broken off. The abacus superimposed might be on a very thin, little more than formal, as at b; but on c must be thick, as at d.

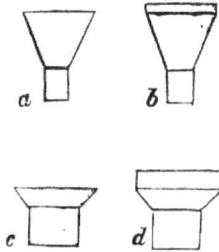

Fig. XXVI.

§ XVIII. These four rules are all that are necessary for general criticism; and observe that these are only semi-imperative,—rules of permission, not of compulsion. Thus Law 1 asserts that the slender shaft may have greater excess of capital than the thick shaft; but it need not, unless the architect chooses; his thick shafts must have small excess, but his slender ones need not have large. So Law 2 says, that as the building is smaller, the excess may be greater; but it need not, for the excess which is safe in the large is still safer in the small. So Law 3 says that capitals of great excess must have steep slopes; but it does not say that capitals of small excess may not have steep slopes also, if we choose. And lastly, Law 4 asserts the necessity of the thick abacus for the shallow bell; but the steep bell may have a thick abacus also.

§ XIX. It will be found, however, that in practice some confession of these laws will always be useful, and especially of the two first. The eye always requires, on a slender shaft, a more spreading capital than it does on a massy one, and a bolder mass of capital on a small scale than on a large. And, in the application of the first rule, it is to be noted that a shaft becomes slender either by diminution of diameter or increase of height; that either mode of change presupposes the weight above it diminished, and requires an expansion of abacus. I know no mode of spoiling a noble building more frequent in actual practice than the imposition of flat and slightly expanded capitals on tall shafts.

§ XX. The reader must observe, also, that, in the demonstration of the four laws, I always assumed the weight above to be given. By the alteration of this weight, therefore, the architect has it in his power to relieve, and therefore alter, the forms of his capitals. By its various distribution on their centres or edges, the slope of their bells and thickness of abaci will be affected also; so that he has countless expedients at his command for the various treatment of his design. He can divide his weights among more shafts; he can throw them in different places and different directions on the abaci; he can alter slope of bells or diameter of shafts; he can use spurred or plain bells, thin or thick abaci; and all these changes admitting of infinity in their degrees, and infinity a thousand times told in their relations: and all this without reference to decoration, merely with the five forms of block capital!

§ XXI. In the harmony of these arrangements, in their fitness, unity, and accuracy, lies the true proportion of every building,—proportion utterly endless in its infinities of change, with unchanged beauty. And yet this connexion of the frame of their building into one harmony has, I believe, never been so much as dreamed of by architects. It has been instinctively done in some degree by many, empirically in some degree by many more; thoughtfully and thoroughly, I believe, by none.

§ XXII. We have hitherto considered the abacus as necessarily a separate stone from the bell: evidently, however, the strength of the capital will be undiminished if both are cut out of one block. This is actually the case in many capitals, especially those on a small scale; and in others the detached upper stone is a mere representative of the abacus, and is much thinner than the form of the capital requires, while the true abacus is united with the bell, and concealed by its decoration, or made part of it.

§ XXIII. Farther. We have hitherto considered bell and abacus as both derived from the concentration of the cornice. But it must at once occur to the reader, that the projection of the under stone and the thickness of the upper, which are quite enough for the work of the continuous cornice, may not be enough always, or rather are seldom likely to be so, for the harder work of the capital. Both may have to be deepened and expanded: but as this would cause a want of harmony in the parts, when they occur on the same level, it is better in such case to let the entire cornice form the abacus of the capital, and put a deep capital bell beneath it.

§ XXIV. The reader will understand both arrangements instantly by two examples. Fig. XXVII. represents two windows, more than usually beautiful examples of a very frequent Venetian form. Here the deep cornice or string course which runs along the wall of the house is quite strong enough for the work of the capitals of the slender shafts: its own upper stone is therefore also theirs; its own lower stone, by its revolution or concentration, forms their bells: but to mark the increased importance of its function in so doing, it receives decoration, as the bell of the capital, which it did not receive as the under stone of the Cornice.

Fig. XXVII.

In Fig. XXVIII., a little bit of the church of Santa Fosca at Torcello, the cornice or string course, which goes round every part of the church, is not strong enough to form the capitals of the shafts. It therefore forms their abaci only; and in order to mark the diminished importance of its function, it ceases to receive, as the abacus of the capital, the decoration which it received as the string course of the wall.

This last arrangement is of great frequency in Venice, occurring most characteristically in St. Mark's: and in the Gothic of St. John and Paul we find the two arrangements beautifully united, though in great simplicity; the string courses of the walls form the capitals of the shafts of the traceries; and the abaci of the vaulting shafts of the apse.

Fig. XXVIII.

§ XXV. We have hitherto spoken of capitals of circular shafts only: those of square piers are more frequently formed by the cornice only; otherwise they are like those of circular piers, without the difficulty of reconciling the base of the bell with its head.

§ XXVI. When two or more shafts are grouped together, their capitals are usually treated as separate, until they come into actual contact. If there be any awkwardness in the junction, it is concealed by the decoration, and one abacus serves, in most cases, for all. The double group, Fig. XXVII., is the simplest possible type of the arrangement. In the richer Northern Gothic groups of eighteen or twenty shafts cluster together, and sometimes the smaller shafts crouch under the capitals of the larger, and hide their heads in the crannies, with small nominal abaci of their own, while the larger shafts carry the serviceable abacus of the whole pier, as in the nave of Rouen. There is, however, evident sacrifice of sound principle in this system, the smaller abaci being of no use. They are the exact contrary of the rude early abacus at Milan, given in Plate XVII. There one poor abacus stretched itself out to do all the work: here there are idle abaci getting up into corners and doing none.

§ XXVII. Finally, we have considered the capital hitherto entirely as an expansion of the bearing power of the shaft, supposing the shaft composed of a single stone. But, evidently, the capital has a function, if possible, yet more important, when the shaft is composed of small masonry. It enables all that masonry to act together, and to receive the pressure from above collectively and with a single strength. And thus, considered merely as a large stone set on the top of the shaft, it is a feature of the highest architectural importance, irrespective of its expansion, which indeed is, in some very noble capitals, exceedingly small. And thus every large stone set at any important point to reassemble the force of smaller masonry and prepare it for the sustaining of weight, is a capital or "head" stone (the true meaning of the word) whether it project or not. Thus at 6, in Plate IV., the stones which support the thrust of the brickwork are capitals, which have no projection at all; and the large stones in the window above are capitals projecting in one direction only.

§ XXVIII. The reader is now master of all he need know respecting construction of capitals; and from what has been laid before him, must assuredly feel that there can never be any new system of architectural forms invented; but that all vertical support must be, to the end of time, best obtained by shafts and capitals. It has been so obtained by nearly every nation of builders, with more or less refinement in the management of the details; and the later Gothic builders of the North stand almost alone in their effort to dispense with the natural development of the shaft, and banish the capital from their compositions.

They were gradually led into this error through a series of steps which it is not here our business to trace. But they may be generalised in a few words.

§ XXIX. All classical architecture, and the Romanesque which is legitimately descended from it, is composed of bold independent shafts, plain or fluted, with bold detached capitals, forming arcades or colonnades where they are needed; and of walls whose apertures are surrounded by courses of parallel lines called mouldings, which are continuous round the apertures, and have neither shafts nor capitals. The shaft system and moulding system are entirely separate.

The Gothic architects confounded the two. They clustered the shafts till they looked like a group of mouldings. They shod and capitaled the mouldings till they looked like a group of shafts. So that a pier became merely the side of a door or window rolled up, and the side of the window a pier unrolled (vide last Chapter, § XXX.), both being composed of a series of small shafts, each with base and capital. The architect seemed to have whole mats of shafts at his disposal, like the rush mats which one puts under cream cheese. If he wanted a great pier he rolled up the mat; if he wanted the side of a door he spread out the mat: and now the reader has to add to the other distinctions between the Egyptian and the Gothic shaft, already noted in § XXVI. of Chap. VIII., this one more—the most important of all—that while the Egyptian rush cluster has only one massive capital altogether, the Gothic rush mat has a separate tiny capital to every several rush.

§ XXX. The mats were gradually made of finer rushes, until it became troublesome to give each rush its capital. In fact, when the groups of shafts became excessively complicated, the expansion of their small abaci was of no use: it was dispensed with altogether, and the mouldings of pier and jamb ran up continuously into the arches.

This condition, though in many respects faulty and false, is yet the eminently characteristic state of Gothic: it is the definite formation of it as a distinct style, owing no farther aid to classical models; and its lightness and complexity render it, when well treated, and enriched with Flamboyant decoration, a very glorious means of picturesque effect. It is, in fact, this form of Gothic which commends itself most easily to the general mind, and which has suggested the innumerable foolish theories about the derivation of Gothic from tree trunks and avenues, which have from time to time been brought forward by persons ignorant of the history of architecture.

§ XXXI. When the sense of picturesqueness, as well as that of justness and dignity, had been lost, the spring of the continuous mouldings was replaced by what Professor Willis calls the Discontinuous impost; which, being a barbarism of the basest and most painful kind, and being to architecture what the setting of a saw is to music, I shall not trouble the reader to examine. For it is not in my plan to note for him all the various conditions of error, but only to guide him to the appreciation of the right; and I only note even the true Continuous or Flamboyant Gothic because this is redeemed by its beautiful decoration, afterwards to be considered. For, as far as structure is concerned, the moment the capital vanishes from the shaft, that moment we are in error: all good Gothic has true capitals to the shafts of its jambs and traceries, and all Gothic is debased the instant the shaft vanishes. It matters not how slender, or how small, or how low, the shaft may be: wherever there is indication of concentrated vertical support, then the capital is a necessary termination. I know how much Gothic, otherwise beautiful, this sweeping principle condemns; but it condemns not altogether. We may still take delight in its lovely proportions, its rich decoration, or its elastic and reedy moulding; but be assured, wherever shafts, or any approximations to the forms of shafts, are employed, for whatever office, or on whatever scale, be it in jambs or piers, or balustrades, or traceries, without capitals, there is a defiance of the natural laws of construction; and that, wherever such examples are found in ancient buildings, they are either the experiments of barbarism, or the commencements of decline.

FOOTNOTES:

[47] Appendix 19, "Early English Capitals."

[48] In this case the weight borne is supposed to increase as the abacus widens; the illustration would have been clearer if I had assumed the breadth of abacus to be constant, and that of the shaft to vary.

CHAPTER X

THE ARCH LINE

§ I. We have seen in the last section how our means of vertical support may, for the sake of economy both of space and material, be gathered into piers or shafts, and directed to the sustaining of particular points. The next question is how to connect these points or tops of shafts with each other, so as to be able to lay on them a continuous roof. This the reader, as before, is to favor me by finding out for himself, under these following conditions.

Let s, s, Fig. XXIX. opposite, be two shafts, with their capitals ready prepared for their work; and a, b, b, and c, c, c, be six stones of different sizes, one very long and large, and two smaller, and three smaller still, of which the reader is to choose which he likes best, in order to connect the tops of the shafts.

I suppose he will first try if he can lift the great stone a, and if he can, he will put it very simply on the tops of the two pillars, as at A.

Very well indeed: he has done already what a number of Greek architects have been thought very clever for having done. But suppose he cannot lift the great stone a, or suppose I will not give it to him, but only the two smaller stones at b, b; he will doubtless try to put them up, tilted against each other, as at

d. Very awkward this; worse than card-house building. But if he cuts off the corners of the stones, so as to make each of them of the form e, they will stand up very securely, as at B.

But suppose he cannot lift even these less stones, but can raise those at c, c, c. Then, cutting each of them into the form at e, he will doubtless set them up as at f.

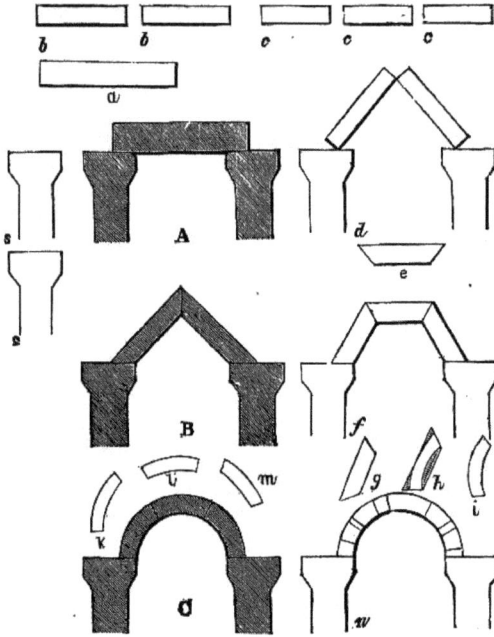

Fig. XXIX.

§ II. This last arrangement looks a little dangerous. Is there not a chance of the stone in the middle pushing the others out, or tilting them up and aside, and slipping down itself between them? There is such a chance: and if by somewhat altering the form of the stones, we can diminish this chance, all the better. I must say "we" now, for perhaps I may have to help the reader a little.

The danger is, observe, that the midmost stone at f pushes out the side ones: then if we can give the side ones such a shape as that, left to themselves, they would fall heavily forward, they will resist this push out by their weight, exactly in proportion to their own particular inclination or desire to tumble in. Take one of them separately, standing up as at g; it is just possible it may stand up as it is, like the Tower of Pisa: but we want it to fall forward. Suppose we cut away the parts that are shaded at h and leave it as at i, it is very certain it cannot stand alone now, but will fall forward to our entire satisfaction.

Farther: the midmost stone at f is likely to be troublesome chiefly by its weight, pushing down between the others; the more we lighten it the better: so we will cut it into exactly the same shape as the side ones, chiselling away the shaded parts, as at h. We shall then have all the three stones k, l, m, of the same shape; and now putting them together, we have, at C, what the reader, I doubt not, will perceive at once to be a much more satisfactory arrangement than that at f.

§ III. We have now got three arrangements; in one using only one piece of stone, in the second two, and in the third three. The first arrangement has no particular name, except the "horizontal:" but the single stone (or beam, it may be,) is called a lintel; the second arrangement is called a "Gable;" the third an "Arch."

We might have used pieces of wood instead of stone in all these arrangements, with no difference in plan, so long as the beams were kept loose, like the stones; but as beams can be securely nailed together at the ends, we need not trouble ourselves so much about their shape or balance, and therefore the plan at f is a peculiarly wooden construction (the reader will doubtless recognise in it the profile of many a farm-house roof): and again, because beams are tough, and light, and long, as compared with stones, they are admirably adapted for the constructions at A and B, the plain lintel and gable, while that at C is, for the most part, left to brick and stone.

§ IV. But farther. The constructions, A, B, and C, though very conveniently to be first considered as composed of one, two, and three pieces, are by no means necessarily so. When we have once cut the stones of the arch into a shape like that of k, l, and m, they will hold together, whatever their number, place, or size, as at n; and the great value of the arch is, that it permits small stones to be used with safety instead of large ones, which are not always to be had. Stones cut into the shape of k, l, and m, whether they be short or long (I have drawn them all sizes at n on purpose), are called Voussoirs; this is a hard, ugly French name; but the reader will perhaps be kind enough to recollect it; it will save us both some trouble: and to make amends for this infliction, I will relieve him of the term keystone. One voussoir is as much a keystone as another; only people usually call the stone which is last put in the keystone; and that one happens generally to be at the top or middle of the arch.

§ V. Not only the arch, but even the lintel, may be built of many stones or bricks. The reader may see lintels built in this way over most of the windows of our brick London houses, and so also the gable: there are, therefore, two distinct questions respecting each arrangement;—First, what is the line or direction of it, which gives it its strength? and, secondly, what is the manner of masonry of it, which gives it its consistence? The first of these I shall consider in this Chapter under the head of the Arch Line, using the term arch as including all manner of construction (though we shall have no trouble except about curves); and in the next Chapter I shall consider the second, under the head, Arch Masonry.

§ VI. Now the arch line is the ghost or skeleton of the arch; or rather it is the spinal marrow of the arch, and the voussoirs are the vertebræ, which keep it safe and sound, and clothe it. This arch line the architect has first to conceive and shape in his mind, as opposed to, or having to bear, certain forces which will try to distort it this way and that; and against which he is first to direct and bend the line itself into as strong resistance as he may, and then, with his voussoirs and what else he can, to guard it, and help it, and keep it to its duty and in its shape. So the arch line is the moral character of the arch, and the adverse forces are its temptations; and the voussoirs, and what else we may help it with, are its armor and its motives to good conduct.

§ VII. This moral character of the arch is called by architects its "Line of Resistance." There is a great deal of nicety in calculating it with precision, just as there is sometimes in finding out very precisely what is a man's true line of moral conduct; but this, in arch morality and in man morality, is a very simple and easily to be understood principle,—that if either arch or man expose themselves to their special temptations or adverse forces, outside of the voussoirs or proper and appointed armor, both will fall. An arch whose line of resistance is in the middle of its voussoirs is perfectly safe: in proportion as the said line runs near the edge of its voussoirs, the arch is in danger, as the man is who nears temptation; and the moment the line of resistance emerges out of the voussoirs the arch falls.

§ VIII. There are, therefore, properly speaking, two arch lines. One is the visible direction or curve of the arch, which may generally be considered as the under edge of its voussoirs, and which has often no more to do with the real stability of the arch, than a man's apparent conduct has with his heart. The other line, which is the line of resistance, or line of good behavior, may or may not be consistent with the outward and apparent curves of the arch; but if not, then the security of the arch depends simply upon this, whether the voussoirs which assume or pretend to the one line are wide enough to include the other.

§ IX. Now when the reader is told that the line of resistance varies with every change either in place or quantity of the weight above the arch, he will see at once that we have no chance of arranging arches by their moral characters: we can only take the apparent arch line, or visible direction, as a ground of arrangement. We shall consider the possible or probable forms or contours of arches in the present Chapter, and in the succeeding one the forms of voussoir and other help which may best fortify these visible lines against every temptation to lose their consistency.

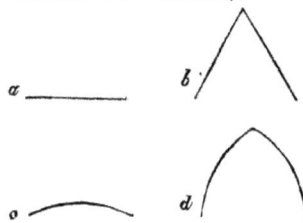

Fig. XXX.

§ X. Look back to Fig. XXIX. Evidently the abstract or ghost line of the arrangement at A is a plain horizontal line, as here at a, Fig. XXX. The abstract line of the arrangement at B, Fig. XXIX., is composed of two straight lines, set against each other, as here at b. The abstract line of C, Fig. XXIX., is a curve of some kind, not at present determined, suppose c, Fig. XXX. Then, as b is two of the straight lines at a, set up against each other, we may conceive an arrangement, d, made up of two of the curved lines at c, set against each other. This is called a pointed arch, which is a contradiction in terms: it ought to be called a curved gable; but it must keep the name it has got.

Now a, b, c, d, Fig. XXX., are the ghosts of the lintel, the gable, the arch, and the pointed arch. With the poor lintel ghost we need trouble ourselves no farther; there are no changes in him: but there is much variety in the other three, and the method of their variety will be best discerned by studying b and d, as subordinate to and connected with the simple arch at c.

§ XI. Many architects, especially the worst, have been very curious in designing out of the way arches,—elliptical arches, and four-centred arches, so called, and other singularities. The good architects have generally been content, and we for the present will be so, with God's arch, the arch of the rainbow and of the apparent heaven, and which the sun shapes for us as it sets and rises. Let us watch the sun for a moment as it climbs: when it is a quarter up, it will give us the arch a, Fig. XXXI.; when it is half up, b, and when three quarters up, c. There will be an infinite number of arches between these, but we will take these as sufficient representatives of all. Then a is the low arch, b the central or pure arch, c the high arch, and the rays of the sun would have drawn for us their voussoirs.

§ XII. We will take these several arches successively, and fixing the top of each accurately, draw two right lines thence to its base, d, e, f, Fig. XXXI. Then these lines give us the relative gables of each of the arches; d is the Italian or southern gable, e the central gable, f the Gothic gable.

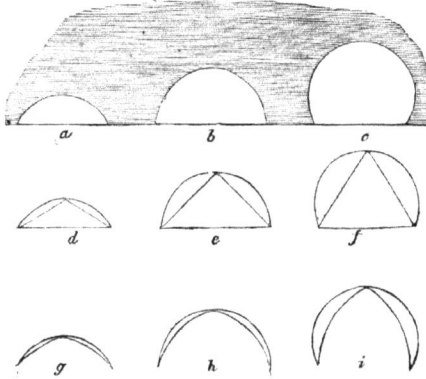

Fig. XXXI.

§ XIII. We will again take the three arches with their gables in succession, and on each of the sides of the gable, between it and the arch, we will describe another arch, as at g, h, i. Then the curves so described give the pointed arches belonging to each of the round arches; g, the flat pointed arch, h, the central pointed arch, and i, the lancet pointed arch.

§ XIV. If the radius with which these intermediate curves are drawn be the base of f, the last is the equilateral pointed arch, one of great importance in Gothic work. But between the gable and circle, in all the three figures, there are an infinite number of pointed arches, describable with different radii; and the three round arches, be it remembered, are themselves representatives of an infinite number, passing from the flattest conceivable curve, through the semicircle and horseshoe, up to the full circle.

The central and the last group are the most important. The central round, or semicircle, is the Roman, the Byzantine, and Norman arch; and its relative pointed includes one wide branch of Gothic. The horseshoe round is the Arabic and Moorish arch, and its relative pointed includes the whole range of Arabic and lancet, or Early English and French Gothics. I mean of course by the relative pointed, the entire group of which the equilateral arch is the representative. Between it and the outer horseshoe, as this latter rises higher, the reader will find, on experiment, the great families of what may be called the horseshoe pointed,—curves of the highest importance, but which are all included, with English lancet, under the term, relative pointed of the horseshoe arch.

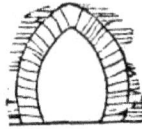

Fig. XXXII.

§ XV. The groups above described are all formed of circular arcs, and include all truly useful and beautiful arches for ordinary work. I believe that singular and complicated curves are made use of in modern engineering, but with these the general reader can have no concern: the Ponte della Trinita at Florence is the most graceful instance I know of such structure; the arch made use of being very subtle, and approximating to the low ellipse; for which, in common work, a barbarous pointed arch, called four-centred, and composed of bits of circles, is substituted by the English builders. The high ellipse, I believe, exists in eastern architecture. I have never myself met with it on a large scale; but it occurs in the niches of the later portions of the Ducal palace at Venice, together with a singular hyperbolic arch, a in Fig. XXXIII., to be described hereafter: with such caprices we are not here concerned.

§ XVI. We are, however, concerned to notice the absurdity of another form of arch, which, with the four-centred, belongs to the English perpendicular Gothic.

Taking the gable of any of the groups in Fig. XXXI. (suppose the equilateral), here at b, in Fig. XXXIII., the dotted line representing the relative pointed arch, we may evidently conceive an arch formed by reversed curves on the inside of the gable, as here shown by the inner curved lines. I imagine the reader by this time knows enough of the nature of arches to understand that, whatever strength or stability was gained by the curve on the outside of the gable, exactly so much is lost by curves on the inside. The natural tendency of such an arch to dissolution by its own mere weight renders it a feature of detestable ugliness, wherever it occurs on a large scale. It is eminently characteristic of Tudor work, and it is the profile of the Chinese roof (I say on a large scale, because this as well as all other capricious arches, may be made secure by their masonry when small, but not otherwise). Some allowable modifications of it will be noticed in the chapter on Roofs.

Fig. XXXIII.

§ XVII. There is only one more form of arch which we have to notice. When the last described arch is used, not as the principal arrangement, but as a mere heading to a common pointed arch, we have the form c, Fig. XXXIII. Now this is better than the entirely reversed arch for two reasons; first, less of the line is weakened by reversing; secondly, the double curve has a very high æsthetic value, not existing in the mere segments of circles. For these reasons arches of this kind are not only admissible, but even of great desirableness, when their scale and masonry render them secure, but above a certain scale they are altogether barbarous; and, with the reversed Tudor arch, wantonly employed, are the characteristics of the worst and meanest schools of architecture, past or present.

This double curve is called the Ogee; it is the profile of many German leaden roofs, of many Turkish domes (there more excusable, because associated and in sympathy with exquisitely managed arches of the same line in the walls below), of Tudor turrets, as in Henry the Seventh's Chapel, and it is at the bottom or top of sundry other blunders all over the world.

§ XVIII. The varieties of the ogee curve are infinite, as the reversed portion of it may be engrafted on every other form of arch, horseshoe, round, or pointed. Whatever is generally worthy of note in these varieties, and in other arches of caprice, we shall best discover by examining their masonry; for it is by their good masonry only that they are rendered either stable or beautiful. To this question, then, let us address ourselves.

CHAPTER XI

THE ARCH MASONRY

§ I. On the subject of the stability of arches, volumes have been written and volumes more are required. The reader will not, therefore, expect from me any very complete explanation of its conditions within the limits of a single chapter. But that which is necessary for him to know is very simple and very easy; and yet, I believe, some part of it is very little known, or noticed.

We must first have a clear idea of what is meant by an arch. It is a curved shell of firm materials, on whose back a burden is to be laid of loose materials. So far as the materials above it are not loose, but themselves hold together, the opening below is not an arch, but an excavation. Note this difference very carefully. If the King of Sardinia tunnels through the Mont Cenis, as he proposes, he will not require to build a brick arch under his tunnel to carry the weight of the Mont Cenis: that would need scientific masonry indeed. The Mont Cenis will carry itself, by its own cohesion, and a succession of invisible granite arches, rather larger than the tunnel. But when Mr. Brunel tunnelled the Thames bottom, he needed to build a brick arch to carry the six or seven feet of mud and the weight of water above. That is a type of all arches proper.

§ II. Now arches, in practice, partake of the nature of the two. So far as their masonry above is Mont-Cenisian, that is to say, colossal in comparison of them, and granitic, so that the arch is a mere hole in the rock substance of it, the form of the arch is of no consequence whatever: it may be rounded, or lozenged, or ogee'd, or anything else; and in the noblest architecture there is always some character of this kind given to the masonry. It is independent enough not to care about the holes cut in it, and does not subside into them like sand. But the theory of arches does not presume on any such condition of things; it allows itself only the shell of the arch proper; the vertebræ, carrying their marrow of resistance; and, above this shell, it assumes the wall to be in a state of flux, bearing down on the arch, like water or sand, with its whole weight. And farther, the problem which is to be solved by the arch builder is not merely to carry this weight, but to carry it with the least thickness of shell. It is easy to carry it by continually thickening your voussoirs: if you have six feet depth of sand or gravel to carry, and you choose to employ granite voussoirs six feet thick, no question but your arch is safe enough. But it is perhaps somewhat too costly: the thing to be done is to carry the sand or gravel with brick voussoirs, six inches thick, or, at any rate, with the least thickness of voussoir which will be safe; and to do this requires peculiar arrangement of the lines of the arch. There are many arrangements, useful all in their way, but we have only to do, in the best architecture, with the simplest and most easily understood. We have first to note those which regard the actual shell of the arch, and then we shall give a few examples of the superseding of such expedients by Mont-Cenisian masonry.

§ III. What we have to say will apply to all arches, but the central pointed arch is the best for general illustration. Let a, Plate III., be the shell of a pointed arch with loose loading above; and suppose you find that shell not quite thick enough; and that the weight bears too heavily on the top of the arch, and is likely to break it in: you proceed to thicken your shell, but need you thicken it all equally? Not so; you would only waste your good voussoirs. If you have any common sense you will thicken it at the top, where a Mylodon's skull is thickened for the same purpose (and some human skulls, I fancy), as at b. The pebbles and gravel above will now shoot off it right and left, as the bullets do off a cuirassier's breastplate, and will have no chance of beating it in.

If still it be not strong enough, a farther addition may be made, as at c, now thickening the voussoirs a little at the base also. But as this may perhaps throw the arch inconveniently high, or occasion a waste of voussoirs at the top, we may employ another expedient.

§ IV. I imagine the reader's common sense, if not his previous knowledge, will enable him to understand that if the arch at a, Plate III., burst in at the top, it must burst out at the sides. Set up two pieces of pasteboard, edge to edge, and press them down with your hand, and you will see them bend out at the sides. Therefore, if you can keep the arch from starting out at the points p, p, it cannot curve in at the top, put what weight on it you will, unless by sheer crushing of the stones to fragments.

§ V. Now you may keep the arch from starting out at p by loading it at p, putting more weight upon it and against it at that point; and this, in practice, is the way it is usually done. But we assume at present that the weight above is sand or water, quite unmanageable, not to be directed to the points we choose; and in practice, it may sometimes happen that we cannot put weight upon the arch at p. We may perhaps want an opening above it, or it may be at the side of the building, and many other circumstances may occur to hinder us.

§ VI. But if we are not sure that we can put weight above it, we are perfectly sure that we can hang weight under it. You may always thicken your shell inside, and put the weight upon it as at x x, in d, Plate III. Not much chance of its bursting out at p, now, is there?

§ VII. Whenever, therefore, an arch has to bear vertical pressure, it will bear it better when its shell is shaped as at b or d, than as at a: b and d are, therefore, the types of arches built to resist vertical pressure, all over the world, and from the beginning of architecture to its end. None others can be compared with them: all are imperfect except these.

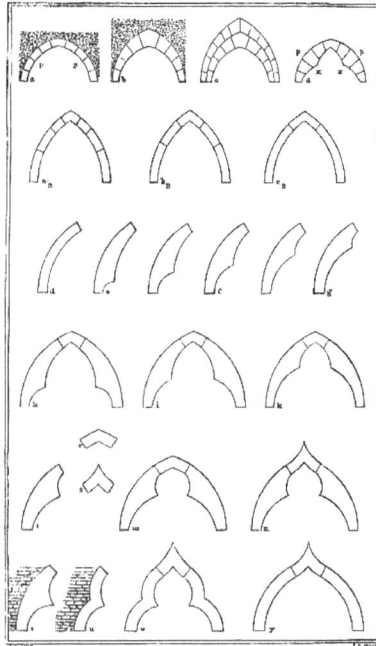

Plate III. ARCH MASONRY.

The added projections at x x, in d, are called CUSPS, and they are the very soul and life of the best northern Gothic; yet never thoroughly understood nor found in perfection, except in Italy, the northern builders working often, even in the best times, with the vulgar form at a.

The form at b is rarely found in the north: its perfection is in the Lombardic Gothic; and branches of it, good and bad according to their use, occur in Saracenic work.

§ VIII. The true and perfect cusp is single only. But it was probably invented (by the Arabs?) not as a constructive, but a decorative feature, in pure fantasy; and in early northern work it is only the application to the arch of the foliation, so called, of penetrated spaces in stone surfaces, already enough explained in the "Seven Lamps," Chap. III., p. 85 et seq. It is degraded in dignity, and loses its usefulness, exactly in proportion to its multiplication on the arch. In later architecture, especially English Tudor, it is sunk into dotage, and becomes a simple excrescence, a bit of stone pinched up out of the arch, as a cook pinches the paste at the edge of a pie.

§ IX. The depth and place of the cusp, that is to say, its exact application to the shoulder of the curve of the arch, varies with the direction of the weight to be sustained. I have spent more than a month, and that in hard work too, in merely trying to get the forms of cusps into perfect order: whereby the reader may guess that I have not space to go into the subject now; but I shall hereafter give a few of the leading and most perfect examples, with their measures and masonry.

§ X. The reader now understands all that he need about the shell of the arch, considered as an united piece of stone.

He has next to consider the shape of the voussoirs. This, as much as is required, he will be able best to comprehend by a few examples; by which I shall be able also to illustrate, or rather which will force me to illustrate, some of the methods of Mont-Cenisian masonry, which were to be the second part of our subject.

§ XI. 1 and 2, Plate IV., are two cornices; 1 from St. Antonio, Padua; 2, from the Cathedral of Sens. I want them for cornices; but I have put them in this plate because, though their arches are filled up behind, and are in fact mere blocks of stone with arches cut into their faces, they illustrate the constant masonry of small arches, both in Italian and Northern Romanesque, but especially Italian, each arch being cut out of its own proper block of stone: this is Mont-Cenisian enough, on a small scale.

3 is a window from Carnarvon Castle, and very primitive and interesting in manner,—one of its arches being of one stone, the other of two. And here we have an instance of a form of arch which would be barbarous enough on a large scale, and of many pieces; but quaint and agreeable thus massively built.

4 is from a little belfry in a Swiss village above Vevay; one fancies the window of an absurd form, seen in the distance, but one is pleased with it on seeing its masonry. It could hardly be stronger.

§ XII. These then are arches cut of one block. The next step is to form them of two pieces, set together at the head of the arch. 6, from the Eremitani, Padua, is very quaint and primitive in manner: it is a curious church altogether, and has some strange traceries cut out of single blocks. One is given in the "Seven Lamps," Plate VII., in the left-hand corner at the bottom.

7, from the Frari, Venice, very firm and fine, and admirably decorated, as we shall see hereafter. 5, the simple two-pieced construction, wrought with the most exquisite proportion and precision of workmanship, as is everything else in the glorious church to which it belongs, San Fermo of Verona. The addition of the top piece, which completes the circle, does not affect the plan of the beautiful arches, with their simple and perfect cusps; but it is highly curious, and serves to show how the idea of the cusp rose out of mere foliation. The whole of the architecture of this church may be characterised as exhibiting the maxima of simplicity in construction, and perfection in workmanship,—a rare unison: for, in general, simple designs are rudely worked, and as the builder perfects his execution, he complicates his plan. Nearly all the arches of San Fermo are two-pieced.

Plate IV. ARCH MASONRY.

§ XIII. We have seen the construction with one and two pieces: a and b, Fig. 8, Plate IV., are the general types of the construction with three pieces, uncusped and cusped; c and d with five pieces, uncusped and cusped. Of these the three-pieced construction is of enormous importance, and must detain us some time. The five-pieced is the three-pieced with a joint added on each side, and is also of great importance. The four-pieced, which is the two-pieced with added joints, rarely occurs, and need not detain us.

§ XIV. It will be remembered that in first working out the principle of the arch, we composed the arch of three pieces. Three is the smallest number which can exhibit the real principle of arch masonry, and it may be considered as representative of all arches built on that principle; the one and two-pieced arches being microscopic Mont-Cenisian, mere caves in blocks of stone, or gaps between two rocks leaning together.

But the three-pieced arch is properly representative of all; and the larger and more complicated constructions are merely produced by keeping the central piece for what is called a keystone, and putting additional joints at the sides. Now so long as an arch is pure circular or pointed, it does not matter how many joints or voussoirs you have, nor where the joints are; nay, you may joint your keystone itself, and make it two-pieced. But if the arch be of any bizarre form, especially ogee, the joints must be in particular places, and the masonry simple, or it will not be thoroughly good and secure; and the fine schools of the ogee arch have only arisen in countries where it was the custom to build arches of few pieces.

§ XV. The typical pure pointed arch of Venice is a five-pieced arch, with its stones in three orders of magnitude, the longest being the lowest, as at b2, Plate III. If the arch be very large, a fourth order of magnitude is added, as at a2. The portals of the palaces of Venice have one or other of these masonries, almost without exception. Now, as one piece is added to make a larger door, one piece is taken away to make a smaller one, or a window, and the masonry type of the Venetian Gothic window is consequently three-pieced, c2.

§ XVI. The reader knows already where a cusp is useful. It is wanted, he will remember, to give weight to those side stones, and draw them inwards against the thrust of the top stone. Take one of the side stones of c2 out for a moment, as at d. Now the proper place of the cusp upon it varies with the weight which it bears or requires; but in practice this nicety is rarely observed; the place of the cusp is almost always determined by æsthetic considerations, and it is evident that the variations in its place may be infinite. Consider the cusp as a wave passing up the side stone from its bottom to its top; then you will have the succession of forms from e to g (Plate III.), with infinite degrees of transition from each to each; but of which you may take e, f, and g, as representing three great families of cusped arches. Use e for your side stones, and you have an arch as that at h below, which may be called a down-cusped arch. Use f for the side stone, and you have i, which may be called a mid-cusped arch. Use g, and you have k, an up-cusped arch.

§ XVII. The reader will observe that I call the arch mid-cusped, not when the cusped point is in the middle of the curve of the arch, but when it is in the middle of the side piece, and also that where the side pieces join the keystone there will be a change, perhaps somewhat abrupt, in the curvature.

I have preferred to call the arch mid-cusped with respect to its side piece than with respect to its own curve, because the most beautiful Gothic arches in the world, those of the Lombard Gothic, have, in all the instances I have examined, a form more or less approximating to this mid-cusped one at i (Plate III.), but having the curvature of the cusp carried up into the keystone, as we shall see presently: where, however, the arch is built of many voussoirs, a mid-cusped arch will mean one which has the point of the cusp midway between its own base and apex.

The Gothic arch of Venice is almost invariably up-cusped, as at k. The reader may note that, in both down-cusped and up-cusped arches, the piece of stone, added to form the cusp, is of the shape of a scymitar, held down in the one case and up in the other.

§ XVIII. Now, in the arches h, i, k, a slight modification has been made in the form of the central piece, in order that it may continue the curve of the cusp. This modification is not to be given to it in practice without considerable nicety of workmanship; and some curious results took place in Venice from this difficulty.

At l (Plate III.) is the shape of the Venetian side stone, with its cusp detached from the arch. Nothing can possibly be better or more graceful, or have the weight better disposed in order to cause it to nod forwards against the keystone, as above explained, Ch. X. § II., where I developed the whole system of the arch from three pieces, in order that the reader might now clearly see the use of the weight of the cusp.

Now a Venetian Gothic palace has usually at least three stories; with perhaps ten or twelve windows in each story, and this on two or three of its sides, requiring altogether some hundred to a hundred and fifty side pieces.

I have no doubt, from observation of the way the windows are set together, that the side pieces were carved in pairs, like hooks, of which the keystones were to be the eyes; that these side pieces were ordered by the architect in the gross, and were used by him sometimes for wider, sometimes for narrower windows; bevelling the two ends as required, fitting in keystones as he best could, and now and then varying the arrangement by turning the side pieces upside down.

There were various conveniences in this way of working, one of the principal being that the side pieces with their cusps were always cut to their complete form, and that no part of the cusp was carried out into the keystone, which followed the curve of the outer arch itself. The ornaments of the cusp might thus be worked without any troublesome reference to the rest of the arch.

§ XIX. Now let us take a pair of side pieces, made to order, like that at l, and see what we can make of them. We will try to fit them first with a keystone which continues the curve of the outer arch, as at m. This the reader assuredly thinks an ugly arch. There are a great many of them in Venice, the ugliest things there, and the Venetian builders quickly began to feel them so. What could they do to better them? The arch at m has a central piece of the form r. Substitute for it a piece of the form s, and we have the arch at n.

§ XX. This arch at n is not so strong as that at m; but, built of good marble, and with its pieces of proper thickness, it is quite strong enough for all practical purposes on a small scale. I have examined at least two thousand windows of this kind and of the other Venetian ogees, of which that at y (in which the plain side-piece d is used instead of the cusped one) is the simplest; and I never found one, even in the most ruinous palaces (in which they had had to sustain the distorted weight of falling walls) in which the central piece was fissured; and this is the only danger to which the window is exposed; in other respects it is as strong an arch as can be built.

It is not to be supposed that the change from the r keystone to the s keystone was instantaneous. It was a change wrought out by many curious experiments, which we shall have to trace hereafter, and to throw the resultant varieties of form into their proper groups.

§ XXI. One step more: I take a mid-cusped side piece in its block form at t, with the bricks which load the back of it. Now, as these bricks support it behind, and since, as far as the use of the cusp is concerned, it matters not whether its weight be in marble or bricks, there is nothing to hinder us from cutting out some of the marble, as at u, and filling up the space with bricks. (Why we should take a fancy to do this, I do not pretend to guess at present; all I have to assert is, that, if the fancy should strike us, there would be no harm in it). Substituting this side piece for the other in the window n, we have that at w, which may, perhaps, be of some service to us afterwards; here we have nothing more to do with it than to note that, thus built, and properly backed by brickwork, it is just as strong and safe a form as that at n; but that this, as well as every variety of ogee arch, depends entirely for its safety, fitness, and beauty, on the masonry which we have just analysed; and that, built on a large scale, and with many voussoirs, all such arches would be unsafe and absurd in general architecture. Yet they may be used occasionally for the sake of the exquisite beauty of which their rich and fantastic varieties admit, and sometimes for the sake of another merit, exactly the opposite of the constructional ones we are at present examining, that they seem to stand by enchantment.

Plate V. Arch Masonry. BRULETTO OF COMO.

§ XXII. In the above reasonings, the inclination of the joints of the voussoirs to the curves of the arch has not been considered. It is a question of much nicety, and which I have not been able as yet fully to investigate: but the natural idea of the arrangement of these lines (which in round arches are of course perpendicular to the curve) would be that every voussoir should have the lengths of its outer and inner arched surface in the same proportion to each other. Either this actual law, or a close approximation to it, is assuredly enforced in the best Gothic buildings.

§ XXIII. I may sum up all that it is necessary for the reader to keep in mind of the general laws connected with this subject, by giving him an example of each of the two forms of the perfect Gothic arch, uncusped and cusped, treated with the most simple and magnificent masonry, and partly, in both cases, Mont-Cenisian.

The first, Plate V., is a window from the Broletto of Como. It shows, in its filling, first, the single-pieced arch, carried on groups of four shafts, and a single slab of marble filling the space above, and pierced with a quatrefoil (Mont-Cenisian, this), while the mouldings above are each constructed with a separate system of voussoirs, all of them shaped, I think, on the principle above stated, § XXII., in alternate serpentine and marble; the outer arch being a noble example of the pure uncusped Gothic construction, b of Plate III.

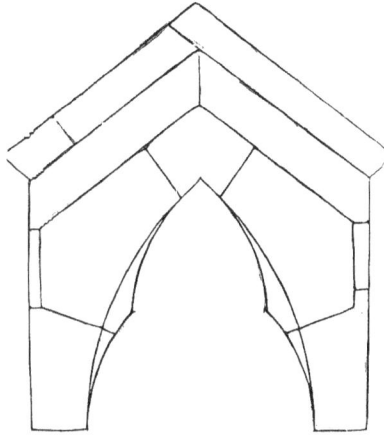

Fig. XXXIV.

§ **XXIV.** Fig. XXXIV. is the masonry of the side arch of, as far as I know or am able to judge, the most perfect Gothic sepulchral monument in the world, the foursquare canopy of the (nameless?)[49] tomb standing over the small cemetery gate of the Church of St. Anastasia at Verona. I shall have frequent occasion to recur to this monument, and, I believe, shall be able sufficiently to justify the terms in which I speak of it: meanwhile, I desire only that the reader should observe the severity and simplicity of the arch lines, the exquisitely delicate suggestion of the ogee curve in the apex, and chiefly the use of the cusp in giving inward weight to the great pieces of stone on the flanks of the arch, and preventing their thrust outwards from being severely thrown on the lowermost stones. The effect of this arrangement is, that the whole massy canopy is sustained safely by four slender pillars (as will be seen hereafter in the careful plate I hope to give of it), these pillars being rather steadied than materially assisted against the thrust, by iron bars, about an inch thick, connecting them at the heads of the abaci; a feature of peculiar importance in this monument, inasmuch as we know it to be part of the original construction, by a beautiful little Gothic wreathed pattern, like one of the hems of garments of Fra Angelico, running along the iron bar itself. So carefully, and so far, is the system of decoration carried out in this pure and lovely monument, my most beloved throughout all the length and breadth of Italy;—chief, as I think, among all the sepulchral marbles of a land of mourning.

FOOTNOTES:

[49] At least I cannot find any account of it in Maffei's "Verona," nor anywhere else, to be depended upon. It is, I doubt not, a work of the beginning of the thirteenth century. Vide Appendix 19, "Tombs at St. Anastasia."

CHAPTER XII

THE ARCH LOAD

§ I. In the preceding enquiry we have always supposed either that the load upon the arch was perfectly loose, as of gravel or sand, or that it was Mont-Cenisian, and formed one mass with the arch voussoirs, of more or less compactness.

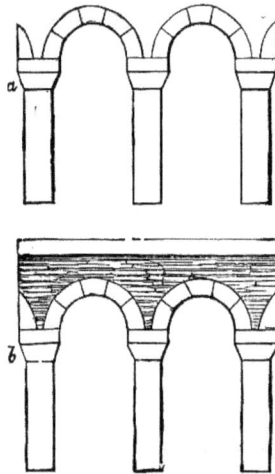

Fig. XXXV.

In practice, the state is usually something between the two. Over bridges and tunnels it sometimes approaches to the condition of mere dust or yielding earth; but in architecture it is mostly firm masonry, not altogether acting with the voussoirs, yet by no means bearing on them with perfectly dead weight, but locking itself together above them, and capable of being thrown into forms which relieve them, in some degree, from its pressure.

§ II. It is evident that if we are to place a continuous roof above the line of arches, we must fill up the intervals between them on the tops of the columns. We have at present nothing granted us but the bare masonry, as here at a, Fig. XXXV., and we must fill up the intervals between the semicircle so as to obtain a level line of support. We may first do this simply as at b, with plain mass of wall; so laying the roof on the top, which is the method of the pure Byzantine and Italian Romanesque. But if we find too much stress is thus laid on the arches, we may introduce small second shafts on the top of the great shaft, a, Fig. XXXVI., which may assist in carrying the roof, conveying great part of its weight at once to the heads of the main shafts, and relieving from its pressure the centres of the arches.

Fig. XXXVI.

§ III. The new shaft thus introduced may either remain lifted on the head of the great shaft, or may be carried to the ground in front of it, or through it, b, Fig. XXXVI.; in which latter case the main shaft divides into two or more minor shafts, and forms a group with the shaft brought down from above.

§ IV. When this shaft, brought from roof to ground, is subordinate to the main pier, and either is carried down the face of it, or forms no large part of the group, the principle is Romanesque or Gothic, b, Fig. XXXVI. When it becomes a bold central shaft, and the main pier splits into two minor shafts on its sides, the principle is Classical or Palladian, c, Fig. XXXVI. Which latter arrangement becomes absurd or unsatisfactory in proportion to the sufficiency of the main shaft to carry the roof without the help of the minor shafts or arch, which in many instances of Palladian work look as if they might be removed without danger to the building.

§ V. The form a is a more pure Northern Gothic type than even b, which is the connecting link between it and the classical type. It is found chiefly in English and other northern Gothic, and in early Lombardic, and is, I doubt not, derived as above explained, Chap. I. § XXVII. b is a general French Gothic and French Romanesque form, as in great purity at Valence.

The small shafts of the form a and b, as being northern, are generally connected with steep vaulted roofs, and receive for that reason the name of vaulting shafts.

§ VI. Of these forms b, Fig. XXXV., is the purest and most sublime, expressing the power of the arch most distinctly. All the others have some appearance of dovetailing and morticing of timber rather than stonework; nor have I ever yet seen a single instance, quite satisfactory, of the management of the capital of the main shaft, when it had either to sustain the base of the vaulting shaft, as in a, or to suffer it to pass through it, as in b, Fig. XXXVI. Nor is the bracket which frequently carries the vaulting shaft in English work a fitting support for a portion of the fabric which is at all events presumed to carry a considerable part of the weight of the roof.

§ VII. The triangular spaces on the flanks of the arch are called Spandrils, and if the masonry of these should be found, in any of its forms, too heavy for the arch, their weight may be diminished, while their strength remains the same, by piercing them with circular holes or lights. This is rarely necessary in ordinary architecture, though sometimes of great use in bridges and iron roofs (a succession of such circles may be seen, for instance, in the spandrils at the Euston Square station); but, from its constructional value, it becomes the best form in which to arrange spandril decorations, as we shall see hereafter.

§ VIII. The height of the load above the arch is determined by the needs of the building and possible length of the shaft; but with this we have at present nothing to do, for we have performed the task which was set us. We have ascertained, as it was required that we should in § VI. of Chap. III. (A), the construction of walls; (B), that of piers; (C), that of piers with lintels or arches prepared for roofing. We have next, therefore, to examine (D) the structure of the roof.

CHAPTER XIII

THE ROOF

§ I. Hitherto our enquiry has been unembarrassed by any considerations relating exclusively either to the exterior or interior of buildings. But it can remain so no longer. As far as the architect is concerned, one side of a wall is generally the same as another; but in the roof there are usually two distinct divisions of the structure; one, a shell, vault, or flat ceiling, internally visible, the other, an upper structure, built of timber, or of some different form, to protect the lower; or of some different form, to support it. Sometimes, indeed, the internally visible structure is the real roof, and sometimes there are more than two divisions, as in St. Paul's, where we have a central shell with a mask below and above. Still it will be convenient to remember the distinction between the part of the roof which is usually visible from within, and whose only business is to stand strongly, and not fall in, which I shall call the Roof Proper; and, secondly, the upper roof, which, being often partly supported by the lower, is not so much concerned with its own stability as with the weather, and is appointed to throw off snow, and get rid of rain, as fast as possible, which I shall call the Roof Mask.

§ II. It is, however, needless for me to engage the reader in the discussion of the various methods of construction of Roofs Proper, for this simple reason, that no person without long experience can tell whether a roof be wisely constructed or not; nor tell at all, even with help of any amount of experience, without examination of the several parts and bearings of it, very different from any observation possible to the general critic: and more than this, the enquiry would be useless to us in our Venetian studies, where the roofs are either not contemporary with the buildings, or flat, or else vaults of the simplest possible constructions, which have been admirably explained by Willis in his "Architecture of the Middle Ages," Chap. VII., to which I may refer the reader for all that it would be well for him to know respecting the connexion of the different parts of the vault with the shafts. He would also do well to read the passages on Tudor vaulting, pp. 185-193, in Mr. Garbett's rudimentary Treatise on Design, before alluded to.[50] I shall content myself therefore with noting one or two points on which neither writer has had occasion to touch, respecting the Roof Mask.

§ III. It was said in § V. of Chapter III. that we should not have occasion, in speaking of roof construction, to add materially to the forms then suggested. The forms which we have to add are only those resulting from the other curves of the arch developed in the last chapter; that is to say, the various eastern domes and cupolas arising out of the revolution of the horseshoe and ogee curves, together with the well-known Chinese concave roof. All these forms are of course purely decorative, the bulging outline, or concave surface, being of no more use, or rather of less, in throwing off snow or rain, than the ordinary spire and gable; and it is rather curious, therefore, that all of them, on a small scale, should have obtained so extensive use in Germany and Switzerland, their native climate being that of the east, where their purpose seems rather to concentrate light upon their orbed surfaces. I much doubt their applicability, on a large scale, to architecture of any admirable dignity; their chief charm is, to the European eye, that of strangeness; and it seems to me possible that in the east the bulging form may be also delightful, from the idea of its enclosing a volume of cool air. I enjoy them in St. Mark's, chiefly because they increase the fantastic and unreal character of St. Mark's Place; and because they appear to sympathise with an expression, common, I think, to all the buildings of that group, of a natural buoyancy, as if they floated in the air or on the surface of the sea. But, assuredly, they are not features to be recommended for imitation.[51]

§ IV. One form, closely connected with the Chinese concave, is, however, often constructively right,—the gable with an inward angle, occurring with exquisitely picturesque effect throughout the domestic architecture of the north, especially Germany and Switzerland; the lower slope being either an attached external penthouse roof, for protection of the wall, as in Fig. XXXVII., or else a kind of buttress set on the angle of the tower; and in either case the roof itself being a simple gable, continuous beneath it.

Fig. XXXVII.

§ V. The true gable, as it is the simplest and most natural, so I esteem it the grandest of roofs; whether rising in ridgy darkness, like a grey slope of slaty mountains, over the precipitous walls of the northern cathedrals, or stretched in burning breadth above the white and square-set groups of the southern architecture. But this difference between its slope in the northern and southern structure is a matter of far greater importance than is commonly supposed, and it is this to which I would especially direct the reader's attention.

§ VI. One main cause of it, the necessity of throwing off snow in the north, has been a thousand times alluded to: another I do not remember having seen noticed, namely, that rooms in a roof are comfortably habitable in the north, which are painful sotto piombi in Italy; and that there is in wet climates a natural tendency in all men to live as high as possible, out of the damp and mist. These two causes, together with accessible quantities of good timber, have induced in the north a general steep pitch of gable, which, when rounded or squared above a tower, becomes a spire or turret; and this feature, worked out with elaborate decoration, is the key-note of the whole system of aspiration, so called, which the German critics have so ingeniously and falsely ascribed to a devotional sentiment pervading the Northern Gothic: I entirely and boldly deny the whole theory; our cathedrals were for the most part built by worldly people, who loved the world, and would have gladly staid in it for ever; whose best hope was the escaping hell, which they thought to do by building cathedrals, but who had very vague conceptions of Heaven in general, and very feeble desires respecting their entrance therein; and the form of the spired cathedral has no more intentional reference to Heaven, as distinguished from the flattened slope of the Greek pediment, than the steep gable of a Norman house has, as distinguished from the flat roof of a Syrian one. We may now, with ingenious pleasure, trace such symbolic characters in the form; we may now use it with such definite meaning; but we only prevent ourselves from all right understanding of history, by attributing much influence to these poetical symbolisms in the formation of a national style. The human race are, for the most part, not to be moved by such silken cords; and the chances of damp in the cellar, or of loose tiles in the roof, have, unhappily, much more to do with the fashions of a man's house building than his ideas of celestial happiness or angelic virtue. Associations of affection have far higher power, and forms which can be no otherwise accounted for may often be explained by reference to the natural features of the country, or to anything which habit must have rendered familiar, and therefore delightful; but the direct symbolisation of a sentiment is a weak motive with all men, and far more so in the practical minds of the north than among the early Christians, who were assuredly quite as heavenly-minded, when they built basilicas, or cut conchas out of the catacombs, as were ever the Norman barons or monks.

§ VII. There is, however, in the north an animal activity which materially aided the system of building begun in mere utility,—an animal life, naturally expressed in erect work, as the languor of the south in reclining or level work. Imagine the difference between the action of a man urging himself to his work in a snow storm, and the inaction of one laid at his length on a sunny bank among cicadas and fallen olives, and you will have the key to a whole group of sympathies which were forcefully expressed in the architecture of both; remembering always that sleep would be to the one luxury, to the other death.

§ VIII. And to the force of this vital instinct we have farther to add the influence of natural scenery; and chiefly of the groups and wildernesses of the tree which is to the German mind what the olive or palm is to the southern, the spruce fir. The eye which has once been habituated to the continual serration of the pine forest, and to the multiplication of its infinite pinnacles, is not easily offended by the repetition of similar forms, nor easily satisfied by the simplicity of flat or massive outlines. Add to the influence of the pine, that of the poplar, more especially in the valleys of France; but think of the spruce chiefly, and meditate on the difference of feeling with which the Northman would be inspired by the frostwork wreathed upon its glittering point, and the Italian by the dark green depth of sunshine on the broad table of the stone-pine[52] (and consider by the way whether the spruce fir be a more heavenly-minded tree than those dark canopies of the Mediterranean isles).

§ IX. Circumstance and sentiment, therefore, aiding each other, the steep roof becomes generally adopted, and delighted in, throughout the north; and then, with the gradual exaggeration with which every pleasant idea is pursued by the human mind, it is raised into all manner of peaks, and points, and ridges; and pinnacle after pinnacle is added on its flanks, and the walls increased in height, in proportion, until we get indeed a very sublime mass, but one which has no more principle of religious aspiration in it than a child's tower of cards. What is more, the desire to build high is complicated with the peculiar love of the grotesque[53] which is characteristic of the north, together with especial delight in multiplication of small forms, as well as in exaggerated points of shade and energy, and a certain degree of consequent insensibility to perfect grace and quiet truthfulness; so that a northern architect could not feel the beauty of the Elgin marbles, and there will always be (in those who have devoted themselves to this particular school) a certain incapacity to taste the finer characters of Greek art, or to understand Titian, Tintoret, or Raphael: whereas among the Italian Gothic workmen, this capacity was never lost, and Nino Pisano and Orcagna could have understood the Theseus in an instant, and would have received from it new life. There can be no question that theirs was the greatest school, and carried out by the greatest men; and that while those who began with this school could perfectly well feel Rouen Cathedral, those who study the Northern Gothic remain in a narrowed field—one of small pinnacles, and dots, and crockets, and twitched faces—and cannot comprehend the meaning of a broad surface or a grand line. Nevertheless the northern school is an admirable and delightful thing, but a lower thing than the southern. The Gothic of the Ducal Palace of Venice is in harmony with all that is grand in all the world: that of the north is in harmony with the grotesque northern spirit only.

§ X. We are, however, beginning to lose sight of our roof structure in its spirit, and must return to our text. As the height of the walls increased, in sympathy with the rise of the roof, while their thickness remained the same, it became more and more necessary to support them by buttresses; but—and this is another point that the reader must specially note—it is not the steep roof mask which requires the buttress, but the vaulting beneath it; the roof mask being a mere wooden frame tied together by cross timbers, and in small buildings often put together on the ground, raised afterwards, and set on the walls like a hat, bearing vertically upon them; and farther, I believe in most cases the northern vaulting requires its great array of external buttress, not so much from any peculiar boldness in its own forms, as from the greater comparative thinness and height of the walls, and more determined throwing of the whole weight of the roof on particular points. Now the connexion of the interior frame-work (or true roof) with the buttress, at such points, is not visible to the spectators from without; but the relation of the roof mask to the top of the wall which it protects, or from which it springs, is perfectly visible; and it is a point of so great importance in the effect of the building, that it will be well to make it a subject of distinct consideration in the following Chapter.

FOOTNOTES:

[50] *Appendix 17*

[51] *I do not speak of the true dome, because I have not studied its construction enough to know at what largeness of scale it begins to be rather a tour de force than a convenient or natural form of roof, and because the ordinary spectator's choice among its various outlines must always be dependent on æsthetic considerations only, and can in no wise be grounded on any conception of its infinitely complicated structural principles.*

[52] *I shall not be thought to have overrated the effect of forest scenery on the northern mind; but I was glad to hear a Spanish gentleman, the other day, describing, together with his own, the regret which the*

peasants in his neighborhood had testified for the loss of a noble stone-pine, one of the grandest in Spain, which its proprietor had suffered to be cut down for small gain. He said that the mere spot where it had grown was still popularly known as "El Pino."

[53] Appendix 8.

CHAPTER XIV

THE ROOF CORNICE

§ I. It will be remembered that in the Sixth Chapter we paused (§ X.) at the point where the addition of brackets to the ordinary wall cornice would have converted it into a structure proper for sustaining a roof. Now the wall cornice was treated throughout our enquiry (compare Chapter VII. § V.) as the capital of the wall, and as forming, by its concentration, the capital of the shaft. But we must not reason back from the capital to the cornice, and suppose that an extension of the principles of the capital to the whole length of the wall, will serve for the roof cornice; for all our conclusions respecting the capital were based on the supposition of its being adapted to carry considerable weight condensed on its abacus: but the roof cornice is, in most cases, required rather to project boldly than to carry weight; and arrangements are therefore to be adopted for it which will secure the projection of large surfaces without being calculated to resist extraordinary pressure. This object is obtained by the use of brackets at intervals, which are the peculiar distinction of the roof cornice.

§ II. Roof cornices are generally to be divided into two great families: the first and simplest, those which are composed merely by the projection of the edge of the roof mask over the wall, sustained by such brackets or spurs as may be necessary; the second, those which provide a walk round the edge of the roof, and which require, therefore, some stronger support, as well as a considerable mass of building above or beside the roof mask, and a parapet. These two families we shall consider in succession.

§ III. 1. The Eaved Cornice. We may give it this name, as represented in the simplest form by cottage eaves. It is used, however, in bold projection, both in north, and south, and east; its use being, in the north, to throw the rain well away from the wall of the building; in the south to give it shade; and it is ordinarily constructed of the ends of the timbers of the roof mask (with their tiles or shingles continued to the edge of the cornice), and sustained by spurs of timber. This is its most picturesque and natural form; not inconsistent with great splendor of architecture in the mediæval Italian domestic buildings, superb in its mass of cast shadow, and giving rich effect to the streets of Swiss towns, even when they have no other claim to interest. A farther value is given to it by its waterspouts, for in order to avoid loading it with weight of water in the gutter at the edge, where it would be a strain on the fastenings of the pipe, it has spouts of discharge at intervals of three or four feet,—rows of magnificent leaden or iron dragons' heads, full of delightful character, except to any person passing along the middle of the street in a heavy shower. I have had my share of their kindness in my time, but owe them no grudge; on the contrary, much gratitude for the delight of their fantastic outline on the calm blue sky, when they had no work to do but to open their iron mouths and pant in the sunshine.

§ IV. When, however, light is more valuable than shadow, or when the architecture of the wall is too fair to be concealed, it becomes necessary to draw the cornice into narrower limits; a change of considerable importance, in that it permits the gutter, instead of being of lead and hung to the edge of the cornice, to be of stone, and supported by brackets in the wall, these brackets becoming proper recipients of after decoration (and sometimes associated with the stone channels of discharge, called gargoyles, which belong, however, more properly to the other family of cornices). The most perfect and beautiful example of this kind of cornice is the Venetian, in which the rain from the tiles is received in a stone gutter supported by small brackets, delicately moulded, and having its outer lower edge decorated with the English dogtooth moulding, whose sharp zigzag mingles richly with the curved edges of the tiling. I know no cornice more beautiful in its extreme simplicity and serviceableness.

§ V. The cornice of the Greek Doric is a condition of the same kind, in which, however, there are no brackets, but useless appendages hung to the bottom of the gutter (giving, however, some impression of support as seen from a distance), and decorated with stone symbolisms of raindrops. The brackets are not allowed, because they would interfere with the sculpture, which in this architecture is put beneath the cornice; and the overhanging form of the gutter is nothing more than a vast dripstone moulding, to keep the rain from such sculpture: its decoration of guttæ, seen in silver points against the shadow, is pretty in feeling, with a kind of continual refreshment and remembrance of rain in it; but the whole arrangement is awkward and meagre, and is only endurable when the eye is quickly drawn away from it to sculpture.

§ VI. In later cornices, invented for the Greek orders, and farther developed by the Romans, the bracket appears in true importance, though of barbarous and effeminate outline: and gorgeous decorations are applied to it, and to the various horizontal mouldings which it carries, some of them of great beauty, and of the highest value to the mediæval architects who imitated them. But a singularly gross mistake was made in the distribution of decoration on these rich cornices (I do not know when first, nor does it matter to me or to the reader), namely, the charging with ornament the under surface of the cornice between the brackets, that is to say, the exact piece of the whole edifice, from top to bottom, where ornament is least visible. I need hardly say much respecting the wisdom of this procedure, excusable only if the whole building were covered with ornament; but it is curious to see the way in which modern architects have copied it, even when they had little enough ornament to spare. For instance, I suppose few persons look at the Athenæum Club-house without feeling vexed at the meagreness and meanness of the windows of the ground floor: if, however, they look up under the cornice, and have good eyes, they will perceive that the architect has reserved his decorations to put between the brackets; and by going up to the first floor, and out on the gallery, they may succeed in obtaining some glimpses of the designs of the said decorations.

§ VII. Such as they are, or were, these cornices were soon considered essential parts of the "order" to which they belonged; and the same wisdom which endeavored to fix the proportions of the orders, appointed also that no order should go without its cornice. The reader has probably heard of the architectural division of superstructure into architrave, frieze, and cornice; parts which have been appointed by great architects to all their work, in the same spirit in which great rhetoricians have ordained that every speech shall have an exordium, and narration, and peroration. The reader will do well to consider that it may be sometimes just as possible to carry a roof, and get rid of rain, without such an arrangement, as it is to tell a plain fact without an exordium or peroration; but he must very absolutely consider that the architectural peroration or cornice is strictly and sternly limited to the end of the wall's speech,—that is, to the edge of the roof; and that it has nothing whatever to do with shafts nor the orders of them. And he will then be able fully to enjoy the farther ordinance of the late Roman and Renaissance architects, who, attaching it to the shaft as if it were part of its shadow, and having to employ their shafts often in places where they came not near the roof, forthwith cut the roof-cornice to pieces and attached a bit of it to every column; thenceforward to be carried by the unhappy shaft wherever it went, in addition to any other work on which it might happen to be employed. I do not recollect among any living beings, except Renaissance architects, any instance of a parallel or comparable stupidity: but one can imagine a savage getting hold of a piece of one of our iron wire ropes, with its rings upon it at intervals to bind it together, and pulling the wires asunder to apply them to separate purposes; but imagining there was magic in the ring that bound them, and so cutting that to pieces also, and fastening a little bit of it to every wire.

§ VIII. Thus much may serve us to know respecting the first family of wall cornices. The second is immeasurably more important, and includes the cornices of all the best buildings in the world. It has derived its best form from mediæval military architecture, which imperatively required two things; first, a parapet which should permit sight and offence, and afford defence at the same time; and secondly, a projection bold enough to enable the defenders to rake the bottom of the wall with falling bodies; projection which, if the wall happened to slope inwards, required not to be small. The thoroughly magnificent forms of cornice thus developed by necessity in military buildings, were adopted, with more or less of boldness or distinctness, in domestic architecture, according to the temper of the times and the circumstances of the individual—decisively in the baron's house, imperfectly in the burgher's: gradually they found their way into ecclesiastical architecture, under wise modifications in the early cathedrals, with infinite absurdity in the imitations of them; diminishing in size as their original purpose sank into a decorative one, until we find battlements, two-and-a-quarter inches square, decorating the gates of the Philanthropic Society.

§ IX. There are, therefore, two distinct features in all cornices of this kind; first, the bracket, now become of enormous importance and of most serious practical service; the second, the parapet: and these two features we shall consider in succession, and in so doing, shall learn all that is needful for us to know, not only respecting cornices, but respecting brackets in general, and balconies.

§ X. 1. The Bracket. In the simplest form of military cornice, the brackets are composed of two or more long stones, supporting each other in gradually increasing projection, with roughly rounded ends, Fig. XXXVIII., and the parapet is simply a low wall carried on the ends of these, leaving, of course, behind, or within it, a hole between each bracket for the convenient dejection of hot sand and lead. This form is best seen, I think, in the old Scotch castles; it is very grand, but has a giddy look, and one is afraid of the whole thing toppling off the wall. The next step was to deepen the brackets, so as to get them propped against a great depth of the main rampart, and to have the inner ends of the stones held by a greater weight of that main wall above; while small arches were thrown from bracket to bracket to carry the parapet wall more securely. This is the most perfect form of cornice, completely satisfying the eye of its security, giving full protection to the wall, and applicable to all architecture, the interstices between the brackets being filled up, when one does not want to throw boiling lead on any body below, and the projection being always delightful, as giving greater command and view of the building, from its angles, to those walking on the rampart. And as, in military buildings, there were usually towers at the angles (round which the battlements swept) in order to flank the walls, so often in the translation into civil or ecclesiastical architecture, a small turret remained at the angle, or a more bold projection of balcony, to give larger prospect to those upon the rampart. This cornice, perfect in all its parts, as arranged for ecclesiastical architecture, and exquisitely decorated, is the one employed in the duomo of Florence and campanile of Giotto, of which I have already spoken as, I suppose, the most perfect architecture in the world.

Fig. XXXVIII.

§ XI. In less important positions and on smaller edifices, this cornice diminishes in size, while it retains its arrangement, and at last we find nothing but the spirit and form of it left; the real practical purpose having ceased, and arch, brackets and all, being cut out of a single stone. Thus we find it used in early buildings throughout the whole of the north and south of Europe, in forms sufficiently represented by the two examples in Plate IV.: 1, from St. Antonio, Padua; 2, from Sens in France.

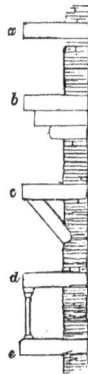

Fig. XXXIX.

§ XII. I wish, however, at present to fix the reader's attention on the form of the bracket itself; a most important feature in modern as well as ancient architecture. The first idea of a bracket is that of a long stone or piece of timber projecting from the wall, as a, Fig. XXXIX., of which the strength depends on the toughness of the stone or wood, and the stability on the weight of wall above it (unless it be the end of a main beam). But let it be supposed that the structure at a, being of the required projection, is found too weak: then we may strengthen it in one of three ways; (1) by putting a second or third stone beneath it, as at b; (2) by giving it a spur, as at c; (3) by giving it a shaft and another bracket below, d; the great use of this arrangement being that the lowermost bracket has the help of the weight of the shaft-length of wall above its insertion, which is, of course, greater than the weight of the small shaft: and then the lower bracket may be farther helped by the structure at b or c.

Fig. XL.

§ XIII. Of these structures, a and c are evidently adapted especially for wooden buildings; b and d for stone ones; the last, of course, susceptible of the richest decoration, and superbly employed in the cornice of the cathedral of Monza: but all are beautiful in their way, and are the means of, I think, nearly half the picturesqueness and power of mediæval building; the forms b and c being, of course, the most frequent; a, when it occurs, being usually rounded off, as at a, Fig. XL.; b, also, as in Fig. XXXVIII., or else itself composed of a single stone cut into the form of the group b here, Fig. XL., or plain, as at c, which is also the proper form of the brick bracket, when stone is not to be had. The reader will at once perceive that the form d is a barbarism (unless when the scale is small and the weight to be carried exceedingly light): it is of course, therefore, a favorite form with the Renaissance architects; and its introduction is one of the first corruptions of the Venetian architecture.

§ XIV. There is one point necessary to be noticed, though bearing on decoration more than construction, before we leave the subject of the bracket. The whole power of the construction depends upon the stones being well let into the wall; and the first function of the decoration should be to give the idea of this insertion, if possible; at all events, not to contradict this idea. If the reader will glance at any of the brackets used in the ordinary architecture of London, he will find them of some such character as Fig. XLI.; not a bad form in itself, but exquisitely absurd in its curling lines, which give the idea of some writhing suspended tendril, instead of a stiff support, and by their careful avoidance of the wall make the bracket look pinned on, and in constant danger of sliding down. This is, also, a Classical and Renaissance decoration.

Fig. XLI.

§ XV. 2. The Parapet. Its forms are fixed in military architecture by the necessities of the art of war at the time of building, and are always beautiful wherever they have been really thus fixed; delightful in the variety of their setting, and in the quaint darkness of their shot-holes, and fantastic changes of elevation and outline. Nothing is more remarkable than the swiftly discerned difference between the masculine irregularity of such true battlements, and the formal pitifulness of those which are set on modern buildings to give them a military air,—as on the jail at Edinburgh.

§ XVI. Respecting the Parapet for mere safeguard upon buildings not military, there are just two fixed laws. It should be pierced, otherwise it is not recognised from below for a parapet at all, and it should not be in the form of a battlement, especially in church architecture.

The most comfortable heading of a true parapet is a plain level on which the arm can be rested, and along which it can glide. Any jags or elevations are disagreeable; the latter, as interrupting the view and disturbing the eye, if they are higher than the arm, the former, as opening some aspect of danger if they are much lower; and the inconvenience, therefore, of the battlemented form, as well as the worse than absurdity, the bad feeling, of the appliance of a military feature to a church, ought long ago to have determined its rejection. Still (for the question of its picturesque value is here so closely connected with that of its practical use, that it is vain to endeavor to discuss it separately) there is a certain agreeableness in the way in which the jagged outline dovetails the shadow of the slated or leaded roof into the top of the wall, which may make the use of the battlement excusable where there is a difficulty in managing some unvaried line, and where the expense of a pierced parapet cannot be encountered: but remember always, that the value of the battlement consists in its letting shadow into the light of the wall, or vice versâ, when it comes against light sky, letting the light of the sky into the shade of the wall; but that the actual outline of the parapet itself, if the eye be arrested upon this, instead of upon the alternation of shadow, is as ugly a succession of line as can by any possibility be invented. Therefore, the battlemented parapet may only be used where this alternation of shade is certain to be shown, under nearly all conditions of effect; and where the lines to be dealt with are on a scale which may admit battlements of bold and manly size. The idea that a battlement is an ornament anywhere, and that a miserable and diminutive imitation of castellated outline will always serve to fill up blanks and Gothicise unmanageable spaces, is one of the great idiocies of the present day. A battlement is in its origin a piece of wall large enough to cover a man's body, and however it may be decorated, or pierced, or finessed away into traceries, as long as so much of its outline is retained as to suggest its origin, so long its size must remain undiminished. To crown a turret six feet high with chopped battlements three inches wide, is children's Gothic: it is one of the paltry falsehoods for which there is no excuse, and part of the system of using models of architecture to decorate architecture, which we shall hereafter note as one of the chief and most destructive follies of the Renaissance;[54] and in the present day the practice may be classed as one which distinguishes the architects of whom there is no hope, who have neither eye nor head for their work, and who must pass their lives in vain struggles against the refractory lines of their own buildings.

§ XVII. As the only excuse for the battlemented parapet is its alternation of shadow, so the only fault of the natural or level parapet is its monotony of line. This is, however, in practice, almost always broken by the pinnacles of the buttresses, and if not, may be varied by the tracery of its penetrations. The forms of these evidently admit every kind of change; for a stone parapet, however pierced, is sure to be strong enough for its purpose of protection, and, as regards the strength of the building in general, the lighter it is the better. More fantastic forms may, therefore, be admitted in a parapet than in any other architectural feature, and for most services, the Flamboyant parapets seem to me preferable to all others; especially when the leaden roofs set off by points of darkness the lace-like intricacy of penetration. These, however, as well as the forms usually given to Renaissance balustrades (of which, by the bye, the best piece of criticism I know is the sketch in "David Copperfield" of the personal appearance of the man who stole Jip), and the other and finer forms invented by Paul Veronese in his architectural backgrounds, together with the pure columnar balustrade of Venice, must be considered as altogether decorative features.

§ XVIII. So also are, of course, the jagged or crown-like finishings of walls employed where no real parapet of protection is desired; originating in the defences of outworks and single walls: these are used much in the east on walls surrounding unroofed courts. The richest examples of such decoration are Arabian; and from Cairo they seem to have been brought to Venice. It is probable that few of my readers, however familiar the general form of the Ducal Palace may have been rendered to them by innumerable drawings, have any distinct idea of its roof, owing to the staying of the eye on its superb parapet, of which we shall give account hereafter. In most of the Venetian cases the parapets which surround roofing are very sufficient for protection, except that the stones of which they are composed appear loose and infirm: but their purpose is entirely decorative; every wall, whether detached or roofed, being indiscriminately fringed with Arabic forms of parapet, more or less Gothicised, according to the lateness of their date.

I think there is no other point of importance requiring illustration respecting the roof itself, or its cornice: but this Venetian form of ornamental parapet connects itself curiously, at the angles of nearly all the buildings on which it occurs, with the pinnacled system of the north, founded on the structure of the buttress. This, it will be remembered, is to be the subject of the fifth division of our inquiry.

FOOTNOTES:

[54] Not of Renaissance alone: the practice of modelling buildings on a minute scale for niches and tabernacle-work has always been more or less admitted, and I suppose authority for diminutive battlements might be gathered from the Gothic of almost every period, as well as for many other faults and mistakes: no Gothic school having ever been thoroughly systematised or perfected, even in its best times. But that a mistaken decoration sometimes occurs among a crowd of noble ones, is no more an excuse for the habitual—far less, the exclusive—use of such a decoration, than the accidental or seeming misconstructions of a Greek chorus are an excuse for a school boy's ungrammatical exercise.

CHAPTER XV

THE BUTTRESS

§ I. We have hitherto supposed ourselves concerned with the support of vertical pressure only; and the arch and roof have been considered as forms of abstract strength, without reference to the means by which their lateral pressure was to be resisted. Few readers will need now to be reminded, that every arch or gable not tied at its base by beams or bars, exercises a lateral pressure upon the walls which sustain it,—pressure which may, indeed, be met and sustained by increasing the thickness of the wall or vertical piers, and which is in reality thus met in most Italian buildings, but may, with less expenditure of material, and with (perhaps) more graceful effect, be met by some particular application of the provisions against lateral pressure called Buttresses. These, therefore, we are next to examine.

§ II. Buttresses are of many kinds, according to the character and direction of the lateral forces they are intended to resist. But their first broad division is into buttresses which meet and break the force before it arrives at the wall, and buttresses which stand on the lee side of the wall, and prop it against the force.

The lateral forces which walls have to sustain are of three distinct kinds: dead weight, as of masonry or still water; moving weight, as of wind or running water; and sudden concussion, as of earthquakes, explosions, &c.

Clearly, dead weight can only be resisted by the buttress acting as a prop; for a buttress on the side of, or towards the weight, would only add to its effect. This, then, forms the first great class of buttressed architecture; lateral thrusts, of roofing or arches, being met by props of masonry outside—the thrust from within, the prop without; or the crushing force of water on a ship's side met by its cross timbers—the thrust here from without the wall, the prop within.

Moving weight may, of course, be resisted by the prop on the lee side of the wall, but is often more effectually met, on the side which is attacked, by buttresses of peculiar forms, cunning buttresses, which do not attempt to sustain the weight, but parry it, and throw it off in directions clear of the wall.

Thirdly: concussions and vibratory motion, though in reality only supported by the prop buttress, must be provided for by buttresses on both sides of the wall, as their direction cannot be foreseen, and is continually changing.

We shall briefly glance at these three systems of buttressing; but the two latter being of small importance to our present purpose, may as well be dismissed first.

§ III. 1. Buttresses for guard against moving weight and set towards the weight they resist.

The most familiar instance of this kind of buttress we have in the sharp piers of a bridge, in the centre of a powerful stream, which divide the current on their edges, and throw it to each side under the arches. A ship's bow is a buttress of the same kind, and so also the ridge of a breastplate, both adding to the strength of it in resisting a cross blow, and giving a better chance of a bullet glancing aside. In Switzerland, projecting buttresses of this kind are often built round churches, heading up hill, to divide and throw off the avalanches. The various forms given to piers and harbor quays, and to the bases of light-houses, in order to meet the force of the waves, are all conditions of this kind of buttress. But in works of ornamental architecture such buttresses are of rare occurrence; and I merely name them in order to mark their place in our architectural system, since in the investigation of our present subject we shall not meet with a single example of them, unless sometimes the angle of the foundation of a palace set against the sweep of the tide, or the wooden piers of some canal bridge quivering in its current.

§ IV. 2. Buttresses for guard against vibratory motion.

The whole formation of this kind of buttress resolves itself into mere expansion of the base of the wall, so as to make it stand steadier, as a man stands with his feet apart when he is likely to lose his balance. This approach to a pyramidal form is also of great use as a guard against the action of artillery; that if a stone or tier of stones be battered out of the lower portions of the wall, the whole upper part may not topple over or crumble down at once. Various forms of this buttress, sometimes applied to particular points of the wall, sometimes forming a great sloping rampart along its base, are frequent in buildings of countries exposed to earthquake. They give a peculiarly heavy outline to much of the architecture of the kingdom of Naples, and they are of the form in which strength and solidity are first naturally sought, in the slope of the Egyptian wall. The base of Guy's Tower at Warwick is a singularly bold example of their military use; and so, in general, bastion and rampart profiles, where, however, the object of stability against a shock is complicated with that of sustaining weight of earth in the rampart behind.

§ V. 3. Prop buttresses against dead weight.

This is the group with which we have principally to do; and a buttress of this kind acts in two ways, partly by its weight and partly by its strength. It acts by its weight when its mass is so great that the weight it sustains cannot stir it, but is lost upon it, buried in it, and annihilated: neither the shape of such a buttress nor the cohesion of its materials are of much consequence; a heap of stones or sandbags, laid up against the wall, will answer as well as a built and cemented mass.

But a buttress acting by its strength is not of mass sufficient to resist the weight by mere inertia; but it conveys the weight through its body to something else which is so capable; as, for instance, a man leaning against a door with his hands, and propping himself against the ground, conveys the force which would open or close the door against him through his body to the ground. A buttress acting in this way must be of perfectly coherent materials, and so strong that though the weight to be borne could easily move it, it cannot break it: this kind of buttress may be called a conducting buttress. Practically, however, the two modes of action are always in some sort united. Again, the weight to be borne may either act generally on the whole wall surface, or with excessive energy on particular points: when it acts on the whole wall surface, the whole wall is generally supported; and the arrangement becomes a continuous rampart, as a dyke, or bank of reservoir.

§ VI. It is, however, very seldom that lateral force in architecture is equally distributed. In most cases the weight of the roof, or the force of any lateral thrust, are more or less confined to certain points and directions. In an early state of architectural science this definiteness of direction is not yet clear, and it is met by uncertain application of mass or strength in the buttress, sometimes by mere thickening of the wall into square piers, which are partly piers, partly buttresses, as in Norman keeps and towers. But as science advances, the weight to be borne is designedly and decisively thrown upon certain points; the direction and degree of the forces which are then received are exactly calculated, and met by conducting buttresses of the smallest possible dimensions; themselves, in their turn, supported by vertical buttresses acting by weight, and these perhaps, in their turn, by another set of conducting buttresses: so that, in the best examples of such arrangements, the weight to be borne may be considered as the shock of an electric fluid, which, by a hundred different rods and channels, is divided and carried away into the ground.

§ VII. In order to give greater weight to the vertical buttress piers which sustain the conducting buttresses, they are loaded with pinnacles, which, however, are, I believe, in all the buildings in which they become very prominent, merely decorative: they are of some use, indeed, by their weight; but if this were all for which they were put there, a few cubic feet of lead would much more securely answer the purpose, without any danger from exposure to wind. If the reader likes to ask any Gothic architect with whom he may happen to be acquainted, to substitute a lump of lead for his pinnacles, he will see by the expression of his face how far he considers the pinnacles decorative members. In the work which seems to me the great type of simple and masculine buttress structure, the apse of Beauvais, the pinnacles are altogether insignificant, and are evidently added just as exclusively to entertain the eye and lighten the aspect of the buttress, as the slight shafts which are set on its angles; while in other very noble Gothic buildings the pinnacles are introduced as niches for statues, without any reference to construction at all: and sometimes even, as in the tomb of Can Signoria at Verona, on small piers detached from the main building.

§ VIII. I believe, therefore, that the development of the pinnacle is merely a part of the general erectness and picturesqueness of northern work above alluded to: and that, if there had been no other place for the pinnacles, the Gothic builders would have put them on the tops of their arches (they often did on the tops of gables and pediments), rather than not have had them; but the natural position of the pinnacle is, of course, where it adds to, rather than diminishes, the stability of the building; that is to say, on its main wall piers and the vertical piers at the buttresses. And thus the edifice is surrounded at last by a complete company of detached piers and pinnacles, each sustaining an inclined prop against the central wall, and looking something like a band of giants holding it up with the butts of their lances. This arrangement would imply the loss of an enormous space of ground, but the intervals of the buttresses are usually walled in below, and form minor chapels.

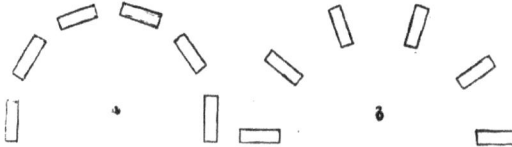

Fig. XLII.

§ IX. The science of this arrangement has made it the subject of much enthusiastic declamation among the Gothic architects, almost as unreasonable, in some respects, as the declamation of the Renaissance architects respecting Greek structure. The fact is, that the whole northern buttress system is based on the grand requirement of tall windows and vast masses of light at the end of the apse. In order to gain this quantity of light, the piers between the windows are diminished in thickness until they are far too weak to bear the roof, and then sustained by external buttresses. In the Italian method the light is rather dreaded than desired, and the wall is made wide enough between the windows to bear the roof, and so left. In fact, the simplest expression of the difference in the systems is, that a northern apse is a southern one with its inter-fenestral piers set edgeways. Thus, a, Fig. XLII., is the general idea of the southern apse; take it to pieces, and set all its piers edgeways, as at b, and you have the northern one. You gain much light for the interior, but you cut the exterior to pieces, and instead of a bold rounded or polygonal surface, ready for any kind of decoration, you have a series of dark and damp cells, which no device that I have yet seen has succeeded in decorating in a perfectly satisfactory manner. If the system be farther carried, and a second or third order of buttresses be added, the real fact is that we have a building standing on two or three rows of concentric piers, with the roof off the whole of it except the central circle, and only ribs left, to carry the weight of the bit of remaining roof in the middle; and after the eye has been accustomed to the bold and simple rounding of the Italian apse, the skeleton character of the disposition is painfully felt. After spending some months in Venice, I thought Bourges Cathedral looked exactly like a half-built ship on its shores. It is useless, however, to dispute respecting the merits of the two systems: both are noble in their place; the Northern decidedly the most scientific, or at least involving the greatest display of science, the Italian the calmest and purest, this having in it the sublimity of a calm heaven or a windless noon, the other that of a mountain flank tormented by the north wind, and withering into grisly furrows of alternate chasm and crag.

§ X. If I have succeeded in making the reader understand the veritable action of the buttress, he will have no difficulty in determining its fittest form. He has to deal with two distinct kinds; one, a narrow vertical pier, acting principally by its weight, and crowned by a pinnacle; the other, commonly called a Flying buttress, a cross bar set from such a pier (when detached from the building) against the main wall. This latter, then, is to be considered as a mere prop or shore, and its use by the Gothic architects might be illustrated by the supposition that we were to build all our houses with walls too thin to stand without wooden props outside, and then to substitute stone props for wooden ones. I have some doubts of the real dignity of such a proceeding, but at all events the merit of the form of the flying buttress depends on its faithfully and visibly performing this somewhat humble office; it is, therefore, in its purity, a mere sloping bar of stone, with an arch beneath it to carry its weight, that is to say, to prevent the action of gravity from in any wise deflecting it, or causing it to break downwards under the lateral thrust; it is thus formed quite simple in Notre Dame of Paris, and in the Cathedral of Beauvais, while at Cologne the sloping bars are pierced with quatrefoils, and at Amiens with traceried arches. Both seem to me effeminate and false in principle; not, of course, that there is any occasion to make the flying buttress heavy, if a light one will answer the purpose; but it seems as if some security were sacrificed to ornament. At Amiens the arrangement is now seen to great disadvantage, for the early traceries have been replaced by base flamboyant ones, utterly weak and despicable. Of the degradations of the original form which took place in after times, I have spoken at p. 35 of the "Seven Lamps."

§ XI. The form of the common buttress must be familiar to the eye of every reader, sloping if low, and thrown into successive steps if they are to be carried to any considerable height. There is much dignity in them when they are of essential service; but even in their best examples, their awkward angles are among the least manageable features of the Northern Gothic, and the whole organisation of its system was destroyed by their unnecessary and lavish application on a diminished scale; until the buttress became actually confused with the shaft, and we find strangely crystallised masses of diminutive buttress applied, for merely vertical support, in the northern tabernacle work; while in some recent copies of it the principle has been so far distorted that the tiny buttressings look as if they carried the superstructure on the points of their pinnacles, as in the Cranmer memorial at Oxford. Indeed, in most modern Gothic, the architects evidently consider buttresses as convenient breaks of blank surface, and general apologies for deadness of wall. They stand in the place of ideas, and I think are supposed also to have something of the odor of sanctity about them; otherwise, one hardly sees why a warehouse seventy feet high should have nothing of the kind, and a chapel, which one can just get into with one's hat off, should have a bunch of them at every corner; and worse than this, they are even thought ornamental when they can be of no possible use; and these stupid penthouse outlines are forced upon the eye in every species of decoration: in St. Margaret's Chapel, West Street, there are actually a couple of buttresses at the end of every pew.

§ XII. It is almost impossible, in consequence of these unwise repetitions of it, to contemplate the buttress without some degree of prejudice; and I look upon it as one of the most justifiable causes of the unfortunate aversion with which many of our best architects regard the whole Gothic school. It may, however, always be regarded with respect when its form is simple and its service clear; but no treason to Gothic can be greater than the use of it in indolence or vanity, to enhance the intricacies of structure, or occupy the vacuities of design.

CHAPTER XVI

FORM OF APERTURE

§ I. We have now, in order, examined the means of raising walls and sustaining roofs, and we have finally to consider the structure of the necessary apertures in the wall veil, the door and window; respecting which there are three main points to be considered.

1. The form of the aperture, i.e., its outline, its size, and the forms of its sides.

2. The filling of the aperture, i.e., valves and glass, and their holdings.

3. The protection of the aperture, and its appliances, i.e., canopies, porches, and balconies. We shall examine these in succession.

§ II. 1. The form of the aperture: and first of doors. We will, for the present, leave out of the question doors and gates in unroofed walls, the forms of these being very arbitrary, and confine ourselves to the consideration of doors of entrance into roofed buildings. Such doors will, for the most part, be at, or near, the base of the building; except when raised for purposes of defence, as in the old Scotch border towers, and our own Martello towers, or, as in Switzerland, to permit access in deep snow, or when stairs are carried up outside the house for convenience or magnificence. But in most cases, whether high or low, a door may be assumed to be considerably lower than the apartments or buildings into which it gives admission, and therefore to have some height of wall above it, whose weight must be carried by the heading of the door. It is clear, therefore, that the best heading must be an arch, because the strongest, and that a square-headed door must be wrong, unless under Mont-Cenisian masonry; or else, unless the top of the door be the roof of the building, as in low cottages. And a square-headed door is just so much more wrong and ugly than a connexion of main shafts by lintels, as the weight of wall above the door is likely to be greater than that above the main shafts. Thus, while I admit the Greek general forms of temple to be admirable in their kind, I think the Greek door always offensive and unmanageable.

§ III. We have it also determined by necessity, that the apertures shall be at least above a man's height, with perpendicular sides (for sloping sides are evidently unnecessary, and even inconvenient, therefore absurd) and level threshold; and this aperture we at present suppose simply cut through the wall without any bevelling of the jambs. Such a door, wide enough for two persons to pass each other easily, and with such fillings or valves as we may hereafter find expedient, may be fit enough for any building into which entrance is required neither often, nor by many persons at a time. But when entrance and egress are constant, or required by crowds, certain further modifications must take place.

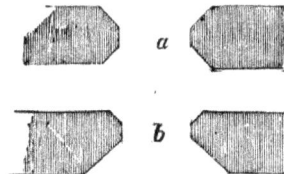

Fig. XLIII.

§ IV. When entrance and egress are constant, it may be supposed that the valves will be absent or unfastened,—that people will be passing more quickly than when the entrance and egress are unfrequent, and that the square angles of the wall will be inconvenient to such quick passers through. It is evident, therefore, that what would be done in time, for themselves, by the passing multitude, should be done for them at once by the architect; and that these angles, which would be worn away by friction, should at once be bevelled off, or, as it is called, splayed, and the most contracted part of the aperture made as short as possible, so that the plan of the entrance should become as at a, Fig. XLIII.

§ V. Farther. As persons on the outside may often approach the door or depart from it, beside the building, so as to turn aside as they enter or leave the door, and therefore touch its jamb, but, on the inside, will in almost every case approach the door, or depart from it in the direct line of the entrance (people generally walking forward when they enter a hall, court, or chamber of any kind, and being forced to do so when they enter a passage), it is evident that the bevelling may be very slight on the inside, but should be large on the outside, so that the plan of the aperture should become as at b, Fig. XLIII. Farther, as the bevelled wall cannot conveniently carry an unbevelled arch, the door arch must be bevelled also, and the aperture, seen from the outside, will have somewhat the aspect of a small cavern diminishing towards the interior.

§ VI. If, however, beside frequent entrance, entrance is required for multitudes at the same time, the size of the aperture either must be increased, or other apertures must be introduced. It may, in some buildings, be optional with the architect whether he shall give many small doors, or few large ones; and in some, as theatres, amphitheatres, and other places where the crowd are apt to be impatient, many doors are by far the best arrangement of the two. Often, however, the purposes of the building, as when it is to be entered by processions, or where the crowd most usually enter in one direction, require the large single entrance; and (for here again the æsthetic and structural laws cannot be separated) the expression and harmony of the building require, in nearly every case, an entrance of largeness proportioned to the multitude which is to meet within. Nothing is more unseemly than that a great multitude should find its way out and in, as ants and wasps do, through holes; and nothing more undignified than the paltry doors of many of our English cathedrals, which look as if they were made, not for the open egress, but for the surreptitious drainage of a stagnant congregation. Besides, the expression of the church door should lead us, as far as possible, to desire at least the western entrance to be single, partly because no man of right feeling would willingly lose the idea of unity and fellowship in going up to worship, which is suggested by the vast single entrance; partly because it is at the entrance that the most serious words of the building are always addressed, by its sculptures or inscriptions, to the worshipper; and it is well, that these words should be spoken to all at once, as by one great voice, not broken up into weak repetitions over minor doors.

In practice the matter has been, I suppose, regulated almost altogether by convenience, the western doors being single in small churches, while in the larger the entrances become three or five, the central door remaining always principal, in consequence of the fine sense of composition which the mediæval builders never lost. These arrangements have formed the noblest buildings in the world. Yet it is worth observing[55] how perfect in its simplicity the single entrance may become, when it is treated as in the Duomo and St. Zeno of Verona, and other such early Lombard churches, having noble porches, and rich sculptures grouped around the entrance.

§ VII. However, whether the entrances be single, triple, or manifold, it is a constant law that one shall be principal, and all shall be of size in some degree proportioned to that of the building. And this size is, of course, chiefly to be expressed in width, that being the only useful dimension in a door (except for pageantry, chairing of bishops and waving of banners, and other such vanities, not, I hope, after this century, much to be regarded in the building of Christian temples); but though the width is the only necessary dimension, it is well to increase the height also in some proportion to it, in order that there may be less weight of wall above, resting on the increased span of the arch. This is, however, so much the necessary result of the broad curve of the arch itself, that there is no structural necessity of elevating the jamb; and I believe that beautiful entrances might be made of every span of arch, retaining the jamb at a little more than a man's height, until the sweep of the curves became so vast that the small vertical line became a part of them, and one entered into the temple as under a great rainbow.

§ VIII. On the other hand, the jamb may be elevated indefinitely, so that the increasing entrance retains at least the proportion of width it had originally; say 4 ft. by 7 ft. 5 in. But a less proportion of width than this has always a meagre, inhospitable, and ungainly look except in military architecture, where the narrowness of the entrance is necessary, and its height adds to its grandeur, as between the entrance towers of our British castles. This law however, observe, applies only to true doors, not to the arches of porches, which may be of any proportion, as of any number, being in fact intercolumniations, not doors; as in the noble example of the west front of Peterborough, which, in spite of the destructive absurdity of its central arch being the narrowest, would still, if the paltry porter's lodge, or gatehouse, or turnpike, or whatever it is, were knocked out of the middle of it, be the noblest west front in England.

§ IX. Further, and finally. In proportion to the height and size of the building, and therefore to the size of its doors, will be the thickness of its walls, especially at the foundation, that is to say, beside the doors; and also in proportion to the numbers of a crowd will be the unruliness and pressure of it. Hence, partly in necessity and partly in prudence, the splaying or chamfering of the jamb of the larger door will be deepened, and, if possible, made at a larger angle for the large door than for the small one; so that the large door will always be encompassed by a visible breadth of jamb proportioned to its own magnitude. The decorative value of this feature we shall see hereafter.

§ X. The second kind of apertures we have to examine are those of windows.

Window apertures are mainly of two kinds; those for outlook, and those for inlet of light, many being for both purposes, and either purpose, or both, combined in military architecture with those of offence and defence. But all window apertures, as compared with door apertures, have almost infinite licence of form and size: they may be of any shape, from the slit or cross slit to the circle;[56] of any size, from the loophole of the castle to the pillars of light of the cathedral apse. Yet, according to their place and purpose, one or two laws of fitness hold respecting them, which let us examine in the two classes of windows successively, but without reference to military architecture, which here, as before, we may dismiss as a subject of separate science, only noticing that windows, like all other features, are always delightful, if not beautiful, when their position and shape have indeed been thus necessarily determined, and that many of their most picturesque forms have resulted from the requirements of war. We should also find in military architecture the typical forms of the two classes of outlet and inlet windows in their utmost development; the greatest sweep of sight and range of shot on the one hand, and the fullest entry of light and air on the other, being constantly required at the smallest possible apertures. Our business, however, is to reason out the laws for ourselves, not to take the examples as we find them.

§ XI. 1. Outlook apertures. For these no general outline is determinable by the necessities or inconveniences of outlooking, except only that the bottom or sill of the windows, at whatever height, should be horizontal, for the convenience of leaning on it, or standing on it if the window be to the ground. The form of the upper part of the window is quite immaterial, for all windows allow a greater range of sight when they are approached than that of the eye itself: it is the approachability of the window, that is to say, the annihilation of the thickness of the wall, which is the real point to be attended to. If, therefore, the aperture be inaccessible, or so small that the thickness of the wall cannot be entered, the wall is to be bevelled[57] on the outside, so as to increase the range of sight as far as possible; if the aperture can be entered, then bevelled from the point to which entrance is possible. The bevelling will, if possible, be in every direction, that is to say, upwards at the top, outwards at the sides, and downwards at the bottom, but essentially downwards; the earth and the doings upon it being the chief object in outlook windows, except of observatories; and where the object is a distinct and special view downwards, it will be of advantage to shelter the eye as far as possible from the rays of light coming from above, and the head of the window may be left horizontal, or even the whole aperture sloped outwards, as the slit in a letter-box is inwards.

The best windows for outlook are, of course, oriels and bow windows, but these are not to be considered under the head of apertures merely; they are either balconies roofed and glazed, and to be considered under the head of external appliances, or they are each a story of an external semi-tower, having true aperture windows on each side of it.

§ XII. 2. Inlet windows. These windows may, of course, be of any shape and size whatever, according to the other necessities of the building, and the quantity and direction of light desired, their purpose being now to throw it in streams on particular lines or spots; now to diffuse it everywhere; sometimes to introduce it in broad masses, tempered in strength, as in the cathedral colored window; sometimes in starry showers of scattered brilliancy, like the apertures in the roof of an Arabian bath; perhaps the most beautiful of all forms being the rose, which has in it the unity of both characters, and sympathy with that of the source of light itself. It is noticeable, however, that while both the circle and pointed oval are beautiful window forms, it would be very painful to cut either of them in half and connect them by vertical lines, as in Fig. XLIV. The reason is, I believe, that so treated, the upper arch is not considered as connected with the lower, and forming an entire figure, but as the ordinary arch roof of the aperture, and the lower arch as an arch floor, equally unnecessary and unnatural. Also, the elliptical oval is generally an unsatisfactory form, because it gives the idea of useless trouble in building it, though it occurs quaintly and pleasantly in the former windows of France: I believe it is also objectionable because it has an indeterminate, slippery look, like that of a bubble rising through a fluid. It, and all elongated forms, are still more objectionable placed horizontally, because this is the weakest position they can structurally have; that is to say, less light is admitted, with greater loss of strength to the building, than by any other form. If admissible anywhere, it is for the sake of variety at the top of the building, as the flat parallelogram sometimes not ungracefully in Italian Renaissance.

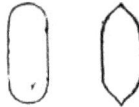

Fig. XLIV.

§ XIII. The question of bevelling becomes a little more complicated in the inlet than the outlook window, because the mass or quantity of light admitted is often of more consequence than its direction, and often vice versâ; and the outlook window is supposed to be approachable, which is far from being always the case with windows for light, so that the bevelling which in the outlook window is chiefly to open range of sight, is in the inlet a means not only of admitting the light in greater quantity, but of directing it to the spot on which it is to fall. But, in general, the bevelling of the one window will reverse that of the other; for, first, no natural light will strike on the inlet window from beneath, unless reflected light, which is (I believe) injurious to the health and the sight; and thus, while in the outlook window the outside bevel downwards is essential, in the inlet it would be useless: and the sill is to be flat, if the window be on a level with the spot it is to light; and sloped downwards within, if above it. Again, as the brightest rays of light are the steepest, the outside bevel upwards is as essential in the roof of the inlet as it was of small importance in that of the outlook window.

§ XIV. On the horizontal section the aperture will expand internally, a somewhat larger number of rays being thus reflected from the jambs; and the aperture being thus the smallest possible outside, this is the favorite military form of inlet window, always found in magnificent development in the thick walls of mediæval castles and convents. Its effect is tranquil, but cheerless and dungeon-like in its fullest development, owing to the limitation of the range of sight in the outlook, which, if the window be unapproachable, reduces it to a mere point of light. A modified condition of it, with some combination of the outlook form, is probably the best for domestic buildings in general (which, however, in modern architecture, are unhappily so thin walled, that the outline of the jambs becomes a matter almost of indifference), it being generally noticeable that the depth of recess which I have observed to be essential to nobility of external effect has also a certain dignity of expression, as appearing to be intended rather to admit light to persons quietly occupied in their homes, than to stimulate or favor the curiosity of idleness.

FOOTNOTES:

[55] *And worth questioning, also, whether the triple porch has not been associated with Romanist views of mediatorship; the Redeemer being represented as presiding over the central door only, and the lateral entrances being under the protection of saints, while the Madonna almost always has one or both of the transepts. But it would be wrong to press this, for, in nine cases out of ten, the architect has been merely influenced in his placing of the statues by an artist's desire of variety in their forms and dress; and very naturally prefers putting a canonisation over one door, a martyrdom over another, and an assumption over a third, to repeating a crucifixion or a judgment above all. The architect's doctrine is only, therefore, to be noted with indisputable reprobation when the Madonna gets possession of the main door.*

[56] *The arch heading is indeed the best where there is much incumbent weight, but a window frequently has very little weight above it, especially when placed high, and the arched form loses light in a low room: therefore the square-headed window is admissible where the square-headed door is not.*

[57] *I do not like the sound of the word "splayed;" I always shall use "bevelled" instead.*

CHAPTER XVII

FILLING OF APERTURE

§ I. Thus far we have been concerned with the outline only of the aperture: we were next, it will be remembered, to consider the necessary modes of filling it with valves in the case of the door, or with glass or tracery in that of the window.

1. Fillings of doors. We concluded, in the previous Chapter, that doors in buildings of any importance or size should have headings in the form of an arch. This is, however, the most inconvenient form we could choose, as respects the fitting of the valves of the doorway; for the arch-shaped head of the valves not

only requires considerable nicety in fitting to the arch, but adds largely to the weight of the door,—a double disadvantage, straining the hinges and making it cumbersome in opening. And this inconvenience is so much perceived by the eye, that a door valve with a pointed head is always a disagreeable object. It becomes, therefore, a matter of true necessity so to arrange the doorway as to admit of its being fitted with rectangular valves.

§ II. Now, in determining the form of the aperture, we supposed the jamb of the door to be of the utmost height required for entrance. The extra height of the arch is unnecessary as an opening, the arch being required for its strength only, not for its elevation. There is, therefore, no reason why it should not be barred across by a horizontal lintel, into which the valves may be fitted, and the triangular or semicircular arched space above the lintel may then be permanently closed, as we choose, either with bars, or glass, or stone.

This is the form of all good doors, without exception, over the whole world and in all ages, and no other can ever be invented.

§ III. In the simplest doors the cross lintel is of wood only, and glass or bars occupy the space above, a very frequent form in Venice. In more elaborate doors the cross lintel is of stone, and the filling sometimes of brick, sometimes of stone, very often a grand single stone being used to close the entire space: the space thus filled is called the Tympanum. In large doors the cross lintel is too long to bear the great incumbent weight of this stone filling without support; it is, therefore, carried by a pier in the centre; and two valves are used, fitted to the rectangular spaces on each side of the pier. In the most elaborate examples of this condition, each of these secondary doorways has an arch heading, a cross lintel, and a triangular filling or tympanum of its own, all subordinated to the main arch above.

§ IV. 2. Fillings of windows.

When windows are large, and to be filled with glass, the sheet of glass, however constructed, whether of large panes or small fragments, requires the support of bars of some kind, either of wood, metal, or stone. Wood is inapplicable on a large scale, owing to its destructibility; very fit for door-valves, which can be easily refitted, and in which weight would be an inconvenience, but very unfit for window-bars, which, if they decayed, might let the whole window be blown in before their decay was observed, and in which weight would be an advantage, as offering more resistance to the wind.

Iron is, however, fit for window-bars, and there seems no constructive reason why we should not have iron traceries, as well as iron pillars, iron churches, and iron steeples. But I have, in the "Seven Lamps," given reasons for not considering such structures as architecture at all.

The window-bars must, therefore, be of stone, and of stone only.

§ V. The purpose of the window being always to let in as much light, and command as much view, as possible, these bars of stone are to be made as slender and as few as they can be, consistently with their due strength.

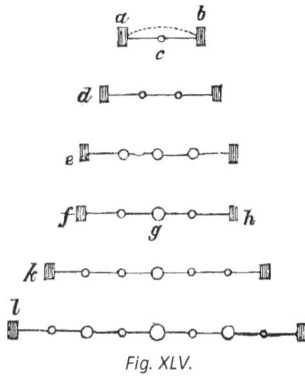

Fig. XLV.

Let it be required to support the breadth of glass, a, b, Fig. XLV. The tendency of the glass sustaining any force, as of wind from without, is to bend into an arch inwards, in the dotted line, and break in the centre. It is to be supported, therefore, by the bar put in its centre, c.

But this central bar, c, may not be enough, and the spaces a c, c b, may still need support. The next step will be to put two bars instead of one, and divide the window into three spaces as at d.

But this may still not be enough, and the window may need three bars. Now the greatest stress is always on the centre of the window. If the three bars are equal in strength, as at e, the central bar is either too slight for its work, or the lateral bars too thick for theirs. Therefore, we must slightly increase the thickness of the central bar, and diminish that of the lateral ones, so as to obtain the arrangement at f h. If the window enlarge farther, each of the spaces f g, g h, is treated as the original space a b, and we have the groups of bars k and l.

So that, whatever the shape of the window, whatever the direction and number of the bars, there are to be central or main bars; second bars subordinated to them; third bars subordinated to the second, and so on to the number required. This is called the subordination of tracery, a system delightful to the eye and mind, owing to its anatomical framing and unity, and to its expression of the laws of good government in all fragile and unstable things. All tracery, therefore, which is not subordinated, is barbarous, in so far as this part of its structure is concerned.

§ VI. The next question will be the direction of the bars. The reader will understand at once, without any laborious proof, that a given area of glass, supported by its edges, is stronger in its resistance to violence when it is arranged in a long strip or band than in a square; and that, therefore, glass is generally to be arranged, especially in windows on a large scale, in oblong areas: and if the bars so dividing it be placed horizontally, they will have less power of supporting themselves, and will need to be thicker in consequence, than if placed vertically. As far, therefore, as the form of the window permits, they are to be vertical.

§ VII. But even when so placed, they cannot be trusted to support themselves beyond a certain height, but will need cross bars to steady them. Cross bars of stone are, therefore, to be introduced at necessary intervals, not to divide the glass, but to support the upright stone bars. The glass is always to be divided longitudinally as far as possible, and the upright bars which divide it supported at proper intervals. However high the window, it is almost impossible that it should require more than two cross bars.

§ VIII. It may sometimes happen that when tall windows are placed very close to each other for the sake of more light, the masonry between them may stand in need, or at least be the better of, some additional support. The cross bars of the windows may then be thickened, in order to bond the intermediate piers more strongly together, and if this thickness appear ungainly, it may be modified by decoration.

§ IX. We have thus arrived at the idea of a vertical frame work of subordinated bars, supported by cross bars at the necessary intervals, and the only remaining question is the method of insertion into the aperture. Whatever its form, if we merely let the ends of the bars into the voussoirs of its heading, the least settlement of the masonry would distort the arch, or push up some of its voussoirs, or break the window bars, or push them aside. Evidently our object should be to connect the window bars among themselves, so framing them together that they may give the utmost possible degree of support to the whole window head in case of any settlement. But we know how to do this already: our window bars are nothing but small shafts. Capital them; throw small arches across between the smaller bars, large arches over them between the larger bars, one comprehensive arch over the whole, or else a horizontal lintel, if the window have a flat head; and we have a complete system of mutual support, independent of the aperture head, and yet assisting to sustain it, if need be. But we want the spandrils of this arch system to be themselves as light, and to let as much light through them, as possible: and we know already how to pierce them (Chap. XII. § VII.). We pierce them with circles; and we have, if the circles are small and the stonework strong, the traceries of Giotto and the Pisan school; if the circles are as large as possible and the bars slender, those which I have already figured and described as the only perfect traceries of the Northern Gothic.[58] The varieties of their design arise partly from the different size of window and consequent number of bars; partly from the different heights of their pointed arches, as well as the various positions of the window head in relation to the roof, rendering one or another arrangement better for dividing the light, and partly from æsthetic and expressional requirements, which, within certain limits, may be allowed a very important influence: for the strength of the bars is ordinarily so much greater than is absolutely necessary, that some portion of it may be gracefully sacrificed to the attainment of variety in the plans of tracery—a variety which, even within its severest limits, is perfectly endless; more especially in the pointed arch, the proportion of the tracery being in the round arch necessarily more fixed.

§ X. The circular window furnishes an exception to the common law, that the bars shall be vertical through the greater part of their length: for if they were so, they could neither have secure perpendicular footing, nor secure heading, their thrust being perpendicular to the curve of the voussoirs only in the centre of the window; therefore, a small circle, like the axle of a wheel, is put into the centre of the window, large enough to give footing to the necessary number of radiating bars; and the bars are arranged as spokes, being all of course properly capitaled and arch-headed. This is the best form of tracery for circular windows, naturally enough called wheel windows when so filled.

§ XI. Now, I wish the reader especially to observe that we have arrived at these forms of perfect Gothic tracery without the smallest reference to any practice of any school, or to any law of authority whatever. They are forms having essentially nothing whatever to do either with Goths or Greeks. They are eternal forms, based on laws of gravity and cohesion; and no better, nor any others so good, will ever be invented, so long as the present laws of gravity and cohesion subsist.

§ XII. It does not at all follow that this group of forms owes its origin to any such course of reasoning as that which has now led us to it. On the contrary, there is not the smallest doubt that tracery began, partly, in the grouping of windows together (subsequently enclosed within a large arch[59]), and partly in the fantastic penetrations of a single slab of stones under the arch, as the circle in Plate V. above. The perfect form seems to have been accidentally struck in passing from experiment on the one side, to affectation on the other; and it was so far from ever becoming systematised, that I am aware of no type of tracery for which a less decided preference is shown in the buildings in which it exists. The early pierced traceries are multitudinous and perfect in their kind,—the late Flamboyant, luxuriant in detail, and lavish in quantity,—but the perfect forms exist in comparatively few churches, generally in portions of the church only, and are always connected, and that closely, either with the massy forms out of which they have emerged, or with the enervated types into which they are instantly to degenerate.

§ XIII. Nor indeed are we to look upon them as in all points superior to the more ancient examples. We have above conducted our reasoning entirely on the supposition that a single aperture is given, which it is the object to fill with glass, diminishing the power of the light as little as possible. But there are many cases, as in triforium and cloister lights, in which glazing is not required; in which, therefore, the bars, if there be any, must have some more important function than that of merely holding glass, and in which their actual use is to give steadiness and tone, as it were, to the arches and walls above and beside them; or to give the idea of protection to those who pass along the triforium, and of seclusion to those who walk in the cloister. Much thicker shafts, and more massy arches, may be properly employed in work of this kind; and many groups of such tracery will be found resolvable into true colonnades, with the arches in pairs, or in triple or quadruple groups, and with small rosettes pierced above them for light. All this is just as right in its place, as the glass tracery is in its own function, and often much more grand. But the same indulgence is not to be shown to the affectations which succeeded the developed forms. Of these there are three principal conditions: the Flamboyant of France, the Stump tracery of Germany, and the Perpendicular of England.

§ XIV. Of these the first arose, by the most delicate and natural transitions, out of the perfect school. It was an endeavor to introduce more grace into its lines, and more change into its combinations; and the æsthetic results are so beautiful, that for some time after the right road had been left, the aberration was more to be admired than regretted. The final conditions became fantastic and effeminate, but, in the country where they had been invented, never lost their peculiar grace until they were replaced by the Renaissance. The copies of the school in England and Italy have all its faults and none of its beauties; in France, whatever it lost in method or in majesty, it gained in fantasy: literally Flamboyant, it breathed away its strength into the air; but there is not more difference between the commonest doggrel that ever broke prose into unintelligibility, and the burning mystery of Coleridge, or spirituality of Elizabeth Barrett, than there is between the dissolute dulness of English Flamboyant, and the flaming undulations of the wreathed lines of delicate stone, that confuse themselves with the clouds of every morning sky that brightens above the valley of the Seine.

§ XV. The second group of traceries, the intersectional or German group, may be considered as including the entire range of the absurd forms which were invented in order to display dexterity in stone-cutting and ingenuity in construction. They express the peculiar character of the German mind, which cuts the frame of every truth joint from joint, in order to prove the edge of its instruments; and, in all cases, prefers a new or a strange thought to a good one, and a subtle thought to a useful one. The point and value of the German tracery consists principally in turning the features of good traceries upside down, and cutting them in two where they are properly continuous. To destroy at once foundation and membership, and suspend everything in the air, keeping out of sight, as far as possible, the evidences of a beginning and the probabilities of an end, are the main objects of German architecture, as of modern German divinity.

§ XVI. This school has, however, at least the merit of ingenuity. Not so the English Perpendicular, though a very curious school also in its way. In the course of the reasoning which led us to the determination of the perfect Gothic tracery, we were induced successively to reject certain methods of arrangement as weak, dangerous, or disagreeable. Collect all these together, and practise them at once, and you have the English Perpendicular.

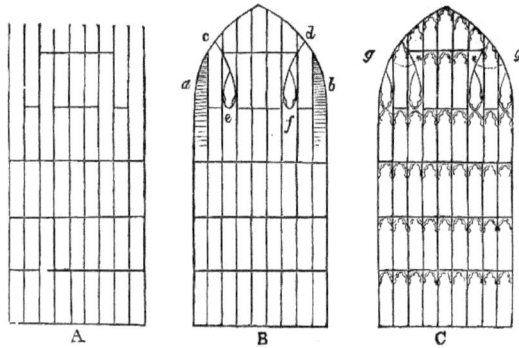

Fig. XLVI.

As thus. You find, in the first place (§ V.), that your tracery bars are to be subordinated, less to greater; so you take a group of, suppose, eight, which you make all exactly equal, giving you nine equal spaces in the window, as at A, Fig. XLVI. You found, in the second place (§ VII.), that there was no occasion for more than two cross bars; so you take at least four or five (also represented at A, Fig. XLVI.), also carefully equalised, and set at equal spaces. You found, in the third place (§ VIII.), that these bars were to be strengthened, in order to support the main piers; you will therefore cut the ends off the uppermost, and the fourth into three pieces (as also at A). In the fourth place, you found (§ IX.) that you were never to run a vertical bar into the arch head; so you run them all into it (as at B, Fig. XLVI.); and this last arrangement will be useful in two ways, for it will not only expose both the bars and the archivolt to an apparent probability of every species of dislocation at any moment, but it will provide you with two pleasing interstices at the flanks, in the shape of carving-knives, a, b, which, by throwing across the curves c, d, you may easily multiply into four; and these, as you can put nothing into their sharp tops, will afford you a more than usually rational excuse for a little bit of Germanism, in filling them with arches upside down, e, f. You will now have left at your disposal two and forty similar interstices, which, for the sake of variety, you will proceed to fill with two and forty similar arches: and, as you were told that the moment a bar received an arch heading, it was to be treated as a shaft and capitalled, you will take care to give your bars no capitals nor bases, but to run bars, foliations and all, well into each other after the fashion of cast-iron, as at C. You have still two triangular spaces occurring in an important part of your window, g g, which, as they are very conspicuous, and you cannot make them uglier than they are, you will do wisely to let alone;—and you will now have the west window of the cathedral of Winchester, a very perfect example of English Perpendicular. Nor do I think that you can, on the whole, better the arrangement, unless, perhaps, by adding buttresses to some of the bars, as is done in the cathedral at Gloucester; these buttresses having the double advantage of darkening the window when seen from within, and suggesting, when it is seen from without, the idea of its being divided by two stout party walls, with a heavy thrust against the glass.

§ XVII. Thus far we have considered the plan of the tracery only: we have lastly to note the conditions under which the glass is to be attached to the bars; and the sections of the bars themselves.

Fig. XLVII.

These bars we have seen, in the perfect form, are to become shafts; but, supposing the object to be the admission of as much light as possible, it is clear that the thickness of the bar ought to be chiefly in the depth of the window, and that by increasing the depth of the bar we may diminish its breadth: clearly, therefore, we should employ the double group of shafts, b, of Fig. XIV., setting it edgeways in the window: but as the glass would then come between the two shafts, we must add a member into which it is to be fitted, as at a, Fig. XLVII., and uniting these three members together in the simplest way, with a curved instead of a sharp recess behind the shafts, we have the section b, the perfect, but simplest type of the main tracery bars in good Gothic. In triforium and cloister tracery, which has no glass to hold, the central member is omitted, and we have either the pure double shaft, always the most graceful, or a single and more massy shaft, which is the simpler and more usual form.

§ XVIII. Finally: there is an intermediate arrangement between the glazed and the open tracery, that of the domestic traceries of Venice. Peculiar conditions, hereafter to be described, require the shafts of these traceries to become the main vertical supports of the floors and walls. Their thickness is therefore enormous; and yet free egress is required between them (into balconies) which is obtained by doors in their lattice glazing. To prevent the inconvenience and ugliness of driving the hinges and fastenings of them into the shafts, and having the play of the doors in the intervals, the entire glazing is thrown behind the pillars, and attached to their abaci and bases with iron. It is thus securely sustained by their massy bulk, and leaves their symmetry and shade undisturbed.

§ XIX. The depth at which the glass should be placed, in windows without traceries, will generally be fixed by the forms of their bevelling, the glass occupying the narrowest interval; but when its position is not thus fixed, as in many London houses, it is to be remembered that the deeper the glass is set (the wall being of given thickness), the more light will enter, and the clearer the prospect will be to a person sitting quietly in the centre of the room; on the contrary, the farther out the glass is set, the more convenient the window will be for a person rising and looking out of it. The one, therefore, is an arrangement for the idle and curious, who care only about what is going on upon the earth: the other for those who are willing to remain at rest, so that they have free admission of the light of Heaven. This might be noted as a curious expressional reason for the necessity (of which no man of ordinary feeling would doubt for a moment) of a deep recess in the window, on the outside, to all good or architectural effect: still, as there is no reason why people should be made idle by having it in their power to look out of window, and as the slight increase of light or clearness of view in the centre of a room is more than balanced by the loss of space, and the greater chill of the nearer glass and outside air, we can, I fear, allege no other structural reason for the picturesque external recess, than the expediency of a certain degree of protection, for the glass, from the brightest glare of sunshine, and heaviest rush of rain.

FOOTNOTES:

[58] "Seven Lamps," p. 53.

[59] On the north side of the nave of the cathedral of Lyons, there is an early French window, presenting one of the usual groups of foliated arches and circles, left, as it were, loose, without any enclosing curve. The effect is very painful. This remarkable window is associated with others of the common form.

CHAPTER XVIII

PROTECTION OF APERTURE

§ I. We have hitherto considered the aperture as merely pierced in the thickness of the walls; and when its masonry is simple and the fillings of the aperture are unimportant, it may well remain so. But when the fillings are delicate and of value, as in the case of colored glass, finely wrought tracery, or sculpture, such as we shall often find occupying the tympanum of doorways, some protection becomes necessary against the run of the rain down the walls, and back by the bevel of the aperture to the joints or surface of the fillings.

§ II. The first and simplest mode of obtaining this is by channelling the jambs and arch head; and this is the chief practical service of aperture mouldings, which are otherwise entirely decorative. But as this very decorative character renders them unfit to be made channels for rain water, it is well to add some external roofing to the aperture, which may protect it from the run of all the rain, except that which necessarily beats into its own area. This protection, in its most usual form, is a mere dripstone moulding carried over or round the head of the aperture. But this is, in reality, only a contracted form of a true roof, projecting from the wall over the aperture; and all protections of apertures whatsoever are to be conceived as portions of small roofs, attached to the wall behind; and supported by it, so long as their scale admits of their being so with safety, and afterwards in such manner as may be most expedient. The proper forms of these, and modes of their support, are to be the subject of our final enquiry.

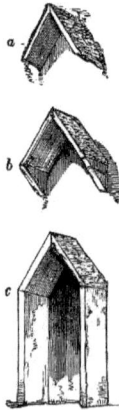

Fig. XLVIII.

§ III. Respecting their proper form we need not stay long in doubt. A deep gable is evidently the best for throwing off rain; even a low gable being better than a high arch. Flat roofs, therefore, may only be used when the nature of the building renders the gable unsightly; as when there is not room for it between the stories; or when the object is rather shade than protection from rain, as often in verandahs and balconies. But for general service the gable is the proper and natural form, and may be taken as representative of the rest. Then this gable may either project unsupported from the wall, a, Fig. XLVIII., or be carried by brackets or spurs, b, or by walls or shafts, c, which shafts or walls may themselves be, in windows, carried on a sill; and this, in its turn, supported by brackets or spurs. We shall glance at the applications of each of these forms in order.

§ IV. There is not much variety in the case of the first, a, Fig. XLVIII. In the Cumberland and border cottages the door is generally protected by two pieces of slate arranged in a gable, giving the purest possible type of the first form. In elaborate architecture such a projection hardly ever occurs, and in large architecture cannot with safety occur, without brackets; but by cutting away the greater part of the projection, we shall arrive at the idea of a plain gabled cornice, of which a perfect example will be found in Plate VII. of the folio series. With this first complete form we may associate the rude, single, projecting, penthouse roof; imperfect, because either it must be level and the water lodge lazily upon it, or throw off the drip upon the persons entering.

§ V. 2. b, Fig. XLVIII. This is a most beautiful and natural type, and is found in all good architecture, from the highest to the most humble: it is a frequent form of cottage door, more especially when carried on spurs, being of peculiarly easy construction in wood: as applied to large architecture, it can evidently be built, in its boldest and simplest form, either of wood only, or on a scale which will admit of its sides being each a single slab of stone. If so large as to require jointed masonry, the gabled sides will evidently require support, and an arch must be thrown across under them, as in Fig. XLIX., from Fiesole.

Fig. XLIX.

If we cut the projection gradually down, we arrive at the common Gothic gable dripstone carried on small brackets, carved into bosses, heads, or some other ornamental form; the sub-arch in such case being useless, is removed or coincides with the arch head of the aperture.

§ VI. 3. c, Fig. XLVIII. Substituting walls or pillars for the brackets, we may carry the projection as far out as we choose, and form the perfect porch, either of the cottage or village church, or of the cathedral. As we enlarge the structure, however, certain modifications of form become necessary, owing to the increased boldness of the required supporting arch. For, as the lower end of the gabled roof and of the arch cannot coincide, we have necessarily above the shafts one of the two forms a or b, in Fig. L., of which the latter is clearly the best, requiring less masonry and shorter roofing; and when the arch becomes so large as to cause a heavy lateral thrust, it may become necessary to provide for its farther safety by pinnacles, c.

This last is the perfect type of aperture protection. None other can ever be invented so good. It is that once employed by Giotto in the cathedral of Florence, and torn down by the proveditore, Benedetto Uguccione, to erect a Renaissance front instead; and another such has been destroyed, not long since, in Venice, the porch of the church of St. Apollinare, also to put up some Renaissance upholstery: for Renaissance, as if it were not nuisance enough in the mere fact of its own existence, appears invariably as a beast of prey, and founds itself on the ruin of all that is best and noblest. Many such porches, however, happily still exist in Italy, and are among its principal glories.

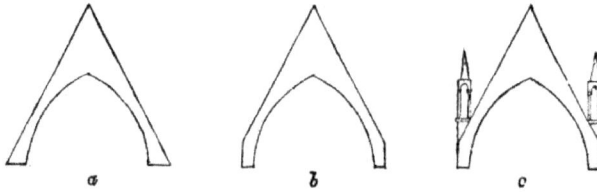

Fig. L.

§ VII. When porches of this kind, carried by walls, are placed close together, as in cases where there are many and large entrances to a cathedral front, they would, in their general form, leave deep and uncomfortable intervals, in which damp would lodge and grass grow; and there would be a painful feeling in approaching the door in the midst of a crowd, as if some of them might miss the real doors, and be driven into the intervals, and embayed there. Clearly it will be a natural and right expedient, in such cases, to open the walls of the porch wider, so that they may correspond in slope, or nearly so, with the bevel of the doorway, and either meet each other in the intervals, or have the said intervals closed up with an intermediate wall, so that nobody may get embayed in them. The porches will thus be united, and form one range of great open gulphs or caverns, ready to receive all comers, and direct the current of the crowd into the narrower entrances. As the lateral thrust of the arches is now met by each other, the pinnacles, if there were any, must be removed, and waterspouts placed between each arch to discharge the double drainage of the gables. This is the form of all the noble northern porches, without exception, best represented by that of Rheims.

§ VIII. Contracted conditions of the pinnacle porch are beautifully used in the doors of the cathedral of Florence; and the entire arrangement, in its most perfect form, as adapted to window protection and decoration, is applied by Giotto with inconceivable exquisiteness in the windows of the campanile; those of the cathedral itself being all of the same type. Various singular and delightful conditions of it are applied in Italian domestic architecture (in the Broletto of Monza very quaintly), being associated with balconies for speaking to the people, and passing into pulpits. In the north we glaze the sides of such projections, and they become bow-windows, the shape of roofing being then nearly immaterial and very fantastic, often a conical cap. All these conditions of window protection, being for real service, are endlessly delightful (and I believe the beauty of the balcony, protected by an open canopy supported by light shafts, never yet to have been properly worked out). But the Renaissance architects destroyed all of them, and introduced the magnificent and witty Roman invention of a model of a Greek pediment, with its cornices of monstrous thickness, bracketed up above the window. The horizontal cornice of the pediment is thus useless, and of course, therefore, retained; the protection to the head of the window being constructed on the principle of a hat with its crown sewn up. But the deep and dark triangular cavity thus obtained affords farther opportunity for putting ornament out of sight, of which the Renaissance architects are not slow to avail themselves.

A more rational condition is the complete pediment with a couple of shafts, or pilasters, carried on a bracketed sill; and the windows of this kind, which have been well designed, are perhaps the best things which the Renaissance schools have produced: those of Whitehall are, in their way, exceedingly beautiful; and those of the Palazzo Ricardi at Florence, in their simplicity and sublimity, are scarcely unworthy of their reputed designer, Michael Angelo.

CHAPTER XIX

SUPERIMPOSITION

§ I. The reader has now some knowledge of every feature of all possible architecture. Whatever the nature of the building which may be submitted to his criticism, if it be an edifice at all, if it be anything else than a mere heap of stones like a pyramid or breakwater, or than a large stone hewn into shape, like an obelisk, it will be instantly and easily resolvable into some of the parts which we have been hitherto considering: its pinnacles will separate themselves into their small shafts and roofs; its supporting members into shafts and arches, or walls penetrated by apertures of various shape, and supported by various kinds of buttresses. Respecting each of these several features I am certain that the reader feels himself prepared, by understanding their plain function, to form something like a reasonable and definite judgment, whether they be good or bad; and this right judgment of parts will, in most cases, lead him to just reverence or condemnation of the whole.

§ II. The various modes in which these parts are capable of combination, and the merits of buildings of different form and expression, are evidently not reducible into lists, nor to be estimated by general laws. The nobility of each building depends on its special fitness for its own purposes; and these purposes vary with every climate, every soil, and every national custom: nay, there were never, probably, two edifices erected in which some accidental difference of condition did not require some difference of plan or of structure; so that, respecting plan and distribution of parts, I do not hope to collect any universal law of right; but there are a few points necessary to be noticed respecting the means by which height is attained in buildings of various plans, and the expediency and methods of superimposition of one story or tier of architecture above another.

§ III. For, in the preceding inquiry, I have always supposed either that a single shaft would reach to the top of the building, or that the farther height required might be added in plain wall above the heads of the arches; whereas it may often be rather expedient to complete the entire lower series of arches, or finish the lower wall, with a bold string course or cornice, and build another series of shafts, or another wall, on the top of it.

§ IV. This superimposition is seen in its simplest form in the interior shafts of a Greek temple; and it has been largely used in nearly all countries where buildings have been meant for real service. Outcry has often been raised against it, but the thing is so sternly necessary that it has always forced itself into acceptance; and it would, therefore, be merely losing time to refute the arguments of those who have attempted its disparagement. Thus far, however, they have reason on their side, that if a building can be kept in one grand mass, without sacrificing either its visible or real adaptation to its objects, it is not well to divide it into stories until it has reached proportions too large to be justly measured by the eye. It ought then to be divided in order to mark its bulk; and decorative divisions are often possible, which rather increase than destroy the expression of general unity.

§ V. Superimposition, wisely practised, is of two kinds, directly contrary to each other, of weight on lightness, and of lightness on weight; while the superimposition of weight on weight, or lightness on lightness, is nearly always wrong.

1. Weight on lightness: I do not say weight on weakness. The superimposition of the human body on its limbs I call weight on lightness: the superimposition of the branches on a tree trunk I call lightness on weight: in both cases the support is fully adequate to the work, the form of support being regulated by the differences of requirement. Nothing in architecture is half so painful as the apparent want of sufficient support when the weight above is visibly passive: for all buildings are not passive; some seem to rise by their own strength, or float by their own buoyancy; a dome requires no visibility of support, one fancies it supported by the air. But passive architecture without help for its passiveness is unendurable. In a lately built house, No. 86, in Oxford Street, three huge stone pillars in the second story are carried apparently by the edges of three sheets of plate glass in the first. I hardly know anything to match the painfulness of this and some other of our shop structures, in which the iron-work is concealed; nor, even when it is apparent, can the eye ever feel satisfied of their security, when built, as at present, with fifty or sixty feet of wall above a rod of iron not the width of this page.

§ VI. The proper forms of this superimposition of weight on lightness have arisen, for the most part, from the necessity or desirableness, in many situations, of elevating the inhabited portions of buildings considerably above the ground level, especially those exposed to damp or inundation, and the consequent abandonment of the ground story as unserviceable, or else the surrender of it to public purposes. Thus, in many market and town houses, the ground story is left open as a general place of sheltered resort, and the enclosed apartments raised on pillars. In almost all warm countries the luxury, almost the necessity, of arcades to protect the passengers from the sun, and the desirableness of large space in the rooms above, lead to the same construction. Throughout the Venetian islet group, the houses seem to have been thus, in the first instance, universally built, all the older palaces appearing to have had the rez de chaussée perfectly open, the upper parts of the palace being sustained on magnificent arches, and the smaller houses sustained in the same manner on wooden piers, still retained in many of the cortiles, and exhibited characteristically throughout the main street of Murano. As ground became more valuable and house-room more scarce, these ground-floors were enclosed with wall veils between the original shafts, and so remain; but the type of the structure of the entire city is given in the Ducal Palace.

§ VII. To this kind of superimposition we owe the most picturesque street effects throughout the world, and the most graceful, as well as the most grotesque, buildings, from the many-shafted fantasy of the Alhambra (a building as beautiful in disposition as it is base in ornamentation) to the four-legged stolidity of the Swiss Chalet:[60] nor these only, but great part of the effect of our cathedrals, in which, necessarily, the close triforium and clerestory walls are superimposed on the nave piers; perhaps with most majesty where with greatest simplicity, as in the old basilican types, and the noble cathedral of Pisa.

§ VIII. In order to the delightfulness and security of all such arrangements, this law must be observed:—that in proportion to the height of wall above them, the shafts are to be short. You may take your given height of wall, and turn any quantity of that wall into shaft that you like; but you must not turn it all into tall shafts, and then put more wall above. Thus, having a house five stories high, you may turn the lower story into shafts, and leave the four stories in wall; or the two lower stories into shafts, and leave three in wall; but, whatever you add to the shaft, you must take from the wall. Then also, of course, the shorter the shaft the thicker will be its proportionate, if not its actual, diameter. In the Ducal Palace of Venice the shortest shafts are always the thickest.[61]

§ IX. The second kind of superimposition, lightness on weight, is, in its most necessary use, of stories of houses one upon another, where, of course, wall veil is required in the lower ones, and has to support wall veil above, aided by as much of shaft structure as is attainable within the given limits. The greatest, if not the only, merit of the Roman and Renaissance Venetian architects is their graceful management of this kind of superimposition; sometimes of complete courses of external arches and shafts one above the other; sometimes of apertures with intermediate cornices at the levels of the floors, and large shafts from top to bottom of the building; always observing that the upper stories shall be at once lighter and richer than the lower ones. The entire value of such buildings depends upon the perfect and easy expression of the relative strength of the stories, and the unity obtained by the varieties of their proportions, while yet the fact of superimposition and separation by floors is frankly told.

§ X. In churches and other buildings in which there is no separation by floors, another kind of pure shaft superimposition is often used, in order to enable the builder to avail himself of short and slender shafts. It has been noted that these are often easily attainable, and of precious materials, when shafts large enough and strong enough to do the work at once, could not be obtained except at unjustifiable expense, and of coarse stone. The architect has then no choice but to arrange his work in successive stories; either frankly completing the arch work and cornice of each, and beginning a new story above it, which is the honester and nobler way, or else tying the stories together by supplementary shafts from floor to roof,—the general practice of the Northern Gothic, and one which, unless most gracefully managed, gives the look of a scaffolding, with cross-poles tied to its uprights, to the whole clerestory wall. The best method is that which avoids all chance of the upright shafts being supposed continuous, by increasing their number and changing their places in the upper stories, so that the whole work branches from the ground like a tree. This is the superimposition of the Byzantine and the Pisan Romanesque; the most beautiful examples of it being, I think, the Southern portico of St. Mark's, the church of S. Giovanni at Pistoja, and the apse of the cathedral of Pisa. In Renaissance work the two principles are equally distinct, though the shafts are (I think) always one above the other. The reader may see one of the best examples of the separately superimposed story in Whitehall (and another far inferior in St. Paul's), and by turning himself round at Whitehall may compare with it the system of connecting shafts in the Treasury; though this is a singularly bad example, the window cornices of the first floor being like shelves in a cupboard, and cutting the mass of the building in two, in spite of the pillars.

§ XI. But this superimposition of lightness on weight is still more distinctly the system of many buildings of the kind which I have above called Architecture of Position, that is to say, architecture of which the greater part is intended merely to keep something in a peculiar position; as in light-houses, and many towers and belfries. The subject of spire and tower architecture, however, is so interesting and extensive, that I have thoughts of writing a detached essay upon it, and, at all events, cannot enter upon it here: but this much is enough for the reader to note for our present purpose, that, although many towers do in reality stand on piers or shafts, as the central towers of cathedrals, yet the expression of all of them, and the real structure of the best and strongest, are the elevation of gradually diminishing weight on massy or even solid foundation. Nevertheless, since the tower is in its origin a building for strength of defence, and faithfulness of watch, rather than splendor of aspect, its true expression is of just so much diminution of weight upwards as may be necessary to its fully balanced strength, not a jot more. There must be no light-headedness in your noble tower: impregnable foundation, wrathful crest, with the vizor down, and the dark vigilance seen through the clefts of it; not the filigree crown or embroidered cap. No towers are so grand as the square-browed ones, with massy cornices and rent battlements: next to these come the fantastic towers, with their various forms of steep roof; the best, not the cone, but the plain gable thrown very high; last of all in my mind (of good towers), those with spires or crowns, though these, of course, are fittest for ecclesiastical purposes, and capable of the richest ornament. The paltry four or eight pinnacled things we call towers in England (as in York Minster), are mere confectioner's Gothic, and not worth classing.

§ XII. But, in all of them, this I believe to be a point of chief necessity,—that they shall seem to stand, and shall verily stand, in their own strength; not by help of buttresses nor artful balancings on this side and on that. Your noble tower must need no help, must be sustained by no crutches, must give place to no suspicion of decrepitude. Its office may be to withstand war, look forth for tidings, or to point to heaven: but it must have in its own walls the strength to do this; it is to be itself a bulwark, not to be sustained by other bulwarks; to rise and look forth, "the tower of Lebanon that looketh toward Damascus," like a stern sentinel, not like a child held up in its nurse's arms. A tower may, indeed, have a kind of buttress, a projection, or subordinate tower at each of its angles; but these are to its main body like the satellites to a shaft, joined with its strength, and associated in its uprightness, part of the tower itself: exactly in the proportion in which they lose their massive unity with its body and assume the form of true buttress walls set on its angles, the tower loses its dignity.

§ XIII. These two characters, then, are common to all noble towers, however otherwise different in purpose or feature,—the first, that they rise from massy foundation to lighter summits, frowning with battlements perhaps, but yet evidently more pierced and thinner in wall than beneath, and, in most ecclesiastical examples, divided into rich open work: the second, that whatever the form of the tower, it shall not appear to stand by help of buttresses. It follows from the first condition, as indeed it would have followed from ordinary æsthetic requirements, that we shall have continual variation in the arrangements of the stories, and the larger number of apertures towards the top,—a condition exquisitely carried out in the old Lombardic towers, in which, however small they may be, the number of apertures is always regularly increased towards the summit; generally one window in the lowest stories, two in the second, then three, five, and six; often, also, one, two, four, and six, with beautiful symmetries of placing, not at present to our purpose. We may sufficiently exemplify the general laws of tower building by placing side by side, drawn to the same scale, a mediæval tower, in which most of them are simply and unaffectedly observed, and one of our own modern towers, in which every one of them is violated, in small space, convenient for comparison. (Plate VI.)

Plate VI. TYPES OF TOWERS. BRITISH VENETIAN.

§ XIV. The old tower is that of St. Mark's at Venice, not a very perfect example, for its top is Renaissance, but as good Renaissance as there is in Venice; and it is fit for our present purpose, because it owes none of its effect to ornament. It is built as simply as it well can be to answer its purpose: no buttresses; no external features whatever, except some huts at the base, and the loggia, afterwards built, which, on purpose, I have not drawn; one bold square mass of brickwork; double walls, with an ascending inclined plane between them, with apertures as small as possible, and these only in necessary places, giving just the light required for ascending the stair or slope, not a ray more; and the weight of the whole relieved only by the double pilasters on the sides, sustaining small arches at the top of the mass, each decorated with the scallop or cockle shell, presently to be noticed as frequent in Renaissance ornament, and here, for once, thoroughly well applied. Then, when the necessary height is reached, the belfry is left open, as in the ordinary Romanesque campanile, only the shafts more slender, but severe and simple, and the whole crowned by as much spire as the tower would carry, to render it more serviceable as a landmark. The arrangement is repeated in numberless campaniles throughout Italy.

§ XV. The one beside it is one of those of the lately built college at Edinburgh. I have not taken it as worse than many others (just as I have not taken the St. Mark's tower as better than many others); but it happens to compress our British system of tower building into small space. The Venetian tower rises 350 feet,[62] and has no buttresses, though built of brick; the British tower rises 121 feet, and is built of stone, but is supposed to be incapable of standing without two huge buttresses on each angle. The St. Mark's tower has a high sloping roof, but carries it simply, requiring no pinnacles at its angles; the British tower has no visible roof, but has four pinnacles for mere ornament. The Venetian tower has its lightest part at the top, and is massy at the base; the British tower has its lightest part at the base, and shuts up its windows into a mere arrowslit at the top. What the tower was built for at all must therefore, it seems to me, remain a mystery to every beholder; for surely no studious inhabitant of its upper chambers will be conceived to be pursuing his employments by the light of the single chink on each side; and, had it been intended for a belfry, the sound of its bells would have been as effectually prevented from getting out as the light from getting in.

§ XVI. In connexion with the subject of towers and of superimposition, one other feature, not conveniently to be omitted from our house-building, requires a moment's notice,—the staircase.

In modern houses it can hardly be considered an architectural feature, and is nearly always an ugly one, from its being apparently without support. And here I may not unfitly note the important distinction, which perhaps ought to have been dwelt upon in some places before now, between the marvellous and the perilous in apparent construction. There are many edifices which are awful or admirable in their height, and lightness, and boldness of form, respecting which, nevertheless, we have no fear that they should fall. Many a mighty dome and aërial aisle and arch may seem to stand, as I said, by miracle, but by steadfast miracle notwithstanding; there is no fear that the miracle should cease. We have a sense of inherent power in them, or, at all events, of concealed and mysterious provision for their safety. But in leaning towers, as of Pisa or Bologna, and in much minor architecture, passive architecture, of modern times, we feel that there is but a chance between the building and destruction; that there is no miraculous life in it, which animates it into security, but an obstinate, perhaps vain, resistance to immediate danger. The appearance of this is often as strong in small things as in large; in the sounding-boards of pulpits, for instance, when sustained by a single pillar behind them, so that one is in dread, during the whole sermon, of the preacher being crushed if a single nail should give way; and again, the modern geometrical unsupported staircase. There is great disadvantage, also, in the arrangement of this latter, when room is of value; and excessive ungracefulness in its awkward divisions of the passage walls, or windows. In mediæval architecture, where there was need of room, the staircase was spiral, and enclosed generally in an exterior tower, which added infinitely to the picturesque effect of the building; nor was the stair itself steeper nor less commodious than the ordinary compressed straight staircase of a modern dwelling-house. Many of the richest towers of domestic architecture owe their origin to this arrangement. In Italy the staircase is often in the open air, surrounding the interior court of the house, and giving access to its various galleries or loggias: in this case it is almost always supported by bold shafts and arches, and forms a most interesting additional feature of the cortile, but presents no peculiarity of construction requiring our present examination.

We may here, therefore, close our inquiries into the subject of construction; nor must the reader be dissatisfied with the simplicity or apparent barrenness of their present results. He will find, when he begins to apply them, that they are of more value than they now seem; but I have studiously avoided letting myself be drawn into any intricate question, because I wished to ask from the reader only so much attention as it seemed that even the most indifferent would not be unwilling to pay to a subject which is hourly becoming of greater practical interest. Evidently it would have been altogether beside the purpose of this essay to have entered deeply into the abstract science, or closely into the mechanical detail, of construction: both have been illustrated by writers far more capable of doing so than I, and may be studied at the reader's discretion; all that has been here endeavored was the leading him to appeal to something like definite principle, and refer to the easily intelligible laws of convenience and necessity, whenever he found his judgment likely to be overborne by authority on the one hand, or dazzled by novelty on the other. If he has time to do more, and to follow out in all their brilliancy the mechanical inventions of the great engineers and architects of the day, I, in some sort, envy him, but must part company with him: for my way lies not along the viaduct, but down the quiet valley which its arches cross, nor through the tunnel, but up the hill-side which its cavern darkens, to see what gifts Nature will give us, and with what imagery she will fill our thoughts, that the stones we have ranged in rude order may now be touched with life; nor lose for ever, in their hewn nakedness, the voices they had of old, when the valley streamlet eddied round them in palpitating light, and the winds of the hill-side shook over them the shadows of the fern.

FOOTNOTES:

[60] *I have spent much of my life among the Alps; but I never pass, without some feeling of new surprise, the Chalet, standing on its four pegs (each topped with a flat stone), balanced in the fury of Alpine winds. It is not, perhaps, generally known that the chief use of the arrangement is not so much to raise the building above the snow, as to get a draught of wind beneath it, which may prevent the drift from rising against its sides.*

[61] *Appendix 20, "Shafts of the Ducal Palace."*

[62] *I have taken Professor Willis's estimate; there being discrepancy among various statements. I did not take the trouble to measure the height myself, the building being one which does not come within the range of our future inquiries; and its exact dimensions, even here, are of no importance as respects the question at issue.*

CHAPTER XX

THE MATERIAL OF ORNAMENT

§ I. We enter now on the second division of our subject. We have no more to do with heavy stones and hard lines; we are going to be happy: to look round in the world and discover (in a serious manner always, however, and under a sense of responsibility) what we like best in it, and to enjoy the same at our leisure: to gather it, examine it, fasten all we can of it into imperishable forms, and put it where we may see it for ever.

This is to decorate architecture.

§ II. There are, therefore, three steps in the process: first, to find out in a grave manner what we like best; secondly, to put as much of this as we can (which is little enough) into form; thirdly, to put this formed abstraction into a proper place.

And we have now, therefore, to make these three inquiries in succession: first, what we like, or what is the right material of ornament; then how we are to present it, or its right treatment; then, where we are to put it, or its right place. I think I can answer that first inquiry in this Chapter, the second inquiry in the next Chapter, and the third I shall answer in a more diffusive manner, by taking up in succession the several parts of architecture above distinguished, and rapidly noting the kind of ornament fittest for each.

§ III. I said in chapter II. § XIV., that all noble ornamentation was the expression of man's delight in God's work. This implied that there was an ignoble ornamentation, which was the expression of man's delight in his own. There is such a school, chiefly degraded classic and Renaissance, in which the ornament is composed of imitations of tilings made by man. I think, before inquiring what we like best of God's work, we had better get rid of all this imitation of man's, and be quite sure we do not like that.

§ IV. We shall rapidly glance, then, at the material of decoration hence derived. And now I cannot, as I before have done respecting construction, convince the reader of one thing being wrong, and another right. I have confessed as much again and again; I am now only to make appeal to him, and cross-question him, whether he really does like things or not. If he likes the ornament on the base of the column of the Place Vendôme, composed of Wellington boots and laced frock coats, I cannot help it; I can only say I differ from him, and don't like it. And if, therefore, I speak dictatorially, and say this is base, or degraded, or ugly, I mean, only that I believe men of the longest experience in the matter would either think it so, or would be prevented from thinking it so only by some morbid condition of their minds; and I believe that the reader, if he examine himself candidly, will usually agree in my statements.

§ V. The subjects of ornament found in man's work may properly fall into four heads: 1. Instruments of art, agriculture, and war; armor, and dress; 2. Drapery; 3. Shipping; 4. Architecture itself.

1. Instruments, armor, and dress.

The custom of raising trophies on pillars, and of dedicating arms in temples, appears to have first suggested the idea of employing them as the subjects of sculptural ornament: thenceforward, this abuse has been chiefly characteristic of classical architecture, whether true or Renaissance. Armor is a noble thing in its proper service and subordination to the body; so is an animal's hide on its back; but a heap of cast skins, or of shed armor, is alike unworthy of all regard or imitation. We owe much true sublimity, and more of delightful picturesqueness, to the introduction of armor both in painting and sculpture: in poetry it is better still,—Homer's undressed Achilles is less grand than his crested and shielded Achilles, though Phidias would rather have had him naked; in all mediæval painting, arms, like all other parts of costume, are treated with exquisite care and delight; in the designs of Leonardo, Raffaelle, and Perugino, the armor sometimes becomes almost too conspicuous from the rich and endless invention bestowed upon it; while Titian and Rubens seek in its flash what the Milanese and Perugian sought in its form, sometimes subordinating heroism to the light of the steel, while the great designers wearied themselves in its elaborate fancy.

But all this labor was given to the living, not the dead armor; to the shell with its animal in it, not the cast shell of the beach; and even so, it was introduced more sparingly by the good sculptors than the good painters; for the former felt, and with justice, that the painter had the power of conquering the over prominence of costume by the expression and color of the countenance, and that by the darkness of the eye, and glow of the cheek, he could always conquer the gloom and the flash of the mail; but they could hardly, by any boldness or energy of the marble features, conquer the forwardness and conspicuousness of the sharp armorial forms. Their armed figures were therefore almost always subordinate, their principal figures draped or naked, and their choice of subject was much influenced by this feeling of necessity. But the Renaissance sculptors displayed the love of a Camilla for the mere crest and plume. Paltry and false alike in every feeling of their narrowed minds, they attached themselves, not only to costume without the person, but to the pettiest details of the costume itself. They could not describe Achilles, but they could describe his shield; a shield like those of dedicated spoil, without a handle, never to be waved in the face of war. And then we have helmets and lances, banners and swords, sometimes with men to hold them, sometimes without; but always chiselled with a tailor-like love of the chasing or the embroidery,—show helmets of the stage, no Vulcan work on them, no heavy hammer strokes, no Etna fire in the metal of them, nothing but pasteboard crests and high feathers. And these, cast together in disorderly heaps, or grinning vacantly over keystones, form one of the leading decorations of Renaissance architecture, and that one of the best; for helmets and lances, however loosely laid, are better than violins, and pipes, and books of music, which were another of the Palladian and Sansovinian sources of ornament. Supported by ancient authority, the abuse soon became a matter of pride, and since it was easy to copy a heap of cast clothes, but difficult to manage an arranged design of human figures, the indolence of architects came to the aid of their affectation, until by the moderns we find the practice carried out to its most interesting results, and, as above noted, a large pair of boots occupying the principal place in the bas-reliefs on the base of the Colonne Vendôme.

§ VI. A less offensive, because singularly grotesque, example of the abuse at its height, occurs in the Hôtel des Invalides, where the dormer windows are suits of armor down to the bottom of the corselet, crowned by the helmet, and with the window in the middle of the breast.

Instruments of agriculture and the arts are of less frequent occurrence, except in hieroglyphics, and other work, where they are not employed as ornaments, but represented for the sake of accurate knowledge, or as symbols. Wherever they have purpose of this kind, they are of course perfectly right; but they are then part of the building's conversation, not conducive to its beauty. The French have managed, with great dexterity, the representation of the machinery for the elevation of their Luxor obelisk, now sculptured on its base.

§ VII. 2. Drapery. I have already spoken of the error of introducing drapery, as such, for ornament, in the "Seven Lamps." I may here note a curious instance of the abuse in the church of the Jesuiti at Venice (Renaissance). On first entering you suppose that the church, being in a poor quarter of the city, has been somewhat meanly decorated by heavy green and white curtains of an ordinary upholsterer's pattern: on looking closer, they are discovered to be of marble, with the green pattern inlaid. Another remarkable instance is in a piece of not altogether unworthy architecture at Paris (Rue Rivoli), where the columns are supposed to be decorated with images of handkerchiefs tied in a stout knot round the middle of them. This shrewd invention bids fair to become a new order. Multitudes of massy curtains and various upholstery, more or less in imitation of that of the drawing-room, are carved and gilt, in wood or stone, about the altars and other theatrical portions of Romanist churches; but from these coarse and senseless vulgarities we may well turn, in all haste, to note, with respect as well as regret, one of the errors of the great school of Niccolo Pisano,—an error so full of feeling as to be sometimes all but redeemed, and altogether forgiven,—the sculpture, namely, of curtains around the recumbent statues upon tombs, curtains which angels are represented as withdrawing, to gaze upon the faces of those who are at rest. For some time the idea was simply and slightly expressed, and though there was always a painfulness in finding the shafts of stone, which were felt to be the real supporters of the canopy, represented as of yielding drapery, yet the beauty of the angelic figures, and the tenderness of the thought, disarmed all animadversion. But the scholars of the Pisani, as usual, caricatured when they were unable to invent; and the quiet curtained canopy became a huge marble tent, with a pole in the centre of it. Thus vulgarised, the idea itself soon disappeared, to make room for urns, torches, and weepers, and the other modern paraphernalia of the churchyard.

§ VIII. 3. Shipping. I have allowed this kind of subject to form a separate head, owing to the importance of rostra in Roman decoration, and to the continual occurrence of naval subjects in modern monumental bas-relief. Mr. Fergusson says, somewhat doubtfully, that he perceives a "kind of beauty" in a ship: I say, without any manner of doubt, that a ship is one of the loveliest things man ever made, and one of the noblest; nor do I know any lines, out of divine work, so lovely as those of the head of a ship, or even as the sweep of the timbers of a small boat, not a race boat, a mere floating chisel, but a broad, strong, sea boat, able to breast a wave and break it: and yet, with all this beauty, ships cannot be made subjects of sculpture. No one pauses in particular delight beneath the pediments of the Admiralty; nor does scenery of shipping ever become prominent in bas-relief without destroying it: witness the base of the Nelson pillar. It may be, and must be sometimes, introduced in severe subordination to the figure subject, but just enough to indicate the scene; sketched in the lightest lines on the background; never with any attempt at realisation, never with any equality to the force of the figures, unless the whole purpose of the subject be picturesque. I shall explain this exception presently, in speaking of imitative architecture.

§ IX. There is one piece of a ship's fittings, however, which may be thought to have obtained acceptance as a constant element of architectural ornament,—the cable: it is not, however, the cable itself, but its abstract form, a group of twisted lines (which a cable only exhibits in common with many natural objects), which is indeed beautiful as an ornament. Make the resemblance complete, give to the stone the threads and character of the cable, and you may, perhaps, regard the sculpture with curiosity, but never more with admiration. Consider the effect of the base of the statue of King William IV. at the end of London Bridge.

§ X. 4. Architecture itself. The erroneous use of armor, or dress, or instruments, or shipping, as decorative subject, is almost exclusively confined to bad architecture—Roman or Renaissance. But the false use of architecture itself, as an ornament of architecture, is conspicuous even in the mediæval work of the best times, and is a grievous fault in some of its noblest examples.

It is, therefore, of great importance to note exactly at what point this abuse begins, and in what it consists.

§ XI. In all bas-relief, architecture may be introduced as an explanation of the scene in which the figures act; but with more or less prominence in the inverse ratio of the importance of the figures.

The metaphysical reason of this is, that where the figures are of great value and beauty, the mind is supposed to be engaged wholly with them; and it is an impertinence to disturb its contemplation of them by any minor features whatever. As the figures become of less value, and are regarded with less intensity, accessory subjects may be introduced, such as the thoughts may have leisure for.

Thus, if the figures be as large as life, and complete statues, it is gross vulgarity to carve a temple above them, or distribute them over sculptured rocks, or lead them up steps into pyramids: I need hardly instance Canova's works,[63] and the Dutch pulpit groups, with fishermen, boats, and nets, in the midst of church naves.

If the figures be in bas-relief, though as large as life, the scene may be explained by lightly traced outlines: this is admirably done in the Ninevite marbles.

If the figures be in bas-relief, or even alto-relievo, but less than life, and if their purpose is rather to enrich a space and produce picturesque shadows, than to draw the thoughts entirely to themselves, the scenery in which they act may become prominent. The most exquisite examples of this treatment are the gates of Ghiberti. What would that Madonna of the Annunciation be, without the little shrine into which she shrinks back? But all mediæval work is full of delightful examples of the same kind of treatment: the gates of hell and of paradise are important pieces, both of explanation and effect, in all early representations of the last judgment, or of the descent into Hades. The keys of St. Peter, and the crushing flat of the devil under his own door, when it is beaten in, would hardly be understood without the respective gate-ways above. The best of all the later capitals of the Ducal Palace of Venice depends for great part of its value on the richness of a small campanile, which is pointed to proudly by a small emperor in a turned-up hat, who, the legend informs us, is "Numa Pompilio, imperador, edifichador di tempi e chiese."

§ XII. Shipping may be introduced, or rich fancy of vestments, crowns, and ornaments, exactly on the same conditions as architecture; and if the reader will look back to my definition of the picturesque in the "Seven Lamps," he will see why I said, above, that they might only be prominent when the purpose of the subject was partly picturesque; that is to say, when the mind is intended to derive part of its enjoyment from the parasitical qualities and accidents of the thing, not from the heart of the thing itself.

And thus, while we must regret the flapping sails in the death of Nelson in Trafalgar Square, we may yet most heartily enjoy the sculpture of a storm in one of the bas-reliefs of the tomb of St. Pietro Martire in the church of St. Eustorgio at Milan, where the grouping of the figures is most fancifully complicated by the undercut cordage of the vessel.

§ XIII. In all these instances, however, observe that the permission to represent the human work as an ornament, is conditional on its being necessary to the representation of a scene, or explanation of an action. On no terms whatever could any such subject be independently admissible.

Observe, therefore, the use of manufacture as ornament is—

1. With heroic figure sculpture, not admissible at all.
2. With picturesque figure sculpture, admissible in the degree of its picturesqueness.
3. Without figure sculpture, not admissible at all.

So also in painting: Michael Angelo, in the Sistine Chapel, would not have willingly painted a dress of figured damask or of watered satin; his was heroic painting, not admitting accessories.

Tintoret, Titian, Veronese, Rubens, and Vandyck, would be very sorry to part with their figured stuffs and lustrous silks; and sorry, observe, exactly in the degree of their picturesque feeling. Should not we also be sorry to have Bishop Ambrose without his vest, in that picture of the National Gallery?

But I think Vandyck would not have liked, on the other hand, the vest without the bishop. I much doubt if Titian or Veronese would have enjoyed going into Waterloo House, and making studies of dresses upon the counter.

§ XIV. So, therefore, finally, neither architecture nor any other human work is admissible as an ornament, except in subordination to figure subject. And this law is grossly and painfully violated by those curious examples of Gothic, both early and late, in the north, (but late, I think, exclusively, in Italy,) in which the minor features of the architecture were composed of small models of the larger: examples which led the way to a series of abuses materially affecting the life, strength, and nobleness of the Northern Gothic,—abuses which no Ninevite, nor Egyptian, nor Greek, nor Byzantine, nor Italian of the earlier ages would have endured for an instant, and which strike me with renewed surprise whenever I pass beneath a portal of thirteenth century Northern Gothic, associated as they are with manifestations of exquisite feeling and power in other directions. The porches of Bourges, Amiens, Notre Dame of Paris, and Notre Dame of Dijon, may be noted as conspicuous in error: small models of feudal towers with diminutive windows and battlements, of cathedral spires with scaly pinnacles, mixed with temple pediments and nondescript edifices of every kind, are crowded together over the recess of the niche into a confused fool's cap for the saint below. Italian Gothic is almost entirely free from the taint of this barbarism until the Renaissance period, when it becomes rampant in the cathedral of Como and Certosa of Pavia; and at Venice we find the Renaissance churches decorated with models of fortifications like those in the Repository at Woolwich, or inlaid with mock arcades in pseudo-perspective, copied from gardeners' paintings at the ends of conservatories.

§ XV. I conclude, then, with the reader's leave, that all ornament is base which takes for its subject human work, that it is utterly base,—painful to every rightly-toned mind, without perhaps immediate sense of the reason, but for a reason palpable enough when we do think of it. For to carve our own work, and set it up for admiration, is a miserable self-complacency, a contentment in our own wretched doings, when we might have been looking at God's doings. And all noble ornament is the exact reverse of this. It is the expression of man's delight in God's work.

§ XVI. For observe, the function of ornament is to make you happy. Now in what are you rightly happy? Not in thinking of what you have done yourself; not in your own pride, not your own birth; not in your own being, or your own will, but in looking at God; watching what He does, what He is; and obeying His law, and yielding yourself to His will.

You are to be made happy by ornaments; therefore they must be the expression of all this. Not copies of your own handiwork; not boastings of your own grandeur; not heraldries; not king's arms, nor any creature's arms, but God's arm, seen in His work. Not manifestation of your delight in your own laws, or your own liberties, or your own inventions; but in divine laws, constant, daily, common laws;—not Composite laws, nor Doric laws, nor laws of the five orders, but of the Ten Commandments.

§ XVII. Then the proper material of ornament will be whatever God has created; and its proper treatment, that which seems in accordance with or symbolical of His laws. And, for material, we shall therefore have, first, the abstract lines which are most frequent in nature; and then, from lower to higher, the whole range of systematised inorganic and organic forms. We shall rapidly glance in order at their kinds; and, however absurd the elemental division of inorganic matter by the ancients may seem to the modern chemist, it is one so grand and simple for arrangements of external appearances, that I shall here follow it; noticing first, after abstract lines, the imitable forms of the four elements, of Earth, Water, Fire, and Air, and then those of animal organisms. It may be convenient to the reader to have the order stated in a clear succession at first, thus:—

1. Abstract lines.
2. Forms of Earth (Crystals).
3. Forms of Water (Waves).
4. Forms of Fire (Flames and Rays).
5. Forms of Air (Clouds).
6. (Organic forms.) Shells.
7. Fish.
8. Reptiles and insects.
9. Vegetation (A.) Stems and Trunks.
10. Vegetation (B.) Foliage.
11. Birds.

12. Mammalian animals and Man.

It may be objected that clouds are a form of moisture, not of air. They are, however, a perfect expression of aërial states and currents, and may sufficiently well stand for the element they move in. And I have put vegetation apparently somewhat out of its place, owing to its vast importance as a means of decoration, and its constant association with birds and men.

§ XVIII. 1. Abstract lines. I have not with lines named also shades and colors, for this evident reason, that there are no such things as abstract shadows, irrespective of the forms which exhibit them, and distinguished in their own nature from each other; and that the arrangement of shadows, in greater or less quantity, or in certain harmonical successions, is an affair of treatment, not of selection. And when we use abstract colors, we are in fact using a part of nature herself,—using a quality of her light, correspondent with that of the air, to carry sound; and the arrangement of color in harmonious masses is again a matter of treatment, not selection. Yet even in this separate art of coloring, as referred to architecture, it is very notable that the best tints are always those of natural stones. These can hardly be wrong; I think I never yet saw an offensive introduction of the natural colors of marble and precious stones, unless in small mosaics, and in one or two glaring instances of the resolute determination to produce something ugly at any cost. On the other hand, I have most assuredly never yet seen a painted building, ancient or modern, which seemed to me quite right.

§ XIX. Our first constituents of ornament will therefore be abstract lines, that is to say, the most frequent contours of natural objects, transferred to architectural forms when it is not right or possible to render such forms distinctly imitative. For instance, the line or curve of the edge of a leaf may be accurately given to the edge of a stone, without rendering the stone in the least like a leaf, or suggestive of a leaf; and this the more fully, because the lines of nature are alike in all her works; simpler or richer in combination, but the same in character; and when they are taken out of their combinations it is impossible to say from which of her works they have been borrowed, their universal property being that of ever-varying curvature in the most subtle and subdued transitions, with peculiar expressions of motion, elasticity, or dependence, which I have already insisted upon at some length in the chapters on typical beauty in "Modern Painters." But, that the reader may here be able to compare them for himself as deduced from different sources, I have drawn, as accurately as I can, on the opposite plate, some ten or eleven lines from natural forms of very different substances and scale: the first, a b, is in the original, I think, the most beautiful simple curve I have ever seen in my life; it is a curve about three quarters of a mile long, formed by the surface of a small glacier of the second order, on a spur of the Aiguille de Blaitière (Chamouni). I have merely outlined the crags on the right of it, to show their sympathy and united action with the curve of the glacier, which is of course entirely dependent on their opposition to its descent; softened, however, into unity by the snow, which rarely melts on this high glacier surface.

The line d c is some mile and a half or two miles long; it is part of the flank of the chain of the Dent d'Oche above the lake of Geneva, one or two of the lines of the higher and more distant ranges being given in combination with it.

Plate VII. ABSTRACT LINES.

h is a line about four feet long, a branch of spruce fir. I have taken this tree because it is commonly supposed to be stiff and ungraceful; its outer sprays are, however, more noble in their sweep than almost any that I know: but this fragment is seen at great disadvantage, because placed upside down, in order that the reader may compare its curvatures with c d, e g, and i k, which are all mountain lines; e g, about five hundred feet of the southern edge of the Matterhorn; i k, the entire slope of the Aiguille Bouchard, from its summit into the valley of Chamouni, a line some three miles long; l m is the line of the side of a willow leaf traced by laying the leaf on the paper; n o, one of the innumerable groups of curves at the lip of a paper Nautilus; p, a spiral, traced on the paper round a Serpula; q r, the leaf of the Alisma Plantago with its interior ribs, real size; s t, the side of a bay-leaf; u w, of a salvia leaf; and it is to be carefully noted that these last curves, being never intended by nature to be seen singly, are more heavy and less agreeable than any of the others which would be seen as independent lines. But all agree in their character of changeful curvature, the mountain and glacier lines only excelling the rest in delicacy and richness of transition.

§ XX. Why lines of this kind are beautiful, I endeavored to show in the "Modern Painters;" but one point, there omitted, may be mentioned here,—that almost all these lines are expressive of action of force of some kind, while the circle is a line of limitation or support. In leafage they mark the forces of its growth and expansion, but some among the most beautiful of them are described by bodies variously in motion, or subjected to force; as by projectiles in the air, by the particles of water in a gentle current, by planets in motion in an orbit, by their satellites, if the actual path of the satellite in space be considered instead of its relation to the planet; by boats, or birds, turning in the water or air, by clouds in various action upon the wind, by sails in the curvatures they assume under its force, and by thousands of other objects moving or bearing force. In the Alisma leaf, q r, the lines through its body, which are of peculiar beauty, mark the different expansions of its fibres, and are, I think, exactly the same as those which would be traced by the currents of a river entering a lake of the shape of the leaf, at the end where the stalk is, and passing out at its point. Circular curves, on the contrary, are always, I think, curves of limitation or support; that is to say, curves of perfect rest. The cylindrical curve round the stem of a plant binds its fibres together; while the ascent of the stem is in lines of various curvature: so the curve of the horizon and of the apparent heaven, of the rainbow, etc.: and though the reader might imagine that the circular orbit of any moving body, or the curve described by a sling, was a curve of motion, he should observe that the circular character is given to the curve not by the motion, but by the confinement: the circle is the consequence not of the energy of the body, but of its being forbidden to leave the centre; and whenever the whirling or circular motion can be fully impressed on it we obtain instant balance and rest with respect to the centre of the circle.

Hence the peculiar fitness of the circular curve as a sign of rest, and security of support, in arches; while the other curves, belonging especially to action, are to be used in the more active architectural features—the hand and foot (the capital and base), and in all minor ornaments; more freely in proportion to their independence of structural conditions.

§ XXI. We need not, however, hope to be able to imitate, in general work, any of the subtly combined curvatures of nature's highest designing: on the contrary, their extreme refinement renders them unfit for coarse service or material. Lines which are lovely in the pearly film of the Nautilus shell, are lost in the grey roughness of stone; and those which are sublime in the blue of far away hills, are weak in the substance of incumbent marble. Of all the graceful lines assembled on Plate VII., we shall do well to be content with two of the simplest. We shall take one mountain line (e g) and one leaf line (u w), or rather fragments of them, for we shall perhaps not want them all. I will mark off from u w the little bit x y, and from e g the piece e f; both which appear to me likely to be serviceable: and if hereafter we need the help of any abstract lines, we will see what we can do with these only.

§ XXII. 2. Forms of Earth (Crystals). It may be asked why I do not say rocks or mountains? Simply, because the nobility of these depends, first, on their scale, and, secondly, on accident. Their scale cannot be represented, nor their accident systematised. No sculptor can in the least imitate the peculiar character of accidental fracture: he can obey or exhibit the laws of nature, but he cannot copy the felicity of her fancies, nor follow the steps of her fury. The very glory of a mountain is in the revolutions which raised it into power, and the forces which are striking it into ruin. But we want no cold and careful imitation of catastrophe; no calculated mockery of convulsion; no delicate recommendation of ruin. We are to follow the labor of Nature, but not her disturbance; to imitate what she has deliberately ordained,[64] not what she has violently suffered, or strangely permitted. The only uses, therefore, of rock form which are wise in the architect, are its actual introduction (by leaving untouched such blocks as are meant for rough service), and that noble use of the general examples of mountain structure of which I have often heretofore spoken. Imitations of rock form have, for the most part, been confined to periods of degraded feeling and to architectural toys or pieces of dramatic effect,—the Calvaries and holy sepulchres of Romanism, or the grottoes and fountains of English gardens. They were, however, not unfrequent in mediæval bas-reliefs; very curiously and elaborately treated by Ghiberti on the doors of Florence, and in religious sculpture necessarily introduced wherever the life of the anchorite was to be expressed. They were rarely introduced as of ornamental character, but for particular service and expression; we shall see an interesting example in the Ducal Palace at Venice.

§ XXIII. But against crystalline form, which is the completely systematised natural structure of the earth, none of these objections hold good, and, accordingly, it is an endless element of decoration, where higher conditions of structure cannot be represented. The four-sided pyramid, perhaps the most frequent of all natural crystals, is called in architecture a dogtooth; its use is quite limitless, and always beautiful: the cube and rhomb are almost equally frequent in chequers and dentils: and all mouldings of the middle Gothic are little more than representations of the canaliculated crystals of the beryl, and such other minerals:

§ XXIV. Not knowingly. I do not suppose a single hint was ever actually taken from mineral form; not even by the Arabs in their stalactite pendants and vaults: all that I mean to allege is, that beautiful ornament, wherever found, or however invented, is always either an intentional or unintentional copy of some constant natural form; and that in this particular instance, the pleasure we have in these geometrical figures of our own invention, is dependent for all its acuteness on the natural tendency impressed on us by our Creator to love the forms into which the earth He gave us to tread, and out of which He formed our bodies, knit itself as it was separated from the deep.

§ XXV. 3. Forms of Water (Waves).

The reasons which prevent rocks from being used for ornament repress still more forcibly the portraiture of the sea. Yet the constant necessity of introducing some representation of water in order to explain the scene of events, or as a sacred symbol, has forced the sculptors of all ages to the invention of some type or letter for it, if not an actual imitation. We find every degree of conventionalism or of naturalism in these types, the earlier being, for the most part, thoughtful symbols; the latter, awkward attempts at portraiture.[65] The most conventional of all types is the Egyptian zigzag, preserved in the astronomical sign of Aquarius; but every nation, with any capacities of thought, has given, in some of its work, the same great definition of open water, as "an undulatory thing with fish in it." I say open water, because inland nations have a totally different conception of the element. Imagine for an instant the different feelings of an husbandman whose hut is built by the Rhine or the Po, and who sees, day by day, the same giddy succession of silent power, the same opaque, thick, whirling, irresistible labyrinth of rushing lines and twisted eddies, coiling themselves into serpentine race by the reedy banks, in omne volubilis ævum,—and the image of the sea in the mind of the fisher upon the rocks of Ithaca, or by the Straits of Sicily, who sees how, day by day, the morning winds come coursing to the shore, every breath of them with a green wave rearing before it; clear, crisp, ringing, merry-minded waves, that fall over and over each other, laughing like children as they near the beach, and at last clash themselves all into dust of crystal over the dazzling sweeps of sand. Fancy the difference of the image of water in those two minds, and then compare the sculpture of the coiling eddies of the Tigris and its reedy branches in those slabs of Nineveh, with the crested curls of the Greek sea on the coins of Camerina or Tarentum. But both agree in the undulatory lines, either of the currents or the surface, and in the introduction of fish as explanatory of the meaning of those lines (so also the Egyptians in their frescoes, with most elaborate realisation of the fish). There is a very curious instance on a Greek mirror in the British Museum, representing Orion on the Sea; and multitudes of examples with dolphins on the Greek vases: the type is preserved without alteration in mediæval painting and sculpture. The sea in that Greek mirror (at least 400 B.C.), in the mosaics of Torcello and St. Mark's, on the font of St. Frediano at Lucca, on the gate of the fortress of St. Michael's Mount in Normandy, on the Bayeux tapestry, and on the capitals of the Ducal Palace at Venice (under Arion on his Dolphin), is represented in a manner absolutely identical. Giotto, in the frescoes of Avignon, has, with his usual strong feeling for naturalism, given the best example I remember, in painting, of the unity of the conventional system with direct imitation, and that both in sea and river; giving in pure blue color the coiling whirlpool of the stream, and the curled crest of the breaker. But in all early sculptural examples, both imitation and decorative effect are subordinate to easily understood symbolical language; the undulatory lines are often valuable as an enrichment of surface, but are rarely of any studied gracefulness. One of the best examples I know of their expressive arrangement is around some figures in a spandril at Bourges, representing figures sinking in deep sea (the deluge): the waved lines yield beneath the bodies and wildly lave the edge of the moulding, two birds, as if to mark the reverse of all order of nature, lowest of all sunk in the depth of them. In later times of debasement, water began to be represented with its waves, foam, etc., as on the Vendramin tomb at Venice, above cited; but even there, without any definite ornamental purpose, the sculptor meant partly to explain a story, partly to display dexterity of chiselling, but not to produce beautiful forms pleasant to the eye. The imitation is vapid and joyless, and it has often been matter of surprise to me that sculptors, so fond of exhibiting their skill, should have suffered this imitation to fall so short, and remain so cold,—should not have taken more pains to curl the waves clearly, to edge them sharply, and to express, by drill-holes or other artifices, the character of foam. I think in one of the Antwerp churches something of this kind is done in wood, but in general it is rare.

§ XXVI. 4. Forms of Fire (Flames and Rays). If neither the sea nor the rock can be imagined, still less the devouring fire. It has been symbolised by radiation both in painting and sculpture, for the most part in the latter very unsuccessfully. It was suggested to me, not long ago,[66] that zigzag decorations of Norman architects were typical of light springing from the half-set orb of the sun; the resemblance to the ordinary sun type is indeed remarkable, but I believe accidental. I shall give you, in my large plates, two curious instances of radiation in brick ornament above arches, but I think these also without any very luminous intention. The imitations of fire in the torches of Cupids and genii, and burning in tops of urns, which attest and represent the mephitic inspirations of the seventeenth century in most London churches, and in monuments all over civilised Europe, together with the gilded rays of Romanist altars, may be left to such mercy as the reader is inclined to show them.

§ XXVII. 5. Forms of Air (Clouds). Hardly more manageable than flames, and of no ornamental use, their majesty being in scale and color, and inimitable in marble. They are lightly traced in much of the cinque cento sculpture; very boldly and grandly in the strange Last Judgment in the porch of St. Maclou at Rouen, described in the "Seven Lamps." But the most elaborate imitations are altogether of recent date, arranged in concretions like flattened sacks, forty or fifty feet above the altars of continental churches, mixed with the gilded truncheons intended for sunbeams above alluded to.

§ XXVIII. 6. Shells. I place these lowest in the scale (after inorganic forms) as being moulds or coats of organism; not themselves organic. The sense of this, and of their being mere emptiness and deserted houses, must always prevent them, however beautiful in their lines, from being largely used in ornamentation. It is better to take the line and leave the shell. One form, indeed, that of the cockle, has been in all ages used as the decoration of half domes, which were named conchas from their shell form: and I believe the wrinkled lip of the cockle, so used, to have been the origin, in some parts of Europe at least, of the exuberant foliation of the round arch. The scallop also is a pretty radiant form, and mingles well with other symbols when it is needed. The crab is always as delightful as a grotesque, for here we suppose the beast inside the shell; and he sustains his part in a lively manner among the other signs of the zodiac, with the scorpion; or scattered upon sculptured shores, as beside the Bronze Boar of Florence. We shall find him in a basket at Venice, at the base of one of the Piazzetta shafts.

§ XXIX. 7. Fish. These, as beautiful in their forms as they are familiar to our sight, while their interest is increased by their symbolic meaning, are of great value as material of ornament. Love of the picturesque has generally induced a choice of some supple form with scaly body and lashing tail, but the simplest fish form is largely employed in mediæval work. We shall find the plain oval body and sharp head of the Thunny constantly at Venice; and the fish used in the expression of sea-water, or water generally, are always plain bodied creatures in the best mediæval sculpture. The Greek type of the dolphin, however, sometimes but slightly exaggerated from the real outline of the Delphinus Delphis,[67] is one of the most picturesque of animal forms; and the action of its slow revolving plunge is admirably caught upon the surface sea represented in Greek vases.

§ XXX. 8. Reptiles and Insects. The forms of the serpent and lizard exhibit almost every element of beauty and horror in strange combination; the horror, which in an imitation is felt only as a pleasurable excitement, has rendered them favorite subjects in all periods of art; and the unity of both lizard and serpent in the ideal dragon, the most picturesque and powerful of all animal forms, and of peculiar symbolical interest to the Christian mind, is perhaps the principal of all the materials of mediæval picturesque sculpture. By the best sculptors it is always used with this symbolic meaning, by the cinque cento sculptors as an ornament merely. The best and most natural representations of mere viper or snake are to be found interlaced among their confused groups of meaningless objects. The real power and horror of the snake-head has, however, been rarely reached. I shall give one example from Verona of the twelfth century.

Other less powerful reptile forms are not unfrequent. Small frogs, lizards, and snails almost always enliven the foregrounds and leafage of good sculpture. The tortoise is less usually employed in groups. Beetles are chiefly mystic and colossal. Various insects, like everything else in the world, occur in cinque cento work; grasshoppers most frequently. We shall see on the Ducal Palace at Venice an interesting use of the bee.

§ XXXI. 9. Branches and stems of Trees. I arrange these under a separate head; because, while the forms of leafage belong to all architecture, and ought to be employed in it always, those of the branch and stem belong to a peculiar imitative and luxuriant architecture, and are only applicable at times. Pagan sculptors seem to have perceived little beauty in the stems of trees; they were little else than timber to them; and they preferred the rigid and monstrous triglyph, or the fluted column, to a broken bough or gnarled trunk. But with Christian knowledge came a peculiar regard for the forms of vegetation, from the root upwards. The actual representation of the entire trees required in many scripture subjects,—as in the most frequent of Old Testament subjects, the Fall; and again in the Drunkenness of Noah, the Garden Agony, and many others, familiarised the sculptors of bas-relief to the beauty of forms before unknown; while the symbolical name given to Christ by the Prophets, "the Branch," and the frequent expressions referring to this image throughout every scriptural description of conversion, gave an especial interest to the Christian mind to this portion of vegetative structure. For some time, nevertheless, the sculpture of trees was confined to bas-relief; but it at last affected even the treatment of the main shafts in Lombard Gothic buildings,—as in the western façade of Genoa, where two of the shafts are represented as gnarled trunks: and as bas-relief itself became more boldly introduced, so did tree sculpture, until we find the writhed and knotted stems of the vine and fig used for angle shafts on the Doge's Palace, and entire oaks and appletrees forming, roots and all, the principal decorative sculptures of the Scala tombs at Verona. It was then discovered to be more easy to carve branches than leaves and, much helped by the frequent employment in later Gothic of the "Tree of Jesse," for traceries and other purposes, the system reached full developement in a perfect thicket of twigs, which form the richest portion of the decoration of the porches of Beauvais. It had now been carried to its richest extreme: men wearied of it and abandoned it, and like all other natural and beautiful things, it was ostracised by the mob of Renaissance architects. But it is interesting to observe how the human mind, in its acceptance of this feature of ornament, proceeded from the ground, and followed, as it were, the natural growth of the tree. It began with the rude and solid trunk, as at Genoa; then the branches shot out, and became loaded leaves; autumn came, the leaves were shed, and the eye was directed to the extremities of the delicate branches;—the Renaissance frosts came, and all perished.

§ XXXII. 10. Foliage, Flowers, and Fruit. It is necessary to consider these as separated from the stems; not only, as above noted, because their separate use marks another school of architecture, but because they are the only organic structures which are capable of being so treated, and intended to be so, without strong effort of imagination. To pull animals to pieces, and use their paws for feet of furniture, or their heads for terminations of rods and shafts, is usually the characteristic of feelingless schools; the greatest men like their animals whole. The head may, indeed, be so managed as to look emergent from the stone, rather than fastened to it; and wherever there is throughout the architecture any expression of sternness or severity (severity in its literal sense, as in Romans, XI. 22), such divisions of the living form may be permitted; still, you cannot cut an animal to pieces as you can gather a flower or a leaf. These were intended for our gathering, and for our constant delight: wherever men exist in a perfectly civilised and healthy state, they have vegetation around them; wherever their state approaches that of innocence or perfectness, it approaches that of Paradise,—it is a dressing of garden. And, therefore, where nothing else can be used for ornament, vegetation may; vegetation in any form, however fragmentary, however abstracted. A single leaf laid upon the angle of a stone, or the mere form or frame-work of the leaf drawn upon it, or the mere shadow and ghost of the leaf,—the hollow "foil" cut out of it,—possesses a charm which nothing else can replace; a charm not exciting, nor demanding laborious thought or sympathy, but perfectly simple, peaceful, and satisfying.

§ XXXIII. The full recognition of leaf forms, as the general source of subordinate decoration, is one of the chief characteristics of Christian architecture; but the two roots of leaf ornament are the Greek acanthus, and the Egyptian lotus.[68] The dry land and the river thus each contributed their part; and all the florid capitals of the richest Northern Gothic on the one hand, and the arrowy lines of the severe Lombardic capitals on the other, are founded on these two gifts of the dust of Greece and the waves of the Nile. The leaf which is, I believe, called the Persepolitan water-leaf, is to be associated with the lotus flower and stem, as the origin of our noblest types of simple capital; and it is to be noted that the florid leaves of the dry land are used most by the Northern architects, while the water leaves are gathered for their ornaments by the parched builders of the Desert.

§ XXXIV. Fruit is, for the most part, more valuable in color than form; nothing is more beautiful as a subject of sculpture on a tree; but, gathered and put in baskets, it is quite possible to have too much of it. We shall find it so used very dextrously on the Ducal Palace of Venice, there with a meaning which rendered it right necessary; but the Renaissance architects address themselves to spectators who care for nothing but feasting, and suppose that clusters of pears and pineapples are visions of which their imagination can never weary, and above which it will never care to rise. I am no advocate for image worship, as I believe the reader will elsewhere sufficiently find; but I am very sure that the Protestantism of London would have found itself quite as secure in a cathedral decorated with statues of good men, as in one hung round with bunches of ribston pippins.

§ XXXV. 11. Birds. The perfect and simple grace of bird form, in general, has rendered it a favorite subject with early sculptors, and with those schools which loved form more than action; but the difficulty of expressing action, where the muscular markings are concealed, has limited the use of it in later art. Half the ornament, at least, in Byzantine architecture, and a third of that of Lombardic, is composed of birds, either pecking at fruit or flowers, or standing on either side of a flower or vase, or alone, as generally the symbolical peacock. But how much of our general sense of grace or power of motion, of serenity, peacefulness, and spirituality, we owe to these creatures, it is impossible to conceive; their wings supplying us with almost the only means of representation of spiritual motion which we possess, and with an ornamental form of which the eye is never weary, however meaninglessly or endlessly repeated; whether in utter isolation, or associated with the bodies of the lizard, the horse, the lion, or the man. The heads of the birds of prey are always beautiful, and used as the richest ornaments in all ages.

§ XXXVI. 12. Quadrupeds and Men. Of quadrupeds the horse has received an elevation into the primal rank of sculptural subject, owing to his association with men. The full value of other quadruped forms has hardly been perceived, or worked for, in late sculpture; and the want of science is more felt in these subjects than in any other branches of early work. The greatest richness of quadruped ornament is found in the hunting sculpture of the Lombards; but rudely treated (the most noble examples of treatment being the lions of Egypt, the Ninevite bulls, and the mediæval griffins). Quadrupeds of course form the noblest subjects of ornament next to the human form; this latter, the chief subject of sculpture, being sometimes the end of architecture rather than its decoration.

We have thus completed the list of the materials of architectural decoration, and the reader may be assured that no effort has ever been successful to draw elements of beauty from any other sources than these. Such an effort was once resolutely made. It was contrary to the religion of the Arab to introduce any animal form into his ornament; but although all the radiance of color, all the refinements of proportion, and all the intricacies of geometrical design were open to him, he could not produce any noble work without an abstraction of the forms of leafage, to be used in his capitals, and made the ground plan of his chased ornament. But I have above noted that coloring is an entirely distinct and independent art; and in the "Seven Lamps" we saw that this art had most power when practised in arrangements of simple geometrical form: the Arab, therefore, lay under no disadvantage in coloring, and he had all the noble elements of constructive and proportional beauty at his command: he might not imitate the sea-shell, but he could build the dome. The imitation of radiance by the variegated voussoir, the expression of the sweep of the desert by the barred red lines upon the wall, the starred inshedding of light through his vaulted roof, and all the endless fantasy of abstract line,[69] were still in the power of his ardent and fantastic spirit. Much he achieved; and yet in the effort of his overtaxed invention, restrained from its proper food, he made his architecture a glittering vacillation of undisciplined enchantment, and left the lustre of its edifices to wither like a startling dream, whose beauty we may indeed feel, and whose instruction we may receive, but must smile at its inconsistency, and mourn over its evanescence.

FOOTNOTES:

[63] The admiration of Canova I hold to be one of the most deadly symptoms in the civilisation of the upper classes in the present century.

[64] Thus above, I adduced for the architect's imitation the appointed stories and beds of the Matterhorn, not its irregular forms of crag or fissure.

[65] Appendix 21, "Ancient Representations of Water."

[66] By the friend to whom I owe Appendix 21.

[67] One is glad to hear from Cuvier, that though dolphins in general are "les plus carnassiers, et proportion gardée avec leur taille, les plus cruels de l'ordre;" yet that in the Delphinus Delphis, "tout l'organisation de son cerveau annonce qu'il ne doit pas être dépourvu de la docilité qu'ils (les anciens) lui attribuaient."

[68] Vide Wilkinson, vol. v., woodcut No. 478, fig. 8. The tamarisk appears afterwards to have given the idea of a subdivision of leaf more pure and quaint than that of the acanthus. Of late our botanists have discovered, in the "Victoria regia" (supposing its blossom reversed), another strangely beautiful type of what we may perhaps hereafter find it convenient to call Lily capitals.

[69] Appendix 22, "Arabian Ornamentation."

§ I. We now know where we are to look for subjects of decoration. The next question is, as the reader must remember, how to treat or express these subjects.

There are evidently two branches of treatment: the first being the expression, or rendering to the eye and mind, of the thing itself; and the second, the arrangement of the thing so expressed: both of these being quite distinct from the placing of the ornament in proper parts of the building. For instance, suppose we take a vine-leaf for our subject. The first question is, how to cut the vine-leaf? Shall we cut its ribs and notches on the edge, or only its general outline? and so on. Then, how to arrange the vine-leaves when we have them; whether symmetrically, or at random; or unsymmetrically, yet within certain limits? All these I call questions of treatment. Then, whether the vine-leaves so arranged are to be set on the capital of a pillar or on its shaft, I call a question of place.

§ II. So, then, the questions of mere treatment are twofold, how to express, and how to arrange. And expression is to the mind or the sight. Therefore, the inquiry becomes really threefold:—

1. How ornament is to be expressed with reference to the mind.

2. How ornament is to be arranged with reference to the sight.

3. How ornament is to be arranged with reference to both.

§ III. (1.) How is ornament to be treated with reference to the mind?

If, to produce a good or beautiful ornament, it were only necessary to produce a perfect piece of sculpture, and if a well cut group of flowers or animals were indeed an ornament wherever it might be placed, the work of the architect would be comparatively easy. Sculpture and architecture would become separate arts; and the architect would order so many pieces of such subject and size as he needed, without troubling himself with any questions but those of disposition and proportion. But this is not so. No perfect piece either of painting or sculpture is an architectural ornament at all, except in that vague sense in which any beautiful thing is said to ornament the place it is in. Thus we say that pictures ornament a room; but we should not thank an architect who told us that his design, to be complete, required a Titian to be put in one corner of it, and a Velasquez in the other; and it is just as unreasonable to call perfect sculpture, niched in, or encrusted on a building, a portion of the ornament of that building, as it would be to hang pictures by the way of ornament on the outside of it. It is very possible that the sculptured work may be harmoniously associated with the building, or the building executed with reference to it; but in this latter case the architecture is subordinate to the sculpture, as in the Medicean chapel, and I believe also in the Parthenon. And so far from the perfection of the work conducing to its ornamental purpose, we may say, with entire security, that its perfection, in some degree, unfits it for its purpose, and that no absolutely complete sculpture can be decoratively right. We have a familiar instance in the flower-work of St. Paul's, which is probably, in the abstract, as perfect flower sculpture as could be produced at the time; and which is just as rational an ornament of the building as so many valuable Van Huysums, framed and glazed and hung up over each window.

§ IV. The especial condition of true ornament is, that it be beautiful in its place, and nowhere else, and that it aid the effect of every portion of the building over which it has influence; that it does not, by its richness, make other parts bald, or, by its delicacy, make other parts coarse. Every one of its qualities has reference to its place and use: and it is fitted for its service by what would be faults and deficiencies if it had no especial duty. Ornament, the servant, is often formal, where sculpture, the master, would have been free; the servant is often silent where the master would have been eloquent; or hurried, where the master would have been serene.

§ V. How far this subordination is in different situations to be expressed, or how far it may be surrendered, and ornament, the servant, be permitted to have independent will; and by what means the subordination is best to be expressed when it is required, are by far the most difficult questions I have ever tried to work out respecting any branch of art; for, in many of the examples to which I look as authoritative in their majesty of effect, it is almost impossible to say whether the abstraction or imperfection of the sculpture was owing to the choice, or the incapacity of the workman; and, if to the latter, how far the result of fortunate incapacity can be imitated by prudent self-restraint. The reader, I think, will understand this at once by considering the effect of the illuminations of an old missal. In their bold rejection of all principles of perspective, light and shade, and drawing, they are infinitely more ornamental to the page, owing to the vivid opposition of their bright colors and quaint lines, than if they had been drawn by Da Vinci himself: and so the Arena chapel is far more brightly decorated by the archaic frescoes of Giotti, than the Stanze of the Vatican are by those of Raffaelle. But how far it is possible to recur to such archaicism, or to make up for it by any voluntary abandonment of power, I cannot as yet venture in any wise to determine.

§ VI. So, on the other hand, in many instances of finished work in which I find most to regret or to reprobate, I can hardly distinguish what is erroneous in principle from what is vulgar in execution. For instance, in most Romanesque churches of Italy, the porches are guarded by gigantic animals, lions or griffins, of admirable severity of design; yet, in many cases, of so rude workmanship, that it can hardly be determined how much of this severity was intentional,—how much involuntary: in the cathedral of Genoa two modern lions have, in imitation of this ancient custom, been placed on the steps of its west front; and the Italian sculptor, thinking himself a marvellous great man because he knew what lions were really like, has copied them, in the menagerie, with great success, and produced two hairy and well-whiskered beasts, as like to real lions as he could possibly cut them. One wishes them back in the menagerie for his pains; but it is impossible to say how far the offence of their presence is owing to the mere stupidity and vulgarity of the sculpture, and how far we might have been delighted with a realisation, carried to nearly the same length by Ghiberti or Michael Angelo. (I say nearly, because neither Ghiberti nor Michael Angelo would ever have attempted, or permitted, entire realisation, even in independent sculpture.)

§ VII. In spite of these embarrassments, however, some few certainties may be marked in the treatment of past architecture, and secure conclusions deduced for future practice. There is first, for instance, the assuredly intended and resolute abstraction of the Ninevite and Egyptian sculptors. The men who cut those granite lions in the Egyptian room of the British Museum, and who carved the calm faces of those Ninevite kings, knew much more, both of lions and kings, than they chose to express. Then there is the Greek system, in which the human sculpture is perfect, the architecture and animal sculpture is subordinate to it, and the architectural ornament severely subordinated to this again, so as to be composed of little more than abstract lines: and, finally, there is the peculiarly mediæval system, in which the inferior details are carried to as great or greater imitative perfection as the higher sculpture;

and the subordination is chiefly effected by symmetries of arrangement, and quaintnesses of treatment, respecting which it is difficult to say how far they resulted from intention, and how far from incapacity.

§ VIII. Now of these systems, the Ninevite and Egyptian are altogether opposed to modern habits of thought and action; they are sculptures evidently executed under absolute authorities, physical and mental, such as cannot at present exist. The Greek system presupposes the possession of a Phidias; it is ridiculous to talk of building in the Greek manner; you may build a Greek shell or box, such as the Greek intended to contain sculpture, but you have not the sculpture to put in it. Find your Phidias first, and your new Phidias will very soon settle all your architectural difficulties in very unexpected ways indeed; but until you find him, do not think yourselves architects while you go on copying those poor subordinations, and secondary and tertiary orders of ornament, which the Greek put on the shell of his sculpture. Some of them, beads, and dentils, and such like, are as good as they can be for their work, and you may use them for subordinate work still; but they are nothing to be proud of, especially when you did not invent them: and others of them are mistakes and impertinences in the Greek himself, such as his so-called honeysuckle ornaments and others, in which there is a starched and dull suggestion of vegetable form, and yet no real resemblance nor life, for the conditions of them result from his own conceit of himself, and ignorance of the physical sciences, and want of relish for common nature, and vain fancy that he could improve everything he touched, and that he honored it by taking it into his service: by freedom from which conceits the true Christian architecture is distinguished—not by points to its arches.

§ IX. There remains, therefore, only the mediæval system, in which I think, generally, more completion is permitted (though this often because more was possible) in the inferior than in the higher portions of ornamental subject. Leaves, and birds, and lizards are realised, or nearly so; men and quadrupeds formalised. For observe, the smaller and inferior subject remains subordinate, however richly finished; but the human sculpture can only be subordinate by being imperfect. The realisation is, however, in all cases, dangerous except under most skilful management, and the abstraction, if true and noble, is almost always more delightful.[70]

Plate VIII. DECORATION BY DISKS. PALAZZO DEI BADOARI PARTECIPAZZI.

§ X. What, then, is noble abstraction? It is taking first the essential elements of the thing to be represented, then the rest in the order of importance (so that wherever we pause we shall always have obtained more than we leave behind), and using any expedient to impress what we want upon the mind, without caring about the mere literal accuracy of such expedient. Suppose, for instance, we have to represent a peacock: now a peacock has a graceful neck, so has a swan; it has a high crest, so has a cockatoo; it has a long tail, so has a bird of Paradise. But the whole spirit and power of peacock is in those eyes of the tail. It is true, the argus pheasant, and one or two more birds, have something like them, but nothing for a moment comparable to them in brilliancy: express the gleaming of the blue eyes through the plumage, and you have nearly all you want of peacock, but without this, nothing; and yet those eyes are not in relief; a rigidly true sculpture of a peacock's form could have no eyes,—nothing but feathers. Here, then, enters the stratagem of sculpture; you must cut the eyes in relief, somehow or another; see how it is done in the peacock on the opposite page; it is so done by nearly all the Byzantine sculptors: this particular peacock is meant to be seen at some distance (how far off I know not, for it is an interpolation in the building where it occurs, of which more hereafter), but at all events at a distance of thirty or forty feet; I have put it close to you that you may see plainly the rude rings and rods which stand for the eyes and quills, but at the just distance their effect is perfect.

§ XI. And the simplicity of the means here employed may help us, both to some clear understanding of the spirit of Ninevite and Egyptian work, and to some perception of the kind of enfantillage or archaicism to which it may be possible, even in days of advanced science, legitimately to return. The architect has no right, as we said before, to require of us a picture of Titian's in order to complete his design; neither has he the right to calculate on the co-operation of perfect sculptors, in subordinate capacities. Far from this; his business is to dispense with such aid altogether, and to devise such a system of ornament as shall be capable of execution by uninventive and even unintelligent workmen; for supposing that he required noble sculpture for his ornament, how far would this at once limit the number and the scale of possible buildings? Architecture is the work of nations; but we cannot have nations of great sculptors. Every house in every street of every city ought to be good architecture, but we cannot have Flaxman or Thorwaldsen at work upon it: nor, even if we chose only to devote ourselves to our public buildings, could the mass and majesty of them be great, if we required all to be executed by great men; greatness is not to be had in the required quantity. Giotto may design a campanile, but he cannot carve it; he can only carve one or two of the bas-reliefs at the base of it. And with every increase of your fastidiousness in the execution of your ornament, you diminish the possible number and grandeur of your buildings. Do not think you can educate your workmen, or that the demand for perfection will increase the supply: educated imbecility and finessed foolishness are the worst of all imbecilities and foolishnesses; and there is no free-trade measure, which will ever lower the price of brains,—there is no California of common sense. Exactly in the degree in which you require your decoration to be wrought by thoughtful men, you diminish the extent and number of architectural works. Your business as an architect, is to calculate only on the co-operation of inferior men, to think for them, and to indicate for them such expressions of your thoughts as the weakest capacity can comprehend and the feeblest hand can execute. This is the definition of the purest architectural abstractions. They are the deep and laborious thoughts of the greatest men, put into such easy letters that they can be written by the simplest. They are expressions of the mind of manhood by the hands of childhood.

§ XII. And now suppose one of those old Ninevite or Egyptian builders, with a couple of thousand men—mud-bred, onion-eating creatures—under him, to be set to work, like so many ants, on his temple sculptures. What is he to do with them? He can put them through a granitic exercise of current hand; he can teach them all how to curl hair thoroughly into croche-coeurs, as you teach a bench of school-boys how to shape pothooks; he can teach them all how to draw long eyes and straight noses, and how to copy accurately certain well-defined lines. Then he fits his own great design to their capacities; he takes out of king, or lion, or god, as much as was expressible by croche-coeurs and granitic pothooks; he throws this into noble forms of his own imagining, and having mapped out their lines so that there can be no possibility of error, sets his two thousand men to work upon them, with a will, and so many onions a day.

§ XIII. I said those times cannot now return. We have, with Christianity, recognised the individual value of every soul; and there is no intelligence so feeble but that its single ray may in some sort contribute to the general light. This is the glory of Gothic architecture, that every jot and tittle, every point and niche of it, affords room, fuel, and focus for individual fire. But you cease to acknowledge this, and you refuse to accept the help of the lesser mind, if you require the work to be all executed in a great manner. Your business is to think out all of it nobly, to dictate the expression of it as far as your dictation can assist the less elevated intelligence: then to leave this, aided and taught as far as may be, to its own simple act and effort; and to rejoice in its simplicity if not in its power, and in its vitality if not in its science.

§ XIV. We have, then, three orders of ornament, classed according to the degrees of correspondence of the executive and conceptive minds. We have the servile ornament, in which the executive is absolutely subjected to the inventive,—the ornament of the great Eastern nations, more especially Hamite, and all pre-Christian, yet thoroughly noble in its submissiveness. Then we have the mediæval system, in which the mind of the inferior workman is recognised, and has full room for action, but is guided and ennobled by the ruling mind. This is the truly Christian and only perfect system. Finally, we have ornaments expressing the endeavor to equalise the executive and inventive,—endeavor which is Renaissance and revolutionary, and destructive of all noble architecture.

§ XV. Thus far, then, of the incompleteness or simplicity of execution necessary in architectural ornament, as referred to the mind. Next we have to consider that which is required when it is referred to the sight, and the various modifications of treatment which are rendered necessary by the variation of its distance from the eye. I say necessary: not merely expedient or economical. It is foolish to carve what is to be seen forty feet off with the delicacy which the eye demands within two yards; not merely because such delicacy is lost in the distance, but because it is a great deal worse than lost:—the delicate work has actually worse effect in the distance than rough work. This is a fact well known to painters, and, for the most part, acknowledged by the critics of painters, namely, that there is a certain distance for which a picture is painted; and that the finish, which is delightful if that distance be small, is actually injurious if the distance be great: and, moreover, that there is a particular method of handling which none but consummate artists reach, which has its effects at the intended distance, and is altogether hieroglyphical and unintelligible at any other. This, I say, is acknowledged in painting, but it is not practically acknowledged in architecture; nor until my attention was especially directed to it, had I myself any idea of the care with which this great question was studied by the mediæval architects. On my first careful examination of the capitals of the upper arcade of the Ducal Palace at Venice, I was induced, by their singular inferiority of workmanship, to suppose them posterior to those of the lower arcade. It was not till I discovered that some of those which I thought the worst above, were the best when seen from below, that I obtained the key to this marvellous system of adaptation; a system which I afterwards found carried out in every building of the great times which I had opportunity of examining.

§ **XVI.** There are two distinct modes in which this adaptation is effected. In the first, the same designs which are delicately worked when near the eye, are rudely cut, and have far fewer details when they are removed from it. In this method it is not always easy to distinguish economy from skill, or slovenliness from science. But, in the second method, a different design is adopted, composed of fewer parts and of simpler lines, and this is cut with exquisite precision. This is of course the higher method, and the more satisfactory proof of purpose; but an equal degree of imperfection is found in both kinds when they are seen close; in the first, a bald execution of a perfect design; the second, a baldness of design with perfect execution. And in these very imperfections lies the admirableness of the ornament.

§ **XVII.** It may be asked whether, in advocating this adaptation to the distance of the eye, I obey my adopted rule of observance of natural law. Are not all natural things, it may be asked, as lovely near as far away? Nay, not so. Look at the clouds, and watch the delicate sculpture of their alabaster sides, and the rounded lustre of their magnificent rolling. They are meant to be beheld far away; they were shaped for their place, high above your head; approach them, and they fuse into vague mists, or whirl away in fierce fragments of thunderous vapor. Look at the crest of the Alp, from the far-away plains over which its light is cast, whence human souls have communion with it by their myriads. The child looks up to it in the dawn, and the husbandman in the burden and heat of the day, and the old man in the going down of the sun, and it is to them all as the celestial city on the world's horizon; dyed with the depth of heaven, and clothed with the calm of eternity. There was it set, for holy dominion, by Him who marked for the sun his journey, and bade the moon know her going down. It was built for its place in the far-off sky; approach it, and as the sound of the voice of man dies away about its foundations, and the tide of human life, shallowed upon the vast aërial shore, is at last met by the Eternal "Here shall thy waves be stayed," the glory of its aspect fades into blanched fearfulness; its purple walls are rent into grisly rocks, its silver fretwork saddened into wasting snow, the storm-brands of ages are on its breast, the ashes of its own ruin lie solemnly on its white raiment.

Nor in such instances as these alone, though strangely enough, the discrepancy between apparent and actual beauty is greater in proportion to the unapproachableness of the object, is the law observed. For every distance from the eye there is a peculiar kind of beauty, or a different system of lines of form; the sight of that beauty is reserved for that distance, and for that alone. If you approach nearer, that kind of beauty is lost, and another succeeds, to be disorganised and reduced to strange and incomprehensible means and appliances in its turn. If you desire to perceive the great harmonies of the form of a rocky mountain, you must not ascend upon its sides. All is there disorder and accident, or seems so; sudden starts of its shattered beds hither and thither; ugly struggles of unexpected strength from under the ground; fallen fragments, toppling one over another into more helpless fall. Retire from it, and, as your eye commands it more and more, as you see the ruined mountain world with a wider glance, behold! dim sympathies begin to busy themselves in the disjointed mass; line binds itself into stealthy fellowship with line; group by group, the helpless fragments gather themselves into ordered companies; new captains of hosts and masses of battalions become visible, one by one, and far away answers of foot to foot, and of bone to bone, until the powerless chaos is seen risen up with girded loins, and not one piece of all the unregarded heap could now be spared from the mystic whole.

§ **XVIII.** Now it is indeed true that where nature loses one kind of beauty, as you approach it, she substitutes another; this is worthy of her infinite power: and, as we shall see, art can sometimes follow her even in doing this; but all I insist upon at present is, that the several effects of nature are each worked with means referred to a particular distance, and producing their effect at that distance only. Take a singular and marked instance: When the sun rises behind a ridge of pines, and those pines are seen from a distance of a mile or two, against his light, the whole form of the tree, trunk, branches, and all, becomes one frostwork of intensely brilliant silver, which is relieved against the clear sky like a burning fringe, for some distance on either side of the sun.[71] Now suppose that a person who had never seen pines were, for the first time in his life, to see them under this strange aspect, and, reasoning as to the means by which such effect could be produced, laboriously to approach the eastern ridge, how would he be amazed to find that the fiery spectres had been produced by trees with swarthy and grey trunks, and dark green leaves! We, in our simplicity, if we had been required to produce such an appearance, should have built up trees of chased silver, with trunks of glass, and then been grievously amazed to find that, at two miles off, neither silver nor glass were any more visible; but nature knew better, and prepared for her fairy work with the strong branches and dark leaves, in her own mysterious way.

§ XIX. Now this is exactly what you have to do with your good ornament. It may be that it is capable of being approached, as well as likely to be seen far away, and then it ought to have microscopic qualities, as the pine leaves have, which will bear approach. But your calculation of its purpose is for a glory to be produced at a given distance; it may be here, or may be there, but it is a given distance; and the excellence of the ornament depends upon its fitting that distance, and being seen better there than anywhere else, and having a particular function and form which it can only discharge and assume there. You are never to say that ornament has great merit because "you cannot see the beauty of it here;" but, it has great merit because "you can see its beauty here only." And to give it this merit is just about as difficult a task as I could well set you. I have above noted the two ways in which it is done: the one, being merely rough cutting, may be passed over; the other, which is scientific alteration of design, falls, itself, into two great branches, Simplification and Emphasis.

A word or two is necessary on each of these heads.

§ XX. When an ornamental work is intended to be seen near, if its composition be indeed fine, the subdued and delicate portions of the design lead to, and unite, the energetic parts, and those energetic parts form with the rest a whole, in which their own immediate relations to each other are not perceived. Remove this design to a distance, and the connecting delicacies vanish, the energies alone remain, now either disconnected altogether, or assuming with each other new relations, which, not having been intended by the designer, will probably be painful. There is a like, and a more palpable, effect, in the retirement of a band of music in which the instruments are of very unequal powers; the fluting and fifeing expire, the drumming remains, and that in a painful arrangement, as demanding something which is unheard. In like manner, as the designer at arm's length removes or elevates his work, fine gradations, and roundings, and incidents, vanish, and a totally unexpected arrangement is established between the remainder of the markings, certainly confused, and in all probability painful.

§ XXI. The art of architectural design is therefore, first, the preparation for this beforehand, the rejection of all the delicate passages as worse than useless, and the fixing the thought upon the arrangement of the features which will remain visible far away. Nor does this always imply a diminution of resource; for, while it may be assumed as a law that fine modulation of surface in light becomes quickly invisible as the object retires, there are a softness and mystery given to the harder markings, which enable them to be safely used as media of expression. There is an exquisite example of this use, in the head of the Adam of the Ducal Palace. It is only at the height of 17 or 18 feet above the eye; nevertheless, the sculptor felt it was no use to trouble himself about drawing the corners of the mouth, or the lines of the lips, delicately, at that distance; his object has been to mark them clearly, and to prevent accidental shadows from concealing them, or altering their expression. The lips are cut thin and sharp, so that their line cannot be mistaken, and a good deep drill-hole struck into the angle of the mouth; the eye is anxious and questioning, and one is surprised, from below, to perceive a kind of darkness in the iris of it, neither like color, nor like a circular furrow. The expedient can only be discovered by ascending to the level of the head; it is one which would have been quite inadmissible except in distant work, six drill-holes cut into the iris, round a central one for the pupil.

§ XXII. By just calculation, like this, of the means at our disposal, by beautiful arrangement of the prominent features, and by choice of different subjects for different places, choosing the broadest forms for the farthest distance, it is possible to give the impression, not only of perfection, but of an exquisite delicacy, to the most distant ornament. And this is the true sign of the right having been done, and the utmost possible power attained:—The spectator should be satisfied to stay in his place, feeling the decoration, wherever it may be, equally rich, full, and lovely: not desiring to climb the steeples in order to examine it, but sure that he has it all, where he is. Perhaps the capitals of the cathedral of Genoa are the best instances of absolute perfection in this kind: seen from below, they appear as rich as the frosted silver of the Strada degli Orefici; and the nearer you approach them, the less delicate they seem.

§ XXIII. This is, however, not the only mode, though the best, in which ornament is adapted for distance. The other is emphasis,—the unnatural insisting upon explanatory lines, where the subject would otherwise become unintelligible. It is to be remembered that, by a deep and narrow incision, an architect has the power, at least in sunshine, of drawing a black line on stone, just as vigorously as it can be drawn with chalk on grey paper; and that he may thus, wherever and in the degree that he chooses, substitute chalk sketching for sculpture. They are curiously mingled by the Romans. The bas-reliefs of the Arc d'Orange are small, and would be confused, though in bold relief, if they depended for intelligibility on the relief only; but each figure is outlined by a strong incision at its edge into the background, and all the ornaments on the armor are simply drawn with incised lines, and not cut out at all. A similar use of lines is made by the Gothic nations in all their early sculpture, and with delicious effect. Now, to draw a mere pattern—as, for instance, the bearings of a shield—with these simple incisions, would, I suppose, occupy an able sculptor twenty minutes or half an hour; and the pattern is then clearly seen, under all circumstances of light and shade; there can be no mistake about it, and no missing it. To carve out the bearings in due and finished relief would occupy a long summer's day, and the results would be feeble and indecipherable in the best lights, and in some lights totally and hopelessly invisible, ignored, non-existant. Now the Renaissance architects, and our modern ones, despise the simple expedient of the rough Roman or barbarian. They do not care to be understood. They care only to speak finely, and be thought great orators, if one could only hear them. So I leave you to choose between the old men, who took minutes to tell things plainly, and the modern men, who take days to tell them unintelligibly.

§ XXIV. All expedients of this kind, both of simplification and energy, for the expression of details at a distance where their actual forms would have been invisible, but more especially this linear method, I shall call Proutism; for the greatest master of the art in modern times has been Samuel Prout. He actually takes up buildings of the later times in which the ornament has been too refined for its place, and translates it into the energised linear ornament of earlier art: and to this power of taking the life and essence of decoration, and putting it into a perfectly intelligible form, when its own fulness would have been confused, is owing the especial power of his drawings. Nothing can be more closely analogous than the method with which an old Lombard uses his chisel, and that with which Prout uses the reed-pen; and we shall see presently farther correspondence in their feeling about the enrichment of luminous surfaces.

§ XXV. Now, all that has been hitherto said refers to ornament whose distance is fixed, or nearly so; as when it is at any considerable height from the ground, supposing the spectator to desire to see it, and to get as near it as he can. But the distance of ornament is never fixed to the general spectator. The tower of a cathedral is bound to look well, ten miles off, or five miles, or half a mile, or within fifty yards. The ornaments of its top have fixed distances, compared with those of its base; but quite unfixed distances in their relation to the great world: and the ornaments of the base have no fixed distance at all. They are bound to look well from the other side of the cathedral close, and to look equally well, or better, as we enter the cathedral door. How are we to manage this?

§ XXVI. As nature manages it. I said above, § XVII., that for every distance from the eye there was a different system of form in all natural objects: this is to be so then in architecture. The lesser ornament is to be grafted on the greater, and third or fourth orders of ornaments upon this again, as need may be, until we reach the limits of possible sight; each order of ornament being adapted for a different distance: first, for example, the great masses,—the buttresses and stories and black windows and broad cornices of the tower, which give it make, and organism, as it rises over the horizon, half a score of miles away: then the traceries and shafts and pinnacles, which give it richness as we approach: then the niches and statues and knobs and flowers, which we can only see when we stand beneath it. At this third order of ornament, we may pause, in the upper portions; but on the roofs of the niches, and the robes of the statues, and the rolls of the mouldings, comes a fourth order of ornament, as delicate as the eye can follow, when any of these features may be approached.

§ XXVII. All good ornamentation is thus arborescent, as it were, one class of it branching out of another and sustained by it; and its nobility consists in this, that whatever order or class of it we may be contemplating, we shall find it subordinated to a greater, simpler, and more powerful; and if we then contemplate the greater order, we shall find it again subordinated to a greater still; until the greatest can only be quite grasped by retiring to the limits of distance commanding it.

And if this subordination be not complete, the ornament is bad: if the figurings and chasings and borderings of a dress be not subordinated to the folds of it,—if the folds are not subordinate to the action and mass of the figure,—if this action and mass not to the divisions of the recesses and shafts among which it stands,—if these not to the shadows of the great arches and buttresses of the whole building, in each case there is error; much more if all be contending with each other and striving for attention at the same time.

§ XXVIII. It is nevertheless evident, that, however perfect this distribution, there cannot be orders adapted to every distance of the spectator. Between the ranks of ornament there must always be a bold separation; and there must be many intermediate distances, where we are too far off to see the lesser rank clearly, and yet too near to grasp the next higher rank wholly: and at all these distances the spectator will feel himself ill-placed, and will desire to go nearer or farther away. This must be the case in all noble work, natural or artificial. It is exactly the same with respect to Rouen cathedral or the Mont Blanc. We like to see them from the other side of the Seine, or of the lake of Geneva; from the Marché aux Fleurs, or the Valley of Chamouni; from the parapets of the apse, or the crags of the Montagne de la Côte: but there are intermediate distances which dissatisfy us in either case, and from which one is in haste either to advance or to retire.

§ XXIX. Directly opposed to this ordered, disciplined, well officered and variously ranked ornament, this type of divine, and therefore of all good human government, is the democratic ornament, in which all is equally influential, and has equal office and authority; that is to say, none of it any office nor authority, but a life of continual struggle for independence and notoriety, or of gambling for chance regards. The English perpendicular work is by far the worst of this kind that I know; its main idea, or decimal fraction of an idea, being to cover its walls with dull, successive, eternity of reticulation, to fill with equal foils the equal interstices between the equal bars, and charge the interminable blanks with statues and rosettes, invisible at a distance, and uninteresting near.

The early Lombardic, Veronese, and Norman work is the exact reverse of this; being divided first into large masses, and these masses covered with minute chasing and surface work, which fill them with interest, and yet do not disturb nor divide their greatness. The lights are kept broad and bright, and yet are found on near approach to be charged with intricate design. This, again, is a part of the great system of treatment which I shall hereafter call "Proutism;" much of what is thought mannerism and imperfection in Prout's work, being the result of his determined resolution that minor details shall never break up his large masses of light.

§ XXX. Such are the main principles to be observed in the adaptation of ornament to the sight. We have lastly to inquire by what method, and in what quantities, the ornament, thus adapted to mental contemplation, and prepared for its physical position, may most wisely be arranged. I think the method ought first to be considered, and the quantity last; for the advisable quantity depends upon the method.

§ XXXI. It was said above, that the proper treatment or arrangement of ornament was that which expressed the laws and ways of Deity. Now, the subordination of visible orders to each other, just noted, is one expression of these. But there may also—must also—be a subordination and obedience of the parts of each order to some visible law, out of itself, but having reference to itself only (not to any upper order): some law which shall not oppress, but guide, limit, and sustain.

In the tenth chapter of the second volume of "Modern Painters," the reader will find that I traced one part of the beauty of God's creation to the expression of a self-restrained liberty: that is to say, the image of that perfection of divine action, which, though free to work in arbitrary methods, works always in consistent methods, called by us Laws.

Now, correspondingly, we find that when these natural objects are to become subjects of the art of man, their perfect treatment is an image of the perfection of human action: a voluntary submission to divine law.

It was suggested to me but lately by the friend to whose originality of thought I have before expressed my obligations, Mr. Newton, that the Greek pediment, with its enclosed sculptures, represented to the Greek mind the law of Fate, confining human action within limits not to be overpassed. I do not believe the Greeks ever distinctly thought of this; but the instinct of all the human race, since the world began, agrees in some expression of such limitation as one of the first necessities of good ornament.[72] And this expression is heightened, rather than diminished, when some portion of the design slightly breaks the law to which the rest is subjected; it is like expressing the use of miracles in the divine government; or, perhaps, in slighter degrees, the relaxing of a law, generally imperative, in compliance with some more imperative need—the hungering of David. How eagerly this special infringement of a general law was sometimes sought by the mediæval workmen, I shall be frequently able to point out to the reader; but I remember just now a most curious instance, in an archivolt of a house in the Corte del Remer close to the Rialto at Venice. It is composed of a wreath of flower-work—a constant Byzantine design—with an animal in each coil; the whole enclosed between two fillets. Each animal, leaping or eating, scratching or biting, is kept nevertheless strictly within its coil, and between the fillets. Not the shake of an ear, not the tip of a tail, overpasses this appointed line, through a series of some five-and-twenty or thirty animals; until, on a sudden, and by mutual consent, two little beasts (not looking, for the rest, more rampant than the others), one on each side, lay their small paws across the enclosing fillet at exactly the same point of its course, and thus break the continuity of its line. Two ears of corn, or leaves, do the same thing in the mouldings round the northern door of the Baptistery at Florence.

§ XXXII. Observe, however, and this is of the utmost possible importance, that the value of this type does not consist in the mere shutting of the ornament into a certain space, but in the acknowledgment by the ornament of the fitness of the limitation—of its own perfect willingness to submit to it; nay, of a predisposition in itself to fall into the ordained form, without any direct expression of the command to do so; an anticipation of the authority, and an instant and willing submission to it, in every fibre and spray: not merely willing, but happy submission, as being pleased rather than vexed to have so beautiful a law suggested to it, and one which to follow is so justly in accordance with its own nature. You must not cut out a branch of hawthorn as it grows, and rule a triangle round it, and suppose that it is then submitted to law. Not a bit of it. It is only put in a cage, and will look as if it must get out, for its life, or wither in the confinement. But the spirit of triangle must be put into the hawthorn. It must suck in isoscelesism with its sap. Thorn and blossom, leaf and spray, must grow with an awful sense of triangular necessity upon them, for the guidance of which they are to be thankful, and to grow all the stronger and more gloriously. And though there may be a transgression here and there, and an adaptation to some other need, or a reaching forth to some other end greater even than the triangle, yet this liberty is to be always accepted under a solemn sense of special permission; and when the full form is reached and the entire submission expressed, and every blossom has a thrilling sense of its responsibility down into its tiniest stamen, you may take your terminal line away if you will. No need for it any more. The commandment is written on the heart of the thing.

§ XXXIII. Then, besides this obedience to external law, there is the obedience to internal headship, which constitutes the unity of ornament, of which I think enough has been said for my present purpose in the chapter on Unity in the second vol. of "Modern Painters." But I hardly know whether to arrange as an expression of a divine law, or a representation of a physical fact, the alternation of shade with light which, in equal succession, forms one of the chief elements of continuous ornament, and in some peculiar ones, such as dentils and billet mouldings, is the source of their only charm. The opposition of good and evil, the antagonism of the entire human system (so ably worked out by Lord Lindsay), the alternation of labor with rest, the mingling of life with death, or the actual physical fact of the division of light from darkness, and of the falling and rising of night and day, are all typified or represented by these chains of shade and light of which the eye never wearies, though their true meaning may never occur to the thoughts.

§ XXXIV. The next question respecting the arrangement of ornament is one closely connected also with its quantity. The system of creation is one in which "God's creatures leap not, but express a feast, where all the guests sit close, and nothing wants." It is also a feast, where there is nothing redundant. So, then, in distributing our ornament, there must never be any sense of gap or blank, neither any sense of there being a single member, or fragment of a member, which could be spared. Whatever has nothing to do, whatever could go without being missed, is not ornament; it is deformity and encumbrance. Away with it. And, on the other hand, care must be taken either to diffuse the ornament which we permit, in due relation over the whole building, or so to concentrate it, as never to leave a sense of its having got into knots, and curdled upon some points, and left the rest of the building whey. It is very difficult to give the rules, or analyse the feelings, which should direct us in this matter: for some shafts may be carved and others left unfinished, and that with advantage; some windows may be jewelled like Aladdin's, and one left plain, and still with advantage; the door or doors, or a single turret, or the whole western façade of a church, or the apse or transept, may be made special subjects of decoration, and the rest left plain, and still sometimes with advantage. But in all such cases there is either sign of that feeling which I advocated in the First Chapter of the "Seven Lamps," the desire of rather doing some portion of the building as we would have it, and leaving the rest plain, than doing the whole imperfectly; or else there is choice made of some important feature, to which, as more honorable than the rest, the decoration is confined. The evil is when, without system, and without preference of the nobler members, the ornament alternates between sickly luxuriance and sudden blankness. In many of our Scotch and English abbeys, especially Melrose, this is painfully felt; but the worst instance I have ever seen is the window in the side of the arch under the Wellington statue, next St. George's Hospital. In the first place, a window has no business there at all; in the second, the bars of the window are not the proper place for decoration, especially wavy decoration, which one instantly fancies of cast iron; in the third, the richness of the ornament is a mere patch and eruption upon the wall, and one hardly knows whether to be most irritated at the affectation of severity in the rest, or at the vain luxuriance of the dissolute parallelogram.

§ XXXV. Finally, as regards quantity of ornament I have already said, again and again, you cannot have too much if it be good; that is, if it be thoroughly united and harmonised by the laws hitherto insisted upon. But you may easily have too much if you have more than you have sense to manage. For with every added order of ornament increases the difficulty of discipline. It is exactly the same as in war: you cannot, as an abstract law, have too many soldiers, but you may easily have more than the country is able to sustain, or than your generalship is competent to command. And every regiment which you cannot manage will, on the day of battle, be in your way, and encumber the movements it is not in disposition to sustain.

§ XXXVI. As an architect, therefore, you are modestly to measure your capacity of governing ornament. Remember, its essence,—its being ornament at all, consists in its being governed. Lose your authority over it, let it command you, or lead you, or dictate to you in any wise, and it is an offence, an incumbrance, and a dishonor. And it is always ready to do this; wild to get the bit in its teeth, and rush forth on its own devices. Measure, therefore, your strength; and as long as there is no chance of mutiny, add soldier to soldier, battalion to battalion; but be assured that all are heartily in the cause, and that there is not one of whose position you are ignorant, or whose service you could spare.

FOOTNOTES:

[70] Vide "Seven Lamps," Chap. IV. § 34.

[71] Shakspeare and Wordsworth (I think they only) have noticed this, Shakspeare, in Richard II.:—

"But when, from under this terrestrial ball,
He fires the proud tops of the eastern pines."

And Wordsworth, in one of his minor poems, on leaving Italy:

"My thoughts become bright like yon edging of pines
On the steep's lofty verge—how it blackened the air!
But, touched from behind by the sun, it now shines
With threads that seem part of his own silver hair."

CHAPTER XXII

THE ANGLE

§ I. We have now examined the treatment and specific kinds of ornament at our command. We have lastly to note the fittest places for their disposal. Not but that all kinds of ornament are used in all places; but there are some parts of the building, which, without ornament, are more painful than others, and some which wear ornament more gracefully than others; so that, although an able architect will always be finding out some new and unexpected modes of decoration, and fitting his ornament into wonderful places where it is least expected, there are, nevertheless, one or two general laws which may be noted respecting every one of the parts of a building, laws not (except a few) imperative like those of construction, but yet generally expedient, and good to be understood, if it were only that we might enjoy the brilliant methods in which they are sometimes broken. I shall note, however, only a few of the simplest; to trace them into their ramifications, and class in due order the known or possible methods of decoration for each part of a building, would alone require a large volume, and be, I think, a somewhat useless work; for there is often a high pleasure in the very unexpectedness of the ornament, which would be destroyed by too elaborate an arrangement of its kinds.

§ II. I think that the reader must, by this time, so thoroughly understand the connection of the parts of a building, that I may class together, in treating of decoration, several parts which I kept separate in speaking of construction. Thus I shall put under one head (A) the base of the wall and of the shaft; then (B) the wall veil and shaft itself; then (C) the cornice and capital; then (D) the jamb and archivolt, including the arches both over shafts and apertures, and the jambs of apertures, which are closely connected with their archivolts; finally (E) the roof, including the real roof, and the minor roofs or gables of pinnacles and arches. I think, under these divisions, all may be arranged which is necessary to be generally stated; for tracery decorations or aperture fillings are but smaller forms of application of the arch, and the cusps are merely smaller spandrils, while buttresses have, as far as I know, no specific ornament. The best are those which have least; and the little they have resolves itself into pinnacles, which are common to other portions of the building, or into small shafts, arches, and niches, of still more general applicability. We shall therefore have only five divisions to examine in succession, from foundation to roof.

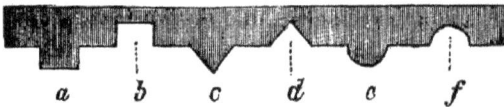

Fig. LI.

§ III. But in the decoration of these several parts, certain minor conditions of ornament occur which are of perfectly general application. For instance, whether, in archivolts, jambs, or buttresses, or in square piers, or at the extremity of the entire building, we necessarily have the awkward (moral or architectural) feature, the corner. How to turn a corner gracefully becomes, therefore, a perfectly general question; to be examined without reference to any particular part of the edifice.

§ IV. Again, the furrows and ridges by which bars of parallel light and shade are obtained, whether these are employed in arches, or jambs, or bases, or cornices, must of necessity present one or more of six forms: square projection, a (Fig. LI.), or square recess, b, sharp projection, c, or sharp recess, d, curved projection, e, or curved recess, f. What odd curves the projection or recess may assume, or how these different conditions may be mixed and run into one another, is not our present business. We note only the six distinct kinds or types.

Now, when these ridges or furrows are on a small scale they often themselves constitute all the ornament required for larger features, and are left smooth cut; but on a very large scale they are apt to become insipid, and they require a sub-ornament of their own, the consideration of which is, of course, in great part, general, and irrespective of the place held by the mouldings in the building itself: which consideration I think we had better undertake first of all.

§ V. But before we come to particular examination of these minor forms, let us see how far we can simplify it. Look back to Fig. LI., above. There are distinguished in it six forms of moulding. Of these, c is nothing but a small corner; but, for convenience sake, it is better to call it an edge, and to consider its decoration together with that of the member a, which is called a fillet; while e, which I shall call a roll (because I do not choose to assume that it shall be only of the semicircular section here given), is also best considered together with its relative recess, f; and because the shape of a recess is of no great consequence, I shall class all the three recesses together, and we shall thus have only three subjects for separate consideration:—

1. The Angle.
2. The Edge and Fillet.
3. The Roll and Recess.

§ VI. There are two other general forms which may probably occur to the reader's mind, namely, the ridge (as of a roof), which is a corner laid on its back, or sloping,—a supine corner, decorated in a very different manner from a stiff upright corner: and the point, which is a concentrated corner, and has wonderfully elaborate decorations all to its insignificant self, finials, and spikes, and I know not what more. But both these conditions are so closely connected with roofs (even the cusp finial being a kind of pendant to a small roof), that I think it better to class them and their ornament under the head of roof decoration, together with the whole tribe of crockets and bosses; so that we shall be here concerned only with the three subjects above distinguished: and, first, the corner or Angle.

§ VII. The mathematician knows there are many kinds of angles; but the one we have principally to deal with now, is that which the reader may very easily conceive as the corner of a square house, or square anything. It is of course the one of most frequent occurrence; and its treatment, once understood, may, with slight modification, be referred to other corners, sharper or blunter, or with curved sides.

§ VIII. Evidently the first and roughest idea which would occur to any one who found a corner troublesome, would be to cut it off. This is a very summary and tyrannical proceeding, somewhat barbarous, yet advisable if nothing else can be done: an amputated corner is said to be chamfered. It can, however, evidently be cut off in three ways: 1. with a concave cut, a; 2. with a straight cut, b; 3. with a convex cut, c, Fig. LII.

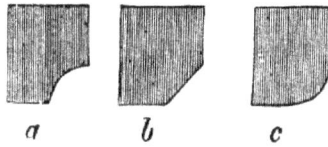

Fig. LII.

The first two methods, the most violent and summary, have the apparent disadvantage that we get by them,—two corners instead of one; much milder corners, however, and with a different light and shade between them; so that both methods are often very expedient. You may see the straight chamfer (b) on most lamp posts, and pillars at railway stations, it being the easiest to cut: the concave chamfer requires more care, and occurs generally in well-finished but simple architecture—very beautifully in the small arches of the Broletto of Como, Plate V.; and the straight chamfer in architecture of every kind, very constantly in Norman cornices and arches, as in Fig. 2, Plate IV., at Sens.

§ IX. The third, or convex chamfer, as it is the gentlest mode of treatment, so (as in medicine and morals) it is very generally the best. For while the two other methods produce two corners instead of one, this gentle chamfer does verily get rid of the corner altogether, and substitutes a soft curve in its place.

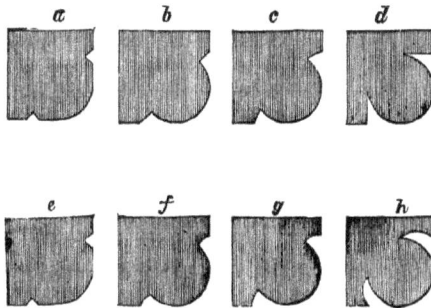

Fig. LIII.

But it has, in the form above given, this grave disadvantage, that it looks as if the corner had been rubbed or worn off, blunted by time and weather, and in want of sharpening again. A great deal often depends, and in such a case as this, everything depends, on the Voluntariness of the ornament. The work of time is beautiful on surfaces, but not on edges intended to be sharp. Even if we needed them blunt, we should not like them blunt on compulsion; so, to show that the bluntness is our own ordaining, we will put a slight incised line to mark off the rounding, and show that it goes no farther than we choose. We shall thus have the section a, Fig. LIII.; and this mode of turning an angle is one of the very best ever invented. By enlarging and deepening the incision, we get in succession the forms b, c, d; and by describing a small equal arc on each of the sloping lines of these figures, we get e, f, g, h.

§ X. I do not know whether these mouldings are called by architects chamfers or beads; but I think bead a bad word for a continuous moulding, and the proper sense of the word chamfer is fixed by Spenser as descriptive not merely of truncation, but of trench or furrow:—

"Tho gin you, fond flies, the cold to scorn,
And, crowing in pipes made of green corn,
You thinken to be lords of the year;
But eft when ye count you freed from fear,
Comes the breme winter with chamfred brows,
Full of wrinkles and frosty furrows."

So I shall call the above mouldings beaded chamfers, when there is any chance of confusion with the plain chamfer, a, or b, of Fig. LII.: and when there is no such chance, I shall use the word chamfer only.

§ XI. Of those above given, b is the constant chamfer of Venice, and a of Verona: a being the grandest and best, and having a peculiar precision and quaintness of effect about it. I found it twice in Venice, used on the sharp angle, as at a and b, Fig. LIV., a being from the angle of a house on the Rio San Zulian, and b from the windows of the church of San Stefano.

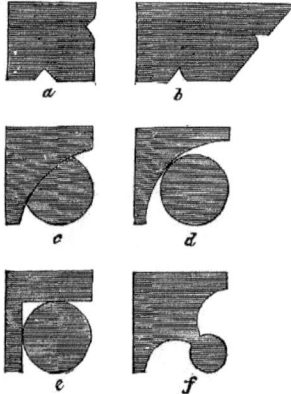

Fig. LIV.

§ XII. There is, however, evidently another variety of the chamfers, f and g, Fig. LIII., formed by an unbroken curve instead of two curves, as c, Fig. LIV.; and when this, or the chamfer d, Fig. LIII., is large, it is impossible to say whether they have been devised from the incised angle, or from small shafts set in a nook, as at e, Fig. LIV., or in the hollow of the curved chamfer, as d, Fig. LIV. In general, however, the shallow chamfers, a, b, e, and f, Fig. LIII., are peculiar to southern work; and may be assumed to have been derived from the incised angle, while the deep chamfers, c, d, g, h, are characteristic of northern work, and may be partly derived or imitated from the angle shaft; while, with the usual extravagance of the northern architects, they are cut deeper and deeper until we arrive at the condition f, Fig. LIV., which is the favorite chamfer at Bourges and Bayeux, and in other good French work.

I have placed in the Appendix[73] a figure belonging to this subject, but which cannot interest the general reader, showing the number of possible chamfers with a roll moulding of given size.

§ XIII. If we take the plain chamfer, b, of Fig. LII., on a large scale, as at a, Fig. LV., and bead both its edges, cutting away the parts there shaded, we shall have a form much used in richly decorated Gothic, both in England and Italy. It might be more simply described as the chamfer a of Fig. LII., with an incision on each edge; but the part here shaded is often worked into ornamental forms, not being entirely cut away.

Fig. LV.

§ XIV. Many other mouldings, which at first sight appear very elaborate, are nothing more than a chamfer, with a series of small echoes of it on each side, dying away with a ripple on the surface of the wall, as in b, Fig. LV., from Coutances (observe, here the white part is the solid stone, the shade is cut away).

Chamfers of this kind are used on a small scale and in delicate work: the coarse chamfers are found on all scales: f and g, Fig. LIII., in Venice, form the great angles of almost every Gothic palace; the roll being a foot or a foot and a half round, and treated as a shaft, with a capital and fresh base at every story, while the stones of which it is composed form alternate quoins in the brickwork beyond the chamfer curve. I need hardly say how much nobler this arrangement is than a common quoined angle; it gives a finish to the aspect of the whole pile attainable in no other way. And thus much may serve concerning angle decoration by chamfer.

FOOTNOTES:

[73] Appendix 23: "Varieties of Chamfer."

CHAPTER XXIII

THE EDGE AND FILLET

§ I. The decoration of the angle by various forms of chamfer and bead, as above described, is the quietest method we can employ; too quiet, when great energy is to be given to the moulding, and impossible, when, instead of a bold angle, we have to deal with a small projecting edge, like c in Fig. LI. In such cases we may employ a decoration, far ruder and easier in its simplest conditions than the bead, far more effective when not used in too great profusion; and of which the complete developments are the source of mouldings at once the most picturesque and most serviceable which the Gothic builders invented.

§ II. The gunwales of the Venetian heavy barges being liable to somewhat rough collision with each other, and with the walls of the streets, are generally protected by a piece of timber, which projects in the form of the fillet, a, Fig. LI.; but which, like all other fillets, may, if we so choose, be considered as composed of two angles or edges, which the natural and most wholesome love of the Venetian boatmen for ornament, otherwise strikingly evidenced by their painted sails and glittering flag-vanes, will not suffer to remain wholly undecorated. The rough service of these timbers, however, will not admit of rich ornament, and the boatbuilder usually contents himself with cutting a series of notches in each edge, one series alternating with the other, as represented at 1, Plate IX.

§ III. In that simple ornament, not as confined to Venetian boats, but as representative of a general human instinct to hack at an edge, demonstrated by all school-boys and all idle possessors of penknives or other cutting instruments on both sides of the Atlantic;—in that rude Venetian gunwale, I say, is the germ of all the ornament which has touched, with its rich successions of angular shadow, the portals and archivolts of nearly every early building of importance, from the North Cape to the Straits of Messina. Nor are the modifications of the first suggestion intricate. All that is generic in their character may be seen on Plate IX. at a glance.

Plate IX. EDGE DECORATION.

§ IV. Taking a piece of stone instead of timber, and enlarging the notches, until they meet each other, we have the condition 2, which is a moulding from the tomb of the Doge Andrea Dandolo, in St. Mark's. Now, considering this moulding as composed of two decorated edges, each edge will be reduced, by the meeting of the notches, to a series of four-sided pyramids (as marked off by the dotted lines), which, the notches here being shallow, will be shallow pyramids; but by deepening the notches, we get them as at 3, with a profile a, more or less steep. This moulding I shall always call "the plain dogtooth;" it is used in profusion in the Venetian and Veronese Gothic, generally set with its front to the spectator, as here at 3; but its effect may be much varied by placing it obliquely (4, and profile as at b); or with one side horizontal (5, and profile c). Of these three conditions, 3 and 5 are exactly the same in reality, only differently placed; but in 4 the pyramid is obtuse, and the inclination of its base variable, the upper side of it being always kept vertical. It is comparatively rare. Of the three, the last, 5, is far the most brilliant in effect, giving in the distance a zigzag form to the high light on it, and a full sharp shadow below. The use of this shadow is sufficiently seen by fig. 7 in this plate (the arch on the left, the number beneath it), in which these levelled dogteeth, with a small interval between each, are employed to set off by their vigor the delicacy of floral ornament above. This arch is the side of a niche from the tomb of Can Signorio della Scala, at Verona; and the value, as well as the distant expression of its dogtooth, may be seen by referring to Prout's beautiful drawing of this tomb in his "Sketches in France and Italy." I have before observed that this artist never fails of seizing the true and leading expression of whatever he touches: he has made this ornament the leading feature of the niche, expressing it, as in distance it is only expressible, by a zigzag.

§ V. The reader may perhaps be surprised at my speaking so highly of this drawing, if he take the pains to compare Prout's symbolism of the work on the niche with the facts as they stand here in Plate IX. But the truth is that Prout has rendered the effect of the monument on the mind of the passer-by;—the effect it was intended to have on every man who turned the corner of the street beneath it: and in this sense there is actually more truth and likeness[74] in Prout's translation than in my fac-simile, made diligently by peering into the details from a ladder. I do not say that all the symbolism in Prout's Sketch is the best possible; but it is the best which any architectural draughtsman has yet invented; and in its application to special subjects it always shows curious internal evidence that the sketch has been made on the spot, and that the artist tried to draw what he saw, not to invent an attractive subject. I shall notice other instances of this hereafter.

§ VI. The dogtooth, employed in this simple form, is, however, rather a foil for other ornament, than itself a satisfactory or generally available decoration. It is, however, easy to enrich it as we choose: taking up its simple form at 3, and describing the arcs marked by the dotted lines upon its sides, and cutting a small triangular cavity between them, we shall leave its ridges somewhat rudely representative of four leaves, as at 8, which is the section and front view of one of the Venetian stone cornices described above, Chap. XIV., § IV., the figure 8 being here put in the hollow of the gutter. The dogtooth is put on the outer lower truncation, and is actually in position as fig. 5; but being always looked up to, is to the spectator as 3, and always rich and effective. The dogteeth are perhaps most frequently expanded to the width of fig. 9.

§ VII. As in nearly all other ornaments previously described, so in this,—we have only to deepen the Italian cutting, and we shall get the Northern type. If we make the original pyramid somewhat steeper, and instead of lightly incising, cut it through, so as to have the leaves held only by their points to the base, we shall have the English dogtooth; somewhat vulgar in its piquancy, when compared with French mouldings of a similar kind.[75] It occurs, I think, on one house in Venice, in the Campo St. Polo; but the ordinary moulding, with light incisions, is frequent in archivolts and architraves, as well as in the roof cornices.

§ VIII. This being the simplest treatment of the pyramid, fig. 10, from the refectory of Wenlock Abbey, is an example of the simplest decoration of the recesses or inward angles between the pyramids; that is to say, of a simple hacked edge like one of those in fig. 2, the cuts being taken up and decorated instead of the points. Each is worked into a small trefoiled arch, with an incision round it to mark its outline, and another slight incision above, expressing the angle of the first cutting. I said that the teeth in fig. 7 had in distance the effect of a zigzag: in fig. 10 this zigzag effect is seized upon and developed, but with the easiest and roughest work; the angular incision being a mere limiting line, like that described in § IX. of the last chapter. But hence the farther steps to every condition of Norman ornament are self evident. I do not say that all of them arose from development of the dogtooth in this manner, many being quite independent inventions and uses of zigzag lines; still, they may all be referred to this simple type as their root and representative, that is to say, the mere hack of the Venetian gunwale, with a limiting line following the resultant zigzag.

§ IX. Fig. 11 is a singular and much more artificial condition, cast in brick, from the church of the Frari, and given here only for future reference. Fig. 12, resulting from a fillet with the cuts on each of its edges interrupted by a bar, is a frequent Venetian moulding, and of great value; but the plain or leaved dogteeth have been the favorites, and that to such a degree, that even the Renaissance architects took them up; and the best bit of Renaissance design in Venice, the side of the Ducal Palace next the Bridge of Sighs, owes great part of its splendor to its foundation, faced with large flat dogteeth, each about a foot wide in the base, with their points truncated, and alternating with cavities which are their own negatives or casts.

§ X. One other form of the dogtooth is of great importance in northern architecture, that produced by oblique cuts slightly curved, as in the margin, Fig. LVI. It is susceptible of the most fantastic and endless decoration; each of the resulting leaves being, in the early porches of Rouen and Lisieux, hollowed out and worked into branching tracery: and at Bourges, for distant effect, worked into plain leaves, or bold bony processes with knobs at the points, and near the spectator, into crouching demons and broad winged owls, and other fancies and intricacies, innumerable and inexpressible.

Fig. LVI.

§ XI. Thus much is enough to be noted respecting edge decoration. We were next to consider the fillet. Professor Willis has noticed an ornament, which he has called the Venetian dentil, "as the most universal ornament in its own district that ever I met with;" but has not noticed the reason for its frequency. It is nevertheless highly interesting.

The whole early architecture of Venice is architecture of incrustation: this has not been enough noticed in its peculiar relation to that of the rest of Italy. There is, indeed, much incrusted architecture throughout Italy, in elaborate ecclesiastical work, but there is more which is frankly of brick, or thoroughly of stone. But the Venetian habitually incrusted his work with nacre; he built his houses, even the meanest, as if he had been a shell-fish,—roughly inside, mother-of-pearl on the surface: he was content, perforce, to gather the clay of the Brenta banks, and bake it into brick for his substance of wall; but he overlaid it with the wealth of ocean, with the most precious foreign marbles. You might fancy early Venice one wilderness of brick, which a petrifying sea had beaten upon till it coated it with marble: at first a dark city—washed white by the sea foam. And I told you before that it was also a city of shafts and arches, and that its dwellings were raised upon continuous arcades, among which the sea waves wandered. Hence the thoughts of its builders were early and constantly directed to the incrustation of arches.

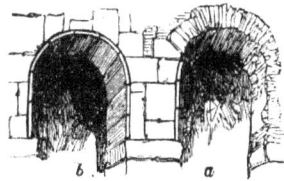

Fig. LVII.

§ XII. In Fig. LVII. I have given two of these Byzantine stilted arches: the one on the right, a, as they now too often appear, in its bare brickwork; that on the left, with its alabaster covering, literally marble defensive armor, riveted together in pieces, which follow the contours of the building. Now, on the wall, these pieces are mere flat slabs cut to the arch outline; but under the soffit of the arch the marble mail is curved, often cut singularly thin, like bent tiles, and fitted together so that the pieces would sustain each other even without rivets. It is of course desirable that this thin sub-arch of marble should project enough to sustain the facing of the wall; and the reader will see, in Fig. LVII., that its edge forms a kind of narrow band round the arch (b), a band which the least enrichment would render a valuable decorative feature. Now this band is, of course, if the soffit-pieces project a little beyond the face of the wall-pieces, a mere fillet, like the wooden gunwale in Plate IX.; and the question is, how to enrich it most wisely. It might easily have been dogtoothed, but the Byzantine architects had not invented the dogtooth, and would not have used it here, if they had; for the dogtooth cannot be employed alone, especially on so principal an angle as this of the main arches, without giving to the whole building a peculiar look, which I can not otherwise describe than as being to the eye, exactly what untempered acid is to the tongue. The mere dogtooth is an acid moulding, and can only be used in certain mingling with others, to give them piquancy; never alone. What, then, will be the next easiest method of giving interest to the fillet?

Fig. LVIII.

§ XIII. Simply to make the incisions square instead of sharp, and to leave equal intervals of the square edge between them. Fig. LVIII. is one of the curved pieces of arch armor, with its edge thus treated; one side only being done at the bottom, to show the simplicity and ease of the work. This ornament gives force and interest to the edge of the arch, without in the least diminishing its quietness. Nothing was ever, nor could be ever invented, fitter for its purpose, or more easily cut. From the arch it therefore found its way into every position where the edge of a piece of stone projected, and became, from its constancy of occurrence in the latest Gothic as well as the earliest Byzantine, most truly deserving of the name of the "Venetian Dentil." Its complete intention is now, however, only to be seen in the pictures of Gentile Bellini and Vittor Carpaccio; for, like most of the rest of the mouldings of Venetian buildings, it was always either gilded or painted—often both, gold being laid on the faces of the dentils, and their recesses colored alternately red and blue.

§ XIV. Observe, however, that the reason above given for the universality of this ornament was by no means the reason of its invention. The Venetian dentil is a particular application (consequent on the incrusted character of Venetian architecture) of the general idea of dentil, which had been originally given by the Greeks, and realised both by them and by the Byzantines in many laborious forms, long before there was need of them for arch armor; and the lower half of Plate IX. will give some idea of the conditions which occur in the Romanesque of Venice, distinctly derived from the classical dentil; and of the gradual transition to the more convenient and simple type, the running-hand dentil, which afterwards became the characteristic of Venetian Gothic. No. 13[76] is the common dentiled cornice, which occurs repeatedly in St. Mark's; and, as late as the thirteenth century, a reduplication of it, forming the abaci of the capitals of the Piazzetta shafts. Fig. 15 is perhaps an earlier type; perhaps only one of more careless workmanship, from a Byzantine ruin in the Rio di Ca' Foscari: and it is interesting to compare it with fig. 14 from the Cathedral of Vienne, in South France. Fig. 17, from St. Mark's, and 18, from the apse of Murano, are two very early examples in which the future true Venetian dentil is already developed in method of execution, though the object is still only to imitate the classical one; and a rude imitation of the bead is joined with it in fig. 17. No. 16 indicates two examples of experimental forms: the uppermost from the tomb of Mastino della Scala, at Verona; the lower from a door in Venice, I believe, of the thirteenth century: 19 is a more frequent arrangement, chiefly found in cast brick, and connecting the dentils with the dogteeth: 20 is a form introduced richly in the later Gothic, but of rare occurrence until the latter half of the thirteenth century. I shall call it the gabled dentil. It is found in the greatest profusion in sepulchral Gothic, associated with several slight variations from the usual dentil type, of which No. 21, from the tomb of Pietro Cornaro, may serve as an example.

§ XV. All the forms given in Plate IX. are of not unfrequent occurrence: varying much in size and depth, according to the expression of the work in which they occur; generally increasing in size in late work (the earliest dentils are seldom more than an inch or an inch and a half long: the fully developed dentil of the later Gothic is often as much as four or five in length, by one and a half in breadth); but they are all somewhat rare, compared to the true or armor dentil, above described. On the other hand, there are one or two unique conditions, which will be noted in the buildings where they occur.[77] The Ducal Palace furnishes three anomalies in the arch, dogtooth, and dentil: it has a hyperbolic arch, as noted above, Chap. X., § XV.; it has a double-fanged dogtooth in the rings of the spiral shafts on its angles; and, finally, it has a dentil with concave sides, of which the section and two of the blocks, real size, are given in Plate XIV. The labor of obtaining this difficult profile has, however, been thrown away; for the effect of the dentil at ten feet distance is exactly the same as that of the usual form: and the reader may consider the dogtooth and dentil in that plate as fairly representing the common use of them in the Venetian Gothic.

§ XVI. I am aware of no other form of fillet decoration requiring notice: in the Northern Gothic, the fillet is employed chiefly to give severity or flatness to mouldings supposed to be too much rounded, and is therefore generally plain. It is itself an ugly moulding, and, when thus employed, is merely a foil for others, of which, however, it at last usurped the place, and became one of the most painful features in the debased Gothic both of Italy and the North.

FOOTNOTES:

[74] I do not here speak of artistical merits, but the play of the light among the lower shafts is also singularly beautiful in this sketch of Prout's, and the character of the wild and broken leaves, half dead, on the stone of the foreground.

[75] Vide the "Seven Lamps," p. 122.

[76] The sections of all the mouldings are given on the right of each; the part which is constantly solid being shaded, and that which is cut into dentils left.

[77] As, however, we shall not probably be led either to Bergamo or Bologna, I may mention here a curiously rich use of the dentil, entirely covering the foliation and tracery of a niche on the outside of the duomo of Bergamo; and a roll, entirely incrusted, as the handle of a mace often is with nails, with massy dogteeth or nail-heads, on the door of the Pepoli palace of Bologna.

CHAPTER XXIV

THE ROLL AND RECESS

§ I. I have classed these two means of architectural effect together, because the one is in most cases the negative of the other, and is used to relieve it exactly as shadow relieves light; recess alternating with roll, not only in lateral, but in successive order; not merely side by side with each other, but interrupted the one by the other in their own lines. A recess itself has properly no decoration; but its depth gives value to the decoration which flanks, encloses, or interrupts it, and the form which interrupts it best is the roll.

§ II. I use the word roll generally for any mouldings which present to the eye somewhat the appearance of being cylindrical, and look like round rods. When upright, they are in appearance, if not in fact, small shafts; and are a kind of bent shaft, even when used in archivolts and traceries;—when horizontal, they confuse themselves with cornices, and are, in fact, generally to be considered as the best means of drawing an architectural line in any direction, the soft curve of their side obtaining some shadow at nearly all times of the day, and that more tender and grateful to the eye than can be obtained either by an incision or by any other form of projection.

§ III. Their decorative power is, however, too slight for rich work, and they frequently require, like the angle and the fillet, to be rendered interesting by subdivision or minor ornament of their own. When the roll is small, this is effected, exactly as in the case of the fillet, by cutting pieces out of it; giving in the simplest results what is called the Norman billet moulding: and when the cuts are given in couples, and the pieces rounded into spheres and almonds, we have the ordinary Greek bead, both of them too well known to require illustration. The Norman billet we shall not meet with in Venice; the bead constantly occurs in Byzantine, and of course in Renaissance work. In Plate IX., Fig. 17, there is a remarkable example of its early treatment, where the cuts in it are left sharp.

§ IV. But the roll, if it be of any size, deserves better treatment. Its rounded surface is too beautiful to be cut away in notches; and it is rather to be covered with flat chasing or inlaid patterns. Thus ornamented, it gradually blends itself with the true shaft, both in the Romanesque work of the North, and in the Italian connected schools; and the patterns used for it are those used for shaft decoration in general.

§ V. But, as alternating with the recess, it has a decoration peculiar to itself. We have often, in the preceding chapters, noted the fondness of the Northern builders for deep shade and hollowness in their mouldings; and in the second chapter of the "Seven Lamps," the changes are described which reduced the massive roll mouldings of the early Gothic to a series of recesses, separated by bars of light. The shape of these recesses is at present a matter of no importance to us: it was, indeed, endlessly varied; but needlessly, for the value of a recess is in its darkness, and its darkness disguises its form. But it was not in mere wanton indulgence of their love of shade that the Flamboyant builders deepened the furrows of their mouldings: they had found a means of decorating those furrows as rich as it was expressive, and the entire frame-work of their architecture was designed with a view to the effect of this decoration; where the ornament ceases, the frame-work is meagre and mean: but the ornament is, in the best examples of the style, unceasing.

§ VI. It is, in fact, an ornament formed by the ghosts or anatomies of the old shafts, left in the furrows which had taken their place. Every here and there, a fragment of a roll or shaft is left in the recess or furrow: a billet-moulding on a huge scale, but a billet-moulding reduced to a skeleton; for the fragments of roll are cut hollow, and worked into mere entanglement of stony fibres, with the gloom of the recess shown through them. These ghost rolls, forming sometimes pedestals, sometimes canopies, sometimes covering the whole recess with an arch of tracery, beneath which it runs like a tunnel, are the peculiar decorations of the Flamboyant Gothic.

§ VII. Now observe, in all kinds of decoration, we must keep carefully under separate heads, the consideration of the changes wrought in the mere physical form, and in the intellectual purpose of ornament. The relations of the canopy to the statue it shelters, are to be considered altogether distinctly from those of the canopy to the building which it decorates. In its earliest conditions the canopy is partly confused with representations of miniature architecture: it is sometimes a small temple or gateway, sometimes a honorary addition to the pomp of a saint, a covering to his throne, or to his shrine; and this canopy is often expressed in bas-relief (as in painting), without much reference to the great requirements of the building. At other times it is a real protection to the statue, and is enlarged into a complete pinnacle, carried on proper shafts, and boldly roofed. But in the late northern system the canopies are neither expressive nor protective. They are a kind of stone lace-work, required for the ornamentation of the building, for which the statues are often little more than an excuse, and of which the physical character is, as above described, that of ghosts of departed shafts.

§ VIII. There is, of course, much rich tabernacle work which will not come literally under this head, much which is straggling or flat in its plan, connecting itself gradually with the ordinary forms of independent shrines and tombs; but the general idea of all tabernacle work is marked in the common phrase of a "niche," that is to say a hollow intended for a statue, and crowned by a canopy; and this niche decoration only reaches its full development when the Flamboyant hollows are cut deepest, and when the manner and spirit of sculpture had so much lost their purity and intensity that it became desirable to draw the eye away from the statue to its covering, so that at last the canopy became the more important of the two, and is itself so beautiful that we are often contented with architecture from which profanity has struck the statues, if only the canopies are left; and consequently, in our modern ingenuity, even set up canopies where we have no intention of setting statues.

§ IX. It is a pity that thus we have no really noble example of the effect of the statue in the recesses of architecture: for the Flamboyant recess was not so much a preparation for it as a gulf which swallowed it up. When statues were most earnestly designed, they were thrust forward in all kinds of places, often in front of the pillars, as at Amiens, awkwardly enough, but with manly respect to the purpose of the figures. The Flamboyant hollows yawned at their sides, the statues fell back into them, and nearly disappeared, and a flash of flame in the shape of a canopy rose as they expired.

§ X. I do not feel myself capable at present of speaking with perfect justice of this niche ornament of the north, my late studies in Italy having somewhat destroyed my sympathies with it. But I once loved it intensely, and will not say anything to depreciate it now, save only this, that while I have studied long at Abbeville, without in the least finding that it made me care less for Verona, I never remained long in Verona without feeling some doubt of the nobility of Abbeville.

§ XI. Recess decoration by leaf mouldings is constantly and beautifully associated in the north with niche decoration, but requires no special notice, the recess in such cases being used merely to give value to the leafage by its gloom, and the difference between such conditions and those of the south being merely that in the one the leaves are laid across a hollow, and in the other over a solid surface; but in neither of the schools exclusively so, each in some degree intermingling the method of the other.

§ XII. Finally the recess decoration by the ball flower is very definite and characteristic, found, I believe, chiefly in English work. It consists merely in leaving a small boss or sphere, fixed, as it were, at intervals in the hollows; such bosses being afterwards carved into roses, or other ornamental forms, and sometimes lifted quite up out of the hollow, on projecting processes, like vertebræ, so as to make them more conspicuous, as throughout the decoration of the cathedral of Bourges.

The value of this ornament is chiefly in the spotted character which it gives to the lines of mouldings seen from a distance. It is very rich and delightful when not used in excess; but it would satiate and weary the eye if it were ever used in general architecture. The spire of Salisbury, and of St. Mary's at Oxford, are agreeable as isolated masses; but if an entire street were built with this spotty decoration at every casement, we could not traverse it to the end without disgust. It is only another example of the constant aim at piquancy of effect which characterised the northern builders; an ingenious but somewhat vulgar effort to give interest to their grey masses of coarse stone, without overtaking their powers either of invention or execution. We will thank them for it without blame or praise, and pass on.

CHAPTER XXV

THE BASE

§ I. We know now as much as is needful respecting the methods of minor and universal decorations, which were distinguished in Chapter XXII., § III., from the ornament which has special relation to particular parts. This local ornament, which, it will be remembered, we arranged in § II. of the same chapter under five heads, we have next, under those heads, to consider. And, first, the ornament of the bases, both of walls and shafts.

It was noticed in our account of the divisions of a wall, that there are something in those divisions like the beginning, the several courses, and the close of a human life. And as, in all well-conducted lives, the hard work, and roughing, and gaining of strength come first, the honor or decoration in certain intervals during their course, but most of all in their close, so, in general, the base of the wall, which is its beginning of labor, will bear least decoration, its body more, especially those epochs of rest called its string courses; but its crown or cornice most of all. Still, in some buildings, all these are decorated richly, though the last most; and in others, when the base is well protected and yet conspicuous, it may probably receive even more decoration than other parts.

§ II. Now, the main things to be expressed in a base are its levelness and evenness. We cannot do better than construct the several members of the base, as developed in Fig. II., p. 55, each of a different colored marble, so as to produce marked level bars of color all along the foundation. This is exquisitely done in all the Italian elaborate wall bases; that of St. Anastasia at Verona is one of the most perfect existing, for play of color; that of Giotto's campanile is on the whole the most beautifully finished. Then, on the vertical portions, a, b, c, we may put what patterns in mosaic we please, so that they be not too rich; but if we choose rather to have sculpture (or must have it for want of stones to inlay), then observe that all sculpture on bases must be in panels, or it will soon be worn away, and that a plain panelling is often good without any other ornament. The member b, which in St. Mark's is subordinate, and c, which is expanded into a seat, are both of them decorated with simple but exquisitely-finished panelling, in red and white or green and white marble; and the member e is in bases of this kind very valuable, as an expression of a firm beginning of the substance of the wall itself. This member has been of no service to us hitherto, and was unnoticed in the chapters on construction; but it was expressed in the figure of the wall base, on account of its great value when the foundation is of stone and the wall of brick (coated or not). In such cases it is always better to add the course e, above the slope of the base, than abruptly to begin the common masonry of the wall.

§ III. It is, however, with the member d, or Xb, that we are most seriously concerned; for this being the essential feature of all bases, and the true preparation for the wall or shaft, it is most necessary that here, if anywhere, we should have full expression of levelness and precision; and farther, that, if possible, the eye should not be suffered to rest on the points of junction of the stones, which would give an effect of instability. Both these objects are accomplished by attracting the eye to two rolls, separated by a deep hollow, in the member d itself. The bold projections of their mouldings entirely prevent the attention from being drawn to the joints of the masonry, and besides form a simple but beautifully connected group of bars of shadow, which express, in their perfect parallelism, the absolute levelness of the foundation.

§ IV. I need hardly give any perspective drawing of an arrangement which must be perfectly familiar to the reader, as occurring under nearly every column of the too numerous classical buildings all over Europe. But I may name the base of the Bank of England as furnishing a very simple instance of the group, with a square instead of a rounded hollow, both forming the base of the wall, and gathering into that of the shafts as they occur; while the bases of the pillars of the façade of the British Museum are as good examples as the reader can study on a larger scale.

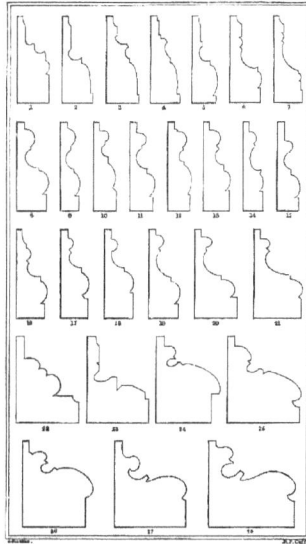

Plate X. PROFILES OF BASES.

§ V. I believe this group of mouldings was first invented by the Greeks, and it has never been materially improved, as far as its peculiar purpose is concerned;[78] the classical attempts at its variation being the ugliest: one, the using a single roll of larger size, as may be seen in the Duke of York's column, which therefore looks as if it stood on a large sausage (the Monument has the same base, but more concealed by pedestal decoration): another, the using two rolls without the intermediate cavetto,—a condition hardly less awkward, and which may be studied to advantage in the wall and shaftbases of the Athenæum Club-house: and another, the introduction of what are called fillets between the rolls, as may be seen in the pillars of Hanover Chapel, Regent Street, which look, in consequence, as if they were standing upon a pile of pewter collection plates. But the only successful changes have been mediæval; and their nature will be at once understood by a glance at the varieties given on the opposite page. It will be well first to give the buildings in which they occur, in order.

1. Santa Fosca, Torcello.
2. North transept, St. Mark's, Venice.
3. Nave, Torcello.
4. Nave, Torcello.
5. South transept, St. Mark's.
6. Northern portico, upper shafts. St. Mark's.
7. Another of the same group.
8. Cortile of St. Ambrogio, Milan.
9. Nave shafts, St. Michele, Pavia.
10. Outside wall base, St. Mark's, Venice
11. Fondaco de' Turchi, Venice.
12. Nave, Vienne, France.

15. Byzantine fragment, Venice.
16. St. Mark's, upper Colonnade.
17. Ducal Palace, Venice (windows.)
18. Ca' Falier, Venice.
19. St. Zeno, Verona.
20. San Stefano, Venice.
21. Ducal Palace, Venice (windows.)
22. Nave, Salisbury.
23. Santa Fosca, Torcello.
24. Nave, Lyons Cathedral.
25. Notre Dame, Dijon.
26. Nave, Bourges Cathedral.

13. Fondaco de' Turchi, Venice.	27. Nave, Mortain (Normandy).
14. Ca' Giustiniani, Venice.	28. Nave, Rouen Cathedral.

§ VI. Eighteen out of the twenty eight varieties are Venetian, being bases to which I shall have need of future reference; but the interspersed examples, 8, 9, 12, and 19, from Milan, Pavia, Vienne (France), and Verona, show the exactly correspondent conditions of the Romanesque base at the period, throughout the centre of Europe. The last five examples show the changes effected by the French Gothic architects: the Salisbury base (22) I have only introduced to show its dulness and vulgarity beside them; and 23, from Torcello, for a special reason, in that place.

§ VII. The reader will observe that the two bases, 8 and 9, from the two most important Lombardic churches of Italy, St. Ambrogio of Milan and St. Michele of Pavia, mark the character of the barbaric base founded on pure Roman models, sometimes approximating to such models very closely; and the varieties 10, 11, 13, 16 are Byzantine types, also founded on Roman models. But in the bases 1 to 7 inclusive, and, still more characteristically, in 23 below, there is evidently an original element, a tendency to use the fillet and hollow instead of the roll, which is eminently Gothic; which in the base 3 reminds one even of Flamboyant conditions, and is excessively remarkable as occurring in Italian work certainly not later than the tenth century, taking even the date of the last rebuilding of the Duomo of Torcello, though I am strongly inclined to consider these bases portions of the original church. And I have therefore put the base 23 among the Gothic group to which it has so strong relationship, though, on the last supposition, five centuries older than the earliest of the five terminal examples; and it is still more remarkable because it reverses the usual treatment of the lower roll, which is in general a tolerably accurate test of the age of a base, in the degree of its projection. Thus, in the examples 2, 3, 4, 5, 9, 10, 12, the lower roll is hardly rounded at all, and diametrically opposed to the late Gothic conditions, 24 to 28, in which it advances gradually, like a wave preparing to break, and at last is actually seen curling over with the long-backed rush of surf upon the shore. Yet the Torcello base resembles these Gothic ones both in expansion beneath and in depth of cavetto above.

§ VIII. There can be no question of the ineffable superiority of these Gothic bases, in grace of profile, to any ever invented by the ancients. But they have all two great faults: They seem, in the first place, to have been designed without sufficient reference to the necessity of their being usually seen from above; their grace of profile cannot be estimated when so seen, and their excessive expansion gives them an appearance of flatness and separation from the shaft, as if they had splashed out under its pressure: in the second place their cavetto is so deeply cut that it has the appearance of a black fissure between the members of the base; and in the Lyons and Bourges shafts, 24 and 26, it is impossible to conquer the idea suggested by it, that the two stones above and below have been intended to join close, but that some pebbles have got in and kept them from fitting; one is always expecting the pebbles to be crushed, and the shaft to settle into its place with a thunder-clap.

§ IX. For these reasons, I said that the profile of the pure classic base had hardly been materially improved; but the various conditions of it are beautiful or commonplace, in proportion to the variety of proportion among their lines and the delicacy of their curvatures; that is to say, the expression of characters like those of the abstract lines in Plate VII.

The five best profiles in Plate X. are 10, 17, 19, 20, 21; 10 is peculiarly beautiful in the opposition between the bold projection of its upper roll, and the delicate leafy curvature of its lower; and this and 21 may be taken as nearly perfect types, the one of the steep, the other of the expansive basic profiles. The characters of all, however, are so dependent upon their place and expression, that it is unfair to judge them thus separately; and the precision of curvature is a matter of so small consequence in general effect, that we need not here pursue the subject farther.

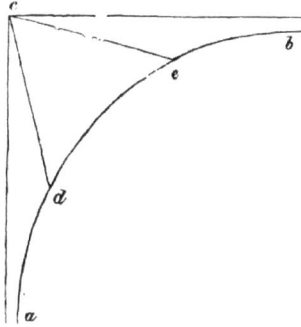

Fig. LIX.

§ X. We have thus far, however, considered only the lines of moulding in the member X b, whether of wall or shaft base. But the reader will remember that in our best shaft base, in Fig. XII. (p. 78), certain props or spurs were applied to the slope of X b; but now that X b is divided into these delicate mouldings, we cannot conveniently apply the spur to its irregular profile; we must be content to set it against the lower roll. Let the upper edge of this lower roll be the curved line here, a, d, e, b, Fig. LIX., and c the angle of the square plinth projecting beneath it. Then the spur, applied as we saw in Chap. VII., will be of some such form as the triangle c e d, Fig. LIX.

§ XI. Now it has just been stated that it is of small importance whether the abstract lines of the profile of a base moulding be fine or not, because we rarely stoop down to look at them. But this triangular spur is nearly always seen from above, and the eye is drawn to it as one of the most important features of the whole base; therefore it is a point of immediate necessity to substitute for its harsh right lines (c d, c e) some curve of noble abstract character.

§ XII. I mentioned, in speaking of the line of the salvia leaf at p. 224, that I had marked off the portion of it, x y, because I thought it likely to be generally useful to us afterwards; and I promised the reader that as he had built, so he should decorate his edifice at his own free will. If, therefore, he likes the above triangular spur, c d e, by all means let him keep it; but if he be on the whole dissatisfied with it, I may be permitted, perhaps, to advise him to set to work like a tapestry bee, to cut off the little bit of line of salvia leaf x y, and try how he can best substitute it for the awkward lines c d c e. He may try it any way that he likes; but if he puts the salvia curvature inside the present lines, he will find the spur looks weak, and I think he will determine at last on placing it as I have done at c d, c e, Fig. LX. (If the reader will be at the pains to transfer the salvia leaf line with tracing paper, he will find it accurately used in this figure.) Then I merely add an outer circular line to represent the outer swell of the roll against which the spur is set, and I put another such spur to the opposite corner of the square, and we have the half base, Fig. LX., which is a general type of the best Gothic bases in existence, being very nearly that of the upper shafts of the Ducal Palace of Venice. In those shafts the quadrant a b, or the upper edge of the lower roll, is 2 feet 1-3/8 inches round, and the base of the spur d e, is 10 inches; the line d e being therefore to a b as 10 to 25-3/8. In Fig. LX. it is as 10 to 24, the measurement being easier and the type somewhat more generally representative of the best, i.e. broadest, spurs of Italian Gothic.

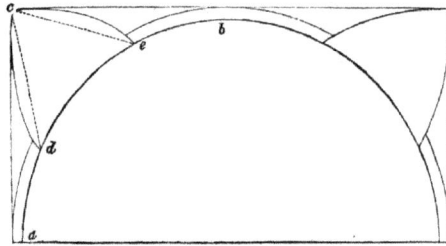

Fig. LX.

§ XIII. Now, the reader is to remember, there is nothing magical in salvia leaves: the line I take from them happened merely to fall conveniently on the page, and might as well have been taken from anything else; it is simply its character of gradated curvature which fits it for our use. On Plate XI., opposite, I have given plans of the spurs and quadrants of twelve Italian and three Northern bases; these latter (13), from Bourges, (14) from Lyons, (15) from Rouen, are given merely to show the Northern disposition to break up bounding lines, and lose breadth in picturesqueness. These Northern bases look the prettiest in this plate, because this variation of the outline is nearly all the ornament they have, being cut very rudely; but the Italian bases above them are merely prepared by their simple outlines for far richer decoration at the next step, as we shall see presently. The Northern bases are to be noted also for another grand error: the projection of the roll beyond the square plinth, of which the corner is seen, in various degrees of advancement, in the three examples. 13 is the base whose profile is No. 26 in Plate X.; 14 is 24 in the same plate; and 15 is 28.

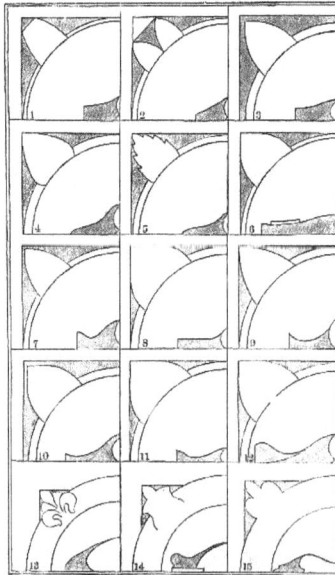

Plate XI. PLANS OF BASES.

§ XIV. The Italian bases are the following; all, except 7 and 10, being Venetian: 1 and 2, upper colonnade, St. Mark's; 3, Ca' Falier; 4, lower colonnade, and 5, transept, St. Mark's; 6, from the Church of St. John and Paul; 7, from the tomb near St. Anastasia, Verona, described above (p. 142); 8 and 9, Fon daco de' Turchi, Venice; 10, tomb of Can Mastino della Scala, Verona; 11, San Stefano, Venice; 12, Ducal Palace, Venice, upper colonnade. The Nos. 3, 8, 9, 11 are the bases whose profiles are respectively Nos. 18, 11, 13, and 20 in Plate X. The flat surfaces of the basic plinths are here shaded; and in the lower corner of the square occupied by each quadrant is put, also shaded, the central profile of each spur, from its root at the roll of the base to its point; those of Nos. 1 and 2 being conjectural, for their spurs were so rude and ugly, that I took no note of their profiles; but they would probably be as here given. As these bases, though here, for the sake of comparison, reduced within squares of equal size, in reality belong to shafts of very different size, 9 being some six or seven inches in diameter, and 6, three or four feet, the proportionate size of the roll varies accordingly, being largest, as in 9, where the base is smallest, and in 6 and 12 the leaf profile is given on a larger scale than the plan, or its character could not have been exhibited.

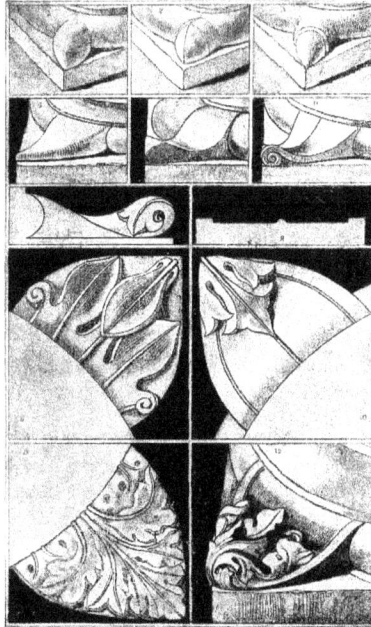

Plate XII. DECORATION OF BASES.

§ XV. Now, in all these spurs, the reader will observe that the narrowest are for the most part the earliest. No. 2, from the upper colonnade of St. Mark's, is the only instance I ever saw of the double spur, as transitive between the square and octagon plinth; the truncated form, 1, is also rare and very ugly. Nos. 3, 4, 5, 7 and 9 are the general conditions of the Byzantine spur; 8 is a very rare form of plan in

Byzantine work, but proved to be so by its rude level profile; while 7, on the contrary, Byzantine in plan, is eminently Gothic in the profile. 9 to 12 are from formed Gothic buildings, equally refined in their profile and plan.

§ XVI. The character of the profile is indeed much altered by the accidental nature of the surface decoration; but the importance of the broad difference between the raised and flat profile will be felt on glancing at the examples 1 to 6 in Plate XII. The three upper examples are the Romanesque types, which occur as parallels with the Byzantine types, 1 to 3 of Plate XI. Their plans would be nearly the same; but instead of resembling flat leaves, they are literally spurs, or claws, as high as they are broad; and the third, from St. Michele of Pavia, appears to be intended to have its resemblance to a claw enforced by the transverse fillet. 1 is from St. Ambrogio, Milan; 2 from Vienne, France. The 4th type, Plate XII., almost like the extremity of a man's foot, is a Byzantine form (perhaps worn on the edges), from the nave of St. Mark's; and the two next show the unity of the two principles, forming the perfect Italian Gothic types,—5, from tomb of Can Signorio della Scala, Verona; 6, from San Stefano, Venice (the base 11 of Plate XI., in perspective). The two other bases, 10 and 12 of Plate XI., are conditions of the same kind, showing the varieties of rise and fall in exquisite modulation; the 10th, a type more frequent at Verona than Venice, in which the spur profile overlaps the roll, instead of rising out of it, and seems to hold it down, as if it were a ring held by sockets. This is a character found both in early and late work; a kind of band, or fillet, appears to hold, and even compress, the centre of the roll in the base of one of the crypt shafts of St. Peter's, Oxford, which has also spurs at its angles; and long bands flow over the base of the angle shaft of the Ducal Palace of Venice, next the Porta della Carta.

§ XVII. When the main contours of the base are once determined, its decoration is as easy as it is infinite. I have merely given, in Plate XII., three examples to which I shall need to refer, hereafter. No. 9 is a very early and curious one; the decoration of the base 6 in Plate XI., representing a leaf turned over and flattened down; or, rather, the idea of the turned leaf, worked as well as could be imagined on the flat contour of the spur. Then 10 is the perfect, but simplest possible development of the same idea, from the earliest bases of the upper colonnade of the Ducal Palace, that is to say, the bases of the sea façade; and 7 and 8 are its lateral profile and transverse section. Finally, 11 and 12 are two of the spurs of the later shafts of the same colonnade on the Piazzetta side (No. 12 of Plate XI.). No. 11 occurs on one of these shafts only, and is singularly beautiful. I suspect it to be earlier than the other, which is the characteristic base of the rest of the series, and already shows the loose, sensual, ungoverned character of fifteenth century ornament in the dissoluteness of its rolling.

§ XVIII. I merely give these as examples ready to my hand, and necessary for future reference; not as in anywise representative of the variety of the Italian treatment of the general contour, far less of the endless caprices of the North. The most beautiful base I ever saw, on the whole, is a Byzantine one in the Baptistery of St. Mark's, in which the spur profile approximates to that of No. 10 in Plate XI.; but it is formed by a cherub, who sweeps downwards on the wing. His two wings, as they half close, form the upper part of the spur, and the rise of it in the front is formed by exactly the action of Alichino, swooping on the pitch lake: "quei drizzo, volando, suso il petto." But it requires noble management to confine such a fancy within such limits. The greater number of the best bases are formed of leaves; and the reader may amuse himself as he will by endless inventions of them, from types which he may gather among the weeds at the nearest roadside. The value of the vegetable form is especially here, as above noted, Chap. XX., § XXXII., its capability of unity with the mass of the base, and of being suggested by few lines; none but the Northern Gothic architects are able to introduce entire animal forms in this position with perfect success. There is a beautiful instance at the north door of the west front of Rouen; a lizard pausing and curling himself round a little in the angle; one expects him the next instant to lash round the shaft and vanish: and we may with advantage compare this base with those of Renaissance Scuola di San Rocca[79] at Venice, in which the architect, imitating the mediæval bases, which he did not understand, has put an elephant, four inches higher, in the same position.

§ XIX. I have not in this chapter spoken at all of the profiles which are given in Northern architecture to the projections of the lower members of the base, b and c in Fig. II., nor of the methods in which both these, and the rolls of the mouldings in Plate X., are decorated, especially in Roman architecture, with superadded chain work or chasing of various patterns. Of the first I have not spoken, because I shall have no occasion to allude to them in the following essay; nor of the second, because I consider them barbarisms. Decorated rolls and decorated ogee profiles, such, for instance, as the base of the Arc de l'Etoile at Paris, are among the richest and farthest refinements of decorative appliances; and they ought always to be reserved for jambs, cornices, and archivolts: if you begin with them in the base, you have no power of refining your decorations as you ascend, and, which is still worse, you put your most delicate work on the jutting portions of the foundation,—the very portions which are most exposed to abrasion. The best expression of a base is that of stern endurance,—the look of being able to bear roughing; or, if the whole building is so delicate that no one can be expected to treat even its base with unkindness,[80] then at least the expression of quiet, prefatory simplicity. The angle spur may receive such decoration as we have seen, because it is one of the most important features in the whole building; and the eye is always so attracted to it that it cannot be in rich architecture left altogether blank; the eye is stayed upon it by its position, but glides, and ought to glide, along the basic rolls to take measurement of their length: and even with all this added fitness, the ornament of the basic spur is best, in the long run, when it is boldest and simplest. The base above described, § XVIII., as the most beautiful I ever saw, was not for that reason the best I ever saw: beautiful in its place, in a quiet corner of a Baptistery sheeted with jasper and alabaster, it would have been utterly wrong, nay, even offensive, if used in sterner work, or repeated along a whole colonnade. The base No. 10 of Plate XII. is the richest with which I was ever perfectly satisfied for general service; and the basic spurs of the building which I have named as the best Gothic monument in the world (p. 141), have no ornament upon them whatever. The adaptation, therefore, of rich cornice and roll mouldings to the level and ordinary lines of bases, whether of walls or shafts, I hold to be one of the worst barbarisms which the Roman and Renaissance architects ever committed; and that nothing can afterwards redeem the effeminacy and vulgarity of the buildings in which it prominently takes place.

§ XX. I have also passed over, without present notice, the fantastic bases formed by couchant animals, which sustain many Lombardic shafts. The pillars they support have independent bases of the ordinary kind; and the animal form beneath is less to be considered as a true base (though often exquisitely combined with it, as in the shaft on the south-west angle of the cathedral of Genoa) than as a piece of sculpture, otherwise necessary to the nobility of the building, and deriving its value from its special positive fulfilment of expressional purposes, with which we have here no concern. As the embodiment of a wild superstition, and the representation of supernatural powers, their appeal to the imagination sets at utter defiance all judgment based on ordinary canons of law; and the magnificence of their treatment atones, in nearly every case, for the extravagance of their conception. I should not admit this appeal to the imagination, if it had been made by a nation in whom the powers of body and mind had been languid; but by the Lombard, strong in all the realities of human life, we need not fear being led astray: the visions of a distempered fancy are not indeed permitted to replace the truth, or set aside the laws of science: but the imagination which is thoroughly under the command of the intelligent will,[81] has a dominion indiscernible by science, and illimitable by law; and we may acknowledge the authority of the Lombardic gryphons in the mere splendor of their presence, without thinking idolatry an excuse for mechanical misconstruction, or dreading to be called upon, in other cases, to admire a systemless architecture, because it may happen to have sprung from an irrational religion.

FOOTNOTES:

[78] *Another most important reason for the peculiar sufficiency and value of this base, especially as opposed to the bulging forms of the single or double roll, without the cavetto, has been suggested by the writer of the Essay on the Æsthetics of Gothic Architecture in the British Quarterly for August, 1849:—"The Attic base recedes at the point where, if it suffered from superincumbent weight, it would bulge out."*

[79] *I have put in Appendix 24, "Renaissance Bases," my memorandum written respecting this building on the spot. But the reader had better delay referring to it, until we have completed our examination of ornaments in shafts and capitals.*

[80] *Appendix 25, "Romanist Decoration of Bases."*

[81] *In all the wildness of the Lombardic fancy (described in Appendix 8), this command of the will over its action is as distinct as it is stern. The fancy is, in the early work of the nation, visibly diseased; but never the will, nor the reason.*

CHAPTER XXVI

THE WALL VEIL AND SHAFT

§ I. No subject has been more open ground of dispute among architects than the decoration of the wall veil, because no decoration appeared naturally to grow out of its construction; nor could any curvatures be given to its surface large enough to produce much impression on the eye. It has become, therefore, a kind of general field for experiments of various effects of surface ornament, or has been altogether abandoned to the mosaicist and fresco painter. But we may perhaps conclude, from what was advanced in the Fifth Chapter, that there is one kind of decoration which will, indeed, naturally follow on its construction. For it is perfectly natural that the different kinds of stone used in its successive courses should be of different colors; and there are many associations and analogies which metaphysically justify the introduction of horizontal bands of color, or of light and shade. They are, in the first place, a kind of expression of the growth or age of the wall, like the rings in the wood of a tree; then they are a farther symbol of the alternation of light and darkness, which was above noted as the source of the charm of many inferior mouldings: again, they are valuable as an expression of horizontal space to the imagination, space of which the conception is opposed, and gives more effect by its opposition, to the enclosing power of the wall itself (this I spoke of as probably the great charm of these horizontal bars to the Arabian mind): and again they are valuable in their suggestion of the natural courses of rocks, and beds of the earth itself. And to all these powerful imaginative reasons we have to add the merely ocular charm of interlineal opposition of color; a charm so great, that all the best colorists, without a single exception, depend upon it for the most piquant of their pictorial effects, some vigorous mass of alternate stripes or bars of color being made central in all their richest arrangements. The whole system of Tintoret's great picture of the Miracle of St. Mark is poised on the bars of blue, which cross the white turban of the executioner.

Plate XIII. WALL VEIL DECORATIONS.

§ II. There are, therefore, no ornaments more deeply suggestive in their simplicity than these alternate bars of horizontal colors; nor do I know any buildings more noble than those of the Pisan Romanesque, in which they are habitually employed; and certainly none so graceful, so attractive, so enduringly delightful in their nobleness. Yet, of this pure and graceful ornamentation, Professor Willis says, "a practice more destructive of architectural grandeur can hardly be conceived:" and modern architects have substituted for it the ingenious ornament of which the reader has had one specimen above, Fig. III., p. 61, and with which half the large buildings in London are disfigured, or else traversed by mere straight lines, as, for instance, the back of the Bank. The lines on the Bank may, perhaps, be considered typical of accounts; but in general the walls, if left destitute of them, would have been as much fairer than the walls charged with them, as a sheet of white paper is than the leaf of a ledger. But that the reader may have free liberty of judgment in this matter, I place two examples of the old and the Renaissance ornament side by side on the opposite page. That on the right is Romanesque, from St. Pietro of Pistoja; that on the left, modern English, from the Arthur Club-house, St. James's Street.

§ III. But why, it will be asked, should the lines which mark the division of the stones be wrong when they are chiselled, and right when they are marked by color? First, because the color separation is a natural one. You build with different kinds of stone, of which, probably, one is more costly than another; which latter, as you cannot construct your building of it entirely, you arrange in conspicuous bars. But the chiselling of the stones is a wilful throwing away of time and labor in defacing the building: it costs much to hew one of those monstrous blocks into shape; and, when it is done, the building is weaker than it was before, by just as much stone as has been cut away from its joints. And, secondly, because, as I have repeatedly urged, straight lines are ugly things as lines, but admirable as limits of colored spaces; and the joints of the stones, which are painful in proportion to their regularity, if drawn as lines, are perfectly agreeable when marked by variations of hue.

§ IV. What is true of the divisions of stone by chiselling, is equally true of divisions of bricks by pointing. Nor, of course, is the mere horizontal bar the only arrangement in which the colors of brickwork or masonry can be gracefully disposed. It is rather one which can only be employed with advantage when the courses of stone are deep and bold. When the masonry is small, it is better to throw its colors into chequered patterns. We shall have several interesting examples to study in Venice besides the well-known one of the Ducal Palace. The town of Moulins, in France, is one of the most remarkable on this side the Alps for its chequered patterns in bricks. The church of Christchurch, Streatham, lately built, though spoiled by many grievous errors (the iron work in the campanile being the grossest), yet affords the inhabitants of the district a means of obtaining some idea of the variety of effects which are possible with no other material than brick.

§ V. We have yet to notice another effort of the Renaissance architects to adorn the blank spaces of their walls by what is called Rustication. There is sometimes an obscure trace of the remains of the imitation of something organic in this kind of work. In some of the better French eighteenth century buildings it has a distinctly floral character, like a final degradation of Flamboyant leafage; and some of our modern English architects appear to have taken the decayed teeth of elephants for their type; but, for the most part, it resembles nothing so much as worm casts; nor these with any precision. If it did, it would not bring it within the sphere of our properly imitative ornamentation. I thought it unnecessary to warn the reader that he was not to copy forms of refuse or corruption; and that, while he might legitimately take the worm or the reptile for a subject of imitation, he was not to study the worm cast or coprolite.

§ VI. It is, however, I believe, sometimes supposed that rustication gives an appearance of solidity to foundation stones. Not so; at least to any one who knows the look of a hard stone. You may, by rustication, make your good marble or granite look like wet slime, honeycombed by sand-eels, or like half-baked tufo covered with slow exudation of stalactite, or like rotten claystone coated with concretions of its own mud; but not like the stones of which the hard world is built. Do not think that nature rusticates her foundations. Smooth sheets of rock, glistening like sea waves, and that ring under the hammer like a brazen bell,—that is her preparation for first stories. She does rusticate sometimes: crumbly sand-stones, with their ripple-marks filled with red mud; dusty lime-stones, which the rains wash into labyrinthine cavities; spongy lavas, which the volcano blast drags hither and thither into ropy coils and bubbling hollows;—these she rusticates, indeed, when she wants to make oyster-shells and magnesia of them; but not when she needs to lay foundations with them. Then she seeks the polished surface and iron heart, not rough looks and incoherent substance.

§ VII. Of the richer modes of wall decoration it is impossible to institute any general comparison; they are quite infinite, from mere inlaid geometrical figures up to incrustations of elaborate bas-relief. The architect has perhaps more license in them, and more power of producing good effect with rude design than in any other features of the building; the chequer and hatchet work of the Normans and the rude bas-reliefs of the Lombards being almost as satisfactory as the delicate panelling and mosaic of the Duomo of Florence. But this is to be noted of all good wall ornament, that it retains the expression of firm and massive substance, and of broad surface, and that architecture instantly declined when linear design was substituted for massive, and the sense of weight of wall was lost in a wilderness of upright or undulating rods. Of the richest and most delicate wall veil decoration by inlaid work, as practised in Italy from the twelfth to the fifteenth century, I have given the reader two characteristic examples in Plates XX. and XXI.

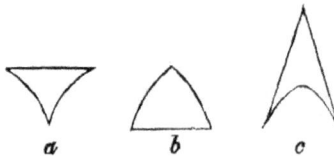

a   *b*   *c*

Fig. LXI.

§ VIII. There are, however, three spaces in which the wall veil, peculiarly limited in shape, was always felt to be fitted for surface decoration of the most elaborate kind; and in these spaces are found the most majestic instances of its treatment, even to late periods. One of these is the spandril space, or the filling between any two arches, commonly of the shape a, Fig. LXI.; the half of which, or the flank filling of any arch, is called a spandril. In Chapter XVII., on Filling of Apertures, the reader will find another of these spaces noted, called the tympanum, and commonly of the form b, Fig. LXI.: and finally, in Chapter XVIII., he will find the third space described, that between an arch and its protecting gable, approximating generally to the form c, Fig. LXI.

§ IX. The methods of treating these spaces might alone furnish subject for three very interesting essays; but I shall only note the most essential points respecting them.

(1.) The Spandril. It was observed in Chapter XII., that this portion of the arch load might frequently be lightened with great advantage by piercing it with a circle, or with a group of circles; and the roof of the Euston Square railroad station was adduced as an example. One of the spandril decorations of Bayeux Cathedral is given in the "Seven Lamps," Plate VII. fig. 4. It is little more than one of these Euston Square spandrils, with its circles foliated.

Plate XIV. SPANDRIL DECORATION. THE DUCAL PALACE.

Sometimes the circle is entirely pierced; at other times it is merely suggested by a mosaic or light tracery on the wall surface, as in the plate opposite, which is one of the spandrils of the Ducal Palace at Venice. It was evidently intended that all the spandrils of this building should be decorated in this manner, but only two of them seem to have been completed.[82]

§ X. The other modes of spandril filling may be broadly reduced to four heads. 1. Free figure sculpture, as in the Chapter-house of Salisbury, and very superbly along the west front of Bourges, the best Gothic spandrils I know. 2. Radiated foliage, more or less referred to the centre, or to the bottom of the spandril for its origin; single figures with expanded wings often answering the same purpose. 3. Trefoils; and 4, ordinary wall decoration continued into the spandril space, as in Plate XIII., above, from St. Pietro at Pistoja, and in Westminster Abbey. The Renaissance architects introduced spandril fillings composed of colossal human figures reclining on the sides of the arch, in precarious lassitude; but these cannot come under the head of wall veil decoration.

§ XI. (2.) The Tympanum. It was noted that, in Gothic architecture, this is for the most part a detached slab of stone, having no constructional relation to the rest of the building. The plan of its sculpture is therefore quite arbitrary; and, as it is generally in a conspicuous position, near the eye, and above the entrance, it is almost always charged with a series of rich figure sculptures, solemn in feeling and consecutive in subject. It occupies in Christian sacred edifices very nearly the position of the pediment in Greek sculpture. This latter is itself a kind of tympanum, and charged with sculpture in the same manner.

§ XII. (3.) The Gable. The same principles apply to it which have been noted respecting the spandril, with one more of some importance. The chief difficulty in treating a gable lies in the excessive sharpness of its upper point. It may, indeed, on its outside apex, receive a finial; but the meeting of the inside lines of its terminal mouldings is necessarily both harsh and conspicuous, unless artificially concealed. The most beautiful victory I have ever seen obtained over this difficulty was by placing a sharp shield, its point, as usual, downwards, at the apex of the gable, which exactly reversed the offensive lines, yet without actually breaking them; the gable being completed behind the shield. The same thing is done in the Northern and Southern Gothic: in the porches of Abbeville and the tombs of Verona.

§ XIII. I believe there is little else to be noted of general laws of ornament respecting the wall veil. We have next to consider its concentration in the shaft.

Now the principal beauty of a shaft is its perfect proportion to its work,—its exact expression of necessary strength. If this has been truly attained, it will hardly need, in some cases hardly bear, more decoration than is given to it by its own rounding and taper curvatures; for, if we cut ornaments in intaglio on its surface, we weaken it; if we leave them in relief, we overcharge it, and the sweep of the line from its base to its summit, though deduced in Chapter VIII., from necessities of construction, is already one of gradated curvature, and of high decorative value.

§ XIV. It is, however, carefully to be noted, that decorations are admissible on colossal and on diminutive shafts, which are wrong upon those of middle size. For, when the shaft is enormous, incisions or sculpture on its sides (unless colossal also), do not materially interfere with the sweep of its curve, nor diminish the efficiency of its sustaining mass. And if it be diminutive, its sustaining function is comparatively of so small importance, the injurious results of failure so much less, and the relative strength and cohesion of its mass so much greater, that it may be suffered in the extravagance of ornament or outline which would be unendurable in a shaft of middle size, and impossible in one of colossal. Thus, the shafts drawn in Plate XIII., of the "Seven Lamps," though given as examples of extravagance, are yet pleasing in the general effect of the arcade they support; being each some six or seven feet high. But they would have been monstrous, as well as unsafe, if they had been sixty or seventy.

§ XV. Therefore, to determine the general rule for shaft decoration, we must ascertain the proportions representative of the mean bulk of shafts: they might easily be calculated from a sufficient number of examples, but it may perhaps be assumed, for our present general purpose, that the mean standard would be of some twenty feet in height, by eight or nine in circumference: then this will be the size on which decoration is most difficult and dangerous: and shafts become more and more fit subjects for decoration, as they rise farther above, or fall farther beneath it, until very small and very vast shafts will both be found to look blank unless they receive some chasing or imagery; blank, whether they support a chair or table on the one side, or sustain a village on the ridge of an Egyptian architrave on the other.

§ XVI. Of the various ornamentation of colossal shafts, there are no examples so noble as the Egyptian; these the reader can study in Mr. Roberts' work on Egypt nearly as well, I imagine, as if he were beneath their shadow, one of their chief merits, as examples of method, being the perfect decision and visibility of their designs at the necessary distance: contrast with these the incrustations of bas-relief on the Trajan pillar, much interfering with the smooth lines of the shaft, and yet themselves untraceable, if not invisible.

§ XVII. On shafts of middle size, the only ornament which has ever been accepted as right, is the Doric fluting, which, indeed, gave the effect of a succession of unequal lines of shade, but lost much of the repose of the cylindrical gradation. The Corinthian fluting, which is a mean multiplication and deepening of the Doric, with a square instead of a sharp ridge between each hollow, destroyed the serenity of the shaft altogether, and is always rigid and meagre. Both are, in fact, wrong in principle; they are an elaborate weakening[83] of the shaft, exactly opposed (as above shown) to the ribbed form, which is the result of a group of shafts bound together, and which is especially beautiful when special service is given to each member.

Fig. LXII.

§ XVIII. On shafts of inferior size, every species of decoration may be wisely lavished, and in any quantity, so only that the form of the shaft be clearly visible. This I hold to be absolutely essential, and that barbarism begins wherever the sculpture is either so bossy, or so deeply cut, as to break the contour of the shaft, or compromise its solidity. Thus, in Plate XXI. (Appendix 8), the richly sculptured shaft of the lower story has lost its dignity and definite function, and become a shapeless mass, injurious to the symmetry of the building, though of some value as adding to its imaginative and fantastic character. Had all the shafts been like it, the façade would have been entirely spoiled; the inlaid pattern, on the contrary, which is used on the shortest shaft of the upper story, adds to its preciousness without interfering with its purpose, and is every way delightful, as are all the inlaid shaft ornaments of this noble church (another example of them is given in Plate XII. of the "Seven Lamps"). The same rule would condemn the Caryatid; which I entirely agree with Mr. Fergusson in thinking (both for this and other reasons) one of the chief errors of the Greek schools; and, more decisively still, the Renaissance inventions of shaft ornament, almost too absurd and too monstrous to be seriously noticed, which consist in leaving square blocks between the cylinder joints, as in the portico of No. 1, Regent Street, and many other buildings in London; or in rusticating portions of the shafts, or wrapping fleeces about them, as at the entrance of Burlington House, in Piccadilly; or tying drapery round them in knots, as in the new buildings above noticed (Chap. 20, § VII.), at Paris. But, within the limits thus defined, there is no feature capable of richer decoration than the shaft; the most beautiful examples of all I have seen, are the slender pillars, encrusted with arabesques, which flank the portals of the Baptistery and Duomo at Pisa, and some others of the Pisan and Lucchese churches; but the varieties of sculpture and inlaying, with which the small Romanesque shafts, whether Italian or Northern, are adorned when they occupy important positions, are quite endless, and nearly all admirable. Mr. Digby Wyatt has given a beautiful example of inlaid work so employed, from the cloisters of the Lateran, in his work on early mosaic; an example which unites the surface decoration of the shaft with the adoption of the spiral contour. This latter is often all the decoration which is needed, and none can be more beautiful; it has been spoken against, like many other good and lovely things, because it has been too often used in extravagant degrees, like the well-known twisting of the pillars in Raffaelle's "Beautiful gate." But that extravagant condition was a Renaissance barbarism: the old Romanesque builders kept their spirals slight and pure; often, as in the example from St. Zeno, in Plate XVII. below, giving only half a turn from the base of the shaft to its head, and nearly always observing what I hold to be an imperative law, that no twisted shaft shall be single, but composed of at least two distinct members, twined with each other. I suppose they followed their own right feeling in doing this, and had never studied natural shafts; but the type they might have followed was caught by one of the few great painters who were not affected by the evil influence of the fifteenth century, Benozzo Gozzoli, who, in the frescoes of the Ricardi Palace, among stems of trees for the most part as vertical as stone shafts, has suddenly introduced one of the shape given in Fig. LXII. Many forest trees present, in their accidental contortions, types of most complicated spiral shafts, the plan being originally of a grouped shaft rising from several roots; nor, indeed, will the reader ever find models for every kind of shaft decoration, so graceful or so gorgeous, as he will find in the great forest aisle, where the strength of the earth itself seems to rise from the roots into the vaulting; but the shaft surface, barred as it expands with rings of ebony and silver, is fretted with traceries of ivy, marbled with purple moss, veined with grey lichen, and tesselated, by the rays of the rolling heaven, with flitting fancies of blue shadow and burning gold.

FOOTNOTES:

[82] *Vide end of Appendix 20.*

[83] *Vide, however, their defence in the Essay above quoted, p. 251.*

CHAPTER XXVII

THE CORNICE AND CAPITAL

§ I. There are no features to which the attention of architects has been more laboriously directed, in all ages, than these crowning members of the wall and shaft; and it would be vain to endeavor, within any moderate limits, to give the reader any idea of the various kinds of admirable decoration which have been invented for them. But, in proportion to the effort and straining of the fancy, have been the extravagances into which it has occasionally fallen; and while it is utterly impossible severally to enumerate the instances either of its success or its error, it is very possible to note the limits of the one and the causes of the other. This is all that we shall attempt in the present chapter, tracing first for ourselves, as in previous instances, the natural channels by which invention is here to be directed or confined, and afterwards remarking the places where, in real practice, it has broken bounds.

§ II. The reader remembers, I hope, the main points respecting the cornice and capital, established above in the Chapters on Construction. Of these I must, however, recapitulate thus much:—

1. That both the cornice and capital are, with reference to the slope of their profile or bell, to be divided into two great orders; in one of which the ornament is convex, and in the other concave. (Ch. VI., § V.)

2. That the capital, with reference to the method of twisting the cornice round to construct it, and to unite the circular shaft with the square abacus, falls into five general forms, represented in Fig. XXII., p. 119.

3. That the most elaborate capitals were formed by true or simple capitals with a common cornice added above their abacus. (Ch. IX., § XXIV.)

We have then, in considering decoration, first to observe the treatment of the two great orders of the cornice; then their gathering into the five of the capital; then the addition of the secondary cornice to the capital when formed.

§ III. The two great orders or families of cornice were above distinguished in Fig. V., p. 69.; and it was mentioned in the same place that a third family arose from their combination. We must deal with the two great opposed groups first.

They were distinguished in Fig. V. by circular curves drawn on opposite sides of the same line. But we now know that in these smaller features the circle is usually the least interesting curve that we can use; and that it will be well, since the capital and cornice are both active in their expression, to use some of the more abstract natural lines. We will go back, therefore, to our old friend the salvia leaf; and taking the same piece of it we had before, x y, Plate VII., we will apply it to the cornice line; first within it, giving the concave cornice, then without, giving the convex cornice. In all the figures, a, b, c, d, Plate XV., the dotted line is at the same slope, and represents an average profile of the root of cornices (a, Fig. V., p. 69); the curve of the salvia leaf is applied to it in each case, first with its roundest curvature up, then with its roundest curvature down; and we have thus the two varieties, a and b, of the concave family, and c and d, of the convex family.

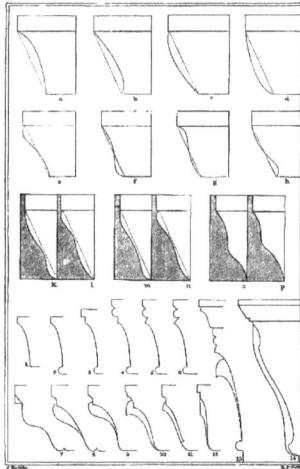

Plate XV. CORNICE PROFILES.

§ IV. These four profiles will represent all the simple cornices in the world; represent them, I mean, as central types: for in any of the profiles an infinite number of slopes may be given to the dotted line of the root (which in these four figures is always at the same angle); and on each of these innumerable slopes an innumerable variety of curves may be fitted, from every leaf in the forest, and every shell on the shore, and every movement of the human fingers and fancy; therefore, if the reader wishes to obtain something like a numerical representation of the number of possible and beautiful cornices which may be based upon these four types or roots, and among which the architect has leave to choose according to the circumstances of his building and the method of its composition, let him set down a figure 1 to begin with, and write ciphers after it as fast as he can, without stopping, for an hour.

§ V. None of the types are, however, found in perfection of curvature, except in the best work. Very often cornices are worked with circular segments (with a noble, massive effect, for instance, in St. Michele of Lucca), or with rude approximation to finer curvature, especially a, Plate XV., which occurs often so small as to render it useless to take much pains upon its curve. It occurs perfectly pure in the condition represented by 1 of the series 1-6, in Plate XV., on many of the Byzantine and early Gothic buildings of Venice; in more developed form it becomes the profile of the bell of the capital in the later Venetian Gothic, and in much of the best Northern Gothic. It also represents the Corinthian capital, in which the curvature is taken from the bell to be added in some excess to the nodding leaves. It is the most graceful of all simple profiles of cornice and capital.

§ VI. b is a much rarer and less manageable type: for this evident reason, that while a is the natural condition of a line rooted and strong beneath, but bent out by superincumbent weight, or nodding over in freedom, b is yielding at the base and rigid at the summit. It has, however, some exquisite uses, especially in combination, as the reader may see by glancing in advance at the inner line of the profile 14 in Plate XV.

§ VII. c is the leading convex or Doric type, as a is the leading concave or Corinthian. Its relation to the best Greek Doric is exactly what the relation of a is to the Corinthian; that is to say, the curvature must be taken from the straighter limb of the curve and added to the bolder bend, giving it a sudden turn inwards (as in the Corinthian a nod outwards), as the reader may see in the capital of the Parthenon in the British Museum, where the lower limb of the curve is all but a right line.[84] But these Doric and Corinthian lines are mere varieties of the great families which are represented by the central lines a and c, including not only the Doric capital, but all the small cornices formed by a slight increase of the curve of c, which are of so frequent occurrence in Greek ornaments.

§ VIII. d is the Christian Doric, which I said (Chap. I., § XX.) was invented to replace the antique: it is the representative of the great Byzantine and Norman families of convex cornice and capital, and, next to the profile a, the most important of the four, being the best profile for the convex capital, as a is for the concave; a being the best expression of an elastic line inserted vertically in the shaft, and d of an elastic line inserted horizontally and rising to meet vertical pressure.

If the reader will glance at the arrangements of boughs of trees, he will find them commonly dividing into these two families, a and d: they rise out of the trunk and nod from it as a, or they spring with sudden curvature out from it, and rise into sympathy with it, as at d; but they only accidentally display tendencies to the lines b or c. Boughs which fall as they spring from the tree also describe the curve d in the plurality of instances, but reversed in arrangement; their junction with the stem being at the top of it, their sprays bending out into rounder curvature.

§ IX. These then being the two primal groups, we have next to note the combined group, formed by the concave and convex lines joined in various proportions of curvature, so as to form together the reversed or ogee curve, represented in one of its most beautiful states by the glacier line a, on Plate VII. I would rather have taken this line than any other to have formed my third group of cornices by, but as it is too large, and almost too delicate, we will take instead that of the Matterhorn side, e f, Plate VII. For uniformity's sake I keep the slope of the dotted line the same as in the primal forms; and applying this Matterhorn curve in its four relative positions to that line, I have the types of the four cornices or capitals of the third family, e, f, g, h, on Plate XV.

These are, however, general types only thus far, that their line is composed of one short and one long curve, and that they represent the four conditions of treatment of every such line; namely, the longest curve concave in e and f, and convex in g and h; and the point of contrary flexure set high in e and g, and low in f and h. The relative depth of the arcs, or nature of their curvature, cannot be taken into consideration without a complexity of system which my space does not admit.

Of the four types thus constituted, e and f are of great importance; the other two are rarely used, having an appearance of weakness in consequence of the shortest curve being concave: the profiles e and f, when used for cornices, have usually a fuller sweep and somewhat greater equality between the branches of the curve; but those here given are better representatives of the structure applicable to capitals and cornices indifferently.

§ X. Very often, in the farther treatment of the profiles e or f, another limb is added to their curve in order to join it to the upper or lower members of the cornice or capital. I do not consider this addition as forming another family of cornices, because the leading and effective part of the curve is in these, as in the others, the single ogee; and the added bend is merely a less abrupt termination of it above or below: still this group is of so great importance in the richer kinds of ornamentation that we must have it sufficiently represented. We shall obtain a type of it by merely continuing the line of the Matterhorn side, of which before we took only a fragment. The entire line e to g on Plate VII., is evidently composed of three curves of unequal lengths, which if we call the shortest 1, the intermediate one 2, and the longest 3, are there arranged in the order 1, 3, 2, counting upwards. But evidently we might also have had the arrangements 1, 2, 3, and 2, 1, 3, giving us three distinct lines, altogether independent of position, which being applied to one general dotted slope will each give four cornices, or twelve altogether. Of these the six most important are those which have the shortest curve convex: they are given in light relief from k to p, Plate XV., and, by turning the page upside down, the other six will be seen in dark relief, only the little upright bits of shadow at the bottom are not to be considered as parts of them, being only admitted in order to give the complete profile of the more important cornices in light.

§ XI. In these types, as in e and f, the only general condition is, that their line shall be composed of three curves of different lengths and different arrangements (the depth of arcs and radius of curvatures being unconsidered). They are arranged in three couples, each couple being two positions of the same entire line; so that numbering the component curves in order of magnitude and counting upwards, they will read—

k 1, 2, 3,

l 3, 2, 1,
m 1, 3, 2,
n 2, 3, 1,
o 2, 1, 3,
p 3, 1, 2.

m and n, which are the Matterhorn line, are the most beautiful and important of all the twelve; k and l the next; o and p are used only for certain conditions of flower carving on the surface. The reverses (dark) of k and l are also of considerable service; the other four hardly ever used in good work.

§ XII. If we were to add a fourth curve to the component series, we should have forty-eight more cornices: but there is no use in pursuing the system further, as such arrangements are very rare and easily resolved into the simpler types with certain arbitrary additions fitted to their special place; and, in most cases, distinctly separate from the main curve, as in the inner line of No. 14, which is a form of the type e, the longest curve, i.e., the lowest, having deepest curvature, and each limb opposed by a short contrary curve at its extremities, the convex limb by a concave, the concave by a convex.

§ XIII. Such, then, are the great families of profile lines into which all cornices and capitals may be divided; but their best examples unite two such profiles in a mode which we cannot understand till we consider the further ornament with which the profiles are charged. And in doing this we must, for the sake of clearness, consider, first the nature of the designs themselves, and next the mode of cutting them.

Plate XVI. CORNICE DECORATION.

§ XIV. In Plate XVI., opposite, I have thrown together a few of the most characteristic mediæval examples of the treatment of the simplest cornice profiles: the uppermost, a, is the pure root of cornices from St. Mark's. The second, d, is the Christian Doric cornice, here lettered d in order to avoid confusion, its profile being d of Plate XV. in bold development, and here seen on the left-hand side, truly drawn, though filled up with the ornament to show the mode in which the angle is turned. This is also from St. Mark's. The third, b, is b of Plate XV., the pattern being inlaid in black because its office was in the interior of St. Mark's, where it was too dark to see sculptured ornament at the required distance. (The other two simple profiles, a and c of Plate XV., would be decorated in the same manner, but require no example here, for the profile a is of so frequent occurrence that it will have a page to itself alone in the next volume; and c may be seen over nearly every shop in London, being that of the common Greek egg cornice.) The fourth, e in Plate XVI., is a transitional cornice, passing from Byzantine into Venetian Gothic: f is a fully developed Venetian Gothic cornice founded on Byzantine traditions; and g the perfect Lombardic-Gothic cornice, founded on the Pisan Romanesque traditions, and strongly marked with the noblest Northern element, the Lombardic vitality restrained by classical models. I consider it a perfect cornice, and of the highest order.

§ XV. Now in the design of this series of ornaments there are two main points to be noted; the first, that they all, except b, are distinctly rooted in the lower part of the cornice, and spring to the top. This arrangement is constant in all the best cornices and capitals; and it is essential to the expression of the supporting power of both. It is exactly opposed to the system of running cornices and banded[85] capitals, in which the ornament flows along them horizontally, or is twined round them, as the mouldings are in the early English capital, and the foliage in many decorated ones. Such cornices have arisen from a mistaken appliance of the running ornaments, which are proper to archivolts, jambs, &c., to the features which have definite functions of support. A tendril may nobly follow the outline of an arch, but must not creep along a cornice, nor swathe or bandage a capital; it is essential to the expression of these features that their ornament should have an elastic and upward spring; and as the proper profile for the curve is that of a tree bough, as we saw above, so the proper arrangement of its farther ornament is that which best expresses rooted and ascendant strength like that of foliage.

There are certain very interesting exceptions to the rule (we shall see a curious one presently); and in the carrying out of the rule itself, we may see constant licenses taken by the great designers, and momentary violations of it, like those above spoken of, respecting other ornamental laws—violations which are for our refreshment, and for increase of delight in the general observance; and this is one of the peculiar beauties of the cornice g, which, rooting itself in strong central clusters, suffers some of its leaves to fall languidly aside, as the drooping outer leaves of a natural cluster do so often; but at the very instant that it does this, in order that it may not lose any of its expression of strength, a fruit-stalk is thrown up above the languid leaves, absolutely vertical, as much stiffer and stronger than the rest of the plant as the falling leaves are weaker. Cover this with your finger, and the cornice falls to pieces, like a bouquet which has been untied.

§ XVI. There are some instances in which, though the real arrangement is that of a running stem, throwing off leaves up and down, the positions of the leaves give nearly as much elasticity and organisation to the cornice, as if they had been rightly rooted; and others, like b, where the reversed portion of the ornament is lost in the shade, and the general expression of strength is got by the lower member. This cornice will, nevertheless, be felt at once to be inferior to the rest; and though we may often be called upon to admire designs of these kinds, which would have been exquisite if not thus misplaced, the reader will find that they are both of rare occurrence, and significative of declining style;

while the greater mass of the banded capitals are heavy and valueless, mere aggregations of confused sculpture, swathed round the extremity of the shaft, as if she had dipped it into a mass of melted ornament, as the glass-blower does his blow-pipe into the metal, and brought up a quantity adhering glutinously to its extremity. We have many capitals of this kind in England: some of the worst and heaviest in the choir of York. The later capitals of the Italian Gothic have the same kind of effect, but owing to another cause: for their structure is quite pure, and based on the Corinthian type: and it is the branching form of the heads of the leaves which destroys the effect of their organisation. On the other hand, some of the Italian cornices which are actually composed by running tendrils, throwing off leaves into oval interstices, are so massive in their treatment, and so marked and firm in their vertical and arched lines, that they are nearly as suggestive of support as if they had been arranged on the rooted system. A cornice of this kind is used in St. Michele of Lucca (Plate VI. in the "Seven Lamps," and XXI. here), and with exquisite propriety; for that cornice is at once a crown to the story beneath it and a foundation to that which is above it, and therefore unites the strength and elasticity of the lines proper to the cornice with the submission and prostration of those proper to the foundation.

§ XVII. This, then, is the first point needing general notice in the designs in Plate XVI. The second is the difference between the freedom of the Northern and the sophistication of the classical cornices, in connection with what has been advanced in Appendix 8. The cornices, a, d, and b, are of the same date, but they show a singular difference in the workman's temper: that at b is a single copy of a classical mosaic; and many carved cornices occur, associated with it, which are, in like manner, mere copies of the Greek and Roman egg and arrow mouldings. But the cornices a and d are copies of nothing of the kind: the idea of them has indeed been taken from the Greek honeysuckle ornament, but the chiselling of them is in no wise either Greek, or Byzantine, in temper. The Byzantines were languid copyists: this work is as energetic as its original; energetic, not in the quantity of work, but in the spirit of it: an indolent man, forced into toil, may cover large spaces with evidence of his feeble action, or accumulate his dulness into rich aggregation of trouble, but it is gathered weariness still. The man who cut those two uppermost cornices had no time to spare: did as much cornice as he could in half an hour; but would not endure the slightest trace of error in a curve, or of bluntness in an edge. His work is absolutely unreproveable; keen, and true, as Nature's own; his entire force is in it, and fixed on seeing that every line of it shall be sharp and right: the faithful energy is in him: we shall see something come of that cornice: The fellow who inlaid the other (b), will stay where he is for ever; and when he has inlaid one leaf up, will inlay another down,—and so undulate up and down to all eternity: but the man of a and d will cut his way forward, or there is no truth in handicrafts, nor stubbornness in stone.

§ XVIII. But there is something else noticeable in those two cornices, besides the energy of them: as opposed either to b, or the Greek honeysuckle or egg patterns, they are natural designs. The Greek egg and arrow cornice is a nonsense cornice, very noble in its lines, but utterly absurd in meaning. Arrows have had nothing to do with eggs (at least since Leda's time), neither are the so-called arrows like arrows, nor the eggs like eggs, nor the honeysuckles like honeysuckles; they are all conventionalised into a monotonous successiveness of nothing,—pleasant to the eye, useless to the thought. But those Christian cornices are, as far as may be, suggestive; there is not the tenth of the work in them that there is in the Greek arrows, but, as far as that work will go, it has consistent intention; with the fewest possible incisions, and those of the easiest shape, they suggest the true image, of clusters of leaves, each leaf with its central depression from root to point, and that distinctly visible at almost any distance from the eye, and in almost any light.

§ XIX. Here, then, are two great new elements visible; energy and naturalism:—Life, with submission to the laws of God, and love of his works; this is Christianity, dealing with her classical models. Now look back to what I said in Chap. 1. § XX. of this dealing of hers, and invention of the new Doric line; then to what is above stated (§ VIII.) respecting that new Doric, and the boughs of trees; and now to the evidence in the cutting of the leaves on the same Doric section, and see how the whole is beginning to come together.

§ XX. We said that something would come of these two cornices, a and d. In e and f we see that something has come of them: e is also from St. Mark's, and one of the earliest examples in Venice of the transition from the Byzantine to the Gothic cornice. It is already singularly developed; flowers have been added between the clusters of leaves, and the leaves themselves curled over: and observe the well-directed thought of the sculptor in this curling;—the old incisions are retained below, and their excessive rigidity is one of the proofs of the earliness of the cornice; but those incisions now stand for the under surface of the leaf; and behold, when it turns over, on the top of it you see true ribs. Look at the upper and under surface of a cabbage-leaf, and see what quick steps we are making.

§ XXI. The fifth example (f) was cut in 1347; it is from the tomb of Marco Giustiniani, in the church of St. John and Paul, and it exhibits the character of the central Venetian Gothic fully developed. The lines are all now soft and undulatory, though elastic; the sharp incisions have become deeply-gathered folds; the hollow of the leaf is expressed completely beneath, and its edges are touched with light, and incised into several lobes, and their ribs delicately drawn above. (The flower between is only accidentally absent; it occurs in most cornices of the time.)

But in both these cornices the reader will notice that while the naturalism of the sculpture is steadily on the increase, the classical formalism is still retained. The leaves are accurately numbered, and sternly set in their places; they are leaves in office, and dare not stir nor wave. They have the shapes of leaves, but not the functions, "having the form of knowledge, but denying the power thereof." What is the meaning of this?

§ XXII. Look back to the XXXIIIrd paragraph of the first chapter, and you will see the meaning of it. These cornices are the Venetian Ecclesiastical Gothic; the Christian element struggling with the Formalism of the Papacy,—the Papacy being entirely heathen in all its principles. That officialism of the leaves and their ribs means Apostolic succession, and I don't know how much more, and is already preparing for the transition to old Heathenism again, and the Renaissance.[86]

§ XXIII. Now look to the last cornice (g). That is Protestantism,—a slight touch of Dissent, hardly amounting to schism, in those falling leaves, but true life in the whole of it. The forms all broken through, and sent heaven knows where, but the root held fast; and the strong sap in the branches; and, best of all, good fruit ripening and opening straight towards heaven, and in the face of it, even though some of the leaves lie in the dust.

Now, observe. The cornice f represents Heathenism and Papistry, animated by the mingling of Christianity and nature. The good in it, the life of it, the veracity and liberty of it, such as it has, are Protestantism in its heart; the rigidity and saplessness are the Romanism of it. It is the mind of Fra Angelico in the monk's dress,—Christianity before the Reformation. The cornice g has the Lombardic life element in its fulness, with only some color and shape of Classicalism mingled with it—the good of classicalism; as much method and Formalism as are consistent with life, and fitting for it: The continence within certain border lines, the unity at the root, the simplicity of the great profile,—all these are the healthy classical elements retained: the rest is reformation, new strength, and recovered liberty.

§ XXIV. There is one more point about it especially noticeable. The leaves are thoroughly natural in their general character, but they are of no particular species: and after being something like cabbage-leaves in the beginning, one of them suddenly becomes an ivy-leaf in the end. Now I don't know what to say of this. I know it, indeed, to be a classical character;—it is eminently characteristic of Southern work; and markedly distinctive of it from the Northern ornament, which would have been oak, or ivy, or apple, but not anything, nor two things in one. It is, I repeat, a clearly classical element; but whether a good or bad element, I am not sure;—whether it is the last trace of Centaurism and other monstrosity dying away; or whether it has a figurative purpose, legitimate in architecture (though never in painting), and has been rightly retained by the Christian sculptor, to express the working of that spirit which grafts one nature upon another, and discerns a law in its members warring against the law of its mind.

§ XXV. These, then, being the points most noticeable in the spirit both of the designs and the chiselling, we have now to return to the question proposed in § XIII., and observe the modifications of form of profile which resulted from the changing contours of the leafage; for up to § XIII., we had, as usual, considered the possible conditions of form in the abstract;—the modes in which they have been derived from each other in actual practice require to be followed in their turn. How the Greek Doric or Greek ogee cornices were invented is not easy to determine, and, fortunately, is little to our present purpose; for the mediæval ogee cornices have an independent development of their own, from the first type of the concave cornice a in Plate XV.

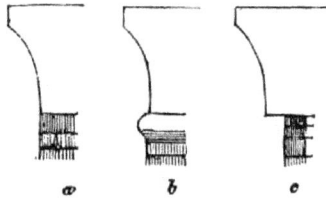

Fig. LXIII.

§ XXVI. That cornice occurs, in the simplest work, perfectly pure, but in finished work it was quickly felt that there was a meagreness in its junction with the wall beneath it, where it was set as here at a, Fig. LXIII., which could only be conquered by concealing such junction in a bar of shadow. There were two ways of getting this bar: one by a projecting roll at the foot of the cornice (b, Fig. LXIII.), the other by slipping the whole cornice a little forward (c. Fig. LXIII.). From these two methods arise two groups of cornices and capitals, which we shall pursue in succession.

§ XXVII. First group. With the roll at the base (b, Fig. LXIII.). The chain of its succession is represented from 1 to 6, in Plate XV.: 1 and 2 are the steps already gained, as in Fig. LXIII.; and in them the profile of cornice used is a of Plate XV., or a refined condition of b of Fig. V., p. 69, above. Now, keeping the same refined profile, substitute the condition of it, f of Fig. V. (and there accounted for), above the roll here, and you have 3, Plate XV. This superadded abacus was instantly felt to be harsh in its projecting angle; but you know what to do with an angle when it is harsh. Use your simplest chamfer on it (a or b, Fig. LIII., page 287, above), but on the visible side only, and you have fig. 4, Plate XV. (the top stone being made deeper that you may have room to chamfer it). Now this fig. 4 is the profile of Lombardic and Venetian early capitals and cornices, by tens of thousands; and it continues into the late Venetian Gothic, with this only difference, that as times advances, the vertical line at the top of the original cornice begins to slope outwards, and through a series of years rises like the hazel wand in the hand of a diviner:—but how slowly! a stone dial which marches but 45 degrees in three centuries, and through the intermediate condition 5 arrives at 6, and so stays.

In tracing this chain I have kept all the profiles of the same height in order to make the comparison more easy; the depth chosen is about intermediate between that which is customary in cornices on the one hand, which are often a little shorter, and capitals on the other, which are often a little deeper.[87] And it is to be noted that the profiles 5 and 6 establish themselves in capitals chiefly, while 4 is retained in cornices to the latest times.

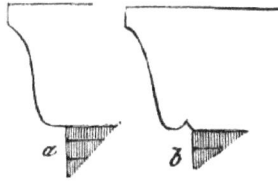

Fig. LXIV.

§ XXVIII. Second group (c, Fig. LXIII.). If the lower angle, which was quickly felt to be hard, be rounded off, we have the form a, Fig. LXIV. The front of the curved line is then decorated, as we have seen; and the termination of the decorated surface marked by an incision, as in an ordinary chamfer, as at b here. This I believe to have been the simple origin of most of the Venetian ogee cornices; but they are farther complicated by the curves given to the leafage which flows over them. In the ordinary Greek cornices, and in a and d of Plate XVI., the decoration is incised from the outside profile, without any suggestion of an interior surface of a different contour. But in the leaf cornices which follow, the decoration is represented as overlaid on one of the early profiles, and has another outside contour of its own; which is, indeed, the true profile of the cornice, but beneath which, more or less, the simpler profile is seen or suggested, which terminates all the incisions of the chisel. This under profile will often be found to be some condition of the type a or b, Fig. LXIV.; and the leaf profile to be another ogee with its fullest curve up instead of down, lapping over the cornice edge above, so that the entire profile might be considered as made up of two ogee curves laid, like packed herrings, head to tail. Figures 8 and 9 of Plate XV. exemplify this arrangement. Fig. 7 is a heavier contour, doubtless composed in the same manner, but of which I had not marked the innermost profile, and which I have given here only to complete the series which, from 7 to 12 inclusive, exemplifies the gradual restriction of the leaf outline, from its boldest projection in the cornice to its most modest service in the capital. This change, however, is not one which indicates difference of age, but merely of office and position: the cornice 7 is from the tomb of the Doge Andrea Dandolo (1350) in St. Mark's, 8 from a canopy over a door of about the same period, 9 from the tomb of the Dogaressa Agnese Venier (1411), 10 from that of Pietro Cornaro (1361),[88] and 11 from that of Andrea Morosini (1347), all in the church of San Giov. and Paola, all these being cornice profiles; and, finally, 12 from a capital of the Ducal Palace, of fourteen century work.

§ XXIX. Now the reader will doubtless notice that in the three examples, 10 to 12, the leaf has a different contour from that of 7, 8, or 9. This difference is peculiarly significant. I have always desired that the reader should theoretically consider the capital as a concentration of the cornice; but in practice it often happens that the cornice is, on the contrary, an unrolled capital; and one of the richest early forms of the Byzantine cornice (not given in Plate XV., because its separate character and importance require examination apart) is nothing more than an unrolled continuation of the lower range of acanthus leaves on the Corinthian capital. From this cornice others appear to have been derived, like e in Plate XVI., in which the acanthus outline has become confused with that of the honeysuckle, and the rosette of the centre of the Corinthian capital introduced between them; and thus their forms approach more and more to those derived from the cornice itself. Now if the leaf has the contour of 10, 11, or 12, Plate XV., the profile is either actually of a capital, or of a cornice derived from a capital; while, if the leaf have the contour of 7 or 8, the profile is either actually of a cornice or of a capital derived from a cornice. Where the Byzantines use the acanthus, the Lombards use the Persepolitan water-leaf; but the connection of the cornices and capitals is exactly the same.

§ XXX. Thus far, however, we have considered the characters of profile which are common to the cornice and capital both. We have now to note what farther decorative features or peculiarities belong to the capital itself, or result from the theoretical gathering of the one into the other.

Look back to Fig. XXII., p. 110. The five types there given, represented the five different methods of concentration of the root of cornices, a of Fig. V. Now, as many profiles of cornices as were developed in Plate XV. from this cornice root, there represented by the dotted slope, so many may be applied to each of the five types in Fig. XXII.,—applied simply in a and b, but with farther modifications, necessitated by their truncations or spurs, in c, d, and e.

Then, these cornice profiles having been so applied in such length and slope as is proper for capitals, the farther condition comes into effect described in Chapter IX. § XXIV., and any one of the cornices in Plate XV. may become the abacus of a capital formed out of any other, or out of itself. The infinity of forms thus resultant cannot, as may well be supposed, be exhibited or catalogued in the space at present permitted to us: but the reader, once master of the principle, will easily be able to investigate for himself the syntax of all examples that may occur to him, and I shall only here, as a kind of exercise, put before him a few of those which he will meet with most frequently in his Venetian inquiries, or which illustrate points, not hitherto touched upon, in the disposition of the abacus.

§ XXXI. In Plate XVII. the capital at the top, on the left hand, is the rudest possible gathering of the plain Christian Doric cornice, d of Plate XV. The shaft is octagonal, and the capital is not cut to fit it, but is square at the base; and the curve of its profile projects on two of its sides more than on the other two, so as to make the abacus oblong, in order to carry an oblong mass of brickwork, dividing one of the upper lights of a Lombard campanile at Milan. The awkward stretching of the brickwork, to do what the capital ought to have done, is very remarkable. There is here no second superimposed abacus.

§ XXXII. The figure on the right hand, at the top, shows the simple but perfect fulfilment of all the requirements in which the first example fails. The mass of brickwork to be carried is exactly the same in size and shape; but instead of being trusted to a single shaft, it has two of smaller area (compare Chap. VIII., § XIII.), and all the expansion necessary is now gracefully attained by their united capitals, hewn out of one stone. Take the section of these capitals through their angle, and nothing can be simpler or purer; it is composed of 2, in Plate XV., used for the capital itself, with c of Fig. LXIII. used for the abacus; the reader could hardly have a neater little bit of syntax for a first lesson. If the section be taken through the side of the bell, the capital profile is the root of cornices, a of Fig. V., with the added roll. This capital is somewhat remarkable in having its sides perfectly straight, some slight curvature being usual on so bold a scale; but it is all the better as a first example, the method of reduction being of order d, in Fig. XXII., p. 110, and with a concave cut, as in Fig. XXI., p. 109. These two capitals are from the cloister of the duomo of Verona.

Plate XVII. CAPITALS CONCAVE GROUP.

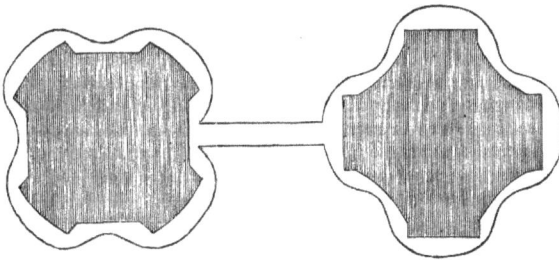

Fig. LXV.

§ XXXIII. The lowermost figure in Plate XVII. represents an exquisitely finished example of the same type, from St. Zeno of Verona. Above, at 2, in Plate II., the plan of the shafts was given, but I inadvertently reversed their position: in comparing that plan with Plate XVII., Plate II. must be held upside down. The capitals, with the band connecting them, are all cut out of one block; their profile is an adaptation of 4 of Plate XV., with a plain headstone superimposed. This method of reduction is that of order d in Fig. XXII., but the peculiarity of treatment of their truncation is highly interesting. Fig. LXV. represents the plans of the capitals at the base, the shaded parts being the bells: the open line, the roll with its connecting band. The bell of the one, it will be seen, is the exact reverse of that of the other: the angle truncations are, in both, curved horizontally as well as uprightly; but their curve is convex in the one, and in the other concave. Plate XVII. will show the effect of both, with the farther incisions, to the same depth, on the flank of the one with the concave truncation, which join with the rest of its singularly bold and keen execution in giving the impression of its rather having been cloven into its form by the sweeps of a sword, than by the dull travail of a chisel. Its workman was proud of it, as well he might be: he has written his name upon its front (I would that more of his fellows had been as kindly vain), and the goodly stone proclaims for ever, ADAMINUS DE SANCTO GIORGIO ME FECIT.

§ XXXIV. The reader will easily understand that the gracefulness of this kind of truncation, as he sees it in Plate XVII., soon suggested the idea of reducing it to a vegetable outline, and laying four healing leaves, as it were, upon the wounds which the sword had made. These four leaves, on the truncations of the capital, correspond to the four leaves which we saw, in like manner, extend themselves over the spurs of the base, and, as they increase in delicacy of execution, form one of the most lovely groups of capitals which the Gothic workmen ever invented; represented by two perfect types in the capitals of the Piazzetta columns of Venice. But this pure group is an isolated one; it remains in the first simplicity of its conception far into the thirteenth century, while around it rise up a crowd of other forms, imitative of the old Corinthian, and in which other and younger leaves spring up in luxuriant growth among the primal four. The varieties of their grouping we shall enumerate hereafter: one general characteristic of them all must be noted here.

§ XXXV. The reader has been told repeatedly[89] that there are two, and only two, real orders of capitals, originally represented by the Corinthian and the Doric; and distinguished by the concave or convex contours of their bells, as shown by the dotted lines at e, Fig. V., p. 65. And hitherto, respecting the capital, we have been exclusively concerned with the methods in which these two families of simple contours have gathered themselves together, and obtained reconciliation to the abacus above, and the shaft below. But the last paragraph introduces us to the surface ornament disposed upon these, in the chiselling of which the characters described above, § XXVIII., which are but feebly marked in the cornice, boldly distinguish and divide the families of the capital.

§ XXXVI. Whatever the nature of the ornament be, it must clearly have relief of some kind, and must present projecting surfaces separated by incisions. But it is a very material question whether the contour, hitherto broadly considered as that of the entire bell, shall be that of the outside of the projecting and relieved ornaments, or of the bottoms of the incisions which divide them; whether, that is to say, we shall first cut out the bell of our capital quite smooth, and then cut farther into it, with incisions, which shall leave ornamental forms in relief, or whether, in originally cutting the contour of the bell, we shall leave projecting bits of stone, which we may afterwards work into the relieved ornament.

§ XXXVII. Now, look back to Fig. V., p. 65. Clearly, if to ornament the already hollowed profile, b, we cut deep incisions into it, we shall so far weaken it at the top, that it will nearly lose all its supporting power. Clearly, also, if to ornament the already bulging profile c we were to leave projecting pieces of stone outside of it, we should nearly destroy all its relation to the original sloping line X, and produce an unseemly and ponderous mass, hardly recognizable as a cornice profile. It is evident, on the other hand, that we can afford to cut into this profile without fear of destroying its strength, and that we can afford to leave projections outside of the other, without fear of destroying its lightness. Such is, accordingly, the natural disposition of the sculpture, and the two great families of capitals are therefore distinguished, not merely by their concave and convex contours, but by the ornamentation being left outside the bell of the one, and cut into the bell of the other; so that, in either case, the ornamental portions will fall between the dotted lines at e, Fig. V., and the pointed oval, or vesica piscis, which is traced by them, may be called the Limit of ornamentation.

§ XXXVIII. Several distinctions in the quantity and style of the ornament must instantly follow from this great distinction in its position. First, in its quantity. For, observe: since in the Doric profile, c of Fig. V., the contour itself is to be composed of the surface of the ornamentation, this ornamentation must be close and united enough to form, or at least suggest, a continuous surface; it must, therefore, be rich in quantity and close in aggregation; otherwise it will destroy the massy character of the profile it adorns, and approximate it to its opposite, the concave. On the other hand, the ornament left projecting from the concave, must be sparing enough, and dispersed enough, to allow the concave bell to be clearly seen beneath it; otherwise it will choke up the concave profile, and approximate it to its opposite, the convex.

§ XXXIX. And, secondly, in its style. For, clearly, as the sculptor of the concave profile must leave masses of rough stone prepared for his outer ornament, and cannot finish them at once, but must complete the cutting of the smooth bell beneath first, and then return to the projecting masses (for if he were to finish these latter first, they would assuredly, if delicate or sharp, be broken as he worked on; since, I say, he must work in this foreseeing and predetermined method, he is sure to reduce the system of his ornaments to some definite symmetrical order before he begins); and the habit of conceiving beforehand all that he has to do, will probably render him not only more orderly in its arrangement, but more skilful and accurate in its execution, than if he could finish all as he worked on. On the other hand, the sculptor of the convex profile has its smooth surface laid before him, as a piece of paper on which he can sketch at his pleasure; the incisions he makes in it are like touches of a dark pencil; and he is at liberty to roam over the surface in perfect freedom, with light incisions or with deep; finishing here, suggesting there, or perhaps in places leaving the surface altogether smooth. It is ten to one, therefore, but that, if he yield to the temptation, he becomes irregular in design, and rude in handling; and we shall assuredly find the two families of capitals distinguished, the one by its symmetrical, thoroughly organised, and exquisitely executed ornament, the other by its rambling, confused, and rudely chiselled ornament: But, on the other hand, while we shall often have to admire the disciplined precision of the one, and as often to regret the irregular rudeness of the other, we shall not fail to find balancing qualities in both. The severity of the disciplinarian capital represses the power of the imagination; it gradually degenerates into Formalism; and the indolence which cannot escape from its stern demand of accurate workmanship, seeks refuge in copyism of established forms, and loses itself at last in lifeless mechanism. The license of the other, though often abused, permits full exercise to the imagination: the mind of the sculptor, unshackled by the niceties of chiselling, wanders over its orbed field in endless fantasy; and, when generous as well as powerful, repays the liberty which has been granted to it with interest, by developing through the utmost wildness and fulness of its thoughts, an order as much more noble than the mechanical symmetry of the opponent school, as the domain which it regulates is vaster.

Plate XVIII. CAPITALS CONVEX GROUP.

§ **XL.** And now the reader shall judge whether I had not reason to cast aside the so-called Five orders of the Renaissance architects, with their volutes and fillets, and to tell him that there were only two real orders, and that there could never be more.[90] For we now find that these two great and real orders are representative of the two great influences which must for ever divide the heart of man: the one of Lawful Discipline, with its perfection and order, but its danger of degeneracy into Formalism; the other of Lawful Freedom, with its vigor and variety, but its danger of degeneracy into Licentiousness.

§ **XLI.** I shall not attempt to give any illustrations here of the most elaborate developments of either order; they will be better given on a larger scale: but the examples in Plate XVII. and XVIII. represent the two methods of ornament in their earliest appliance. The two lower capitals in Plate XVII. are a pure type of the concave school; the two in the centre of Plate XVIII., of the convex. At the top of Plate XVIII. are two Lombardic capitals; that on the left from Sta. Sofia at Padua, that on the right from the cortile of St. Ambrogio at Milan. They both have the concave angle truncation; but being of date prior to the time when the idea of the concave bell was developed, they are otherwise left square, and decorated with the surface ornament characteristic of the convex school. The relation of the designs to each other is interesting; the cross being prominent in the centre of each, but more richly relieved in that from St. Ambrogio. The two beneath are from the southern portico of St. Mark's; the shafts having been of different lengths, and neither, in all probability, originally intended for their present place, they have double abaci, of which the uppermost is the cornice running round the whole façade. The zigzagged capital is highly curious, and in its place very effective and beautiful, although one of the exceptions which it was above noticed that we should sometimes find to the law stated in § XV. above.

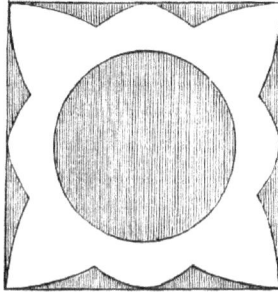

Fig. LXVI.

§ XLII. The lower capital, which is also of the true convex school, exhibits one of the conditions of the spurred type, e of Fig. XXII., respecting which one or two points must be noticed.

If we were to take up the plan of the simple spur, represented at e in Fig. XXII., p. 110, and treat it, with the salvia leaf, as we did the spur of the base, we should have for the head of our capital a plan like Fig. LXVI., which is actually that of one of the capitals of the Fondaco de' Turchi at Venice; with this only difference, that the intermediate curves between the spurs would have been circular: the reason they are not so, here, is that the decoration, instead of being confined to the spur, is now spread over the whole mass, and contours are therefore given to the intermediate curves which fit them for this ornament; the inside shaded space being the head of the shaft, and the outer, the abacus. The reader has in Fig. LXVI. a characteristic type of the plans of the spurred capitals, generally preferred by the sculptors of the convex school, but treated with infinite variety, the spurs often being cut into animal forms, or the incisions between them multiplied, for richer effect; and in our own Norman capital the type c of Fig. XXII. is variously subdivided by incisions on its slope, approximating in general effect to many conditions of the real spurred type, e, but totally differing from them in principle.

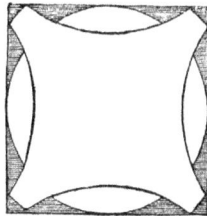

Fig. LXVII.

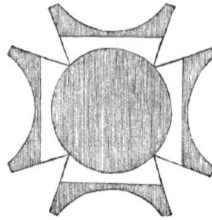

Fig. LXVIII.

§ XLIII. The treatment of the spur in the concave school is far more complicated, being borrowed in nearly every case from the original Corinthian. Its plan may be generally represented by Fig. LXVII. The spur itself is carved into a curling tendril or concave leaf, which supports the projecting angle of a four-sided abacus, whose hollow sides fall back behind the bell, and have generally a rosette or other ornament in their centres. The mediæval architects often put another square abacus above all, as represented by the shaded portion of Fig. LXVII., and some massy conditions of this form, elaborately ornamented, are very beautiful; but it is apt to become rigid and effeminate, as assuredly it is in the original Corinthian, which is thoroughly mean and meagre in its upper tendrils and abacus.

§ XLIV. The lowest capital in Plate XVIII. is from St. Mark's, and singular in having double spurs; it is therefore to be compared with the doubly spurred base, also from St Mark's, in Plate XI. In other respects it is a good example of the union of breadth of mass with subtlety of curvature, which characterises nearly all the spurred capitals of the convex school. Its plan is given in Fig. LXVIII.: the inner shaded circle is the head of the shaft; the white cross, the bottom of the capital, which expands itself into the external shaded portions at the top. Each spur, thus formed, is cut like a ship's bow, with the Doric profile; the surfaces so obtained are then charged with arborescent ornament.

§ XLV. I shall not here farther exemplify the conditions of the treatment of the spur, because I am afraid of confusing the reader's mind, and diminishing the distinctness of his conception of the differences between the two great orders, which it has been my principal object to develope throughout this chapter. If all my readers lived in London, I could at once fix this difference in their minds by a simple, yet somewhat curious illustration. In many parts of the west end of London, as, for instance, at the corners of Belgrave Square, and the north side of Grosvenor Square, the Corinthian capitals of newly-built houses are put into cages of wire. The wire cage is the exact form of the typical capital of the convex school; the Corinthian capital, within, is a finished and highly decorated example of the concave. The space between the cage and capital is the limit of ornamentation.

§ XLVI. Those of my readers, however, to whom this illustration is inaccessible, must be content with the two profiles, 13 and 14, on Plate XV. If they will glance along the line of sections from 1 to 6, they will see that the profile 13 is their final development, with a superadded cornice for its abacus. It is taken from a capital in a very important ruin of a palace, near the Rialto of Venice, and hereafter to be described; the projection, outside of its principal curve, is the profile of its superadded leaf ornamentation; it may be taken as one of the simplest, yet a perfect type of the concave group.

§ XLVII. The profile 14 is that of the capital of the main shaft of the northern portico of St. Mark's, the most finished example I ever met with of the convex family, to which, in spite of the central inward bend of its profile, it is marked as distinctly belonging, by the bold convex curve at its root, springing from the shaft in the line of the Christian Doric cornice, and exactly reversing the structure of the other profile, which rises from the shaft, like a palm leaf from its stem. Farther, in the profile 13, the innermost line is that of the bell; but in the profile 14, the outermost line is that of the bell, and the inner line is the limit of the incisions of the chisel, in undercutting a reticulated veil of ornament, surrounding a flower like a lily; most ingeniously, and, I hope, justly, conjectured by the Marchese Selvatico to have been intended for an imitation of the capitals of the temple of Solomon, which Hiram made, with "nets of checker work, and wreaths of chain work for the chapiters that were on the top of the pillars ... and the chapiters that were upon the top of the pillars were of lily work in the porch." (1 Kings, vii. 17, 19.)

§ XLVIII. On this exquisite capital there is imposed an abacus of the profile with which we began our investigation long ago, the profile a of Fig. V. This abacus is formed by the cornice already given, a, of Plate XVI.: and therefore we have, in this lovely Venetian capital, the summary of the results of our investigation, from its beginning to its close: the type of the first cornice; the decoration of it, in its emergence from the classical models; the gathering into the capital; the superimposition of the secondary cornice, and the refinement of the bell of the capital by triple curvature in the two limits of chiselling. I cannot express the exquisite refinements of the curves on the small scale of Plate XV.; I will give them more accurately in a larger engraving; but the scale on which they are here given will not prevent the reader from perceiving, and let him note it thoughtfully, that the outer curve of the noble capital is the one which was our first example of associated curves; that I have had no need, throughout the whole of our inquiry, to refer to any other ornamental line than the three which I at first chose, the simplest of those which Nature set by chance before me; and that this lily, of the delicate Venetian marble, has but been wrought, by the highest human art, into the same line which the clouds disclose, when they break from the rough rocks of the flank of the Matterhorn.

FOOTNOTES:

[84] In very early Doric it was an absolute right line; and that capital is therefore derived from the pure cornice root, represented by the dotted line.

[85] The word banded is used by Professor Willis in a different sense; which I would respect, by applying it in his sense always to the Impost, and in mine to the capital itself. (This note is not for the general reader, who need not trouble himself about the matter.)

[86] The Renaissance period being one of return to formalism on the one side, of utter licentiousness on the other, so that sometimes, as here, I have to declare its lifelessness, at other times (Chap. XXV., § XVII.) its lasciviousness. There is, of course, no contradiction in this: but the reader might well ask how I knew the change from the base 11 to the base 12, in Plate XII., to be one from temperance to luxury; and from the cornice f to the cornice g, in Plate XVI., to be one from formalism to vitality. I know it, both by certain internal evidences, on which I shall have to dwell at length hereafter, and by the context of the works of the time. But the outward signs might in both ornaments be the same, distinguishable only as signs of opposite tendencies by the event of both. The blush of shame cannot always be told from the blush of indignation.

[87] The reader must always remember that a cornice, in becoming a capital, must, if not originally bold and deep, have depth added to its profile, in order to reach the just proportion of the lower member of the shaft head; and that therefore the small Greek egg cornices are utterly incapable of becoming capitals till they have totally changed their form and depth. The Renaissance architects, who never obtained hold of a right principle but they made it worse than a wrong one by misapplication, caught the

idea of turning the cornice into a capital, but did not comprehend the necessity of the accompanying change of depth. Hence we have pilaster heads formed of small egg cornices, and that meanest of all mean heads of shafts, the coarse Roman Doric profile chopped into a small egg and arrow moulding, both which may be seen disfiguring half the buildings in London.

[88] I have taken these dates roughly from Selvatico; their absolute accuracy to within a year or two, is here of no importance.

[89] Chap. I. § XIX., Appendix 7: and Chap. VI. § V.

[90] Chap. I., § XIX.

CHAPTER XXVIII

THE ARCHIVOLT AND APERTURE

Plate XIX. ARCHIVOLT DECORATION. AT VERONA.

§ I. If the windows and doors of some of our best northern Gothic buildings were built up, and the ornament of their archivolts concealed, there would often remain little but masses of dead wall and unsightly buttress; the whole vitality of the building consisting in the graceful proportions or rich mouldings of its apertures. It is not so in the south, where, frequently, the aperture is a mere dark spot on the variegated wall; but there the column, with its horizontal or curved architrave, assumes an importance of another kind, equally dependent upon the methods of lintel and archivolt decoration. These, though in their richness of minor variety they defy all exemplification, may be very broadly generalized.

Of the mere lintel, indeed, there is no specific decoration, nor can be; it has no organism to direct its ornament, and therefore may receive any kind and degree of ornament, according to its position. In a

Greek temple, it has meagre horizontal lines; in a Romanesque church, it becomes a row of upright niches, with an apostle in each; and may become anything else at the architect's will. But the arch head has a natural organism, which separates its ornament into distinct families, broadly definable.

§ II. In speaking of the arch-line and arch masonry, we considered the arch to be cut straight through the wall; so that, if half built, it would have the appearance at a, Fig. LXIX. But in the chapter on Form of Apertures, we found that the side of the arch, or jamb of the aperture, might often require to be bevelled, so as to give the section b, Fig. LXIX. It is easily conceivable that when two ranges of voussoirs were used, one over another, it would be easier to leave those beneath, of a smaller diameter, than to bevel them to accurate junction with those outside. Whether influenced by this facility, or by decorative instinct, the early northern builders often substitute for the bevel the third condition, c, of Fig. LXIX.; so that, of the three forms in that figure, a belongs principally to the south, c to the north, and b indifferently to both.

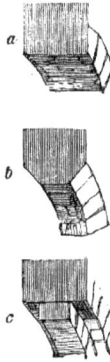

Fig. LXIX.

§ III. If the arch in the northern building be very deep, its depth will probably be attained by a succession of steps, like that in c; and the richest results of northern archivolt decoration are entirely based on the aggregation of the ornament of these several steps; while those of the south are only the complete finish and perfection of the ornament of one. In this ornament of the single arch, the points for general note are very few.

§ IV. It was, in the first instance, derived from the classical architrave,[91] and the early Romanesque arches are nothing but such an architrave, bent round. The horizontal lines of the latter become semicircular, but their importance and value remain exactly the same; their continuity is preserved across all the voussoirs, and the joints and functions of the latter are studiously concealed. As the builders get accustomed to the arch, and love it better, they cease to be ashamed of its structure: the voussoirs begin to show themselves confidently, and fight for precedence with the architrave lines; and there is an entanglement of the two structures, in consequence, like the circular and radiating lines of a cobweb, until at last the architrave lines get worsted, and driven away outside of the voussoirs; being permitted to stay at all only on condition of their dressing themselves in mediæval costume, as in the plate opposite.

§ V. In other cases, however, before the entire discomfiture of the architrave, a treaty of peace is signed between the adverse parties on these terms: That the architrave shall entirely dismiss its inner three meagre lines, and leave the space of them to the voussoirs, to display themselves after their manner; but that, in return for this concession, the architrave shall have leave to expand the small cornice which usually terminates it (the reader had better look at the original form in that of the Erechtheum, in the middle of the Elgin room of the British Museum) into bolder prominence, and even to put brackets under it, as if it were a roof cornice, and thus mark with a bold shadow the terminal line of the voussoirs. This condition is seen in the arch from St. Pietro of Pistoja, Plate XIII., above.

§ VI. If the Gothic spirit of the building be thoroughly determined, and victorious, the architrave cornice is compelled to relinquish its classical form, and take the profile of a Gothic cornice or dripstone; while, in other cases, as in much of the Gothic of Verona, it is forced to disappear altogether. But the voussoirs then concede, on the other hand, so much of their dignity as to receive a running ornament of foliage or animals, like a classical frieze, and continuous round the arch. In fact, the contest between the adversaries may be seen running through all the early architecture of Italy: success inclining sometimes to the one, sometimes to the other, and various kinds of truce or reconciliation being effected between them: sometimes merely formal, sometimes honest and affectionate, but with no regular succession in time. The greatest victory of the voussoir is to annihilate the cornice, and receive an ornament of its own outline, and entirely limited by its own joints: and yet this may be seen in the very early apse of Murano.

§ VII. The most usual condition, however, is that unity of the two members above described, § V., and which may be generally represented by the archivolt section a, Fig. LXX.; and from this descend a family of Gothic archivolts of the highest importance. For the cornice, thus attached to the arch, suffers exactly the same changes as the level cornice, or capital; receives, in due time, its elaborate ogee profile and leaf ornaments, like Fig. 8 or 9 of Plate XV.; and, when the shaft loses its shape, and is lost in the later Gothic jamb, the archivolt has influence enough to introduce this ogee profile in the jamb also, through the banded impost: and we immediately find ourselves involved in deep successions of ogee mouldings in sides of doors and windows, which never would have been thought of, but for the obstinate resistance of the classical architrave to the attempts of the voussoir at its degradation or banishment.

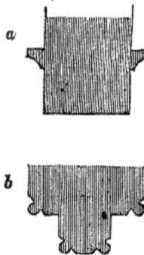

Fig. LXX.

§ VIII. This, then, will be the first great head under which we shall in future find it convenient to arrange a large number of archivolt decorations. It is the distinctively Southern and Byzantine form, and typically represented by the section a, of Fig. LXX.; and it is susceptible of almost every species of surface ornament, respecting which only this general law may be asserted: that, while the outside or vertical surface may properly be decorated, and yet the soffit or under surface left plain, the soffit is never to be decorated, and the outer surface left plain. Much beautiful sculpture is, in the best Byzantine buildings, half lost by being put under soffits; but the eye is led to discover it, and even to demand it, by the rich chasing of the outside of the voussoirs. It would have been an hypocrisy to carve them externally only. But there is not the smallest excuse for carving the soffit, and not the outside; for, in that case, we approach the building under the idea of its being perfectly plain; we do not look for the soffit decoration, and, of course, do not see it: or, if we do, it is merely to regret that it should not be in a better place. In the Renaissance architects, it may, perhaps, for once, be considered a merit, that they put their bad decoration systematically in the places where we should least expect it, and can seldomest see it:—Approaching the Scuola di San Rocco, you probably will regret the extreme plainness and barrenness of the window traceries; but, if you will go very close to the wall beneath the windows, you may, on sunny days, discover a quantity of panel decorations which the ingenious architect has concealed under the soffits.

The custom of decorating the arch soffit with panelling is a Roman application of the Greek roof ornament, which, whatever its intrinsic merit (compare Chap. XXIX. § IV.), may rationally be applied to waggon vaults, as of St. Peter's, and to arch soffits under which one walks. But the Renaissance architects had not wit enough to reflect that people usually do not walk through windows.

§ IX. So far, then, of the Southern archivolt: In Fig. LXIX., above, it will be remembered that c represents the simplest form of the Northern. In the farther development of this, which we have next to consider, the voussoirs, in consequence of their own negligence or over-confidence, sustain a total and irrecoverable defeat. That archivolt is in its earliest conditions perfectly pure and undecorated,—the simplest and rudest of Gothic forms. Necessarily, when it falls on the pier, and meets that of the opposite arch, the entire section of masonry is in the shape of a cross, and is carried by the crosslet shaft, which we above stated to be distinctive of Northern design. I am more at a loss to account for the sudden and fixed development of this type of archivolt than for any other architectural transition with which I am acquainted. But there it is, pure and firmly established, as early as the building of St. Michele of Pavia; and we have thenceforward only to observe what comes of it.

§ X. We find it first, as I said, perfectly barren; cornice and architrave altogether ignored, the existence of such things practically denied, and a plain, deep-cut recess with a single mighty shadow occupying their place. The voussoirs, thinking their great adversary utterly defeated, are at no trouble to show themselves; visible enough in both the upper and under archivolts, they are content to wait the time when, as might have been hoped, they should receive a new decoration peculiar to themselves.

§ XI. In this state of paralysis, or expectation, their flank is turned by an insidious chamfer. The edges of the two great blank archivolts are felt to be painfully conspicuous; all the four are at once beaded or chamfered, as at b, Fig. LXX.; a rich group of deep lines, running concentrically with the arch, is the result on the instant, and the fate of the voussoirs is sealed. They surrender at once without a struggle, and unconditionally; the chamfers deepen and multiply themselves, cover the soffit, ally themselves with other forms resulting from grouped shafts or traceries, and settle into the inextricable richness of the fully developed Gothic jamb and arch; farther complicated in the end by the addition of niches to their recesses, as above described.

§ XII. The voussoirs, in despair, go over to the classical camp, in hope of receiving some help or tolerance from their former enemies. They receive it indeed: but as traitors should, to their own eternal dishonor. They are sharply chiselled at the joints, or rusticated, or cut into masks and satyrs' heads, and so set forth and pilloried in the various detestable forms of which the simplest is given above in Plate XIII. (on the left); and others may be seen in nearly every large building in London, more especially in the bridges; and, as if in pure spite at the treatment they had received from the archivolt, they are now not content with vigorously showing their lateral joints, but shape themselves into right-angled steps at their heads, cutting to pieces their limiting line, which otherwise would have had sympathy with that of the arch, and fitting themselves to their new friend, the Renaissance Ruled Copy-book wall. It had been better they had died ten times over, in their own ancient cause, than thus prolonged their existence.

§ XIII. We bid them farewell in their dishonor, to return to our victorious chamfer. It had not, we said, obtained so easy a conquest, unless by the help of certain forms of the grouped shaft. The chamfer was quite enough to decorate the archivolts, if there were no more than two; but if, as above noticed in § III., the archivolt was very deep, and composed of a succession of such steps, the multitude of chamferings were felt to be weak and insipid, and instead of dealing with the outside edges of the archivolts, the group was softened by introducing solid shafts in their dark inner angles. This, the manliest and best condition of the early northern jamb and archivolt, is represented in section at fig. 12 of Plate II.; and its simplest aspect in Plate V., from the Broletto of Como,—an interesting example, because there the voussoirs being in the midst of their above-described southern contest with the architrave, were better prepared for the flank attack upon them by the shaft and chamfer, and make a noble resistance, with the help of color, in which even the shaft itself gets slightly worsted, and cut across in several places, like General Zach's column at Marengo.

§ XIV. The shaft, however, rapidly rallies, and brings up its own peculiar decorations to its aid; and the intermediate archivolts receive running or panelled ornaments, also, until we reach the exquisitely rich conditions of our own Norman archivolts, and of the parallel Lombardic designs, such as the entrance of the Duomo, and of San Fermo, at Verona. This change, however, occupies little time, and takes place principally in doorways, owing to the greater thickness of wall, and depth of archivolt; so that we find the rich shafted succession of ornament, in the doorway and window aperture, associated with the earliest and rudest double archivolt, in the nave arches, at St. Michele of Pavia. The nave arches, therefore, are most usually treated by the chamfer, and the voussoirs are there defeated much sooner than by the shafted arrangements, which they resist, as we saw, in the south by color; and even in the north, though forced out of their own shape, they take that of birds' or monsters' heads, which for some time peck and pinch the rolls of the archivolt to their hearts' content; while the Norman zigzag ornament allies itself with them, each zigzag often restraining itself amicably between the joints of each voussoir in the ruder work, and even in the highly finished arches, distinctly presenting a concentric or sunlike arrangement of lines; so much so, as to prompt the conjecture, above stated, Chap. XX. § XXVI., that all such ornaments were intended to be typical of light issuing from the orb of the arch. I doubt the intention, but acknowledge the resemblance; which perhaps goes far to account for the never-failing delightfulness of this zigzag decoration. The diminution of the zigzag, as it gradually shares the defeat of the voussoir, and is at last overwhelmed by the complicated, railroad-like fluency of the later Gothic mouldings, is to me one of the saddest sights in the drama of architecture.

§ XV. One farther circumstance is deserving of especial note in Plate V., the greater depth of the voussoirs at the top of the arch. This has been above alluded to as a feature of good construction, Chap. XI., § III.; it is to be noted now as one still more valuable in decoration: for when we arrive at the deep succession of concentric archivolts, with which northern portals, and many of the associated windows, are headed, we immediately find a difficulty in reconciling the outer curve with the inner. If, as is sometimes the case, the width of the group of archivolts be twice or three times that of the inner aperture, the inner arch may be distinctly pointed, and the outer one, if drawn with concentric arcs, approximate very nearly to a round arch. This is actually the case in the later Gothic of Verona; the outer line of the archivolt having a hardly perceptible point, and every inner arch of course forming the point more distinctly, till the innermost becomes a lancet. By far the nobler method, however, is that of the pure early Italian Gothic; to make every outer arch a magnified fac-simile of the innermost one, every arc including the same number of degrees, but degrees of a larger circle. The result is the condition represented in Plate V., often found in far bolder development; exquisitely springy and elastic in its expression, and entirely free from the heaviness and monotony of the deep northern archivolts.

§ XVI. We have not spoken of the intermediate form, b, of Fig. LXIX. (which its convenience for admission of light has rendered common in nearly all architectures), because it has no transitions peculiar to itself: in the north it sometimes shares the fate of the outer architrave, and is channelled into longitudinal mouldings; sometimes remains smooth and massy, as in military architecture, or in the simpler forms of domestic and ecclesiastical. In Italy it receives surface decoration like the architrave, but has, perhaps, something of peculiar expression in being placed between the tracery of the window within, and its shafts and tabernacle work without, as in the Duomo of Florence: in this position it is always kept smooth in surface, and inlaid (or painted) with delicate arabesques; while the tracery and the tabernacle work are richly sculptured. The example of its treatment by colored voussoirs, given in Plate XIX., may be useful to the reader as a kind of central expression of the aperture decoration of the pure Italian Gothic;—aperture decoration proper; applying no shaft work to the jambs, but leaving the bevelled opening unenriched; using on the outer archivolt the voussoirs and concentric architrave in reconcilement (the latter having, however, some connection with the Norman zigzag); and beneath them, the pure Italian two-pieced and mid-cusped arch, with rich cusp decoration. It is a Veronese arch, probably of the thirteenth century, and finished with extreme care; the red portions are all in brick, delicately cast: and the most remarkable feature of the whole is the small piece of brick inlaid on the angle of each stone voussoir, with a most just feeling, which every artist will at once understand, that the color ought not to be let go all at once.

§ XVII. We have traced the various conditions of treatment in the archivolt alone; but, except in what has been said of the peculiar expression of the voussoirs, we might throughout have spoken in the same terms of the jamb. Even a parallel to the expression of the voussoir may be found in the Lombardic and Norman divisions of the shafts, by zigzags and other transverse ornamentation, which in the end are all swept away by the canaliculated mouldings. Then, in the recesses of these and of the archivolts alike, the niche and statue decoration develops itself; and the vaulted and cavernous apertures are covered with incrustations of fretwork, and with every various application of foliage to their fantastic mouldings.

§ XVIII. I have kept the inquiry into the proper ornament of the archivolt wholly free from all confusion with the questions of beauty in tracery; for, in fact, all tracery is a mere multiplication and entanglement of small archivolts, and its cusp ornament is a minor condition of that proper to the spandril. It does not reach its completely defined form until the jamb and archivolt have been divided into longitudinal mouldings; and then the tracery is formed by the innermost group of the shafts or fillets, bent into whatever forms or foliations the designer may choose; but this with a delicacy of adaptation which I rather choose to illustrate by particular examples, of which we shall meet with many in the course of our inquiry, than to delay the reader by specifying here. As for the conditions of beauty in the disposition of the tracery bars, I see no hope of dealing with the subject fairly but by devoting, if I can find time, a separate essay to it—which, in itself, need not be long, but would involve, before it could be completed, the examination of the whole mass of materials lately collected by the indefatigable industry of the English architects who have devoted their special attention to this subject, and which are of the highest value as illustrating the chronological succession or mechanical structure of tracery, but which, in most cases, touch on their æsthetic merits incidentally only. Of works of this kind, by far the best I have met with is Mr. Edmund Sharpe's, on Decorated Windows, which seems to me, as far as a cursory glance can enable me to judge, to exhaust the subject as respects English Gothic; and which may be recommended to the readers who are interested in the subject, as containing a clear and masterly enunciation of the general principles by which the design of tracery has been regulated, from its first development to its final degradation.

FOOTNOTES:

[91] The architrave is properly the horizontal piece of stone laid across the tops of the pillars in Greek buildings, and commonly marked with horizontal lines, obtained by slight projections of its surface, while it is protected above in the richer orders, by a small cornice.

CHAPTER XXIX

THE ROOF

§ I. The modes of decoration hitherto considered, have been common to the exteriors and interiors of all noble buildings; and we have taken no notice of the various kinds of ornament which require protection from weather, and are necessarily confined to interior work. But in the case of the roof, the exterior and interior treatments become, as we saw in construction, so also in decoration, separated by broad and bold distinctions. One side of a wall is, in most cases, the same as another, and if its structure be concealed, it is mostly on the inside; but, in the roof, the anatomical structure, out of which decoration should naturally spring, is visible, if at all, in the interior only: so that the subject of internal ornament becomes both wide and important, and that of external, comparatively subordinate.

§ II. Now, so long as we were concerned principally with the outside of buildings, we might with safety leave expressional character out of the question for the time, because it is not to be expected that all persons who pass the building, or see it from a distance, shall be in the temper which the building is properly intended to induce; so that ornaments somewhat at variance with this temper may often be employed externally without painful effect. But these ornaments would be inadmissible in the interior, for those who enter will for the most part either be in the proper temper which the building requires, or desirous of acquiring it. (The distinction is not rigidly observed by the mediæval builders, and grotesques, or profane subjects, occur in the interior of churches, in bosses, crockets, capitals, brackets, and such other portions of minor ornament: but we do not find the interior wall covered with hunting and battle pieces, as often the Lombardic exteriors.) And thus the interior expression of the roof or ceiling becomes necessarily so various, and the kind and degree of fitting decoration so dependent upon particular circumstances, that it is nearly impossible to classify its methods, or limit its application.

§ III. I have little, therefore, to say here, and that touching rather the omission than the selection of decoration, as far as regards interior roofing. Whether of timber or stone, roofs are necessarily divided into surfaces, and ribs or beams;—surfaces, flat or carved; ribs, traversing these in the directions where main strength is required; or beams, filling the hollow of the dark gable with the intricate roof-tree, or supporting the flat ceiling. Wherever the ribs and beams are simply and unaffectedly arranged, there is no difficulty about decoration; the beams may be carved, the ribs moulded, and the eye is satisfied at once; but when the vaulting is unribbed, as in plain waggon vaults and much excellent early Gothic, or when the ceiling is flat, it becomes a difficult question how far their services may receive ornamentation independent of their structure. I have never myself seen a flat ceiling satisfactorily decorated, except by painting: there is much good and fanciful panelling in old English domestic architecture, but it always is in some degree meaningless and mean. The flat ceilings of Venice, as in the Scuola di San Rocco and Ducal Palace, have in their vast panellings some of the noblest paintings (on stretched canvas) which the world possesses: and this is all very well for the ceiling; but one would rather have the painting in a better place, especially when the rain soaks through its canvas, as I have seen it doing through many a noble Tintoret. On the whole, flat ceilings are as much to be avoided as possible; and, when necessary, perhaps a panelled ornamentation with rich colored patterns is the most satisfying, and loses least of valuable labor. But I leave the question to the reader's thought, being myself exceedingly undecided respecting it: except only touching one point—that a blank ceiling is not to be redeemed by a decorated ventilator.

§ IV. I have a more confirmed opinion, however, respecting the decoration of curved surfaces. The majesty of a roof is never, I think, so great, as when the eye can pass undisturbed over the course of all its curvatures, and trace the dying of the shadows along its smooth and sweeping vaults. And I would rather, myself, have a plain ridged Gothic vault, with all its rough stones visible, to keep the sleet and wind out of a cathedral aisle, than all the fanning and pendanting and foliation that ever bewildered Tudor weight. But mosaic or fresco may of course be used as far as we can afford or obtain them; for these do not break the curvature. Perhaps the most solemn roofs in the world are the apse conchas of the Romanesque basilicas, with their golden ground and severe figures. Exactly opposed to these are the decorations which disturb the serenity of the curve without giving it interest, like the vulgar panelling of St. Peter's and the Pantheon; both, I think, in the last degree detestable.

§ V. As roofs internally may be divided into surfaces and ribs, externally they may be divided into surfaces, and points, or ridges; these latter often receiving very bold and distinctive ornament. The outside surface is of small importance in central Europe, being almost universally low in slope, and tiled throughout Spain, South France, and North Italy: of still less importance where it is flat, as a terrace; as often in South Italy and the East, mingled with low domes: but the larger Eastern and Arabian domes become elaborate in ornamentation: I cannot speak of them with confidence; to the mind of an inhabitant of the north, a roof is a guard against wild weather; not a surface which is forever to bask in serene heat, and gleam across deserts like a rising moon. I can only say, that I have never seen any drawing of a richly decorated Eastern dome that made me desire to see the original.

§ VI. Our own northern roof decoration is necessarily simple. Colored tiles are used in some cases with quaint effect; but I believe the dignity of the building is always greater when the roof is kept in an undisturbed mass, opposing itself to the variegation and richness of the walls. The Italian round tile is itself decoration enough, a deep and rich fluting, which all artists delight in; this, however, is fitted exclusively for low pitch of roofs. On steep domestic roofs, there is no ornament better than may be obtained by merely rounding, or cutting to an angle, the lower extremities of the flat tiles or shingles, as in Switzerland: thus the whole surface is covered with an appearance of scales, a fish-like defence against water, at once perfectly simple, natural, and effective at any distance; and the best decoration of sloping stone roofs, as of spires, is a mere copy of this scale armor; it enriches every one of the spires and pinnacles of the cathedral of Coutances, and of many Norman and early Gothic buildings. Roofs covered or edged with lead have often patterns designed upon the lead, gilded and relieved with some dark color, as on the house of Jaques Coeur at Bourges; and I imagine the effect of this must have been singularly delicate and beautiful, but only traces of it now remain. The northern roofs, however, generally stand in little need of surface decoration, the eye being drawn to the fantastic ranges of their dormer windows, and to the finials and fringes on their points and ridges.

§ VII. Whether dormer windows are legitimately to be classed as decorative features, seems to me to admit of doubt. The northern spire system is evidently a mere elevation and exaggeration of the domestic turret with its look-out windows, and one can hardly part with the grotesque lines of the projections, though nobody is to be expected to live in the spire: but, at all events, such windows are never to be allowed in places visibly inaccessible, or on less than a natural and serviceable scale.

§ VIII. Under the general head of roof-ridge and point decoration, we may include, as above noted, the entire race of fringes, finials, and crockets. As there is no use in any of these things, and as they are visible additions and parasitical portions of the structure, more caution is required in their use than in any other features of ornament, and the architect and spectator must both be in felicitous humor before they can be well designed or thoroughly enjoyed. They are generally most admirable where the grotesque Northern spirit has most power; and I think there is almost always a certain spirit of playfulness in them, adverse to the grandest architectural effects, or at least to be kept in severe subordination to the serener character of the prevalent lines. But as they are opposed to the seriousness of majesty on the one hand, so they are to the weight of dulness on the other; and I know not any features which make the contrast between continental domestic architecture, and our own, more humiliatingly felt, or which give so sudden a feeling of new life and delight, when we pass from the streets of London to those of Abbeville or Rouen, as the quaint points and pinnacles of the roof gables and turrets. The commonest and heaviest roof may be redeemed by a spike at the end of it, if it is set on with any spirit; but the foreign builders have (or had, at least) a peculiar feeling in this, and gave animation to the whole roof by the fringe of its back, and the spike on its forehead, so that all goes together, like the dorsal fins and spines of a fish: but our spikes have a dull, screwed on, look; a far-off relationship to the nuts of machinery; and our roof fringes are sure to look like fenders, as if they were meant to catch ashes out of the London smoke-clouds.

§ IX. Stone finials and crockets are, I think, to be considered in architecture, what points and flashes of light are in the color of painting, or of nature. There are some landscapes whose best character is sparkling, and there is a possibility of repose in the midst of brilliancy, or embracing it,—as on the fields of summer sea, or summer land:

"Calm, and deep peace, on this high wold,
And on the dews that drench the furze,
And on the silvery gossamers,
That twinkle into green and gold."

And there are colorists who can keep their quiet in the midst of a jewellery of light; but, for the most part, it is better to avoid breaking up either lines or masses by too many points, and to make the few points used exceedingly precious. So the best crockets and finials are set, like stars, along the lines, and at the points, which they adorn, with considerable intervals between them, and exquisite delicacy and fancy of sculpture in their own designs; if very small, they may become more frequent, and describe lines by a chain of points; but their whole value is lost if they are gathered into bunches or clustered into tassels and knots; and an over-indulgence in them always marks lowness of school. In Venice, the addition of the finial to the arch-head is the first sign of degradation; all her best architecture is entirely without either crockets or finials; and her ecclesiastical architecture may be classed, with fearless accuracy, as better or worse, in proportion to the diminution or expansion of the crocket. The absolutely perfect use of the crocket is found, I think, in the tower of Giotto, and in some other buildings of the Pisan school. In the North they generally err on one side or other, and are either florid and huge, or mean in outline, looking as if they had been pinched out of the stonework, as throughout the entire cathedral of Amiens; and are besides connected with the generally spotty system which has been spoken of under the head of archivolt decoration.

§ X. Employed, however, in moderation, they are among the most delightful means of delicate expression; and the architect has more liberty in their individual treatment than in any other feature of the building. Separated entirely from the structural system, they are subjected to no shadow of any other laws than those of grace and chastity; and the fancy may range without rebuke, for materials of their design, through the whole field of the visible or imaginable creation.

§ I. I have hardly kept my promise. The reader has decorated but little for himself as yet; but I have not, at least, attempted to bias his judgment. Of the simple forms of decoration which have been set before him, he has always been left free to choose; and the stated restrictions in the methods of applying them have been only those which followed on the necessities of construction previously determined. These having been now defined, I do indeed leave my reader free to build; and with what a freedom! All the lovely forms of the universe set before him, whence to choose, and all the lovely lines that bound their substance or guide their motion; and of all these lines,—and there are myriads of myriads in every bank of grass and every tuft of forest; and groups of them divinely harmonized, in the bell of every flower, and in every several member of bird and beast,—of all these lines, for the principal forms of the most important members of architecture, I have used but Three! What, therefore, must be the infinity of the treasure in them all! There is material enough in a single flower for the ornament of a score of cathedrals, but suppose we were satisfied with less exhaustive appliance, and built a score of cathedrals, each to illustrate a single flower? that would be better than trying to invent new styles, I think. There is quite difference of style enough, between a violet and a harebell, for all reasonable purposes.

§ II. Perhaps, however, even more strange than the struggle of our architects to invent new styles, is the way they commonly speak of this treasure of natural infinity. Let us take our patience to us for an instant, and hear one of them, not among the least intelligent:—

"It is not true that all natural forms are beautiful. We may hardly be able to detect this in Nature herself; but when the forms are separated from the things, and exhibited alone (by sculpture or carving), we then see that they are not all fitted for ornamental purposes; and indeed that very few, perhaps none, are so fitted without correction. Yes, I say correction, for though it is the highest aim of every art to imitate nature, this is not to be done by   imitating any natural form, but by criticising and correcting it,—criticising it by Nature's rules gathered from all her works, but never completely carried out by her in any one work; correcting it, by rendering it more natural, i.e. more conformable to the general tendency of Nature, according to that noble maxim recorded of Raffaelle, 'that the artist's object was to make things not as Nature makes them, but as she WOULD make them;' as she ever tries to make them, but never succeeds, though her aim may be deduced from a comparison of her efforts; just as if a number of archers had aimed unsuccessfully at a mark upon a wall, and this mark were then removed, we could by the examination of their arrow marks point out the most probable position of the spot aimed at, with a certainty of being nearer to it than any of their shots."[92]

§ III. I had thought that, by this time, we had done with that stale, second-hand, one-sided, and misunderstood saying of Raffaelle's; or that at least, in these days of purer Christian light, men might have begun to get some insight into the meaning of it: Raffaelle was a painter of humanity, and assuredly there is something the matter with humanity, a few dovrebbe's, more or less, wanting in it. We have most of us heard of original sin, and may perhaps, in our modest moments, conjecture that we are not quite what God, or nature, would have us to be. Raffaelle had something to mend in Humanity: I should have liked to have seen him mending a daisy!—or a pease-blossom, or a moth, or a mustard seed, or any other of God's slightest works. If he had accomplished that, one might have found for him more respectable employment,—to set the stars in better order, perhaps (they seem grievously scattered as they are, and to be of all manner of shapes and sizes,—except the ideal shape, and the proper size); or to give us a corrected view of the ocean; that, at least, seems a very irregular and improveable thing; the very fishermen do not know, this day, how far it will reach, driven up before the west wind:—perhaps Some One else does, but that is not our business. Let us go down and stand by the beach of it,—of the great irregular sea, and count whether the thunder of it is not out of time. One,—two:—here comes a well-formed wave at last, trembling a little at the top, but, on the whole, orderly. So, crash among the shingle, and up as far as this grey pebble; now stand by and watch! Another:—Ah, careless wave! why couldn't you have kept your crest on? it is all gone away into spray, striking up against the cliffs there—I thought as much—missed the mark by a couple of feet! Another:—How now, impatient one! couldn't you have waited till your friend's reflux was done with, instead of rolling yourself up with it in that unseemly manner? You go for nothing. A fourth, and a goodly one at last. What think we of yonder slow rise, and crystalline hollow, without a flaw? Steady, good wave; not so fast; not so fast; where are you coming to?—By our architectural word, this is too bad; two yards over the mark, and ever so much of you in our face besides; and a wave which we had some hope of, behind there, broken all to pieces out at sea, and laying a great white table-cloth of foam all the way to the shore, as if the marine gods were to dine off it! Alas, for these unhappy arrow shots of Nature; she will never hit her mark with those unruly waves of hers, nor get one of them, into the ideal shape, if we wait for a thousand years. Let us send for a Greek architect to do it for her. He comes—the great Greek architect, with measure and rule. Will he not also make the weight for the winds? and weigh out the waters by measure? and make a decree for the rain, and a way for the lightning of the thunder? He sets himself orderly to his work, and behold! this is the mark of nature, and this is the thing into which the great Greek architect improves the sea—

[Greek: Thalatta, thalatta]: Was it this, then, that they wept to see from the sacred mountain—those wearied ones?

§ IV. But the sea was meant to be irregular! Yes, and were not also the leaves, and the blades of grass; and, in a sort, as far as may be without mark of sin, even the countenance of man? Or would it be pleasanter and better to have us all alike, and numbered on our foreheads, that we might be known one from the other?

§ V. Is there, then, nothing to be done by man's art? Have we only to copy, and again copy, for ever, the imagery of the universe? Not so. We have work to do upon it; there is not any one of us so simple, nor so feeble, but he has work to do upon it. But the work is not to improve, but to explain. This infinite universe is unfathomable, inconceivable, in its whole; every human creature must slowly spell out, and long contemplate, such part of it as may be possible for him to reach; then set forth what he has learned of it for those beneath him; extricating it from infinity, as one gathers a violet out of grass; one does not improve either violet or grass in gathering it, but one makes the flower visible; and then the human being has to make its power upon his own heart visible also, and to give it the honor of the good thoughts it has raised up in him, and to write upon it the history of his own soul. And sometimes he may be able to do more than this, and to set it in strange lights, and display it in a thousand ways before unknown: ways specially directed to necessary and noble purposes, for which he had to choose instruments out of the wide armory of God. All this he may do: and in this he is only doing what every Christian has to do with the written, as well as the created word, "rightly dividing the word of truth." Out of the infinity of the written word, he has also to gather and set forth things new and old, to choose them for the season and the work that are before him, to explain and manifest them to others, with such illustration and enforcement as may be in his power, and to crown them with the history of what, by them, God has done for his soul. And, in doing this, is he improving the Word of God? Just such difference as there is between the sense in which a minister may be said to improve a text, to the people's comfort, and the sense in which an atheist might declare that he could improve the Book, which, if any man shall add unto, there shall be added unto him the plagues that are written therein; just such difference is there between that which, with respect to Nature, man is, in his humbleness, called upon to do, and that which, in his insolence, he imagines himself capable of doing.

§ VI. Have no fear, therefore, reader, in judging between nature and art, so only that you love both. If you can love one only, then let it be Nature; you are safe with her: but do not then attempt to judge the art, to which you do not care to give thought, or time. But if you love both, you may judge between them fearlessly; you may estimate the last, by its making you remember the first, and giving you the same kind of joy. If, in the square of the city, you can find a delight, finite, indeed, but pure and intense, like that which you have in a valley among the hills, then its art and architecture are right; but if, after fair trial, you can find no delight in them, nor any instruction like that of nature, I call on you fearlessly to condemn them.

We are forced, for the sake of accumulating our power and knowledge, to live in cities; but such advantage as we have in association with each other is in great part counterbalanced by our loss of fellowship with nature. We cannot all have our gardens now, nor our pleasant fields to meditate in at eventide. Then the function of our architecture is, as far as may be, to replace these; to tell us about nature; to possess us with memories of her quietness; to be solemn and full of tenderness, like her, and rich in portraitures of her; full of delicate imagery of the flowers we can no more gather, and of the living creatures now far away from us in their own solitude. If ever you felt or found this in a London Street,—if ever it furnished you with one serious thought, or one ray of true and gentle pleasure,—if there is in your heart a true delight in its grim railings and dark casements, and wasteful finery of shops, and feeble coxcombry of club-houses,—it is well: promote the building of more like them. But if they never taught you anything, and never made you happier as you passed beneath them, do not think they have any mysterious goodness nor occult sublimity. Have done with the wretched affectation, the futile barbarism, of pretending to enjoy: for, as surely as you know that the meadow grass, meshed with fairy rings, is better than the wood pavement, cut into hexagons; and as surely as you know the fresh winds and sunshine of the upland are better than the choke-damp of the vault, or the gas-light of the ball-room, you may know, as I told you that you should, that the good architecture, which has life, and truth, and joy in it, is better than the bad architecture, which has death, dishonesty, and vexation of heart in it, from the beginning to the end of time.

§ VII. And now come with me, for I have kept you too long from your gondola: come with me, on an autumnal morning, through the dark gates of Padua, and let us take the broad road leading towards the East.

It lies level, for a league or two, between its elms, and vine festoons full laden, their thin leaves veined into scarlet hectic, and their clusters deepened into gloomy blue; then mounts an embankment above the Brenta, and runs between the river and the broad plain, which stretches to the north in endless lines of mulberry and maize. The Brenta flows slowly, but strongly; a muddy volume of yellowish-grey water, that neither hastens nor slackens, but glides heavily between its monotonous banks, with here and there a short, babbling eddy twisted for an instant into its opaque surface, and vanishing, as if something had been dragged into it and gone down. Dusty and shadeless, the road fares along the dyke on its northern side; and the tall white tower of Dolo is seen trembling in the heat mist far away, and never seems nearer than it did at first. Presently you pass one of the much vaunted "villas on the Brenta:" a glaring, spectral shell of brick and stucco, its windows with painted architraves like picture-frames, and a court-yard paved with pebbles in front of it, all burning in the thick glow of the feverish sunshine, but fenced from the high road, for magnificence sake, with goodly posts and chains; then another, of Kew Gothic, with Chinese variations, painted red and green; a third composed for the greater part of dead-wall, with fictitious windows painted upon it, each with a pea-green blind, and a classical architrave in bad perspective; and a fourth, with stucco figures set on the top of its garden-wall: some antique, like the kind to be seen at the corner of the New Road, and some of clumsy grotesque dwarfs, with fat bodies and large boots. This is the architecture to which her studies of the Renaissance have conducted modern Italy.

§ VIII. The sun climbs steadily, and warms into intense white the walls of the little piazza of Dolo, where we change horses. Another dreary stage among the now divided branches of the Brenta, forming irregular and half-stagnant canals; with one or two more villas on the other side of them, but these of the old Venetian type, which we may have recognised before at Padua, and sinking fast into utter ruin, black, and rent, and lonely, set close to the edge of the dull water, with what were once small gardens beside them, kneaded into mud, and with blighted fragments of gnarled hedges and broken stakes for their fencing; and here and there a few fragments of marble steps, which have once given them graceful access from the water's edge, now settling into the mud in broken joints, all aslope, and slippery with green weed. At last the road turns sharply to the north, and there is an open space, covered with bent grass, on the right of it: but do not look that way.

§ IX. Five minutes more, and we are in the upper room of the little inn at Mestre, glad of a moment's rest in shade. The table is (always, I think) covered with a cloth of nominal white and perennial grey, with plates and glasses at due intervals, and small loaves of a peculiar white bread, made with oil, and more like knots of flour than bread. The view from its balcony is not cheerful: a narrow street, with a solitary brick church and barren campanile on the other side of it; and some coventual buildings, with a few crimson remnants of fresco about their windows; and, between them and the street, a ditch with some slow current in it, and one or two small houses beside it, one with an arbor of roses at its door, as in an English tea-garden; the air, however, about us having in it nothing of roses, but a close smell of garlic and crabs, warmed by the smoke of various stands of hot chestnuts. There is much vociferation also going on beneath the window respecting certain wheelbarrows which are in rivalry for our baggage: we appease their rivalry with our best patience, and follow them down the narrow street.

§ X. We have but walked some two hundred yards when we come to a low wharf or quay, at the extremity of a canal, with long steps on each side down to the water, which latter we fancy for an instant has become black with stagnation; another glance undeceives us,—it is covered with the black boats of Venice. We enter one of them, rather to try if they be real boats or not, than with any definite purpose, and glide away; at first feeling as if the water were yielding continually beneath the boat and letting her sink into soft vacancy. It is something clearer than any water we have seen lately, and of a pale green; the banks only two or three feet above it, of mud and rank grass, with here and there a stunted tree; gliding swiftly past the small casement of the gondola, as if they were dragged by upon a painted scene.

Stroke by stroke we count the plunges of the oar, each heaving up the side of the boat slightly as her silver beak shoots forward. We lose patience, and extricate ourselves from the cushions: the sea air blows keenly by, as we stand leaning on the roof of the floating cell. In front, nothing to be seen but long canal and level bank; to the west, the tower of Mestre is lowering fast, and behind it there have risen purple shapes, of the color of dead rose-leaves, all round the horizon, feebly defined against the afternoon sky,—the Alps of Bassano. Forward still: the endless canal bends at last, and then breaks into intricate angles about some low bastions, now torn to pieces and staggering in ugly rents towards the water,—the bastions of the fort of Malghera. Another turn, and another perspective of canal; but not interminable. The silver beak cleaves it fast,—it widens: the rank grass of the banks sinks lower, and lower, and at last dies in tawny knots along an expanse of weedy shore. Over it, on the right, but a few years back, we might have seen the lagoon stretching to the horizon, and the warm southern sky bending over Malamocco to the sea. Now we can see nothing but what seems a low and monotonous dock-yard wall, with flat arches to let the tide through it;—this is the railroad bridge, conspicuous above all things. But at the end of those dismal arches, there rises, out of the wide water, a straggling line of low and confused brick buildings, which, but for the many towers which are mingled among them, might be the suburbs of an English manufacturing town. Four or five domes, pale, and apparently at a greater distance, rise over the centre of the line; but the object which first catches the eye is a sullen cloud of black smoke brooding over the northern half of it, and which issues from the belfry of a church.

It is Venice.

FOOTNOTES:

[92] *Garbett on Design, p. 74.*

1. FOUNDATION OF VENICE

I find the chroniclers agree in fixing the year 421, if any: the following sentence from De Monaci may perhaps interest the reader.

"God, who punishes the sins of men by war sorrows, and whose ways are past finding out, willing both to save the innocent blood, and that a great power, beneficial to the whole world, should arise in a spot strange beyond belief, moved the chief men of the cities of the Venetian province (which from the border of Pannonia, extended as far as the Adda, a river of Lombardy), both in memory of past, and in dread of future distress, to establish states upon the nearer islands of the inner gulphs of the Adriatic, to which, in the last necessity, they might retreat for refuge. And first Galienus de Fontana, Simon de Glauconibus, and Antonius Calvus, or, as others have it, Adalburtus Falerius, Thomas Candiano, Comes Daulus, Consuls of Padua, by the command of their King and the desire of the citizens, laid the foundations of the new commonwealth, under good auspices, on the island of the Rialto, the highest and nearest to the mouth of the deep river now called the Brenta, in the year of Our Lord, as many writers assure us, four hundred and twenty-one, on the 25th day of March."[93]

It is matter also of very great satisfaction to know that Venice was founded by good Christians: "La qual citade è stada hedificada da veri e boni Christiani:" which information I found in the MS. copy of the Zancarol Chronicle, in the library of St. Mark's.

Finally the conjecture as to the origin of her name, recorded by Sansovino, will be accepted willingly by all who love Venice: "Fu interpretato da alcuni, che questa voce VENETIA voglia dire VENI ETIAM, cioè, vieni ancora, e ancora, percioche quante volte verrai, sempre vedrai nuove cose, enuove bellezze."

2. POWER OF THE DOGES

The best authorities agree in giving the year 697 as that of the election of the first doge, Paul Luke Anafeste. He was elected in a general meeting of the commonalty, tribunes, and clergy, at Heraclea, "divinis rebus procuratis," as usual, in all serious work, in those times. His authority is thus defined by Sabellico, who was not likely to have exaggerated it:—"Penes quem decus omne imperii ac majestas esset: cui jus concilium cogendi quoties de republica aliquid referri oporteret; qui tribunos annuos in singulas insulas legeret, a quibus ad Ducem esset provocatio. Cæterum, si quis dignitatem, ecclesiam, sacerdotumve cleri populique suffragio esset adeptus, ita demum id ratum haberetur si dux ipse auctor factus esset." (Lib. I.) The last clause is very important, indicating the subjection of the ecclesiastical to the popular and ducal (or patrician) powers, which, throughout her career, was one of the most remarkable features in the policy of Venice. The appeal from the tribunes to the doge is also important; and the expression "decus omne imperii," if of somewhat doubtful force, is at least as energetic as could have been expected from an historian under the influence of the Council of Ten.

3. SERRAR DEL CONSIGLIO

The date of the decree which made the right of sitting in the grand council hereditary, is variously given; the Venetian historians themselves saying as little as they can about it. The thing was evidently not accomplished at once, several decrees following in successive years: the Council of Ten was established without any doubt in 1310, in consequence of the conspiracy of Tiepolo. The Venetian verse, quoted by Mutinelli (Annali Urbani di Venezia, p. 153), is worth remembering.

"Del mille tresento e diese
A mezzo el mese delle ceriese
Bagiamonte passò el ponte
E per esso fo fatto el Consegio di diese."

The reader cannot do better than take 1297 as the date of the beginning of the change of government, and this will enable him exactly to divide the 1100 years from the election of the first doge into 600 of monarchy and 500 of aristocracy. The coincidence of the numbers is somewhat curious; 697 the date of the establishment of the government, 1297 of its change, and 1797 of its fall.

4. S. PIETRO DI CASTELLO

It is credibly reported to have been founded in the seventh century, and (with somewhat less of credibility) in a place where the Trojans, conducted by Antenor, had, after the destruction of Troy, built "un castello, chiamato prima Troja, poscia Olivolo, interpretato, luogo pieno." It seems that St. Peter appeared in person to the Bishop of Heraclea, and commanded him to found in his honor, a church in that spot of the rising city on the Rialto: "ove avesse veduto una mandra di buoi e di pecore pascolare unitamente. Questa fu la prodigiosa origine della Chiesa di San Pietro, che poscia, o rinovata, o ristaurata, da Orso Participazio IV Vescovo Olivolense, divenne la Cattedrale della Nuova citta." (Notizie Storiche delle Chiese e Monasteri di Venezia. Padua, 1758.) What there was so prodigious in oxen and sheep feeding together, we need St. Peter, I think, to tell us. The title of Bishop of Castello was first taken in 1091: St. Mark's was not made the cathedral church till 1807. It may be thought hardly fair to conclude the small importance of the old St. Pietro di Castello from the appearance of the wretched modernisations of 1620. But these modernisations are spoken of as improvements; and I find no notice of peculiar beauties in the older building, either in the work above quoted, or by Sansovino; who only says that when it was destroyed by fire (as everything in Venice was, I think, about three times in a century), in the reign of Vital Michele, it was rebuilt "with good thick walls, maintaining, for all that, the order of its arrangement taken from the Greek mode of building." This does not seem the description of a very enthusiastic effort to rebuild a highly ornate cathedral. The present church is among the least interesting in Venice; a wooden bridge, something like that of Battersea on a small scale, connects its island, now almost deserted, with a wretched suburb of the city behind the arsenal; and a blank level of lifeless grass, rotted away in places rather than trodden, is extended before its mildewed façade and solitary tower.

5. PAPAL POWER IN VENICE

I may refer the reader to the eleventh chapter of the twenty-eighth book of Daru for some account of the restraints to which the Venetian clergy were subjected. I have not myself been able to devote any time to the examination of the original documents bearing on this matter, but the following extract from a letter of a friend, who will not at present permit me to give his name, but who is certainly better conversant with the records of the Venetian State than any other Englishman, will be of great value to the general reader:—

"In the year 1410, or perhaps at the close of the thirteenth century, churchmen were excluded from the Grand Council and declared ineligible to civil employment; and in the same year, 1410, the Council of Ten, with the Giunta, decreed that whenever in the state's councils matters concerning ecclesiastical affairs were being treated, all the kinsfolk of Venetian beneficed clergymen were to be expelled; and, in the year 1434, the RELATIONS of churchmen were declared ineligible to the post of ambassador at Rome.

"The Venetians never gave possession of any see in their territories to bishops unless they had been proposed to the pope by the senate, which elected the patriarch, who was supposed, at the end of the sixteenth century, to be liable to examination by his Holiness, as an act of confirmation of installation;

but of course, everything depended on the relative power at any given time of Rome and Venice: for instance, a few days after the accession of Julius II., in 1503, he requests the Signory, cap in hand, to ALLOW him to confer the archbishopric of Zara on a dependant of his, one Cipico the Bishop of Famagosta. Six years later, when Venice was overwhelmed by the leaguers of Cambrai, that furious pope would assuredly have conferred Zara on Cipico WITHOUT asking leave. In 1608, the rich Camaldolite Abbey of Vangadizza, in the Polesine, fell vacant through the death of Lionardo Loredano, in whose family it had been since some while. The Venetian ambassador at Rome received the news on the night of the 28th December; and, on the morrow, requested Paul IV. not to dispose of this preferment until he heard from the senate. The pope talked of 'poor cardinals' and of his nephew, but made no positive reply; and, as Francesco Contarini was withdrawing, said to him: 'My Lord ambassador, with this opportunity we will inform you that, to our very great regret, we understand that the chiefs of the Ten mean to turn sacristans; for they order the parish priests to close the church doors at the Ave Maria, and not to ring the bells at certain hours. This is precisely the sacristan's office; we don't know why their lordships, by printed edicts, which we have seen, choose to interfere in this matter. This is pure and mere ecclesiastical jurisdiction; and even, in case of any inconvenience arising, is there not the patriarch, who is at any rate your own; why not apply to him, who could remedy these irregularities? These are matters which cause us very notable displeasure; we say so that they may be written and known: it is decided by the councils and canons, and not uttered by us, that whosoever forms any resolve against the ecclesiastical liberty, cannot do so without incurring censure: and in order that Father Paul [Bacon's correspondent] may not say hereafter, as he did in his past writings, that our predecessors assented either tacitly or by permission, we declare that we do not give our assent, nor do we approve it; nay, we blame it, and let this be announced in Venice, so that, for the rest, every one may take care of his own conscience. St. Thomas à Becket, whose festival is celebrated this very day, suffered martyrdom for the ecclesiastical liberty; it is our duty likewise to support and defend it.' Contarini says: 'This remonstrance was delivered with some marks of anger, which induced me to tell him how the tribunal of the most excellent the Lords chiefs of the Ten is in our country supreme; that it does not do its business unadvisedly, or condescend to unworthy matters; and that, therefore, should those Lords have come to any public declaration of their will, it must be attributed to orders anterior, and to immemorial custom and authority, recollecting that, on former occasions likewise, similar commissions were given to prevent divers incongruities; wherefore an upright intention, such as this, ought not to be taken in any other sense than its own, especially as the parishes of Venice were in her own gift,' &c. &c. The pope persisted in bestowing the abbacy on his nephew, but the republic would not give possession, and a compromise was effected by its being conferred on the Venetian Matteo Priuli, who allowed the cardinal five thousand ducats per annum out of its revenues. A few years before this, this very same pope excommunicated the State, because she had imprisoned two churchmen for heinous crimes; the strife lasted for more than a year, and ended through the mediation of Henry IV., at whose suit the prisoners were delivered to the French ambassador, who made them over to a papal commissioner.

"In January, 1484, a tournament was in preparation on St. Mark's Square: some murmurs had been heard about the distribution of the prizes having been pre-arranged, without regard to the 'best man.' One of the chiefs of the Ten was walking along Rialto on the 28th January, when a young priest, twenty-two years old, a sword-cutlers son, and a Bolognese, and one of Perugia, both men-at-arms under Robert Sansoverino, fell upon a clothier with drawn weapons. The chief of the Ten desired they might be seized, but at the moment the priest escaped; he was, however, subsequently retaken, and in that very evening hanged by torch-light between the columns with the two soldiers. Innocent VIII. was less powerful than Paul IV.; Venice weaker in 1605 than in 1484.

"The exclusion from the Grand Council, whether at the end of the fourteenth or commencement of the following century, of the Venetian ecclesiastics, (as induced either by the republic's acquisitions on the main land then made, and which, through the rich benefices they embraced, might have rendered an ambitious churchman as dangerous in the Grand Council as a victorious condottiere; or from dread of their allegiance being divided between the church and their country, it being acknowledged that no man can serve two masters,) did not render them hostile to their fatherland, whose interests were, with very few exceptions, eagerly fathered by the Venetian prelates at Rome, who, in their turn, received all honor at Venice, where state receptions given to cardinals of the houses of Correr, Grimani, Cornaro, Pisani, Contarini, Zeno, Delfino, and others, vouch for the good understanding that existed between the 'Papalists' and their countrymen. The Cardinal Grimani was instrumental in detaching Julius II. from the league of Cambrai; the Cardinal Cornaro always aided the state to obtain anything required of Leo X.; and, both before and after their times, all Venetians that had a seat in the Sacred College were patriots rather than pluralists: I mean that they cared more for Venice than for their benefices, admitting thus the soundness of that policy which denied them admission into the Grand Council."

To this interesting statement, I shall add, from the twenty-eighth book of Daru, two passages, well deserving consideration by us English in present days:

"Pour être parfaitement assurée contre les envahissements de la puissance ecclésiastique, Venise commença par lui ôter tout prétexte d'intervenir dans les affaires de l'Etat; elle resta invariablement fidèle au dogme. Jamais aucune des opinions nouvelles n'y prit la moindre faveur; jamais aucun hérésiarque ne sortit de Venise. Les conciles, les disputes, les guerres de religion, se passèrent sans qu'elle y prit jamais la moindre part. Inébranlable dans sa foi, elle ne fut pas moins invariable dans son système de tolérance. Non seulement ses sujets de la religion grecque conservèrent l'exercice de leur culte, leurs évêques et leurs prêtres; mais les Protestantes, les Arméniens, les Mahomitans, les Juifs, toutes les religions, toutes les sectes qui se trouvaient dans Venise, avaient des temples, et la sépulture dans les églises n'était point refusé aux hérétiques. Une police vigilante s'appliquait avec le même soin à éteindre les discordes, et à empêcher les fanatiques et les novateurs de troubler l'Etat."

"Si on considère que c'est dans un temps où presque toutes les nations tremblaient devant la puissance pontificale, que les Vénitiens surent tenir leur clergé dans la dépendance, et braver souvent les censures ecclésiastiques et les interdits, sans encourir jamais aucun reproche sur la pureté de leur foi, on sera forcé de reconnaître que cette république avait devancé de loin les autres peuples dans cette partie de la science du gouvernement. La fameuse maxime, 'Siamo veneziani, poi christiani,' n'était qu'une formule énergique qui ne prouvait point quils voulussent placer l'intérêt de la religion après celui de l'Etat, mais qui annonçait leur invariable résolution de ne pas souffrir qu'un pouvoir étranger portât atteinte aux droits de la république.

"Dans toute la durée de son existence, an milieu des revers comme dans la prospérité cet inébranlable gouvernement ne fit qu'une seule fois des concessions à la cour de Borne, et ce fut pour détacher le Pape Jules II. de la ligue de Cambrai.

"Jamais il ne se relâcha du soin de tenir le clergé dans une nullité absolue relativement aux affaires politiques; on peut en juger par la conduite qu'il tint avec l'ordre religieux le plus redoutable et le plus accoutumé à s'immiscer dans les secrets de l'Etat et dans les intérêts temporels."

The main points, next stated, respecting the Jesuits are, that the decree which permitted their establishment in Venice required formal renewal every three years; that no Jesuit could stay in Venice more than three years; that the slightest disobedience to the authority of the government was instantly punished by imprisonment; that no Venetian could enter the order without express permission from the government; that the notaries were forbidden to sanction any testamentary disposal of property to the Jesuits; finally, that the heads of noble families were forbidden to permit their children to be educated in the Jesuits' colleges, on pain of degradation from their rank.

Now, let it be observed that the enforcement of absolute exclusion of the clergy from the councils of the state, dates exactly from the period which I have marked for the commencement of the decline of the Venetian power. The Romanist is welcome to his advantage in this fact, if advantage it be; for I do not bring forward the conduct of the senate of Venice, as Daru does, by way of an example of the general science of government. The Venetians accomplished therein what we ridiculously call a separation of "Church and State" (as if the State were not, in all Christendom, necessarily also the Church[94]), but ought to call a separation of lay and clerical officers. I do not point out this separation as subject of praise, but as the witness borne by the Venetians against the principles of the Papacy. If they were to blame, in yielding to their fear of the ambitious spirit of Rome so far as to deprive their councils of all religious element, what excuse are we to offer for the state, which, with Lords Spiritual of her own faith already in her senate, permits the polity of Rome to be represented by lay members? To have sacrificed religion to mistaken policy, or purchased security with ignominy, would have been no new thing in the world's history; but to be at once impious and impolitic, and seek for danger through dishonor, was reserved for the English parliament of 1829.

I am glad to have this opportunity of referring to, and farther enforcing, the note on this subject which, not without deliberation, I appended to the "Seven Lamps;" and of adding to it the following passage, written by my father in the year 1839, and published in one of the journals of that year:—a passage remarkable as much for its intrinsic value, as for having stated, twelve years ago, truths to which the mind of England seems but now, and that slowly, awakening.

"We hear it said, that it cannot be merely the Roman religion that causes the difficulty [respecting Ireland], for we were once all Roman Catholics, and nations abroad of this faith are not as the Irish. It is totally overlooked, that when we were so, our government was despotic, and fit to cope with this dangerous religion, as most of the Continental governments yet are. In what Roman Catholic state, or in what age of Roman Catholic England, did we ever hear of such agitation as now exists in Ireland by evil men taking advantage of an anomalous state of things—Roman Catholic ignorance in the people, Protestant toleration in the government? We have yet to feel the tremendous difficulty in which Roman Catholic emancipation has involved us. Too late we discover that a Roman Catholic is wholly incapable of being safely connected with the British constitution, as it now exists, in any near relation. The present constitution is no longer fit for Catholics. It is a creature essentially Protestant, growing with the growth, and strengthening with the strength, of Protestantism. So entirely is Protestantism interwoven with the whole frame of our constitution and laws, that I take my stand on this, against all agitators in existence, that the Roman religion is totally incompatible with the British constitution. We have, in trying to combine them, got into a maze of difficulties; we are the worse, and Ireland none the better. It is idle to talk of municipal reform or popular Lords Lieutenant. The mild sway of a constitutional monarchy is not strong enough for a Roman Catholic population. The stern soul of a Republican would not shrink from sending half the misguided population and all the priests into exile, and planting in their place an industrious Protestant people. But you cannot do this, and you cannot convert the Irish, nor by other means make them fit to wear the mild restraints of a Protestant Government. It was, moreover, a strange logic that begot the idea of admitting Catholics to administer any part of our laws or constitution. It was admitted by all that, by the very act of abandoning the Roman religion, we became a free and enlightened people. It was only by throwing off the yoke of that slavish religion that we attained to the freedom of thought which has advanced us in the scale of society. We are so much advanced by adopting and adhering to a reformed religion, that to prove our liberal and unprejudiced views, we throw down the barriers betwixt the two religions, of which the one is the acknowledged cause of light and knowledge, the other the cause of darkness and ignorance. We are so much altered to the better by leaving this people entirely, and giving them neither part nor lot amongst us, that it becomes proper to mingle again with them. We have found so much good in leaving them, that we deem it the best possible reason for returning to be among them. No fear of their Church again shaking us, with all our light and knowledge. It is true, the most enlightened nations fell under the spell of her enchantments, fell into total darkness and superstition; but no fear of us—we are too well informed! What miserable reasoning! infatuated presumption! I fear me, when the Roman religion rolled her clouds of darkness over the earlier ages, that she quenched as much light, and knowledge, and judgment as our modern Liberals have ever displayed. I do not expect a statesman to discuss the point of Transubstantiation betwixt Protestant and Catholic, nor to trace the narrow lines which divide Protestant sectarians from each other; but can any statesman that shall have taken even a cursory glance at the face of Europe, hesitate a moment on the choice of the Protestant religion? If he unfortunately knew nothing of its being the true one in regard to our eternal interests, he is at least bound to see whether it be not the best for the worldly prosperity of a people. He may be but moderately imbued with pious zeal for the salvation of a kingdom, but at least he will be expected to weigh the comparative merits of religion, as of law or government; and blind, indeed, must he be if he does not discern that, in neglecting to cherish the Protestant faith, or in too easily yielding to any encroachments on it, he is foregoing the use of a state engine more powerful than all the laws which the uninspired legislators of the earth have ever promulgated, in promoting the happiness, the peace, prosperity, and the order, the industry, and the wealth, of a people; in forming every quality valuable or desirable in a subject or a citizen; in sustaining the public mind at that point of education and information that forms the best security for the state, and the best preservative for the freedom of a people, whether religious or political."

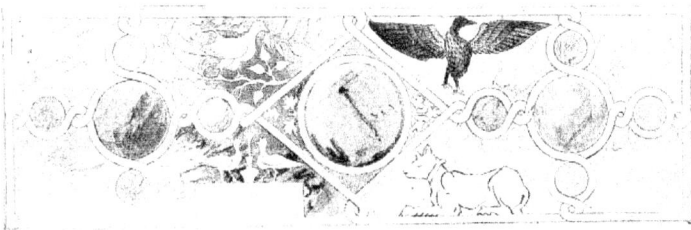

Plate XX. WALL VEIL DECORATION. CA' TREVISAN.

6. RENAISSANCE ORNAMENTS

There having been three principal styles of architecture in Venice,—the Greek or Byzantine, the Gothic, and the Renaissance, it will be shown, in the sequel, that the Renaissance itself is divided into three correspondent families: Renaissance engrafted on Byzantine, which is earliest and best; Renaissance engrafted on Gothic, which is second, and second best; Renaissance on Renaissance, which is double darkness, and worst of all. The palaces in which Renaissance is engrafted on Byzantine are those noticed by Commynes: they are characterized by an ornamentation very closely resembling, and in some cases identical with, early Byzantine work; namely, groups of colored marble circles inclosed in interlacing bands. I have put on the opposite page one of these ornaments, from the Ca' Trevisan, in which a most curious and delicate piece of inlaid design is introduced into a band which is almost exactly copied from the church of Theotocos at Constantinople, and correspondent with others in St. Mark's. There is also much Byzantine feeling in the treatment of the animals, especially in the two birds of the lower compartment, while the peculiar curves of the cinque cento leafage are visible in the leaves above. The dove, alighted, with the olive-branch plucked off, is opposed to the raven with restless expanded wings. Beneath are evidently the two sacrifices "of every clean fowl and of every clean beast." The color is given with green and white marbles, the dove relieved on a ground of greyish green, and all is exquisitely finished.

In Plate I. the upper figure is from the same palace (Ca' Trevisan), and it is very interesting in its proportions. If we take five circles in geometrical proportion, each diameter being two-thirds of the diameter next above it, and arrange the circles so proportioned, in contact with each other, in the manner shown in the plate, we shall find that an increase quite imperceptible in the diameter of the circles in the angles, will enable us to inscribe the whole in a square. The lines so described will then run in the centre of the white bands. I cannot be certain that this is the actual construction of the Trevisan design, because it is on a high wall surface, where I could not get at its measurements; but I found this construction exactly coincide with the lines of my eye sketch. The lower figure in Plate I. is from the front of the Ca' Dario, and probably struck the eye of Commynes in its first brightness. Salvatico, indeed, considers both the Ca' Trevisan (which once belonged to Bianca Cappello) and the Ca' Dario, as buildings of the sixteenth century. I defer the discussion of the question at present, but have, I believe, sufficient reason for assuming the Ca' Dario to have been built about 1486, and the Ca' Trevisan not much later.

7. VARIETIES OF THE ORDERS

Of these phantasms and grotesques, one of some general importance is that commonly called Ionic, of which the idea was taken (Vitruvius says) from a woman's hair, curled; but its lateral processes look more like rams' horns: be that as it may, it is a mere piece of agreeable extravagance, and if, instead of rams' horns, you put ibex horns, or cows' horns, or an ass's head at once, you will have ibex orders, or ass orders, or any number of other orders, one for every head or horn. You may have heard of another order, the Composite, which is Ionic and Corinthian mixed, and is one of the worst of ten thousand forms referable to the Corinthian as their head: it may be described as a spoiled Corinthian. And you may have also heard of another order, called Tuscan (which is no order at all, but a spoiled Doric): and of another called Roman Doric, which is Doric more spoiled, both which are simply among the most stupid variations ever invented upon forms already known. I find also in a French pamphlet upon architecture,[95] as applied to shops and dwelling houses, a sixth order, the "Ordre Français," at least as good as any of the three last, and to be hailed with acclamation, considering whence it comes, there being usually more tendency on the other side of the channel to the confusion of "orders" than their multiplication: but the reader will find in the end that there are in very deed only two orders, of which the Greek, Doric, and Corinthian are the first examples, and they not perfect, nor in anywise sufficiently representative of the vast families to which they belong; but being the first and the best known, they may properly be considered as the types of the rest. The essential distinctions of the two great orders he will find explained in §§ XXXV. and XXXVI. of Chap. XXVII., and in the passages there referred to; but I should rather desire that these passages might be read in the order in which they occur.

I have sketched above, in the First Chapter, the great events of architectural history in the simplest and fewest words I could; but this indraught of the Lombard energies upon the Byzantine rest, like a wild north wind descending into a space of rarified atmosphere, and encountered by an Arab simoom from the south, may well require from us some farther attention; for the differences in all these schools are more in the degrees of their impetuosity and refinement (these qualities being, in most cases, in inverse ratio, yet much united by the Arabs) than in the style of the ornaments they employ. The same leaves, the same animals, the same arrangement, are used by Scandinavians, ancient Britons, Saxons, Normans, Lombards, Romans, Byzantines, and Arabians; all being alike descended through classic Greece from Egypt and Assyria, and some from Phoenicia. The belts which encompass the Assyrian bulls, in the hall of the British Museum, are the same as the belts of the ornaments found in Scandinavian tumuli; their method of ornamentation is the same as that of the gate of Mycenæ, and of the Lombard pulpit of St. Ambrogio of Milan, and of the church of Theotocos at Constantinople; the essential differences among the great schools are their differences of temper and treatment, and science of expression; it is absurd to talk of Norman ornaments, and Lombard ornaments, and Byzantine ornaments, as formally distinguished; but there is irreconcileable separation between Arab temper, and Lombard temper, and Byzantine temper.

Now, as far as I have been able to compare the three schools, it appears to me that the Arab and Lombard are both distinguished from the Byzantine by their energy and love of excitement, but the Lombard stands alone in his love of jest: Neither an Arab nor Byzantine ever jests in his architecture; the Lombard has great difficulty in ever being thoroughly serious; thus they represent three conditions of humanity, one in perfect rest, the Byzantine, with exquisite perception of grace and dignity; the Arab, with the same perception of grace, but with a restless fever in his blood; the Lombard, equally energetic, but not burning himself away, capable of submitting to law, and of enjoying jest. But the Arabian feverishness infects even the Lombard in the South, showing itself, however, in endless invention, with a refreshing firmness and order directing the whole of it. The excitement is greatest in the earliest times, most of all shown in St. Michele of Pavia; and I am strongly disposed to connect much of its peculiar manifestations with the Lombard's habits of eating and drinking, especially his carnivorousness. The Lombard of early times seems to have been exactly what a tiger would be, if you could give him love of a joke, vigorous imagination, strong sense of justice, fear of hell, knowledge of northern mythology, a stone den, and a mallet and chisel; fancy him pacing up and down in the said den to digest his dinner, and striking on the wall, with a new fancy in his head, at every turn, and you have the Lombardic sculptor. As civilisation increases the supply of vegetables, and shortens that of wild beasts, the excitement diminishes; it is still strong in the thirteenth century at Lyons and Rouen; it dies away gradually in the later Gothic, and is quite extinct in the fifteenth century.

I think I shall best illustrate this general idea by simply copying the entries in my diary which were written when, after six months' close study of Byzantine work in Venice, I came again to the Lombard work of Verona and Pavia. There are some other points alluded to in these entries not pertaining to the matter immediately in hand; but I have left them, as they will be of use hereafter.

"(Verona.) Comparing the arabesque and sculpture of the Duomo here with St. Mark's, the first thing that strikes one is the low relief, the second, the greater motion and spirit, with infinitely less grace and science. With the Byzantine, however rude the cutting, every line is lovely, and the animals or men are placed in any attitudes which secure ornamental effect, sometimes impossible ones, always severe, restrained, or languid. With the Romanesque workmen all the figures show the effort (often successful) to express energetic action; hunting chiefly, much fighting, and both spirited; some of the dogs running capitally, straining to it, and the knights hitting hard, while yet the faces and drawing are in the last degree barbarous. At Venice all is graceful, fixed, or languid; the eastern torpor is in every line,—the mark of a school formed on severe traditions, and keeping to them, and never likely or desirous to rise beyond them, but with an exquisite sense of beauty, and much solemn religious faith.

"If the Greek outer archivolt of St. Mark's is Byzantine, the law is somewhat broken by its busy domesticity; figures engaged in every trade, and in the preparation of viands of all kinds; a crowded kind of London Christmas scene, interleaved (literally) by the superb balls of leafage, unique in sculpture; but even this is strongly opposed to the wild war and chase passion of the Lombard. Farther, the Lombard building is as sharp, precise, and accurate, as that of St. Mark's is careless. The Byzantines seem to have been too lazy to put their stones together; and, in general, my first impression on coming to Verona, after four months in Venice, is of the exquisitely neat masonry and perfect feeling here; a style of Gothic formed by a combination of Lombard surface ornament with Pisan Gothic, than which nothing can possibly be more chaste, pure, or solemn."

I have said much of the shafts of the entrance to the crypt of St. Zeno;[96] the following note of the sculptures on the archivolt above them is to our present purpose:

"It is covered by very light but most effective bas-reliefs of jesting subject:—two cocks carrying on their shoulders a long staff to which a fox (?) is tied by the legs, hanging down between them: the strut of the foremost cock, lifting one leg at right angles to the other, is delicious. Then a stag hunt, with a centaur horseman drawing a bow; the arrow has gone clear through the stag's throat, and is sticking there. Several capital hunts with dogs, with fruit trees between, and birds in them; the leaves, considering the early time, singularly well set, with the edges outwards, sharp, and deep cut: snails and frogs filling up the intervals, as if suspended in the air, with some saucy puppies on their hind legs, two or three nondescript beasts; and, finally, on the centre of one of the arches on the south side, an elephant and castle,—a very strange elephant, yet cut as if the carver had seen one."

Observe this elephant and castle; we shall meet with him farther north.

"These sculptures of St. Zeno are, however, quite quiet and tame compared with those of St. Michele of Pavia, which are designed also in a somewhat gloomier mood; significative, as I think, of indigestion. (Note that they are much earlier than St. Zeno; of the seventh century at latest. There is more of nightmare, and less of wit in them.) Lord Lindsay has described them admirably, but has not said half enough; the state of mind represented by the west front is more that of a feverish dream, than resultant from any determined architectural purpose, or even from any definite love and delight in the grotesque. One capital is covered with a mass of grinning heads, other heads grow out of two bodies, or out of and under feet; the creatures are all fighting, or devouring, or struggling which shall be uppermost, and yet in an ineffectual way, as if they would fight for ever, and come to no decision. Neither sphinxes nor centaurs did I notice, nor a single peacock (I believe peacocks to be purely Byzantine), but mermaids with two tails (the sculptor having perhaps seen double at the time), strange, large fish, apes, stags (bulls?), dogs, wolves, and horses, griffins, eagles, long-tailed birds (cocks?), hawks, and dragons, without end, or with a dozen of ends, as the case may be; smaller birds, with rabbits, and small nondescripts, filling the friezes. The actual leaf, which is used in the best Byzantine mouldings at Venice, occurs in parts of these Pavian designs. But the Lombard animals are all alive, and fiercely alive too, all impatience and spring: the Byzantine birds peck idly at the fruit, and the animals hardly touch it with their noses. The cinque cento birds in Venice hold it up daintily, like train-bearers; the birds in the earlier

Gothic peck at it hungrily and naturally; but the Lombard beasts gripe at it like tigers, and tear it off with writhing lips and glaring eyes. They are exactly like Jip with the bit of geranium, worrying imaginary cats in it."

The notice of the leaf in the above extract is important,—it is the vine-leaf; used constantly both by Byzantines and Lombards, but by the latter with especial frequency, though at this time they were hardly able to indicate what they meant. It forms the most remarkable generality of the St. Michele decoration; though, had it not luckily been carved on the façade, twining round a stake, and with grapes, I should never have known what it was meant for, its general form being a succession of sharp lobes, with incised furrows to the point of each. But it is thrown about in endless change; four or five varieties of it might be found on every cluster of capitals: and not content with this, the Lombards hint the same form even in their griffin wings. They love the vine very heartily.

In St. Michele of Lucca we have perhaps the noblest instance in Italy of the Lombard spirit in its later refinement. It is some four centuries later than St. Michele of Pavia, and the method of workmanship is altogether different. In the Pavian church, nearly all the ornament is cut in a coarse sandstone, in bold relief: a darker and harder stone (I think, not serpentine, but its surface is so disguised by the lustre of ages that I could not be certain) is used for the capitals of the western door, which are especially elaborate in their sculpture;—two devilish apes, or apish devils, I know not which, with bristly moustaches and edgy teeth, half-crouching, with their hands impertinently on their knees, ready for a spit or a spring if one goes near them; but all is pure bossy sculpture; there is no inlaying, except of some variegated tiles in the shape of saucers set concave (an ornament used also very gracefully in St. Jacopo of Bologna): and the whole surface of the church is enriched with the massy reliefs, well preserved everywhere above the reach of human animals, but utterly destroyed to some five or six feet from the ground; worn away into large cellular hollows and caverns, some almost deep enough to render the walls unsafe, entirely owing to the uses to which the recesses of the church are dedicated by the refined and high-minded Italians. But St. Michele of Lucca is wrought entirely in white marble and green serpentine; there is hardly any relieved sculpture except in the capitals of the shafts and cornices, and all the designs of wall ornament are inlaid with exquisite precision—white on dark ground; the ground being cut out and filled with serpentine, the figures left in solid marble. The designs of the Pavian church are encrusted on the walls; of the Lucchese, incorporated with them; small portions of real sculpture being introduced exactly where the eye, after its rest on the flatness of the wall, will take most delight in the piece of substantial form. The entire arrangement is perfect beyond all praise, and the morbid restlessness of the old designs is now appeased. Geometry seems to have acted as a febrifuge, for beautiful geometrical designs are introduced amidst the tumult of the hunt; and there is no more seeing double, nor ghastly monstrosity of conception; no more ending of everything in something else; no more disputing for spare legs among bewildered bodies; no more setting on of heads wrong side foremost. The fragments have come together: we are out of the Inferno with its weeping down the spine; we are in the fair hunting-fields of the Lucchese mountains (though they had their tears also),—with horse, and hound, and hawk; and merry blast of the trumpet.—Very strange creatures to be hunted, in all truth; but still creatures with a single head, and that on their shoulders, which is exactly the last place in the Pavian church where a head is to be looked for.

My good friend Mr. Cockerell wonders, in one of his lectures, why I give so much praise to this "crazy front of Lucca." But it is not crazy; not by any means. Altogether sober, in comparison with the early Lombard work, or with our Norman. Crazy in one sense it is: utterly neglected, to the breaking of its old stout heart; the venomous nights and salt frosts of the Maremma winters have their way with it—"Poor Tom's a cold!" The weeds that feed on the marsh air, have twisted themselves into its crannies; the polished fragments of serpentine are spit and rent out of their cells, and lie in green ruins along its ledges; the salt sea winds have eaten away the fair shafting of its star window into a skeleton of crumbling rays. It cannot stand much longer; may Heaven only, in its benignity, preserve it from restoration, and the sands of the Serchio give it honorable grave.

In the "Seven Lamps," Plate VI., I gave a faithful drawing of one of its upper arches, to which I must refer the reader; for there is a marked piece of character in the figure of the horseman on the left of it. And in making this reference, I would say a few words about those much abused plates of the "Seven Lamps." They are black, they are overbitten, they are hastily drawn, they are coarse and disagreeable; how disagreeable to many readers I venture not to conceive. But their truth is carried to an extent never before attempted in architectural drawing. It does not in the least follow that because a drawing is delicate, or looks careful, it has been carefully drawn from the thing represented; in nine instances out of ten, careful and delicate drawings are made at home. It is not so easy as the reader, perhaps, imagines, to finish a drawing altogether on the spot, especially of details seventy feet from the ground; and any one who will try the position in which I have had to do some of my work—standing, namely, on a cornice or window sill, holding by one arm round a shaft, and hanging over the street (or canal, at Venice), with my sketch-book supported against the wall from which I was drawing, by my breast, so as to leave my right hand free—will not thenceforward wonder that shadows should be occasionally carelessly laid in, or lines drawn with some unsteadiness. But, steady, or infirm, the sketches of which those plates in the "Seven Lamps" are fac-similes, were made from the architecture itself, and represent that architecture with its actual shadows at the time of day at which it was drawn, and with every fissure and line of it as they now exist; so that when I am speaking of some new point, which perhaps the drawing was not intended to illustrate, I can yet turn back to it with perfect certainty that if anything be found in it bearing on matters now in hand, I may depend upon it just as securely as if I had gone back to look again at the building.

It is necessary that my readers should understand this thoroughly, and I did not before sufficiently explain it; but I believe I can show them the use of this kind of truth, now that we are again concerned with this front of Lucca. They will find a drawing of the entire front in Gally Knight's "Architecture of Italy." It may serve to give them an idea of its general disposition, and it looks very careful and accurate; but every bit of the ornament on it is drawn out of the artist's head. There is not one line of it that exists on the building. The reader will therefore, perhaps, think my ugly black plate of somewhat more value, upon the whole, in its rough veracity, than the other in its delicate fiction.[97]

Plate XXI. WALL VEIL DECORATION.

As, however, I made a drawing of another part of the church somewhat more delicately, and as I do not choose that my favorite church should suffer in honor by my coarse work, I have had this, as far as might be, fac-similied by line engraving (Plate XXI.). It represents the southern side of the lower arcade of the west front; and may convey some idea of the exquisite finish and grace of the whole; but the old plate, in the "Seven Lamps," gives a nearer view of one of the upper arches, and a more faithful impression of the present aspect of the work, and especially of the seats of the horsemen; the limb straight, and well down on the stirrup (the warrior's seat, observe, not the jockey's), with a single pointed spur on the heel. The bit of the lower cornice under this arch I could not see, and therefore had not drawn; it was supplied from beneath another arch. I am afraid, however, the reader has lost the thread of my story while I have been recommending my veracity to him. I was insisting upon the healthy tone of this Lucca work as compared with the old spectral Lombard friezes. The apes of the Pavian church ride without stirrups, but all is in good order and harness here: civilisation had done its work; there was reaping of corn in the Val d'Arno, though rough hunting still upon its hills. But in the north, though a century or two later, we find the forests of the Rhone, and its rude limestone cotes, haunted by phantasms still (more meat-eating, then, I think). I do not know a more interesting group of cathedrals than that of Lyons, Vienne, and Valencia: a more interesting indeed, generally, than beautiful; but there is a row of niches on the west front of Lyons, and a course of panelled decoration about its doors, which is, without exception, the most exquisite piece of Northern Gothic I ever beheld, and with which I know nothing that is even comparable, except the work of the north transept of Rouen, described in the "Seven Lamps," p. 159; work of about the same date, and exactly the same plan; quatrefoils filled with grotesques, but somewhat less finished in execution, and somewhat less wild in imagination. I wrote down hastily, and in their own course, the subjects of some of the quatrefoils of Lyons; of which I here give the reader the sequence:—

1. Elephant and castle; less graphic than the St. Zeno one.

2. A huge head walking on two legs, turned backwards, hoofed; the head has a horn behind, with drapery over it, which ends in another head.

3. A boar hunt; the boar under a tree, very spirited.

4. A bird putting its head between its legs to bite its own tail, which ends in a head.

5. A dragon with a human head set on the wrong way.

6. St. Peter awakened by the angel in prison; full of spirit, the prison picturesque, with a trefoiled arch, the angel eager, St. Peter startled, and full of motion.

7. St. Peter led out by the angel.

8. The miraculous draught of fishes; fish and all, in the small space.

9. A large leaf, with two snails rampant, coming out of nautilus shells, with grotesque faces, and eyes at the ends of their horns.

10. A man with an axe striking at a dog's head, which comes out of a nautilus shell: the rim of the shell branches into a stem with two large leaves.

11. Martyrdom of St. Sebastian; his body very full of arrows.

12. Beasts coming to ark; Noah opening a kind of wicker cage.

13. Noah building the ark on shores.

14. A vine leaf with a dragon's head and tail, the one biting the other.

15. A man riding a goat, catching a flying devil.

16. An eel or muraena growing into a bunch of flowers, which turns into two wings.

17. A sprig of hazel, with nuts, thrown all around the quatrefoils with a squirrel in centre, apparently attached to the tree only by its enormous tail, richly furrowed into hair, and nobly sweeping.

18. Four hares fastened together by the ears, galloping in a circle. Mingled with these grotesques are many sword and buckler combats, the bucklers being round and conical like a hat; I thought the first I noticed, carried by a man at full gallop on horseback, had been a small umbrella.

This list of subjects may sufficiently illustrate the feverish character of the Northern Energy; but influencing the treatment of the whole there is also the Northern love of what is called the Grotesque, a feeling which I find myself, for the present, quite incapable either of analysing or defining, though we all have a distinct idea attached to the word: I shall try, however, in the next volume.

9. WOODEN CHURCHES OF THE NORTH

I cannot pledge myself to this theory of the origin of the vaulting shaft, but the reader will find some interesting confirmations of it in Dahl's work on the wooden churches of Norway. The inside view of the church of Borgund shows the timber construction of one shaft run up through a crossing architrave, and continued into the clerestory; while the church of Urnes is in the exact form of a basilica; but the wall above the arches is formed of planks, with a strong upright above each capital. The passage quoted from Stephen Eddy's Life of Bishop Wilfrid, at p. 86 of Churton's "Early English Church," gives us one of the transformations or petrifactions of the wooden Saxon churches. "At Ripon he built a new church of polished stone, with columns variously ornamented, and porches." Mr. Churton adds: "It was perhaps in bad imitation of the marble buildings he had seen in Italy, that he washed the walls of this original York Minster, and made them 'whiter than snow.'"

10. CHURCH OF ALEXANDRIA

The very cause which enabled the Venetians to possess themselves of the body of St. Mark, was the destruction of the church by the caliph for the sake of its marbles: the Arabs and Venetians, though bitter enemies, thus building on the same models; these in reverence for the destroyed church, and those with the very pieces of it. In the somewhat prolix account of the matter given in the Notizie Storiche (above quoted) the main points are, that "il Califa de' Saraceni, per fabbricarsi un Palazzo presse di Babilonia, aveva ordinato che dalle Chiese d' Cristiani si togliessero i più scelti marmi;" and that the Venetians, "videro sotto i loro occhi flagellarsi crudelmente un Cristiano per aver infranto un marmo." I heartily wish that the same kind of punishment were enforced to this day, for the same sin.

11. RENAISSANCE LANDSCAPE

I am glad here to re-assert opinions which it has grieved me to be suspected of having changed. The calmer tone of the second volume of "Modern Painters," as compared with the first, induced, I believe, this suspicion, very justifiably, in the minds of many of its readers. The difference resulted, however, from the simple fact, that the first was written in great haste and indignation, for a special purpose and time;—the second, after I had got engaged, almost unawares, in inquiries which could not be hastily nor indignantly pursued; my opinions remaining then, and remaining now, altogether unchanged on the subject which led me into the discussion. And that no farther doubt of them may be entertained by any who may think them worth questioning, I shall here, once for all, express them in the plainest and fewest words I can. I think that J. M. W. Turner is not only the greatest (professed) landscape painter who ever lived, but that he has in him as much as would have furnished all the rest with such power as they had; and that if we put Nicolo Poussin, Salvator, and our own Gainsborough out of the group, he would cut up into Claudes, Cuyps, Ruysdaels, and such others, by uncounted bunches. I hope this is plainly and strongly enough stated. And farther, I like his later pictures, up to the year 1845, the best; and believe that those persons who only like his early pictures do not, in fact, like him at all. They do not like that which is essentially his. They like that in which he resembles other men; which he had learned from Loutherbourg, Claude, or Wilson; that which is indeed his own, they do not care for. Not that there is not much of his own in his early works; they are all invaluable in their way; but those persons who can find no beauty in his strangest fantasy on the Academy walls, cannot distinguish the peculiarly Turneresque characters of the earlier pictures. And, therefore, I again state here, that I think his pictures painted between the years 1830 and 1845 his greatest; and that his entire power is best represented by such pictures as the Temeraire, the Sun of Venice going to Sea, and others, painted exactly at the time when the public and the press were together loudest in abuse of him.

I desire, however, the reader to observe that I said, above, professed landscape painters, among whom, perhaps, I should hardly have put Gainsborough. The landscape of the great figure painters is often majestic in the highest degree, and Tintoret's especially shows exactly the same power and feeling as Turner's. If with Turner I were to rank the historical painters as landscapists, estimating rather the power they show, than the actual value of the landscape they produced, I should class those, whose landscapes I have studied, in some such order as this:

Turner.
Tintoret.
Massaccio.
John Bellini.
Albert Durer.
Giorgione.
Paul Veronese.
Titian.
Rubens.
Correggio.
Orcagna.
Benozzo Gozzoli.
Giotto.
Raffaelle.
Perugino.

—associating with the landscape of Perugino that of Francia and Angelico, and the other severe painters of religious subjects. I have put Turner and Tintoret side by side, not knowing which is, in landscape, the greater; I had nearly associated in the same manner the noble names of John Bellini and Albert Durer; but Bellini must be put first, for his profound religious peace yet not separated from the other, if but that we might remember his kindness to him in Venice; and it is well we should take note of it here, for it furnishes us with a most interesting confirmation of what was said in the text respecting the position of Bellini as the last of the religious painters of Venice. The following passage is quoted in Jackson's "Essay on Wood-engraving," from Albert Durer's Diary:

"I have many good friends among the Italians who warn me not to eat or drink with their painters, of whom several are my enemies, and copy my picture in the church, and others of mine, wherever they can find them, and yet they blame them, and say they are not according to ancient art, and therefore not good. Giovanni Bellini, however, has praised me highly to several gentlemen, and wishes to have something of my doing: he called on me himself, and requested that I would paint a picture for him, for which, he said, he would pay me well. People are all surprised that I should be so much thought of by a person of his reputation: he is very old, but is still the best painter of them all."

A choice little piece of description this, of the Renaissance painters, side by side with the good old Venetian, who was soon to leave them to their own ways. The Renaissance men are seen in perfection, envying, stealing, and lying, but without wit enough to lie to purpose.

12. ROMANIST MODERN ART

It is of the highest importance, in these days, that Romanism should be deprived of the miserable influence which its pomp and picturesqueness have given it over the weak sentimentalism of the English people; I call it a miserable influence, for of all motives to sympathy with the Church of Rome, this I unhesitatingly class as the basest: I can, in some measure, respect the other feelings which have been the beginnings of apostasy; I can respect the desire for unity which would reclaim the Romanist by love, and the distrust of his own heart which subjects the proselyte to priestly power; I say I can respect these feelings, though I cannot pardon unprincipled submission to them, nor enough wonder at the infinite fatuity of the unhappy persons whom they have betrayed:—Fatuity, self-inflicted, and stubborn in resistance to God's Word and man's reason!—to talk of the authority of the Church, as if the Church were anything else than the whole company of Christian men, or were ever spoken of in Scripture[98] as other than a company to be taught and fed, not to teach and feed.—Fatuity! to talk of a separation of Church and State, as if a Christian state, and every officer therein, were not necessarily a part of the Church,[99] and as if any state officer could do his duty without endeavoring to aid and promote religion, or any clerical officer do his duty without seeking for such aid and accepting it:—Fatuity! to seek for the unity of a living body of truth and trust in God, with a dead body of lies and trust in wood, and thence to expect anything else than plague, and consumption by worms undying, for both. Blasphemy as well as fatuity! to ask for any better interpreter of God's Word than God, or to expect knowledge of it in any other way than the plainly ordered way: if any man will do he shall know. But of all these fatuities, the basest is the being lured into the Romanist Church by the glitter of it, like larks into a trap by broken glass; to be blown into a change of religion by the whine of an organ-pipe; stitched into a new creed by gold threads on priests' petticoats; jangled into a change of conscience by the chimes of a belfry. I know nothing in the shape of error so dark as this, no imbecility so absolute, no treachery so contemptible. I had hardly believed that it was a thing possible, though vague stories had been told me of the effect, on some minds, of mere scarlet and candles, until I came on this passage in Pugin's "Remarks on articles in the Rambler":—

"Those who have lived in want and privation are the best qualified to appreciate the blessings of plenty; thus, those who have been devout and sincere members of the separated portion of the English Church; who have prayed, and hoped, and loved, through all the poverty of the maimed rites which it has retained—to them does the realisation of all their longing desires appear truly ravishing. * * * Oh! then, what delight! what joy unspeakable! when one of the solemn piles is presented to them, in all its pristine life and glory!—the stoups are filled to the brim; the rood is raised on high; the screen glows with sacred imagery and rich device; the niches are filled; the altar is replaced, sustained by sculptured shafts, the relics of the saints repose beneath, the body of Our Lord is enshrined on its consecrated stone; the lamps of the sanctuary burn bright; the saintly portraitures in the glass windows shine all gloriously; and the albs hang in the oaken ambries, and the cope chests are filled with orphreyed baudekins; and pix and pax, and chrismatory are there, and thurible, and cross."

One might have put this man under a pix, and left him, one should have thought; but he has been brought forward, and partly received, as an example of the effect of ceremonial splendor on the mind of a great architect. It is very necessary, therefore, that all those who have felt sorrow at this should know at once that he is not a great architect, but one of the smallest possible or conceivable architects; and that by his own account and setting forth of himself. Hear him:—

"I believe, as regards architecture, few men have been so unfortunate as myself. I have passed my life in thinking of fine things, studying fine things, designing fine things, and realising very poor ones. I have never had the chance of producing a single fine ecclesiastical building, except my own church, where I am both paymaster and architect; but everything else, either for want of adequate funds or injudicious interference and control, or some other contingency, is more or less a failure.

"St. George's was spoilt by the very instructions laid down by the committee, that it was to hold 3000 people on the floor at a limited price; in consequence, height, proportion, everything, was sacrificed to meet these conditions. Nottingham was spoilt by the style being restricted to lancet,—a period well suited to a Cistercian abbey in a secluded vale, but very unsuitable for the centre of a crowded town.

"Kirkham was spoilt through several hundred pounds being reduced on the original estimate; to effect this, which was a great sum in proportion to the entire cost, the area of the church was contracted, the walls lowered, tower and spire reduced, the thickness of walls diminished, and stone arches omitted." (Remarks, &c., by A. Welby Pugin: Dolman, 1850.)

Is that so? Phidias can niche himself into the corner of a pediment, and Raffaelle expatiate within the circumference of a clay platter; but Pugin is inexpressible in less than a cathedral? Let his ineffableness be assured of this, once for all, that no difficulty or restraint ever happened to a man of real power, but his power was the more manifested in the contending with, or conquering it; and that there is no field so small, no cranny so contracted, but that a great spirit can house and manifest itself therein. The thunder that smites the Alp into dust, can gather itself into the width of a golden wire. Whatever greatness there was in you, had it been Buonarroti's own, you had room enough for it in a single niche: you might have put the whole power of it into two feet cube of Caen stone. St. George's was not high enough for want of money? But was it want of money that made you put that blunt, overloaded, laborious ogee door into the side of it? Was it for lack of funds that you sunk the tracery of the parapet in its clumsy zigzags? Was it in parsimony that you buried its paltry pinnacles in that eruption of diseased crockets? or in pecuniary embarrassment that you set up the belfry foolscaps, with the mimicry of dormer windows, which nobody can ever reach nor look out of? Not so, but in mere incapability of better things.

I am sorry to have to speak thus of any living architect; and there is much in this man, if he were rightly estimated, which one might both regard and profit by. He has a most sincere love for his profession, a heartily honest enthusiasm for pixes and piscinas; and though he will never design so much as a pix or a piscina thoroughly well, yet better than most of the experimental architects of the day. Employ him by all means, but on small work. Expect no cathedrals from him; but no one, at present, can design a better finial. That is an exceedingly beautiful one over the western door of St. George's; and there is some spirited impishness and switching of tails in the supporting figures at the imposts. Only do not allow his good designing of finials to be employed as an evidence in matters of divinity, nor thence deduce the incompatibility of Protestantism and art. I should have said all that I have said above, of artistical apostasy, if Giotto had been now living in Florence, and if art were still doing all that it did once for Rome. But the grossness of the error becomes incomprehensible as well as unpardonable, when we look to what level of degradation the human intellect has sunk at this instant in Italy. So far from Romanism now producing anything greater in art, it cannot even preserve what has been given to its keeping. I know no abuses of precious inheritance half so grievous, as the abuse of all that is best in art wherever the Romanist priesthood gets possession of it. It amounts to absolute infatuation. The noblest pieces of mediæval sculpture in North Italy, the two griffins at the central (west) door of the cathedral of Verona, were daily permitted to be brought into service, when I was there in the autumn of 1849, by a washerwoman living in the Piazza, who tied her clothes-lines to their beaks: and the shafts of St. Mark's at Venice were used by a salesman of common caricatures to fasten his prints upon (Compare Appendix 25); and this in the face of the continually passing priests: while the quantity of noble art annually destroyed in altarpieces by candle-droppings, or perishing by pure brutality of neglect, passes all estimate. I do not know, as I have repeatedly stated, how far the splendor of architecture, or other art, is compatible with the honesty and usefulness of religious service. The longer I live, the more I incline to severe judgment in this matter, and the less I can trust the sentiments excited by painted glass and colored tiles. But if there be indeed value in such things, our plain duty is to direct our strength against the superstition which has dishonored them; there are thousands who might possibly be benefited by them, to whom they are now merely an offence, owing to their association with idolatrous ceremonies. I have but this exhortation for all who love them,—not to regulate their creeds by their taste in colors, but to hold calmly to the right, at whatever present cost to their imaginative enjoyment; sure that they will one day find in heavenly truth a brighter charm than in earthly imagery, and striving to gather stones for the eternal building, whose walls shall be salvation, and whose gates shall be praise.

13. MR. FERGUSSON'S SYSTEM

The reader may at first suppose this division of the attributes of buildings into action, voice, and beauty, to be the same division as Mr. Fergusson's, now well known, of their merits, into technic, æsthetic and phonetic.

But there is no connection between the two systems; mine, indeed, does not profess to be a system, it is a mere arrangement of my subject, for the sake of order and convenience in its treatment: but, as far as it goes, it differs altogether from Mr. Fergusson's in these two following respects:—

The action of a building, that is to say its standing or consistence, depends on its good construction; and the first part of the foregoing volume has been entirely occupied with the consideration of the constructive merit of buildings: but construction is not their only technical merit. There is as much of technical merit in their expression, or in their beauty, as in their construction. There is no more mechanical or technical admirableness in the stroke of the painter who covers them with fresco, than in the dexterity of the mason who cements their stones: there is just as much of what is technical in their beauty, therefore, as in their construction; and, on the other hand, there is often just as much intellect shown in their construction as there is in either their expression or decoration. Now Mr. Fergusson means by his "Phonetic" division, whatever expresses intellect: my constructive division, therefore, includes part of his phonetic: and my expressive and decorative divisions include part of his technical.

Secondly, Mr. Fergusson tries to make the same divisions fit the subjects of art, and art itself; and therefore talks of technic, æsthetic, and phonetic, arts, (or, translating the Greek,) of artful arts, sensitive arts, and talkative arts; but I have nothing to do with any division of the arts, I have to deal only with the merits of buildings. As, however, I have been led into reference to Mr. Fergusson's system, I would fain say a word or two to effect Mr. Fergusson's extrication from it. I hope to find in him a noble ally, ready to join with me in war upon affectation, falsehood, and prejudice, of every kind: I have derived much instruction from his most interesting work, and I hope for much more from its continuation; but he must disentangle himself from his system, or he will be strangled by it; never was anything so ingeniously and hopelessly wrong throughout; the whole of it is founded on a confusion of the instruments of man with his capacities.

Mr. Fergusson would have us take—

"First, man's muscular action or power." (Technics.)
"Secondly, those developments of sense by which he does!! as much as by his muscles." (Æsthetics.)
"Lastly, his intellect, or to confine this more correctly to its external action, his power of speech!!!" (Phonetics.)

Granting this division of humanity correct, or sufficient, the writer then most curiously supposes that he may arrange the arts as if there were some belonging to each division of man,—never observing that every art must be governed by, and addressed to, one division, and executed by another; executed by the muscular, addressed to the sensitive or intellectual; and that, to be an art at all, it must have in it work of the one, and guidance from the other. If, by any lucky accident, he had been led to arrange the arts, either by their objects, and the things to which they are addressed, or by their means, and the things by which they are executed, he would have discovered his mistake in an instant. As thus:—

These arts are addressed to the,—   Muscles!!
                                     Senses,
                                     Intellect;
or executed by,—   Muscles,
                                     Senses!!
                                     Intellect.

Indeed it is true that some of the arts are in a sort addressed to the muscles, surgery for instance; but this is not among Mr. Fergusson's technic, but his politic, arts! and all the arts may, in a sort, be said to be performed by the senses, as the senses guide both muscles and intellect in their work: but they guide them as they receive information, or are standards of accuracy, but not as in themselves capable of action. Mr. Fergusson is, I believe, the first person who has told us of senses that act or do, they having been hitherto supposed only to sustain or perceive. The weight of error, however, rests just as much in the original division of man, as in the endeavor to fit the arts to it. The slight omission of the soul makes a considerable difference when it begins to influence the final results of the arrangement.

Mr. Fergusson calls morals and religion "Politick arts" (as if religion were an art at all! or as if both were not as necessary to individuals as to societies); and therefore, forming these into a body of arts by themselves, leaves the best of the arts to do without the soul and the moral feeling as rest they may. Hence "expression," or "phonetics," is of intellect only (as if men never expressed their feelings!); and then, strangest and worst of all, intellect is entirely resolved into talking! There can be no intellect but it must talk, and all talking must be intellectual. I believe people do sometimes talk without understanding; and I think the world would fare ill if they never understood without talking. The intellect is an entirely silent faculty, and has nothing to do with parts of speech any more than the moral part has. A man may feel and know things without expressing either the feeling or knowledge; and the talking is a muscular mode of communicating the workings of the intellect or heart—muscular, whether it be by tongue or by sign, or by carving or writing, or by expression of feature; so that to divide a man into muscular and talking parts, is to divide him into body in general, and tongue in particular, the endless confusion resulting from which arrangement is only less marvellous in itself, than the resolution with which Mr. Fergusson has worked through it, and in spite of it, up to some very interesting and suggestive truths; although starting with a division of humanity which does not in the least raise it above the brute, for a rattlesnake has his muscular, æsthetic, and talking part as much as man, only he talks with his tail, and says, "I am angry with you, and should like to bite you," more laconically and effectively than any phonetic biped could, were he so minded. And, in fact, the real difference between the brute and man is not so much that the one has fewer means of expression than the other, as that it has fewer thoughts to express, and that we do not understand its expressions. Animals can talk to one another intelligibly enough when they have anything to say, and their captains have words of command just as clear as ours, and better obeyed. We have indeed, in watching the efforts of an intelligent animal to talk to a human being, a melancholy sense of its dumbness; but the fault is still in its intelligence, more than in its tongue. It has not wit enough to systematise its cries or signs, and form them into language.

But there is no end to the fallacies and confusions of Mr. Fergusson's arrangement. It is a perfect entanglement of gun-cotton, and explodes into vacuity wherever one holds a light to it. I shall leave him to do so with the rest of it for himself, and should perhaps have left it to his own handling altogether, but for the intemperateness of the spirit with which he has spoken on a subject perhaps of all others demanding gentleness and caution. No man could more earnestly have desired the changes lately introduced into the system of the University of Oxford than I did myself: no man can be more deeply sensible than I of grievous failures in the practical working even of the present system: but I believe that these failures may be almost without exception traced to one source, the want of evangelical, and the excess of rubrical religion among the tutors; together with such rustinesses and stiffnesses as necessarily attend the continual operation of any intellectual machine. The fault is, at any rate, far less in the system than in the imperfection of its administration; and had it been otherwise, the terms in which Mr. Fergusson speaks of it are hardly decorous in one who can but be imperfectly acquainted with its working. They are sufficiently answered by the structure of the essay in which they occur; for if the high powers of mind which its author possesses had been subjected to the discipline of the schools, he could not have wasted his time on the development of a system which their simplest formulæ of logic would have shown him to be untenable.

Mr. Fergusson will, however, find it easier to overthrow his system than to replace it. Every man of science knows the difficulty of arranging a reasonable system of classification, in any subject, by any one group of characters; and that the best classifications are, in many of their branches, convenient rather than reasonable: so that, to any person who is really master of his subject, many different modes of classification will occur at different times; one of which he will use rather than another, according to the point which he has to investigate. I need only instance the three arrangements of minerals, by their external characters, and their positive or negative bases, of which the first is the most useful, the second the most natural, the third the most simple; and all in several ways unsatisfactory.

But when the subject becomes one which no single mind can grasp, and which embraces the whole range of human occupation and enquiry, the difficulties become as great, and the methods as various, as the uses to which the classification might be put; and Mr. Fergusson has entirely forgotten to inform us what is the object to which his arrangements are addressed. For observe: there is one kind of arrangement which is based on the rational connection of the sciences or arts with one another; an arrangement which maps them out like the rivers of some great country, and marks the points of their junction, and the direction and force of their united currents; and this without assigning to any one of them a superiority above another, but considering them all as necessary members of the noble unity of human science and effort. There is another kind of classification which contemplates the order of succession in which they might most usefully be presented to a single mind, so that the given mind should obtain the most effective and available knowledge of them all: and, finally, the most usual classification contemplates the powers of mind which they each require for their pursuit, the objects to which they are addressed, or with which they are concerned; and assigns to each of them a rank superior or inferior, according to the nobility of the powers they require, or the grandeur of the subjects they contemplate.

Now, not only would it be necessary to adopt a different classification with respect to each of these great intentions, but it might be found so even to vary the order of the succession of sciences in the case of every several mind to which they were addressed; and that their rank would also vary with the power and specific character of the mind engaged upon them. I once heard a very profound mathematician remonstrate against the impropriety of Wordsworth's receiving a pension from government, on the ground that he was "only a poet." If the study of mathematics had always this narrowing effect upon the sympathies, the science itself would need to be deprived of the rank usually assigned to it; and there could be no doubt that, in the effect it had on the mind of this man, and of such others, it was a very contemptible science indeed. Hence, in estimating the real rank of any art or science, it is necessary for us to conceive it as it would be grasped by minds of every order. There are some arts and sciences which we underrate, because no one has risen to show us with what majesty they may be invested; and others which we overrate, because we are blinded to their general meanness by the magnificence which some one man has thrown around them: thus, philology, evidently the most contemptible of all the sciences, has been raised to unjust dignity by Johnson.[100] And the subject is farther complicated by the question of usefulness; for many of the arts and sciences require considerable intellectual power for their pursuit, and yet become contemptible by the slightness of what they accomplish: metaphysics, for instance, exercising intelligence of a high order, yet useless to the mass of mankind, and, to its own masters, dangerous. Yet, as it has become so by the want of the true intelligence which its inquiries need, and by substitution of vain subtleties in its stead, it may in future vindicate for itself a higher rank than a man of common sense usually concedes to it.

Nevertheless, the mere attempt at arrangement must be useful, even where it does nothing more than develop difficulties. Perhaps the greatest fault of men of learning is their so often supposing all other branches of science dependent upon or inferior to their own best beloved branch; and the greatest deficiency of men comparatively unlearned, their want of perception of the connection of the branches with each other. He who holds the tree only by the extremities, can perceive nothing but the separation of its sprays. It must always be desirable to prove to those the equality of rank, to these the closeness of sequence, of what they had falsely supposed subordinate or separate. And, after such candid admission of the co-equal dignity of the truly noble arts and sciences, we may be enabled more justly to estimate the inferiority of those which indeed seem intended for the occupation of inferior powers and narrower capacities. In Appendix 14, following, some suggestions will be found as to the principles on which classification might be based; but the arrangement of all the arts is certainly not a work which could with discretion be attempted in the Appendix to an essay on a branch of one of them.

14. DIVISIONS OF HUMANITY

The reader will probably understand this part of the subject better if he will take the trouble briefly to consider the actions of the mind and body of man in the sciences and arts, which give these latter the relations of rank usually attributed to them.

It was above observed (Appendix 13) that the arts were generally ranked according to the nobility of the powers they require, that is to say, the quantity of the being of man which they engaged or addressed.

Now their rank is not a very important matter as regards each other, for there are few disputes more futile than that concerning the respective dignity of arts, all of which are necessary and honorable. But it is a very important matter as regards themselves; very important whether they are practised with the devotion and regarded with the respect which are necessary or due to their perfection. It does not at all matter whether architecture or sculpture be the nobler art; but it matters much whether the thought is bestowed upon buildings, or the feeling is expressed in statues, which make either deserving of our admiration. It is foolish and insolent to imagine that the art which we ourselves practise is greater than any other; but it is wise to take care that in our own hands it is as noble as we can make it. Let us take some notice, therefore, in what degrees the faculties of man may be engaged in his several arts: we may consider the entire man as made up of body, soul, and intellect (Lord Lindsay, meaning the same thing, says inaccurately—sense, intellect, and spirit—forgetting that there is a moral sense as well as a bodily sense, and a spiritual body as well as a natural body, and so gets into some awkward confusion, though right in the main points). Then, taking the word soul as a short expression of the moral and responsible part of being, each of these three parts has a passive and active power. The body has senses and muscles; the soul, feeling and resolution; the intellect, understanding and imagination. The scheme may be put into tabular form, thus:—

	Passive or Receptive Part.	Active or Motive Part.
Body	Senses.	Muscles.
Soul	Feeling.	Resolution.
Intellect	Understanding.	Imagination.

In this scheme I consider memory a part of understanding, and conscience I leave out, as being the voice of God in the heart, inseparable from the system, yet not an essential part of it. The sense of beauty I consider a mixture of the Senses of the body and soul.

Now all these parts of the human system have a reciprocal action on one another, so that the true perfection of any of them is not possible without some relative perfection of the others, and yet any one of the parts of the system may be brought into a morbid development, inconsistent with the perfection of the others. Thus, in a healthy state, the acuteness of the senses quickens that of the feelings, and these latter quicken the understanding, and then all the three quicken the imagination, and then all the four strengthen the resolution; while yet there is a danger, on the other hand, that the encouraged and morbid feeling may weaken or bias the understanding, or that the over shrewd and keen understanding may shorten the imagination, or that the understanding and imagination together may take place of, or undermine, the resolution, as in Hamlet. So in the mere bodily frame there is a delightful perfection of the senses, consistent with the utmost health of the muscular system, as in the quick sight and hearing of an active savage: another false delicacy of the senses, in the Sybarite, consequent on their over indulgence, until the doubled rose-leaf is painful; and this inconsistent with muscular perfection. Again; there is a perfection of muscular action consistent with exquisite sense, as in that of the fingers of a musician or of a painter, in which the muscles are guided by the slightest feeling of the strings, or of the pencil: another perfection of muscular action inconsistent with acuteness of sense, as in the effort of battle, in which a soldier does not perceive his wounds. So that it is never so much the question, what is the solitary perfection of a given part of the man, as what is its balanced perfection in relation to the whole of him: and again, the perfection of any single power is not merely to be valued by the mere rank of the power itself, but by the harmony which it indicates among the other powers. Thus, for instance, in an archer's glance along his arrow, or a hunter's raising of his rifle, there is a certain perfection of sense and finger which is the result of mere practice, of a simple bodily perfection; but there is a farther value in the habit which results from the resolution and intellect necessary to the forming of it: in the hunter's raising of his rifle there is a quietness implying far more than mere practice,—implying courage, and habitual meeting of danger, and presence of mind, and many other such noble characters. So also in a musician's way of laying finger on his instrument, or a painter's handling of his pencil, there are many qualities expressive of the special sensibilities of each, operating on the production of the habit, besides the sensibility operating at the moment of action. So that there are three distinct stages of merit in what is commonly called mere bodily dexterity: the first, the dexterity given by practice, called command of tools or of weapons; the second stage, the dexterity or grace given by character, as the gentleness of hand proceeding from modesty or tenderness of spirit, and the steadiness of it resulting from habitual patience coupled with decision, and the thousand other characters partially discernible, even in a man's writing, much more in his general handiwork; and, thirdly, there is the perfection of action produced by the operation of present strength, feeling, or intelligence on instruments thus previously perfected, as the handling of a great painter is rendered more beautiful by his immediate care and feeling and love of his subject, or knowledge of it, and as physical strength is increased by strength of will and greatness of heart. Imagine, for instance, the difference in manner of fighting, and in actual muscular strength and endurance, between a common soldier, and a man in the circumstances of the Horatii, or of the temper of Leonidas.

Mere physical skill, therefore, the mere perfection and power of the body as an instrument, is manifested in three stages:

First, Bodily power by practice;
Secondly, Bodily power by moral habit;
Thirdly, Bodily power by immediate energy;

and the arts will be greater or less, cæteris paribus, according to the degrees of these dexterities which they admit. A smith's work at his anvil admits little but the first; fencing, shooting, and riding, admit something of the second; while the fine arts admit (merely through the channel of the bodily dexterities) an expression almost of the whole man.

Nevertheless, though the higher arts admit this higher bodily perfection, they do not all require it in equal degrees, but can dispense with it more and more in proportion to their dignity. The arts whose chief element is bodily dexterity, may be classed together as arts of the third order, of which the highest will be those which admit most of the power of moral habit and energy, such as riding and the management of weapons; and the rest may be thrown together under the general title of handicrafts, of which it does not much matter which are the most honorable, but rather, which are the most necessary and least injurious to health, which it is not our present business to examine. Men engaged in the practice of these are called artizans, as opposed to artists, who are concerned with the fine arts.

The next step in elevation of art is the addition of the intelligences which have no connection with bodily dexterity; as, for instance, in hunting, the knowledge of the habits of animals and their places of abode; in architecture, of mathematics; in painting, of harmonies of color; in music, of those of sound; all this pure science being joined with readiness of expedient in applying it, and with shrewdness in apprehension of difficulties, either present or probable.

It will often happen that intelligence of this kind is possessed without bodily dexterity, or the need of it; one man directing and another executing, as for the most part in architecture, war, and seamanship. And it is to be observed, also, that in proportion to the dignity of the art, the bodily dexterities needed even in its subordinate agents become less important, and are more and more replaced by intelligence;

as in the steering of a ship, the bodily dexterity required is less than in shooting or fencing, but the intelligence far greater: and so in war, the mere swordsmanship and marksmanship of the troops are of small importance in comparison with their disposition, and right choice of the moment of action. So that arts of this second order must be estimated, not by the quantity of bodily dexterity they require, but by the quantity and dignity of the knowledge needed in their practice, and by the degree of subtlety needed in bringing such knowledge into play. War certainly stands first in the general mind, not only as the greatest of the arts which I have called of the second order, but as the greatest of all arts. It is not, however, easy to distinguish the respect paid to the Power, from that rendered to the Art of the soldier; the honor of victory being more dependent, in the vulgar mind, on its results, than its difficulties. I believe, however, that taking into consideration the greatness of the anxieties under which this art must be practised, the multitude of circumstances to be known and regarded in it, and the subtleties both of apprehension and stratagem constantly demanded by it, as well as the multiplicity of disturbing accidents and doubtful contingencies against which it must make provision on the instant, it must indeed rank as far the first of the arts of the second order; and next to this great art of killing, medicine being much like war in its stratagems and watchings against its dark and subtle death-enemy.

Then the arts of the first order will be those in which the Imaginative part of the intellect and the Sensitive part of the soul are joined: as poetry, architecture, and painting; these forming a kind of cross, in their part of the scheme of the human being, with those of the second order, which wed the Intelligent part of the intellect and Resolute part of the soul. But the reader must feel more and more, at every step, the impossibility of classing the arts themselves, independently of the men by whom they are practised; and how an art, low in itself, may be made noble by the quantity of human strength and being which a great man will pour into it; and an art, great in itself, be made mean by the meanness of the mind occupied in it. I do not intend, when I call painting an art of the first, and war an art of the second, order, to class Dutch landscape painters with good soldiers; but I mean, that if from such a man as Napoleon we were to take away the honor of all that he had done in law and civil government, and to give him the reputation of his soldiership only, his name would be less, if justly weighed, than that of Buonarroti, himself a good soldier also, when need was. But I will not endeavor to pursue the inquiry, for I believe that of all the arts of the first order it would be found that all that a man has, or is, or can be, he can fully express in them, and give to any of them, and find it not enough.

15. INSTINCTIVE JUDGMENTS

The same rapid judgment which I wish to enable the reader to form of architecture, may in some sort also be formed of painting, owing to the close connection between execution and expression in the latter; as between structure and expression in the former. We ought to be able to tell good painting by a side glance as we pass along a gallery; and, until we can do so, we are not fit to pronounce judgment at all: not that I class this easily visible excellence of painting with the great expressional qualities which time and watchfulness only unfold. I have again and again insisted on the supremacy of these last and shall always continue to do so. But I perceive a tendency among some of the more thoughtful critics of the day to forget that the business of a painter is to paint, and so altogether to despise those men, Veronese and Rubens for instance, who were painters, par excellence, and in whom the expressional qualities are subordinate. Now it is well, when we have strong moral or poetical feeling manifested in painting, to mark this as the best part of the work; but it is not well to consider as a thing of small account, the painter's language in which that feeling is conveyed, for if that language be not good and lovely, the man may indeed be a just moralist or a great poet, but he is not a painter, and it was wrong of him to paint. He had much better put his morality into sermons, and his poetry into verse, than into a language of which he was not master. And this mastery of the language is that of which we should be cognizant by a glance of the eye; and if that be not found, it is wasted time to look farther: the man has mistaken his vocation, and his expression of himself will be cramped by his awkward efforts to do what he was not fit to do. On the other hand, if the man be a painter indeed, and have the gift of colors and lines, what is in him will come from his hand freely and faithfully; and the language itself is so difficult and so vast, that the mere possession of it argues the man is great, and that his works are worth reading. So that I have never yet seen the case in which this true artistical excellence, visible by the eye-glance, was not the index of some true expressional worth in the work. Neither have I ever seen a good expressional work without high artistical merit: and that this is ever denied is only owing to the narrow view which men are apt to take both of expression and of art; a narrowness consequent on their own especial practice and habits of thought. A man long trained to love the monk's visions of Fra Angelico, turns in proud and ineffable disgust from the first work of Rubens which he encounters on his return across the Alps. But is he right in his indignation? He has forgotten, that while Angelico prayed and wept in his olive shade, there was different work doing in the dank fields of Flanders;—wild seas to be banked out; endless canals to be dug, and boundless marshes to be drained; hard ploughing and harrowing of the frosty clay; careful breeding of stout horses and fat cattle; close setting of brick walls against cold winds and snow; much hardening of hands and gross stoutening of bodies in all this; gross jovialities of harvest homes and Christmas feasts, which were to be the reward of it; rough affections, and sluggish imagination; fleshy, substantial, ironshod humanities, but humanities still; humanities which God had his eye upon, and which won, perhaps, here and there, as much favor in his sight as the wasted aspects of the whispering monks of Florence (Heaven forbid it should not be so, since the most of us cannot be monks, but must be ploughmen and reapers still). And are we to suppose there is no nobility in Rubens' masculine and universal sympathy with all this, and with his large human rendering of it, Gentleman though he was, by birth, and feeling, and education, and place; and, when he chose, lordly in conception also? He had his faults, perhaps great and lamentable faults, though more those of his time and his country than his own; he has neither cloister breeding nor boudoir breeding, and is very unfit to paint either in missals or annuals; but he has an open sky and wide-world breeding in him, that we may not be offended with, fit alike for king's court, knight's camp, or peasant's cottage. On the other hand, a man trained here in England, in our Sir Joshua school, will not and cannot allow that there is any art at all in the technical work of Angelico. But he is just as wrong as the other. Fra Angelico is as true a master of the art necessary to his purposes, as Rubens was of that necessary for his. We have been taught in England to think there can be no virtue but in a loaded brush and rapid hand; but if we can shake our common sense free of such teaching, we shall understand that there is art also in the delicate point and in the hand which trembles as it moves; not because it is more liable to err, but because there is more danger in its error, and more at stake upon its precision. The art of Angelico, both as a colorist and a draughtsman, is consummate; so perfect and beautiful, that his work may be recognised at any distance by the rainbow-play and brilliancy of it: However closely it may be surrounded by other works of the same school, glowing with enamel and gold, Angelico's may be told from them at a glance, like so many huge pieces of opal lying among common marbles. So again with Giotto; the Arena chapel is not only the most perfect expressional work, it is the prettiest piece of wall decoration and fair color, in North Italy.

Now there is a correspondence of the same kind between the technical and expressional parts of architecture;—not a true or entire correspondence, so that when the expression is best, the building must be also best; but so much of correspondence as that good building is necessary to good expression, comes before it, and is to be primarily looked for: and the more, because the manner of building is capable of being determinately estimated and classed; but the expressional character not so: we can at once determine the true value of technical qualities, we can only approximate to the value of expressional qualities: and besides this, the looking for the technical qualities first will enable us to cast a large quantity of rubbish aside at once, and so to narrow the difficult field of inquiry into expression: we shall get rid of Chinese pagodas and Indian temples, and Renaissance Palladianisms, and Alhambra stucco and filigree, in one great rubbish heap; and shall not need to trouble ourselves about their expression, or anything else concerning them. Then taking the buildings which have been rightly put together, and which show common sense in their structure, we may look for their farther and higher excellences; but on those which are absurd in their first steps we need waste no time.

16. STRENGTH OF SHAFTS

I could have wished, before writing this chapter, to have given more study to the difficult subject of the strength of shafts of different materials and structure; but I cannot enter into every inquiry which general criticism might suggest, and this I believe to be one which would have occupied the reader with less profit than many others: all that is necessary for him to note is, that the great increase of strength gained by a tubular form in iron shafts, of given solid contents, is no contradiction to the general principle stated in the text, that the strength of materials is most available when they are most concentrated. The strength of the tube is owing to certain properties of the arch formed by its sides, not to the dispersion of its materials: and the principle is altogether inapplicable to stone shafts. No one would think of building a pillar of a succession of sandstone rings; however strong it might be, it would be still stronger filled up, and the substitution of such a pillar for a solid one of the same contents would lose too much space; for a stone pillar, even when solid, must be quite as thick as is either graceful or convenient, and in modern churches is often too thick as it is, hindering sight of the preacher, and checking the sound of his voice.

17. ANSWER TO MR. GARBETT

Some three months ago, and long after the writing of this passage, I met accidentally with Mr. Garbett's elementary Treatise on Design. (Weale, 1850.) If I had cared about the reputation of originality, I should have been annoyed—and was so, at first, on finding Mr. Garbett's illustrations of the subject exactly the same as mine, even to the choice of the elephant's foot for the parallel of the Doric pillar: I even thought of omitting, or rewriting, great part of the chapter, but determined at last to let it stand. I am striving to speak plain truths on many simple and trite subjects, and I hope, therefore, that much of what I say has been said before, and am quite willing to give up all claim to originality in any reasoning or assertion whatsoever, if any one cares to dispute it. I desire the reader to accept what I say, not as mine, but as the truth, which may be all the world's, if they look for it. If I remember rightly, Mr. Frank Howard promised at some discussion respecting the "Seven Lamps," reported in the "Builder," to pluck all my borrowed feathers off me; but I did not see the end of the discussion, and do not know to this day how many feathers I have left: at all events the elephant's foot must belong to Mr. Garbett, though, strictly speaking, neither he nor I can be quite justified in using it, for an elephant in reality stands on tiptoe; and this is by no means the expression of a Doric shaft. As, however, I have been obliged to speak of this treatise of Mr. Garbett's, and desire also to recommend it as of much interest and utility in its statements of fact, it is impossible for me to pass altogether without notice, as if unanswerable, several passages in which the writer has objected to views stated in the "Seven Lamps." I should at any rate have noticed the passage quoted above, (Chap. 30th,) which runs counter to the spirit of all I have ever written, though without referring to me; but the references to the "Seven Lamps" I should not have answered, unless I had desired, generally, to recommend the book, and partly also, because they may serve as examples of the kind of animadversion which the "Seven Lamps" had to sustain from architects, very generally; which examples being once answered, there will be little occasion for my referring in future to other criticisms of the kind.

The first reference to the "Seven Lamps" is in the second page, where Mr. Garbett asks a question, "Why are not convenience and stability enough to constitute a fine building?"—which I should have answered shortly by asking another, "Why we have been made men, and not bees nor termites:" but Mr. Garbett has given a very pretty, though partial, answer to it himself, in his 4th to 9th pages,—an answer which I heartily beg the reader to consider. But, in page 12, it is made a grave charge against me, that I use the words beauty and ornament interchangeably. I do so, and ever shall; and so, I believe, one day, will Mr. Garbett himself; but not while he continues to head his pages thus:—"Beauty not dependent on ornament, or superfluous features." What right has he to assume that ornament, rightly so called, ever was, or can be, superfluous? I have said before, and repeatedly in other places, that the most beautiful things are the most useless; I never said superfluous. I said useless in the well-understood and usual sense, as meaning, inapplicable to the service of the body. Thus I called peacocks and lilies useless; meaning, that roast peacock was unwholesome (taking Juvenal's word for it), and that dried lilies made bad hay: but I do not think peacocks superfluous birds, nor that the world could get on well without its lilies. Or, to look closer, I suppose the peacock's blue eyes to be very useless to him; not dangerous indeed, as to their first master, but of small service, yet I do not think there is a superfluous eye in all his tail; and for lilies, though the great King of Israel was not "arrayed" like one of them, can Mr. Garbett tell us which are their superfluous leaves? Is there no Diogenes among lilies? none to be found content to drink dew, but out of silver? The fact is, I never met with the architect yet who did not think ornament meant a thing to be bought in a shop and pinned on, or left off, at architectural toilets, as the fancy seized them, thinking little more than many women do of the other kind of ornament—the only true kind,—St. Peter's kind,—"Not that outward adorning, but the inner—of the heart." I do not mean that architects cannot conceive this better ornament, but they do not understand that it is the only ornament; that all architectural ornament is this, and nothing but this; that a noble building never has any extraneous or superfluous ornament; that all its parts are necessary to its loveliness, and that no single atom of them could be removed without harm to its life. You do not build a temple and then dress it.[101] You create it in its loveliness, and leave it, as her Maker left Eve. Not unadorned, I believe, but so well adorned as to need no feather crowns. And I use the words ornament and beauty interchangeably, in order that architects may understand this: I assume that their building is to be a perfect creature capable of nothing less than it has, and needing nothing more. It may, indeed, receive additional decoration afterwards, exactly as a woman may gracefully put a bracelet on her arm, or set a flower in her hair: but that additional decoration is not the architecture. It is of curtains, pictures, statues, things that may be taken away from the building, and not hurt it. What has the architect to do with these? He has only to do with what is part of the building itself, that is to say, its own inherent beauty. And because Mr. Garbett does not understand or acknowledge this, he is led on from error to error; for we next find him endeavoring to define beauty as distinct from ornament, and saying that "Positive beauty may be produced by a studious collation of whatever will display design, order, and congruity." (p. 14.) Is that so? There is a highly studious collation of whatever will display design, order, and congruity, in a skull, is there not?—yet small beauty. The nose is a decorative feature,—yet slightly necessary to beauty, it seems to me; now, at least, for I once thought I must be wrong in considering a skull disagreeable. I gave it fair trial: put one on my bed-room chimney-piece, and looked at it by sunrise every morning, and by moonlight every night, and by all the best lights I could think of, for a month, in vain. I found it as ugly at last as I did at first. So, also, the hair is a decoration, and its natural curl is of little use; but can Mr. Garbett conceive a bald beauty; or does he prefer a wig, because that is a "studious collation" of whatever will produce design, order, and congruity? So the flush of the cheek is a decoration,—God's painting of the temple of his spirit,—and the redness of the lip; and yet poor Viola thought it beauty truly blent; and I hold with her.

I have answered enough to this count.

The second point questioned is my assertion, "Ornament cannot be overcharged if it is good, and is always overcharged when it is bad." To which Mr. Garbett objects in these terms: "I must contend, on the contrary, that the very best ornament may be overcharged by being misplaced."

A short sentence with two mistakes in it.

First. Mr. Garbett cannot get rid of his unfortunate notion that ornament is a thing to be manufactured separately, and fastened on. He supposes that an ornament may be called good in itself, in the stonemason's yard or in the ironmonger's shop: Once for all, let him put this idea out of his head. We may say of a thing, considered separately, that it is a pretty thing; but before we can say it is a good ornament, we must know what it is to adorn, and how. As, for instance, a ring of gold is a pretty thing; it is a good ornament on a woman's finger; not a good ornament hung through her under lip. A hollyhock, seven feet high, would be a good ornament for a cottage-garden; not a good ornament for a lady's head-dress. Might not Mr. Garbett have seen this without my showing? and that, therefore, when I said "good" ornament, I said "well-placed" ornament, in one word, and that, also, when Mr. Garbett says "it may be overcharged by being misplaced," he merely says it may be overcharged by being bad.

Secondly. But, granted that ornament were independent of its position, and might be pronounced good in a separate form, as books are good, or men are good.—Suppose I had written to a student in Oxford, "You cannot have too many books, if they be good books;" and he had answered me, "Yes, for if I have many, I have no place to put them in but the coal-cellar." Would that in anywise affect the general principle that he could not have too many books?

Or suppose he had written, "I must not have too many, they confuse my head." I should have written back to him: "Don't buy books to put in the coal-hole, nor read them if they confuse your head; you cannot have too many, if they be good: but if you are too lazy to take care of them, or too dull to profit by them, you are better without them."

Exactly in the same tone, I repeat to Mr. Garbett, "You cannot have too much ornament, if it be good: but if you are too indolent to arrange it, or too dull to take advantage of it, assuredly you are better without it."

The other points bearing on this question have already been stated in the close of the 21st chapter.

The third reference I have to answer, is to my repeated assertion, that the evidence of manual labor is one of the chief sources of value in ornament, ("Seven Lamps," p. 49, "Modern Painters," § 1, Chap. III.,) to which objection is made in these terms: "We must here warn the reader against a remarkable error of Ruskin. The value of ornaments in architecture depends not in the slightest degree on the manual labor they contain. If it did, the finest ornaments ever executed would be the stone chains that hang before certain Indian rock-temples." Is that so? Hear a parallel argument. "The value of the Cornish mines depends not in the slightest degree on the quantity of copper they contain. If it did, the most valuable things ever produced would be copper saucepans." It is hardly worth my while to answer this; but, lest any of my readers should be confused by the objection, and as I hold the fact to be of great importance, I may re-state it for them with some explanation.

Observe, then, the appearance of labor, that is to say, the evidence of the past industry of man, is always, in the abstract, intensely delightful: man being meant to labor, it is delightful to see that he has labored, and to read the record of his active and worthy existence.

The evidence of labor becomes painful only when it is a sign of Evil greater, as Evil, than the labor is great, as Good. As, for instance, if a man has labored for an hour at what might have been done by another man in a moment, this evidence of his labor is also evidence of his weakness; and this weakness is greater in rank of evil, than his industry is great in rank of good.

Again, if a man have labored at what was not worth accomplishing, the signs of his labor are the signs of his folly, and his folly dishonors his industry; we had rather he had been a wise man in rest than a fool in labor.

Again, if a man have labored without accomplishing anything, the signs of his labor are the signs of his disappointment; and we have more sorrow in sympathy with his failure, than pleasure in sympathy with his work.

Now, therefore, in ornament, whenever labor replaces what was better than labor, that is to say, skill and thought; wherever it substitutes itself for these, or negatives these by its existence, then it is positive evil. Copper is an evil when it alloys gold, or poisons food: not an evil, as copper; good in the form of pence, seriously objectionable when it occupies the room of guineas. Let Danaë cast it out of her lap, when the gold comes from heaven; but let the poor man gather it up carefully from the earth.

Farther, the evidence of labor is not only a good when added to other good, but the utter absence of it destroys good in human work. It is only good for God to create without toil; that which man can create without toil is worthless: machine ornaments are no ornaments at all. Consider this carefully, reader: I could illustrate it for you endlessly; but you feel it yourself every hour of your existence. And if you do not know that you feel it, take up, for a little time, the trade which of all manual trades has been most honored: be for once a carpenter. Make for yourself a table or a chair, and see if you ever thought any table or chair so delightful, and what strange beauty there will be in their crooked limbs.

I have not noticed any other animadversions on the "Seven Lamps" in Mr. Garbett's volume; but if there be more, I must now leave it to his own consideration, whether he may not, as in the above instances, have made them incautiously: I may, perhaps, also be permitted to request other architects, who may happen to glance at the preceding pages, not immediately to condemn what may appear to them false in general principle. I must often be found deficient in technical knowledge; I may often err in my statements respecting matters of practice or of special law. But I do not write thoughtlessly respecting principles; and my statements of these will generally be found worth reconnoitring before attacking. Architects, no doubt, fancy they have strong grounds for supposing me wrong when they seek to invalidate my assertions. Let me assure them, at least, that I mean to be their friend, although they may not immediately recognise me as such. If I could obtain the public ear, and the principles I have advocated were carried into general practice, porphyry and serpentine would be given to them instead of limestone and brick; instead of tavern and shop-fronts they would have to build goodly churches and noble dwelling-houses; and for every stunted Grecism and stucco Romanism, into which they are now forced to shape their palsied thoughts, and to whose crumbling plagiarisms they must trust their doubtful fame, they would be asked to raise whole streets of bold, and rich, and living architecture, with the certainty in their hearts of doing what was honorable to themselves, and good for all men.

Before I altogether leave the question of the influence of labor on architectural effect, the reader may expect from me a word or two respecting the subject which this year must be interesting to all—the applicability, namely, of glass and iron to architecture in general, as in some sort exemplified by the Crystal Palace.

It is thought by many that we shall forthwith have great part of our architecture in glass and iron, and that new forms of beauty will result from the studied employment of these materials.

It may be told in a few words how far this is possible; how far eternally impossible.

There are two means of delight in all productions of art—color and form.

The most vivid conditions of color attainable by human art are those of works in glass and enamel, but not the most perfect. The best and noblest coloring possible to art is that attained by the touch of the human hand on an opaque surface, upon which it can command any tint required, without subjection to alteration by fire or other mechanical means. No color is so noble as the color of a good painting on canvas or gesso.

This kind of color being, however, impossible, for the most part, in architecture, the next best is the scientific disposition of the natural colors of stones, which are far nobler than any abstract hues producible by human art.

The delight which we receive from glass painting is one altogether inferior, and in which we should degrade ourselves by over indulgence. Nevertheless, it is possible that we may raise some palaces like Aladdin's with colored glass for jewels, which shall be new in the annals of human splendor, and good in their place; but not if they superseded nobler edifices.

Now, color is producible either on opaque or in transparent bodies: but form is only expressible, in its perfection, on opaque bodies, without lustre.

This law is imperative, universal, irrevocable. No perfect or refined form can be expressed except in opaque and lustreless matter. You cannot see the form of a jewel, nor, in any perfection, even of a cameo or bronze. You cannot perfectly see the form of a humming-bird, on account of its burnishing; but you can see the form of a swan perfectly. No noble work in form can ever, therefore, be produced in transparent or lustrous glass or enamel. All noble architecture depends for its majesty on its form: therefore you can never have any noble architecture in transparent or lustrous glass or enamel. Iron is, however, opaque; and both it and opaque enamel may, perhaps, be rendered quite lustreless; and, therefore, fit to receive noble form.

Let this be thoroughly done, and both the iron and enamel made fine in paste or grain, and you may have an architecture as noble as cast or struck architecture even can be: as noble, therefore, as coins can be, or common cast bronzes, and such other multiplicable things;[102]—eternally separated from all good and great things by a gulph which not all the tubular bridges nor engineering of ten thousand nineteenth centuries cast into one great bronze-foreheaded century, will ever overpass one inch of. All art which is worth its room in this world, all art which is not a piece of blundering refuse, occupying the foot or two of earth which, if unencumbered by it, would have grown corn or violets, or some better thing, is art which proceeds from an individual mind, working through instruments which assist, but do not supersede, the muscular action of the human hand, upon the materials which most tenderly receive, and most securely retain, the impressions of such human labor.

And the value of every work of art is exactly in the ratio of the quantity of humanity which has been put into it, and legibly expressed upon it for ever:—

First, of thought and moral purpose;

Secondly, of technical skill;

Thirdly, of bodily industry.

The quantity of bodily industry which that Crystal Palace expresses is very great. So far it is good.

The quantity of thought it expresses is, I suppose, a single and very admirable thought of Mr. Paxton's, probably not a bit brighter than thousands of thoughts which pass through his active and intelligent brain every hour,—that it might be possible to build a greenhouse larger than ever greenhouse was built before. This thought, and some very ordinary algebra, are as much as all that glass can represent of human intellect. "But one poor half-pennyworth of bread to all this intolerable deal of sack." Alas!

"The earth hath bubbles as the water hath:
And this is of them."

18. EARLY ENGLISH CAPITALS

The depth of the cutting in some of the early English capitals is, indeed, part of a general system of attempts at exaggerated force of effect, like the "black touches" of second-rate draughtsmen, which I have noticed as characteristic of nearly all northern work, associated with the love of the grotesque: but the main section of the capital is indeed a dripstone rolled round, as above described; and dripstone sections are continually found in northern work, where not only they cannot increase force of effect, but are entirely invisible except on close examination; as, for instance, under the uppermost range of stones of the foundation of Whitehall, or under the slope of the restored base of All Souls College, Oxford, under the level of the eye. I much doubt if any of the Fellows be aware of its existence.

Many readers will be surprised and displeased by the disparagement of the early English capital. That capital has, indeed, one character of considerable value; namely, the boldness with which it stops the mouldings which fall upon it, and severs them from the shaft, contrasting itself with the multiplicity of their vertical lines. Sparingly used, or seldom seen, it is thus, in its place, not unpleasing; and we English love it from association, it being always found in connection with our purest and loveliest Gothic arches, and never in multitudes large enough to satiate the eye with its form. The reader who sits in the Temple church every Sunday, and sees no architecture during the week but that of Chancery Lane, may most justifiably quarrel with me for what I have said of it. But if every house in Fleet Street or Chancery Lane were Gothic, and all had early English capitals, I would answer for his making peace with me in a fortnight.

19. TOMBS NEAR ST. ANASTASIA

Whose they are, is of little consequence to the reader or to me, and I have taken no pains to discover; their value being not in any evidence they bear respecting dates, but in their intrinsic merit as examples of composition. Two of them are within the gate, one on the top of it, and this latter is on the whole the best, though all are beautiful; uniting the intense northern energy in their figure sculpture with the most serene classical restraint in their outlines, and unaffected, but masculine simplicity of construction.

I have not put letters to the diagram of the lateral arch at page 154, in order not to interfere with the clearness of the curves, but I shall always express the same points by the same letters, whenever I have to give measures of arches of this simple kind, so that the reader need never have the diagrams lettered at all. The base or span of the centre arch will always be a b; its vertex will always be V; the points of the cusps will be c c; p p will be the bases of perpendiculars let fall from V and c on a b; and d the base of a perpendicular from the point of the cusp to the arch line. Then a b will always be a span of the arch, V p its perpendicular height, V a the chord of its side arcs, d c the depth of its cusps, c c the horizontal interval between the cusps, a c the length of the chord of the lower arc of the cusp, V c the length of the chord of the upper arc of the cusp, (whether continuous or not,) and c p the length of a perpendicular from the point of the cusp on a b.

Of course we do not want all these measures for a single arch, but it often happens that some of them are attainable more easily than others; some are often unattainable altogether, and it is necessary therefore to have expressions for whichever we may be able to determine.

V p or V a, a b, and d c are always essential; then either a c and V c or c c and c p: when I have my choice, I always take a b, V p, d c, c c, and c p, but c p is not to be generally obtained so accurately as the cusp arcs.

The measures of the present arch are:

	Ft.	In.
a b,	3	8
V p,	4	0
V c,	2	4-1/2
a c,	2	0-1/4
d c,	0	3-1/2

20. SHAFTS OF DUCAL PALACE

The shortness of the thicker ones at the angles is induced by the greater depth of the enlarged capitals: thus the 36th shaft is 10 ft. 4-1/3 in. in circumference at its base, and 10 ft. 0-1/2[103] in circumference under the fillet of its capital; but it is only 6 ft. 1-3/4 high, while the minor intermediate shafts, of which the thickest is 7 ft. 8 round at the base, and 7 ft. 4 under capital, are yet on the average 7 ft. 7 high. The angle shaft towards the sea (the 18th) is nearly of the proportions of the 36th, and there are three others, the 15th, 24th, and 26th, which are thicker than the rest, though not so thick as the angle ones. The 24th and 26th have both party walls to bear, and I imagine the 15th must in old time have carried another, reaching across what is now the Sala del Gran Consiglio.

They measure respectively round at the base,

The 15th,	8 ft. 2
The 24th	9 ft. 6-1/2
The 26th	8 ft. 0-1/2

The other pillars towards the sea, and those to the 27th inclusive of the Piazzetta, are all seven feet round at the base, and then there is a most curious and delicate crescendo of circumference to the 36th, thus:

The 28th,	7 ft. 3
The 33rd,	7 ft. 6
The 29th	7 ft. 4
The 34th	7 ft. 8
The 30th	7 ft. 6
The 35th	7 ft. 8
The 31st	7 ft. 7
The 36th	10 ft. 4-1/3
The 32nd	7 ft. 5

The shafts of the upper arcade, which are above these thicker columns, are also thicker than their companions, measuring on the average, 4 ft. 8-1/2 in circumference, while those of the sea façade, except the 29th, average 4 ft. 7-1/2 in circumference. The 29th, which is of course above the 15th of the lower story, is 5 ft. 5 in circumference, which little piece of evidence will be of no small value to us by-and-by. The 35th carries the angle of the palace, and is 6 ft. 0 round. The 47th, which comes above the 24th and carries the party wall of the Sala del Gran Consiglio, is strengthened by a pilaster; and the 51st, which comes over the 26th, is 5 ft. 4-1/2 round, or nearly the same as the 29th; it carries the party wall of the Sala del Scrutinio; a small room containing part of St. Mark's library, coming between the two saloons; a room which, in remembrances of the help I have received in all my inquiries from the kindness and intelligence of its usual occupant, I shall never easily distinguish otherwise than as "Mr. Lorenzi's."[104]

I may as well connect with these notes respecting the arcades of the Ducal Palace, those which refer to Plate XIV., which represents one of its spandrils. Every spandril of the lower arcade was intended to have been occupied by an ornament resembling the one given in that plate. The mass of the building being of Istrian stone, a depth of about two inches is left within the mouldings of the arches, rough hewn, to receive the slabs of fine marble composing the patterns. I cannot say whether the design was ever completed, or the marbles have been since removed, but there are now only two spandrils retaining their fillings, and vestiges of them in a third. The two complete spandrils are on the sea façade, above the 3rd and 10th capitals (vide method of numbering, Chap. I., page 30); that is to say, connecting the 2nd arch with the 3rd, and the 9th with the 10th. The latter is the one given in Plate XIV. The white portions of it are all white marble, the dental band surrounding the circle is in coarse sugary marble, which I believe to be Greek, and never found in Venice to my recollection, except in work at least anterior to the fifteenth century. The shaded fields charged with the three white triangles are of red Verona marble; the inner disc is green serpentine, and the dark pieces of the radiating leaves are grey marble. The three triangles are equilateral. The two uppermost are 1 ,, 5 each side, and the lower 1 ,, 2.

The extreme diameter of the circle is 3 ft. 10-1/2; its field is slightly raised above the red marbles, as shown in the section at A, on the left. A a is part of the red marble field; a b the section of the dentil moulding let into it; b c the entire breadth of the rayed zone, represented on the other side of the spandril by the line C f; c d is the white marble band let in, with the dogtooth on the face of it; b c is 7-3/4 inches across; c d 3-3/4; and at B are given two joints of the dentil (mentioned above, in the chapter on dentils, as unique in Venice) of their actual size. At C is given one of the inlaid leaves; its measure being (in inches) C f 7-3/4; C h 3/4; f g 3/4; f e 4-3/4, the base of the smaller leaves being of course f e - f g = 4. The pattern which occupies the other spandril is similar, except that the field b c, instead of the intersecting arcs, has only triangles of grey marble, arranged like rays, with their bases towards the centre. There being twenty round the circle, the reader can of course draw them for himself; they being isosceles, touching the dentil with their points, and being in contact at their bases: it has lost its central boss. The marbles are, in both, covered with a rusty coating, through which it is excessively difficult to distinguish the colors (another proof of the age of the ornament). But the white marbles are certainly, in places (except only the sugary dentil), veined with purple, and the grey seem warmed with green.

A trace of another of these ornaments may be seen over the 21st capital; but I doubt if the marbles have ever been inserted in the other spandrils, and their want of ornament occasions the slight meagreness in the effect of the lower story, which is almost the only fault of the building.

This decoration by discs, or shield-like ornaments, is a marked characteristic of Venetian architecture in its earlier ages, and is carried into later times by the Byzantine Renaissance, already distinguished from the more corrupt forms of Renaissance, in Appendix 6. Of the disc decoration, so borrowed, we have already an example in Plate I. In Plate VII. we have an earlier condition of it, one of the discs being there sculptured, the others surrounded by sculptured bands: here we have, on the Ducal Palace, the most characteristic of all, because likest to the shield, which was probably the origin of the same ornament among the Arabs, and assuredly among the Greeks. In Mr. Donaldson's restoration of the gate of the treasury of Atreus, this ornament is conjecturally employed, and it occurs constantly on the Arabian buildings of Cairo.

21. ANCIENT REPRESENTATIONS OF WATER

I have long been desirous of devoting some time to an enquiry into the effect of natural scenery upon the pagan, and especially the Greek, mind, and knowing that my friend, Mr. C. Newton, had devoted much thought to the elucidation of the figurative and symbolic language of ancient art, I asked him to draw up for me a few notes of the facts which he considered most interesting, as illustrative of its methods of representing nature. I suggested to him, for an initiative subject, the representation of water; because this is one of the natural objects whose portraiture may most easily be made a test of treatment, for it is one of universal interest, and of more closely similar aspect in all parts of the world than any other. Waves, currents, and eddies are much liker each other, everywhere, than either land or vegetation. Rivers and lakes, indeed, differ widely from the sea, and the clear Pacific from the angry Northern ocean; but the Nile is liker the Danube than a knot of Nubian palms is to a glade of the Black Forest; and the Mediterranean is liker the Atlantic than the Campo Felice is like Solway moss.

Mr. Newton has accordingly most kindly furnished me with the following data. One or two of the types which he describes have been already noticed in the main text; but it is well that the reader should again contemplate them in the position which they here occupy in a general system. I recommend his special attention to Mr. Newton's definitions of the terms "figurative" and "symbolic," as applied to art, in the beginning of the paper.

In ancient art, that is to say, in the art of the Egyptian, Assyrian, Greek, and Roman races, water is, for the most part, represented conventionally rather than naturally.

By natural representation is here meant as just and perfect an imitation of nature as the technical means of art will allow: on the other hand, representation is said to be conventional, either when a confessedly inadequate imitation is accepted in default of a better, or when imitation is not attempted at all, and it is agreed that other modes of representation, those by figures or by symbols, shall be its substitute and equivalent.

In figurative representation there is always impersonation; the sensible form, borrowed by the artist from organic life, is conceived to be actuated by a will, and invested with such mental attributes as constitute personality.

The sensible symbol, whether borrowed from organic or from inorganic nature, is not a personification at all, but the conventional sign or equivalent of some object or notion, to which it may perhaps bear no visible resemblance, but with which the intellect or the imagination has in some way associated it.

For instance, a city may be figuratively represented as a woman crowned with towers; here the artist has selected for the expression of his idea a human form animated with a will and motives of action analogous to those of humanity generally. Or, again, as in Greek art, a bull may be a figurative representation of a river, and, in the conception of the artist, this animal form may contain, and be ennobled by, a human mind.

This is still impersonation; the form only in which personality is embodied is changed.

Again, a dolphin may be used as a symbol of the sea; a man ploughing with two oxen is a well-known symbol of a Roman colony. In neither of these instances is there impersonation. The dolphin is not invested, like the figure of Neptune, with any of the attributes of the human mind; it has animal instincts, but no will; it represents to us its native element, only as a part may be taken for a whole.

Again, the man ploughing does not, like the turreted female figure, personify, but rather typifies the town, standing as the visible representation of a real event, its first foundation. To our mental perceptions, as to our bodily senses, this figure seems no more than man; there is no blending of his personal nature with the impersonal nature of the colony, no transfer of attributes from the one to the other.

Though the conventionally imitative, the figurative, and the symbolic, are three distinct kinds of representation, they are constantly combined in one composition, as we shall see in the following examples, cited from the art of successive races in chronological order.

In Egyptian art the general representation of water is the conventionally imitative. In the British Museum are two frescoes from tombs at Thebes, Nos. 177 and 170: the subject of the first of these is an oblong pond, ground-plan and elevation being strangely confused in the design. In this pond water is represented by parallel zigzag lines, in which fish are swimming about. On the surface are birds and lotos flowers; the herbage at the edge of the pond is represented by a border of symmetrical fan-shaped flowers; the field beyond by rows of trees, arranged round the sides of the pond at right angles to each other, and in defiance of all laws of perspective.

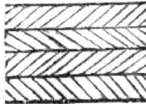

Fig. LXXI.

In the fresco, No. 170, we have the representation of a river with papyrus on its bank. Here the water is rendered by zigzag lines arranged vertically and in parallel lines, so as to resemble herring-bone masonry, thus. There are fish in this fresco as in the preceding, and in both each fish is drawn very distinctly, not as it would appear to the eye viewed through water. The mode of representing this element in Egyptian painting is further abbreviated in their hieroglyphic writing, where the sign of water is a zigzag line; this line is, so to speak, a picture of water written in short hand. In the Egyptian Pantheon there was but one aquatic deity, the god of the Nile; his type is, therefore, the only figurative representation of water in Egyptian art. (Birch, "Gallery of British Museum Antiquities," Pl. 13.) In Assyrian sculpture we have very curious conventionally imitative representations of water. On several of the friezes from Nimroud and Khorsabad, men are seen crossing a river in boats, or in skins, accompanied by horses swimming (see Layard, ii. p. 381). In these scenes water is represented by masses of wavy lines somewhat resembling tresses of hair, and terminating in curls or volutes; these wavy lines express the general character of a deep and rapid current, like that of the Tigris. Fish are but sparingly introduced, the idea of surface being sufficiently expressed by the floating figures and boats. In the representation of these there is the same want of perspective as in the Egyptian fresco which we have just cited.

In the Assyrian Pantheon one aquatic deity has been discovered, the god Dagon, whose human form terminates in a fish's tail. Of the character and attributes of this deity we know but little.

The more abbreviated mode of representing water, the zigzag line, occurs on the large silver coins with the type of a city or a war galley (see Layard, ii. p. 386). These coins were probably struck in Assyria, not long after the conquest of it by the Persians.

In Greek art the modes of representing water are far more varied. Two conventional imitations, the wave moulding and the Mæander, are well known. Both are probably of the most remote antiquity; both have been largely employed as an architectural ornament, and subordinately as a decoration of vases, costume, furniture and implements. In the wave moulding we have a conventional representation of the small crisping waves which break upon the shore of the Mediterranean, the sea of the Greeks.

Their regular succession, and equality of force and volume, are generalised in this moulding, while the minuter varieties which distinguish one wave from another are merged in the general type. The character of ocean waves is to be "for ever changing, yet the same for ever;" it is this eternity of recurrence which the early artist has expressed in this hieroglyphic.

With this profile representation of water may be compared the sculptured waves out of which the head and arms of Hyperion are rising in the pediment of the Parthenon (Elgin Room, No. (65) 91, Museum Marbles, vi. pl. 1). Phidias has represented these waves like a mass of overlapping tiles, thus generalising their rippling movement. In the Mæander pattern the graceful curves of nature are represented by angles, as in the Egyptian hieroglyphic of water: so again the earliest representation of the labyrinth on the coins of the Cnossus is rectangular; on later coins we find the curvilinear form introduced.

In the language of Greek mythography, the wave pattern and the Mæander are sometimes used singly for the idea of water, but more frequently combined with figurative representation. The number of aquatic deities in the Greek Pantheon led to the invention of a great variety of beautiful types. Some of these are very well known. Everybody is familiar with the general form of Poseidon (Neptune), the Nereids, the Nymphs and River Gods; but the modes in which these types were combined with conventional imitation and with accessory symbols deserve careful study, if we would appreciate the surpassing richness and beauty of the language of art formed out of these elements.

This class of representations may be divided into two principal groups, those relating to the sea, and those relating to fresh water.

The power of the ocean and the great features of marine scenery are embodied in such types as Poseidon, Nereus and the Nereids, that is to say, in human forms moving through the liquid element in chariots, or on the back of dolphins, or who combine the human form with that of the fish-like Tritons. The sea-monsters who draw these chariots are called Hippocamps, being composed of the tail of a fish and the fore-part of a horse, the legs terminating in web-feet: this union seems to express speed and power under perfect control, such as would characterise the movements of sea deities. A few examples have been here selected to show how these types were combined with symbols and conventional imitation.

In the British Museum is a vase, No. 1257, engraved (Lenormant et De Witte, Mon. Céram., i. pl. 27), of which the subject is, Europa crossing the sea on the back of the bull. In this design the sea is represented by a variety of expedients. First, the swimming action of the bull suggests the idea of the liquid medium through which he moves. Behind him stands Nereus, his staff held perpendicularly in his hand; the top of his staff comes nearly to the level of the bull's back, and is probably meant as the measure of the whole depth of the sea. Towards the surface line thus indicated a dolphin is rising; in the middle depth is another dolphin; below a shrimp and a cuttle-fish, and the bottom is indicated by a jagged line of rocks, on which are two echini.

On a mosaic found at Oudnah in Algeria (Revue Archéol., iii. pl. 50), we have a representation of the sea, remarkable for the fulness of details with which it is made out.

This, though of the Roman period, is so thoroughly Greek in feeling, that it may be cited as an example of the class of mythography now under consideration. The mosaic lines the floor and sides of a bath, and, as was commonly the case in the baths of the ancients, serves as a figurative representation of the water it contained.

On the sides are hippocamps, figures riding on dolphins, and islands on which fishermen stand; on the floor are fish, crabs, and shrimps.

These, as in the vase with Europa, indicate the bottom of the sea: the same symbols of the submarine world appear on many other ancient designs. Thus in vase pictures, when Poseidon upheaves the island of Cos to overwhelm the Giant Polydotes, the island is represented as an immense mass of rock; the parts which have been under water are indicated by a dolphin, a shrimp, and a sepia, the parts above the water by a goat and a serpent (Lenormant et De Witte, i., tav. 5).

Sometimes these symbols occur singly in Greek art, as the types, for instance, of coins. In such cases they cannot be interpreted without being viewed in relation to the whole context of mythography to which they belong. If we find, for example, on one coin of Tarentum a shell, on another a dolphin, on a third a figure of Tarus, the mythic founder of the town, riding on a dolphin in the midst of the waves, and this latter group expresses the idea of the town itself and its position on the coast, then we know the two former types to be but portions of the greater design, having been detached from it, as we may detach words from sentences.

The study of the fuller and clearer examples, such as we have cited above, enables us to explain many more compendious forms of expression. We have, for instance, on coins several representations of ancient harbors.

Of these, the earliest occurs on the coins of Zancle, the modern Messina in Sicily. The ancients likened the form of this harbor to a sickle, and on the coins of the town we find a curved object, within the area of which is a dolphin. On this curve are four square elevations placed at equal distances. It has been conjectured that these projections are either towers or the large stones to which galleys were moored still to be seen in ancient harbors (see Burgon, Numismatic Chronicle, iii. p. 40). With this archaic representation of a harbor may be compared some examples of the Roman period. On a coin of Sept. Severus struck at Corinth (Millingen, Sylloge of Uned. Coins, 1837, p. 57, Pl. II., No. 30) we have a female figure standing on a rock between two recumbent male figures holding rudders. From an arch at the foot of the rock a stream is flowing: this is a representation of the rock of the Acropolis of Corinth: the female figure is a statue of Aphrodite, whose temple surmounted the rock. The stream is the fountain Pirene. The two recumbent figures are impersonations of the two harbors, Lechreum and Cenchreia, between which Corinth was situated. Philostratus (Icon. ii., c. 16) describes a similar picture of the Isthmus between the two harbors, one of which was in the form of a youth, the other of a nymph.

On another coin of Corinth we have one of the harbors in a semicircular form, the whole arc being marked with small equal divisions, to denote the archways under which the ancient galleys were drawn, subductæ; at the either horn or extremity of the harbor is a temple; in the centre of the mouth, a statue of Neptune. (Millingen, Médailles Inéd., Pl. II., No. 19. Compare also Millingen, Ancient Coins of Cities and Kings, 1831, pp. 50-61, Pl. IV., No. 15; Mionnet, Suppl. vii. p. 79, No. 246; and the harbor of Ostium, on the large brass coins of Nero, in which there is a representation of the Roman fleet and a reclining figure of Neptune.)

In vase pictures we have occasionally an attempt to represent water naturally. On a vase in the British Museum (No. 785), of which the subject is Ulysses and the Sirens, the Sea is rendered by wavy lines drawn in black on a red ground, and something like the effect of light playing on the surface of the water is given. On each side of the ship are shapeless masses of rock on which the Sirens stand.

One of the most beautiful of the figurative representations of the sea is the well-known type of Scylla. She has a beautiful body, terminating in two barking dogs and two serpent tails. Sometimes drowning men, the rari nantes in gurgite vasto, appear caught up in the coils of these tails. Below are dolphins. Scylla generally brandishes a rudder to show the manner in which she twists the course of ships. For varieties of her type see Monum. dell'Inst. Archeol. Rom., iii. Tavv. 52-3.

The representations of fresh water may be arranged under the following heads—rivers, lakes, fountains.

There are several figurative modes of representing rivers very frequently employed in ancient mythography.

In the type which occurs earliest we have the human form combined with that of the bull in several ways. On an archaic coin of Metapontum in Lucania, (see frontispiece to Millingen, Ancient Coins of Greek Cities and Kings,) the river Achelous is represented with the figure of a man with a shaggy beard and bull's horns and ears. On a vase of the best period of Greek art (Brit. Mus. No. 789; Birch, Trans. Roy. Soc. of Lit., New Series, Lond. 1843, i. p. 100) the same river is represented with a satyr's head and long bull's horns on the forehead; his form, human to the waist, terminates in a fish's tail; his hair falls down his back; his beard is long and shaggy. In this type we see a combination of the three forms separately enumerated by Sophocles, in the commencement of the Trachiniæ.

[Greek: Achelôon legô,
os m' en trisin morphaisin exêtei patros,
phoitôn enargês auros allot' aiolos,
drakôn heliktos, allot' andreiô kytei
bouprôros, ek de daskiou geneiados
krounoi dierrhainonto krênaiou potou].

In a third variety of this type the human-headed body is united at the waist with the shoulders of a bull's body, in which it terminates. This occurs on an early vase. (Brit. Mus., No. 452.) On the coins of Oeniadæ in Acarnia, and on those of Ambracia, all of the period after Alexander the Great, the Achelous has a bull's body, and head with a human face. In this variety of the type the human element is almost absorbed, as in the first variety cited above, the coin of Metapontum, the bull portion of the type is only indicated by the addition of the horns and ears to the human head. On the analogy between these, varieties in the type of the Achelous and those under which the metamorphoses of the marine goddess Thetis are represented, see Gerhard, Auserl. Vasenb. ii. pp. 106-113. It is probable that, in the type of Thetis, of Proteus, and also of the Achelous, the singular combinations and transformations are intended to express the changeful nature of the element water.

Numerous other examples may be cited, where rivers are represented by this combination of the bull and human form, which maybe called, for convenience, the Androtauric type. On the coins of Sicily, of the archaic and also of the finest period of art, rivers are most usually represented by a youthful male figure, with small budding horns; the hair has the lank and matted form which characterises aquatic deities in Greek mythography. The name of the river is often inscribed round the head. When the whole figure occurs on the coin, it is always represented standing, never reclining.

The type of the bull on the coins of Sybaris and Thurium, in Magna Græcia, has been considered, with great probability, a representation of this kind. On the coins of Sybaris, which are of a very early period, the head of the bull is turned round; on those of Thurium, he stoops his head, butting: the first of these actions has been thought to symbolise the winding course of the river, the second, its headlong current. On the coins of Thurium, the idea of water is further suggested by the adjunct of dolphins and other fish in the exergue of the coin. The ground on which the bull stands is indicated by herbage or pebbles. This probably represents the river bank. Two bulls' head occur on the coins of Sardis, and it has been ingeniously conjectured by Mr. Burgon that the two rivers of the place are expressed under this type.

The representation of river-gods as human figures in a reclining position, though probably not so much employed in earlier Greek art as the Androtauric type, is very much more familiar to us, from its subsequent adoption in Roman mythography. The earliest example we have of a reclining river-god is in the figure in the Elgin Room commonly called the Ilissus, but more probably the Cephissus. This occupied one angle in the western pediment of the Parthenon; the other Athenian river, the Ilissus, and the fountain Callirrhoe being represented by a male and female figure in the opposite angle; this group, now destroyed, is visible in the drawing made by Carrey in 1678.

It is probable that the necessities of pedimental composition first led the artist to place the river-god in a reclining position. The head of the Ilissus being broken off, we are not sure whether he had bull's horns, like the Sicilian figures already described. His form is youthful, in the folds of the drapery behind him there is a flow like that of waves, but the idea of water is not suggested by any other symbol. When we compare this figure with that of the Nile (Visconti, Mus. Pio Clem., i., Pl. 38), and the figure of the Tiber in the Louvre, both of which are of the Roman period, we see how in these later types the artist multiplied symbols and accessories, ingrafting them on the original simple type of the river-god, as it was conceived by Phidias in the figure of the Ilissus. The Nile is represented as a colossal bearded figure reclining. At his side is a cornucopia, full of the vegetable produce of the Egyptian soil. Round his body are sixteen naked boys, who represent the sixteen cubits, the height to which the river rose in a favorable year. The statue is placed on a basement divided into three compartments, one above another. In the uppermost of these, waves are flowing over in one great sheet from the side of the river-god. In the other two compartments are the animals and plants of the river; the bas-reliefs on this basement are, in fact, a kind of abbreviated symbolic panorama of the Nile.

The Tiber is represented in a very similar manner. On the base are, in two compartments, scenes taken from the early Roman myths; flocks, herds, and other objects on the banks of the river. (Visconti, Mus. P. Cl. i., Pl. 39; Millin, Galerie Mythol., i. p. 77, Pl. 74, Nos. 304, 308.)

In the types of the Greek coins of Camarina, we find two interesting representations of Lakes. On the obverse of one of these we have, within a circle of the wave pattern, a male head, full face, with dishevelled hair, and with a dolphin on either side; on the reverse a female figure sailing on a swan, below which a wave moulding, and above, a dolphin.

On another coin the swan type of the reverse is associated with the youthful head of a river-god, inscribed "Hipparis" on the obverse. On some smaller coins we have the swan flying over the rippling waves, which are represented by the wave moulding. When we examine the chart of Sicily, made by the Admiralty survey, we find marked down at Camarina, a lake through which the river Hipparis flows.

We can hardly doubt that the inhabitants of Camarina represented both their river and their lakes on their coins. The swan flying over the waves would represent a lake; the figure associated with it being no doubt the Aphrodite worshipped at that place: the head, in a circle of wave pattern, may express that part of the river which flows through the lake.

Fountains are usually represented by a stream of water issuing from a lion's head in the rock: see a vase (Gerhard, Auserl. Vasenb., taf. CXXXIV.), where Hercules stands, receiving a shower-bath from a hot spring at Thermæ in Sicily. On the coins of Syracuse the fountain Arethusa is represented by a female head seen to the front; the flowing lines of her dishevelled hair suggest, though they do not directly imitate, the bubbling action of the fresh-water spring; the sea in which it rises is symbolized by the dolphins round the head. This type presents a striking analogy with that of the Camarina head in the circle of wave pattern described above.

These are the principal modes of representing water in Greek mythography. In the art of the Roman period, the same kind of figurative and symbolic language is employed, but there is a constant tendency to multiply accessories and details, as we have shown in the later representations of harbors and river-gods cited above. In these crowded compositions the eye is fatigued and distracted by the quantity it has to examine; the language of art becomes more copious but less terse and emphatic, and addresses itself to minds far less intelligent than the refined critics who were the contemporaries of Phidias.

Rivers in Roman art are usually represented by reclining male figures, generally bearded, holding reeds or other plants in their hands, and leaning on urns from which water is flowing. On the coins of many Syrian cities, struck in imperial times, the city is represented by a turreted female figure seated on rocks, and resting her feet on the shoulder of a youthful male figure, who looks up in her face, stretching out his arms, and who is sunk in the ground as high as the waist. See Müller (Denkmäler d. A. Kunst, i., taf. 49, No. 220) for a group of this kind in the Vatican, and several similar designs on coins.

On the column of Trajan there occur many rude representations of the Danube, and other rivers crossed by the Romans in their military expeditions. The water is imitated by sculptured wavy lines, in which boats are placed. In one scene (Bartoli, Colonna Trajana, Tav. 4) this rude conventional imitation is combined with a figure. In a recess in the river bank is a reclining river-god, terminating at the waist. This is either meant for a statue which was really placed on the bank of the river, and which therefore marks some particular locality, or we have here figurative representation blended with conventional imitation.

On the column of Antoninus (Bartoli, Colon. Anton., Tav. 15) a storm of rain is represented by the head of Jupiter Pluvius, who has a vast outspread beard flowing in long tresses. In the Townley collection, in the British Museum, is a Roman helmet found at Ribchester in Lancashire, with a mask or vizor attached. The helmet is richly embossed with figures in a battle scene; round the brow is a row of turrets; the hair in the forehead is so treated as to give the idea of waves washing the base of the turrets. This head is perhaps a figurative representation of a town girt with fortifications and a moat, near which some great battle was fought. It is engraved (Vetusta Monum. of Soc. Ant. London, iv., Pl. 1-4).

In the Galeria at Florence is a group in alto relievo (Gori, Inscript. Ant. Flor. 1727, p. 76, Tab. 14) of three female figures, one of whom is certainly Demeter Kourotrophos, or the earth; another, Thetis, or the sea; the centre of the three seems to represent Aphrodite associated, as on the coins of Camarina, with the element of fresh water.

This figure is seated on a swan, and holds over her head an arched veil. Her hair is bound with reeds; above her veil grows a tall water plant, and below the swan other water plants, and a stork seated on a hydria, or pitcher, from which water is flowing. The swan, the stork, the water plants, and the hydria must all be regarded as symbols of fresh water, the latter emblem being introduced to show that the element is fit for the use of man.

Fountains in Roman art are generally personified as figures of nymphs reclining with urns, or standing holding before them a large shell.

One of the latest representations of water in ancient art is the mosaic of Palestrina (Barthélemy, in Bartoli, Peint. Antiques) which may be described as a kind of rude panorama of some district of Upper Egypt, a bird's-eye view, half man, half picture, in which the details are neither adjusted to a scale, nor drawn according to perspective, but crowded together, as they would be in an ancient bas-relief.

22. ARABIAN ORNAMENTATION

I do not mean what I have here said of the Inventive power of the Arab to be understood as in the least applying to the detestable ornamentation of the Alhambra.[105] The Alhambra is no more characteristic of Arab work, than Milan Cathedral is of Gothic: it is a late building, a work of the Spanish dynasty in its last decline, and its ornamentation is fit for nothing but to be transferred to patterns of carpets or bindings of books, together with their marbling, and mottling, and other mechanical recommendations. The Alhambra ornament has of late been largely used in shop-fronts, to the no small detriment of Regent Street and Oxford Street.

23. VARIETIES OF CHAMFER

Let B A C, Fig. LXXII., be the original angle of the wall. Inscribe within it a circle, p Q N p, of the size of the bead required, touching A B, A C, in p, p; join p, p, and draw B C parallel to it, touching the circle.

Then the lines B C, p p are the limits of the possible chamfers constructed with curves struck either from centre A, as the line Q q, N d, r u, g c, &c., or from any other point chosen as a centre in the direction Q A produced: and also of all chamfers in straight lines, as a b, e f. There are, of course, an infinite number of chamfers to be struck between B C and p p, from every point in Q A produced to infinity; thus we have infinity multiplied into infinity to express the number of possible chamfers of this species, which are peculiarly Italian chamfers; together with another singly infinite group of the straight chamfers, a b, e f, &c., of which the one formed by the line a b, passing through the centre of the circle, is the universal early Gothic chamfer of Venice.

Again. Either on the line A C, or on any other lines A l or A m, radiating from A, any number of centres may be taken, from which, with any radii not greater than the distance between such points and Q, an infinite number of curves may be struck, such as t u, r s, N n (all which are here struck from centres on the line A C). These lines represent the great class of the northern chamfers, of which the number is infinity raised to its fourth power, but of which the curve N n (for northern) represents the average condition; the shallower chamfers of the same group, r s, t u, &c., occurring often in Italy. The lines r u, t u, and a b may be taken approximating to the most frequent conditions of the southern chamfer.

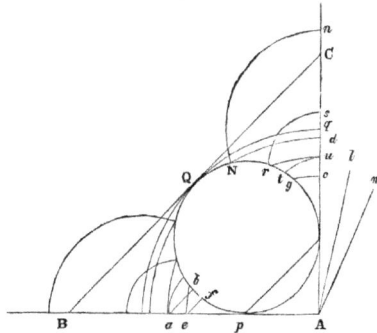

Fig. LXXII.

It is evident that the chords of any of these curves will give a relative group of rectilinear chamfers, occurring both in the North and South; but the rectilinear chamfers, I think, invariably fall within the line Q C, and are either parallel with it, or inclined to A C at an angle greater than A C Q, and often perpendicular to it; but never inclined to it at an angle less than A C Q.

24. RENAISSANCE BASES

The following extract from my note-book refers also to some features of late decoration of shafts.

"The Scuola di San Rocco is one of the most interesting examples of Renaissance work in Venice. Its fluted pillars are surrounded each by a wreath, one of vine, another of laurel, another of oak, not indeed arranged with the fantasticism of early Gothic; but, especially the laurel, reminding one strongly of the laurel sprays, powerful as well as beautiful, of Veronese and Tintoret. Their stems are curiously and richly interlaced—the last vestige of the Byzantine wreathed work—and the vine-leaves are ribbed on the surfaces, I think, nearly as finely as those of the Noah,[106] though more injured by time. The capitals are far the richest Renaissance in Venice, less corrupt and more masculine in plan, than any other, and truly suggestive of support, though of course showing the tendency to error in this respect; and finally, at the angles of the pure Attic bases, on the square plinth, are set couchant animals; one, an elephant four inches high, very curiously and cleverly cut, and all these details worked with a spirit, finish, fancy, and affection quite worthy of the middle ages. But they have all the marked fault of being utterly detached from the architecture. The wreaths round the columns look as if they would drop off the next moment, and the animals at the bases produce exactly the effect of mice who had got there by accident: one feels them ridiculously diminutive, and utterly useless."

The effect of diminutiveness is, I think, chiefly owing to there being no other groups of figures near them, to accustom the eye to the proportion, and to the needless choice of the largest animals, elephants, bears, and lions, to occupy a position so completely insignificant, and to be expressed on so contemptible a scale,—not in a bas-relief or pictorial piece of sculpture, but as independent figures. The whole building is a most curious illustration of the appointed fate of the Renaissance architects,—to caricature whatever they imitated, and misapply whatever they learned.

25. ROMANIST DECORATION OF BASES

I have spoken above (Appendix 12) of the way in which the Roman Catholic priests everywhere suffer their churches to be desecrated. But the worst instances I ever saw of sacrilege and brutality, daily permitted in the face of all men, were the uses to which the noble base of St. Mark's was put, when I was last in Venice. Portions of nearly all cathedrals may be found abandoned to neglect; but this base of St. Mark's is in no obscure position. Full fronting the western sun—crossing the whole breadth of St. Mark's Place—the termination of the most noble square in the world—the centre of the most noble city—its purple marbles were, in the winter of 1849, the customary gambling tables of the idle children of Venice; and the parts which flank the Great Entrance, that very entrance where "Barbarossa flung his mantle off," were the counters of a common bazaar for children's toys, carts, dolls, and small pewter spoons and dishes, German caricatures and books of the Opera, mixed with those of the offices of religion; the caricatures being fastened with twine round the porphyry shafts of the church. One Sunday, the 24th of February, 1850, the book-stall being somewhat more richly laid out than usual, I noted down the titles of a few of the books in the order in which they lay, and I give them below. The irony conveyed by the juxtaposition of the three in Italics appears too shrewd to be accidental; but the fact was actually so.

Along the edge of the white plinth were a row of two kinds of books,

Officium Beatæ Virg. M.; and Officium Hebdomadæ sanctæ, juxta Formam Missalis et Breviarii Romani sub Urbano VIII. correcti.

Behind these lay, side by side, the following:

Don Desiderio. Dramma Giocoso per Musica.
Breve Esposizione della Carattere di vera Religione.

On the top of this latter, keeping its leaves open,

La Figlia del Reggimento. Melodramma comica.
Carteggio di Madama la Marchesa di Pompadour, ossia raccolta di Lettere scritte della Medesima.
Istruzioni di morale Condotta per le Figlie.
Francesca di Rimini. Dramma per Musica.

Then, a little farther on, after a mass of plays:—

Orazioni a Gesu Nazareno e a Maria addolorata.
Semiramide; Melodramma tragico da rappresentarsi nel Gran Teatro il Fenice.
Modo di orare per l'Acquisto del S. Giubileo, conceduto a tutto il Mondo Cattolico da S. S. Gregorio XVI.
Le due illustre Rivali, Melodramma in Tre Atti, da rappresentarsi nel nuovo Gran Teatro il Fenice.
Il Cristiano secondo il Cuore di Gesu, per la Pratica delle sue Virtu.
Traduzione dell'Idioma Italiana.
La chiava Chinese; Commedia del Sig. Abate Pietro Chiari.
La Pelarina; Intermezzo de Tre Parti per Musica.
Il Cavaliero e la Dama; Commedia in Tre Atti in Prosa.

I leave these facts without comment. But this being the last piece of Appendix I have to add to the present volume, I would desire to close its pages with a question to my readers—a statistical question, which, I doubt not, is being accurately determined for us all elsewhere, and which, therefore, it seems to me, our time would not be wasted in determining for ourselves.

There has now been peace between England and the continental powers about thirty-five years, and during that period the English have visited the continent at the rate of many thousands a year, staying there, I suppose, on the average, each two or three months; nor these an inferior kind of English, but the kind which ought to be the best—the noblest born, the best taught, the richest in time and money, having more leisure, knowledge, and power than any other portion of the nation. These, we might suppose, beholding, as they travelled, the condition of the states in which the Papal religion is professed, and being, at the same time, the most enlightened section of a great Protestant nation, would have been animated with some desire to dissipate the Romanist errors, and to communicate to others the better knowledge which they possessed themselves. I doubt not but that He who gave peace upon the earth, and gave it by the hand of England, expected this much of her, and has watched every one of the millions of her travellers as they crossed the sea, and kept count for him of his travelling expenses, and of their distribution, in a manner of which neither the traveller nor his courier were at all informed. I doubt not, I say, but that such accounts have been literally kept for all of us, and that a day will come when they will be made clearly legible to us, and when we shall see added together, on one side of the account book, a great sum, the certain portion, whatever it may be, of this thirty-five years' spendings of the rich English, accounted for in this manner:—

To wooden spoons, nut-crackers, and jewellery, bought at Geneva, and elsewhere among the Alps, so much; to shell cameos and bits of mosaic bought at Rome, so much; to coral horns and lava brooches bought at Naples, so much; to glass beads at Venice, and gold filigree at Genoa, so much; to pictures, and statues, and ornaments, everywhere, so much; to avant-couriers and extra post-horses, for show and magnificence, so much; to great entertainments and good places for seeing sights, so much; to ball-dresses and general vanities, so much. This, I say, will be the sum on one side of the book; and on the other will be written:

To the struggling Protestant Churches of France, Switzerland, and Piedmont, so much.

Had we not better do this piece of statistics for ourselves, in time?

FOOTNOTES:

[93] Ed. Venetis, 1758, Lib. I.

[94] Compare Appendix 12.

[95] L'Artiste en Bâtiments, par Louis Berteaux: Dijon, 1848. My printer writes at the side of the page a note, which I insert with thanks:—"This is not the first attempt at a French order. The writer has a Treatise by Sebastian Le Clerc, a great man in his generation, which contains a Roman order, a Spanish order, which the inventor appears to think very grand, and a new French order nationalised by the Gallic cock crowing and clapping its wings in the capital."

[96] The lower group in Plate XVII.

[97] One of the upper stories is also in Gally Knight's plate represented as merely banded, and otherwise plain: it is, in reality, covered with as delicate inlaying as the rest. The whole front is besides out of proportion, and out of perspective, at once; and yet this work is referred to as of authority, by our architects. Well may our architecture fall from its place among the fine arts, as it is doing rapidly; nearly all our works of value being devoted to the Greek architecture, which is utterly useless to us—or worse. One most noble book, however, has been dedicated to our English abbeys,—Mr. E. Sharpe's "Architectural Parallels"—almost a model of what I should like to see done for the Gothic of all Europe.

[98] Except in the single passage "tell it unto the Church," which is simply the extension of what had been commanded before, i.e., tell the fault first "between thee and him," then taking "with thee one or two more," then, to all Christian men capable of hearing the cause: if he refuse to hear their common voice, "let him be unto thee as a heathen man and publican:" (But consider how Christ treated both.)

[99] One or two remarks on this subject, some of which I had intended to have inserted here, and others in Appendix 5, I have arranged in more consistent order, and published in a separate pamphlet, "Notes on the Construction of Sheep-folds," for the convenience of readers interested in other architecture than that of Venetian palaces.

[100] Not, however, by Johnson's testimony: Vide Adventurer, No. 39. "Such operations as required neither celerity nor strength,—the low drudgery of collating copies, comparing authorities, digesting dictionaries, or accumulating compilations."

[101] We have done so—theoretically; just as one would reason on the human form from the bones outwards: but the Architect of human form frames all at once—bone and flesh.

[102] Of course mere multiplicability, as of an engraving, does not diminish the intrinsic value of the work; and if the casts of sculpture could be as sharp as the sculpture itself, they would hold to it the relation of value which engravings hold to paintings. And, if we choose to have our churches all alike, we might cast them all in bronze—we might actually coin churches, and have mints of Cathedrals. It would be worthy of the spirit of the century to put milled edges for mouldings, and have a popular currency of religious subjects: a new cast of nativities every Christmas. I have not heard this contemplated, however, and I speak, therefore, only of the results which I believe are contemplated, as attainable by mere mechanical applications of glass and iron.

[103] I shall often have occasion to write measures in the current text, therefore the reader will kindly understand that whenever they are thus written, 2 ,, 2, with double commas between, the first figures stand for English feet, the second for English inches.

[104] I cannot suffer this volume to close without also thanking my kind friend, Mr. Rawdon Brown, for help given me in a thousand ways during my stay in Venice: but chiefly for his direction to passages elucidatory of my subject in the MSS. of St. Mark's library.

[105] I have not seen the building itself, but Mr. Owen Jones's work may, I suppose, be considered as sufficiently representing it for all purposes of criticism.

[106] The sculpture of the Drunkenness of Noah on the Ducal Palace, of which we shall have much to say hereafter.

www.ingramcontent.com/pod-product-compliance
Lightning Source LLC
Chambersburg PA
CBHW051950090426

42741CB00008B/1332